Essentials of Organization Development and Change

Essentials of Organization Development and Change

Thomas G. Cummings
University of Southern California

Christopher G. Worley
Pepperdine University

South-Western College Publishing
Thomson Learning™

Australia • Canada • Mexico • Singapore • Spain • United Kingdom • United States

Essentials of Organization Development and Change, 1e,
by Thomas G. Cummings & Christopher G. Worley

Vice President/Publisher: Jack W. Calhoun
Executive Editor: John Szilagyi
Marketing Manager: Rob Bloom
Developmental Editor: Denise Simon
Production Editor: Elizabeth A. Shipp
Media Production Editor: Kristen Meere
Manufacturing Coordinator: Sandee Milewski
Internal Design: Jennifer Martin Lambert
Cover Design: Jennifer Martin Lambert
Cover Illustration: ©1999, PhotoDisc, Inc.
Production House: UpperCase Publication Services, Ltd.
Printer: Westgroup

Printed in the United States of America
1 2 3 4 5 03 02 01 00

For more information contact South-Western College Publishing
5101 Madison Road, Cincinnati, Ohio, 45227
or find us on the Internet at http://www.swcollege.com

For permission to use material from this text or product, contact us by
- **telephone: 1-800-730-2214**
- **fax: 1-800-730-2215**
- **Web: http://www.thomsonrights.com**

Library of Congress Cataloging-in-Publication Data
Cummings, Thomas G.
  Essentials of Organization development and change / Thomas G. Cummings, Christopher G. Worley.
    p. cm.
  A multi-media instructional package, including a Website, is available to supplement the text.
  Includes bibliographical references and index.
  ISBN 0-324-02399-5 (alk. paper)
    1. Organizational change. I. Worley, Christopher G. II. Title.
HD58.8 .C858 2001
658.4'06--dc21
                                          00-041277

To the ones who mentored us:

Will McWhinney, Eric Trist, and Warren Bennis

Jon Atzet, Walter Ross, Pat Williams, and Tom Cummings

Brief Contents

Contents

Part 3
ORGANIZATION DEVELOPMENT INTERVENTIONS   127

Part 4
THE FUTURE OF ORGANIZATION DEVELOPMENT   279

Preface

This book describes the essentials of organization development (OD). OD is the application of behavioral science knowledge to improve organization performance and organization functioning. The distinction between performance and functioning has never been more important. OD's behavioral science orientation traditionally resulted in more attention to functioning than performance. Armed with a set of humanistic values and concerned with the unintended negative social consequences of bureaucratic organizations, OD offered a process for making the organization more hospitable to people. But it usually stopped short of trying to improve performance; it was enough to say that the organization had become more human.

OD, in that context, increasingly was challenged as irrelevant. OD often made people feel better, but questions lingered regarding its ability to influence organization effectiveness and performance. Moreover, the prevalence of fast-paced Internet companies and the emergence of a global, knowledge-based economy have led to pronouncements that leading-edged organizations are the ones creating change. People who profess the ability to manage change are part of the crowd to be left in the dust. Therefore, OD stands at a crossroads. Will it cling to its humanistic traditions and focus on functioning or increase its relevance by integrating more performance-related values? Can it afford not to address the issues that threaten an organization's survival?

The *Essentials of Organization Development and Change,* and its full text and cases companion, *Organization Development and Change,* Seventh Edition, were written to address that dilemma. They contain concepts, frameworks, and practical steps that address a range of relevant issues facing today's organizations. These interventions are aimed not only at improving a system's functioning but at enhancing its performance as well.

Feedback from professors at colleges and universities around the world have suggested that in some cases, a full-service text exceeds the requirements of their courses. Many executive MBA programs, for example, prefer a change-oriented text to supplement their organization behavior, management, or strategy courses. Other groups prefer to use their own favorite cases, additional readings, or other materials. This book offers professors more flexibility in crafting a course to meet their students' needs.

The essentials text provides the key components involved in OD practice and is organized into four parts. Part 1 provides an overview of organization development. It begins with an introduction to OD (Chapter 1) and then discusses the fundamental theories that underlie planned change (Chapter 2). Part 2 is a five-chapter description of the process of planned change. It describes how OD practitioners enter and contract with client systems (Chapter 3); diagnose organizations, groups, and jobs (Chapter 4); collect, analyze, and feed back diagnostic data (Chapter 5); design interventions (Chapter 6); and manage change (Chapter 7). Part 3 then covers the major OD interventions used today. Chapter 8 covers human process interventions; Chapters 9, 10, and 11 describe technostructural approaches, such as structural change, employee involvement, and work design; Chapter 12 presents interventions in human resources management; and Chapters 13 and 14 address strategic change interventions. In the final section, Part 4, we describe directions OD is likely to take, including international OD (Chapter 15) and the future of OD (Chapter 16).

EDUCATIONAL AIDS AND SUPPLEMENTS
Instructor's Manual with Test Bank (ISBN: 0-324-01988-2)

The instructor's manual with test bank to accompany *Organization Development & Change*, Seventh Edition, is available and includes information on how to use the manual with the *Essentials of Organization Development and Change*. The manual contains material that can improve the student's appreciation of OD as well as the professor's effectiveness in the classroom. A variety of multiple choice, true/false, and essay questions are suggested for each chapter. Instructors can use these questions directly or use them to suggest additional questions that reflect the professor's own style.

Video (ISBN: 0-324-06784-4)

A new video library is available to users of *Essentials* to show how organizations and leaders apply organization development to the real world. A tape of Video Examples examines a range of issues. Critical thinking questions appear at appropriate intervals in the ten- to fifteen-minute-long segments.

PowerPoint™ Presentation Slides (ISBN: 0-324-01989-0)

The PowerPoint presentation package consists of tables and figures used in the book. These colorful slides can greatly aid the integration of text material during lectures and discussions.

Web Site

A rich Web site at http://cummings.swcollege.com complements the text, providing many extras for the student.

ACKNOWLEDGMENTS

At the risk of being arrogant (which, to our friends and colleagues, is no risk at all because they know we are), we are proud of this book. Every few years we get the chance to think about a field we believe has relevance and communicate to others what the field is about. That's a lot of fun. This is our third collaboration on the text and although our relationship continues to evolve, one thing has remained constant over time: Clear and concise writing is our passion. We argue over the right word in the right place; we can often finish each other's sentences; we agreed with the criticism that our paragraphs consisted of short, declarative sentences and thought we were being complimented (with a nod to Strunk and White's *Elements of Style*); and we are all too familiar with the admonishment that "there's no such thing as good writing, only good rewriting." But all of the discussions, editing, proofing, and researching do take their toll. We're glad to be done again.

Although it's rewarding to be finished, we would be remiss if we did not acknowledge those who assisted us along the way. To recognize everyone by name is impossible, but we are deeply grateful to and for our families: Nancy, Sarah, and Seth, and Debbie, Sarah, Hannah, and Samuel. We would like to thank our colleagues and students at the University of Southern California and Pepperdine University for their comments on the previous edition and for helping us try out new ideas and perspectives. A particular word of thanks goes to Gordon Brooks and

Peggy Sue Sherman, who took on additional tasks to help us prepare the manuscript, collect data, and generally protect us so we could write. Xochitl Boehm and Christine Mattos graciously performed the task of tracking down recent research and wrote several applications. As well, the following people reviewed the text and influenced our thinking with their honest and constructive feedback:

David F. Elloy	*Gonzaga University*
Coy A. Jones	*University of Memphis*
Craig C. Lundberg	*Cornell University*
Manindra K. Mohapatra	*Indiana State University*
Anne H. Reilly	*Loyola University–Chicago*
Marilyn Sargent	*University of San Francisco*
William C. Sharbrough	*The Citadel*
Diana J. Wong	*Bowling Green State University*

We also would like to express our appreciation to members of the staff at South-Western/Thomson Learning for their aid and encouragement. Special thanks go to John Szilagyi and Denise Simon for their help and guidance throughout the development of this book. Libby Shipp and Christine Cotting patiently took on the task of editing and producing this book.

Thomas G. Cummings
Palos Verdes Estates, California
Winter 2000

Christopher G. Worley
San Juan Capistrano, California

Overview of Organization Development

1

1. General Introduction to Organization Development

This is a book about the essentials of *organization development* (OD)—a process that applies behavioral science knowledge and practices to help organizations achieve greater effectiveness, including increased financial performance and improved quality of work life. Organization development differs from other planned change efforts, such as technological innovation, training and development, or new product development, because the focus is on building the organization's ability to assess its current functioning and to achieve its goals. Moreover, OD is oriented to improving the total system—the organization and its parts in the context of the larger environment that affects them.

This book reviews the broad background of OD and examines assumptions, strategies and models, intervention techniques, and other aspects of OD. This chapter provides an introduction to OD, defining first the concept of OD and then explaining why OD has expanded rapidly in the past fifty years. Next, we discuss the different kinds of people who practice OD today and provide a brief history of the field. Finally we present an overview of the rest of the book.

ORGANIZATION DEVELOPMENT DEFINED

Organization development is both a professional field of social action and an area of scientific inquiry. The practice of OD covers a wide spectrum of activities, with seemingly endless variations upon them. Team building with top corporate management, structural change in a municipality, and job enrichment in a manufacturing firm are all examples of OD. Similarly, the study of OD addresses a broad range of topics, including the effects of change, the methods of organizational change, and the factors influencing OD success.

A number of definitions of OD exist, and the following definition incorporates most of these views and is used in this book: *organization development is a systemwide application of behavioral science knowledge to the planned development, improvement, and reinforcement of the strategies, structures, and processes that lead to organization effectiveness.*

This definition emphasizes several features that differentiate OD from other approaches to organizational change and improvement, such as management consulting, technological innovation, operations management, and training and development. The definition also helps to distinguish OD from two related subjects, change management and organization change, that also are addressed in this book.

First, OD applies to the strategy, structure, and processes of an entire system, such as an organization, a single plant of a multiplant firm, or a department or work group. A change program aimed at modifying an organization's strategy, for example, might focus on how the organization relates to a wider environment and on how those relationships can be improved. It might include changes both in the grouping of people to perform tasks (structure) and in methods of communicating and solving problems (process) to support the changes in strategy. Similarly, an OD program directed at helping a top-management team become more effective might focus on interactions and problem-solving processes within the group. This focus might result in the improved ability of top management to solve company problems in strategy and structure. This contrasts with approaches focusing on one or only a few aspects of a system, such as training and development, technological innovation, or operations management. In these approaches, attention is narrowed to individuals within a system, to improvement of particular products or processes, or to development of production or service delivery functions.

Second, OD is based on behavioral science knowledge and practice, including microconcepts such as leadership, group dynamics, and work design, and macro-approaches such as strategy, organization design, and international relations. These subjects distinguish OD from such applications as management consulting, technological innovation, or operations management that emphasize the economic, financial, and technical aspects of organizations. These approaches tend to neglect the personal and social characteristics of a system.

Third, OD is concerned with managing planned change, but not in the formal sense typically associated with management consulting or technological innovation, which tend to be programmatic and expert-driven approaches to change. Rather, OD is more an adaptive process for planning and implementing change than a blueprint for how things should be done. It involves planning to diagnose and solve organizational problems, but such plans are flexible and often revised as new information is gathered about the progress of the change program. If, for example, there was concern about the performance of a set of international subsidiaries, a reorganization process might begin with plans to assess the current relationships between the international divisions and the corporate headquarters and to redesign them if necessary. These plans would be modified if the assessment discovered that most of the senior management teams were not given adequate cross-cultural training prior to their international assignments.

Fourth, OD involves both the creation and the subsequent reinforcement of change. It moves beyond the initial efforts to implement a change program to a longer-term concern for stabilizing and institutionalizing new activities within the organization. For example, the implementing of self-managed work teams might focus on ways in which supervisors could give workers more control over work methods. After workers had more control, attention would shift to ensuring that supervisors continued to provide that freedom. That assurance might include rewarding supervisors for managing in a participative style. This attention to reinforcement is similar to training and development approaches that address maintenance of new skills or behaviors, but it differs from other change perspectives that do not address how a change can be institutionalized.

Finally, OD is oriented to improving organizational effectiveness. This involves two major assumptions. First, an effective organization is able to solve its own problems and focus its attention and resources on achieving key goals. OD helps organization members gain the skills and knowledge necessary to conduct these activities by involving them in the process. Second, an effective organization has both high performance, including financial returns, quality products and services, high productivity, and continuous improvement, and a high quality of work life. The organization's performance responds to the needs of external groups, such as stockholders, customers, suppliers, and government agencies, that provide the organization with resources and legitimacy. Moreover, it is able to attract and motivate effective employees, who then perform at high levels. Other forms of organization change clearly differ from OD in their focus. Management consulting, for example, is almost solely concerned with financial performance, whereas training and development addresses individual effectiveness.

This definition also helps distinguish OD from two other related subjects of interest in this book: change management and organization change. OD and change management both address the effective implementation of planned change. They are concerned with the sequence of activities, processes, and leadership issues that produce organization improvements. They differ, however, in their underlying value orientation. OD's behavioral science foundation supports values of human potential, participation, and development, whereas change management is more focused on values of economic potential and the creation of competitive advantage.[1] As a result, OD's distinguishing feature is its concern with the transfer of knowledge and skill such that the system is more able to manage change in the future. Change management does not necessarily require the transfer of these skills. In short, all OD involves change management, but change management may not involve OD.

Similarly, organization change is a broader concept than OD. As discussed above, organization development can be applied to managing organizational change. However, it is concerned primarily with managing change in such a way that knowledge and skills are transferred to build the organization's capability to achieve goals and solve problems. It is intended to change the organization in a particular direction, toward improved problem solving, responsiveness, quality of work life, and effectiveness. Organization change, in contrast, is more broadly focused and can apply to *any* kind of change, including technical and managerial innovations, organization decline, or the evolution of a system over time. These changes may or may not be directed at making the organization more developed in the sense implied by OD.

THE GROWTH AND RELEVANCE OF ORGANIZATION DEVELOPMENT

According to several observers, organizations are in the midst of unprecedented uncertainty and chaos, and nothing short of a management revolution will save them.[2] Three major trends are shaping change in organizations: globalization, information technology, and managerial innovation.[3]

First, *globalization* is changing the markets and environments in which organizations operate as well as the way they function. New governments, new leadership, new markets, and new countries are emerging and creating a new global economy. The toppling of the Berlin Wall symbolized and energized the reunification of Germany; entrepreneurs appeared in Russia, the Balkans, and Siberia as the former Soviet Union evolves, in fits and starts, into separate, market-oriented states; and China emerged as an open market and as the governance mechanism over Hong Kong to represent a powerful shift in global economic influence. The establishment of the European Economic Community and the far-reaching impact of the Asian financial crisis clearly demonstrate the interconnectedness of the global economy.

Second, *information technology* is redefining the traditional business model by changing how work is performed, how knowledge is used, and how the cost of doing business is calculated. The way an organization collects, stores, manipulates, uses, and transmits information can lower costs or increase the value and quality of products and services. Information technology, for example, is at the heart of emerging e-commerce strategies and organizations. Amazon.com, E*TRADE, and eBay are among many recent entrants to the information economy, and the amount of business being conducted on the Internet is projected to grow at double-digit rates for well over ten years. Moreover, the underlying rate of innovation is not expected to decline. Electronic data interchange, a state-of-the-art technology application a few years ago, is now considered routine business practice. The ability to move information easily and inexpensively throughout and among organizations has fueled the downsizing, delayering, and restructuring of firms. The Internet and the World Wide Web have enabled a new form of work known as telecommuting; organization members can work from their homes or cars without ever going to the office. Finally, information technology is changing how knowledge is used. Information that is widely shared reduces the concentration of power at the top of the organization. Organization members now share the same key information that senior managers once used to control decision making. Ultimately, information technology will generate new business models in which communication and information sharing is nearly free.

Third, *managerial innovation* has responded to the globalization and information technology trends and has accelerated their impact on organizations. New organizational forms, such as networks, strategic alliances, and virtual corporations, provide organizations with new ways of thinking about how to manufacture goods and deliver services. The strategic alliance, for example, has emerged as one of the indispensable tools in strategy implementation. No single organization, not even IBM, Mitsubishi, or General Electric, can control the environmental and market uncertainty it faces. Sun Microsystems' network is so complex that some products it sells are never touched by a Sun employee. In addition, new methods of change, such as downsizing and reengineering, have radically reduced the size of organizations and increased their flexibility, and new large-group interventions, such as the search conference and open space, have increased the speed with which organizational change can take place.[4] Managers, OD practitioners, and researchers argue that these forces not only are powerful in their own right but are interrelated. Their interaction makes for a highly uncertain and chaotic environment for all kinds of organizations, including manufacturing and service firms and those in the public and private sectors. There is no question that these forces are profoundly affecting organizations.

Fortunately, a growing number of organizations are undertaking the kinds of organizational changes needed to survive and prosper in today's environment. They are making themselves more streamlined and nimble and more responsive to external demands. They are involving employees in key decisions and paying for performance rather than for time. They are taking the initiative in innovating and managing change, rather than simply responding to what has already happened.

Organization development is playing an increasingly key role in helping organizations change themselves. It is helping organizations assess themselves and their environments, and revitalize and rebuild their strategies, structures, and processes. OD is helping organization members go beyond surface changes to transform the underlying assumptions and values governing their behaviors. The different concepts and methods discussed in this book increasingly are finding their way into government agencies, manufacturing firms, multinational corporations, service industries, educational institutions, and not-for-profit organizations. Perhaps at no other time has OD been more responsive and practically relevant to organizations' needs to operate effectively in a highly complex and changing world.

WHO IS THE ORGANIZATION DEVELOPMENT PRACTITIONER?

Throughout this text, the term "organization development practitioner" refers to at least three sets of people. The most obvious group of OD practitioners are those people specializing in OD as a profession. They may be internal or external consultants who offer professional services to organization clients, including top managers, functional department heads, and staff groups. OD professionals traditionally have shared a common set of humanistic values promoting open communications, employee involvement, and personal growth and development. They tend to have common training, skills, and experience in the social processes of organizations (for example, group dynamics, decision making, and communications). In recent years, OD professionals have expanded those traditional values and skill sets to include more concern for organizational effectiveness, competitiveness, and bottom-line results, and greater attention to the technical, structural, and strategic parts of organizations. That expansion, mainly in response to the highly competitive demands facing modern organizations, has resulted in a more diverse set of OD professionals geared to helping organizations cope with those pressures.[5]

Second, the term OD practitioner applies to people specializing in fields related to OD, such as reward systems, organization design, total quality, information technology, and business strategy. These content-oriented fields increasingly are becoming integrated with OD's process orientation, particularly as OD projects have become more comprehensive, involving multiple features and varying parts of organizations. The integrated strategic change intervention described in Chapter 13, for example, is the result of marrying OD with business strategy.[6] A growing number of professionals in these related fields are gaining experience and competence in OD, mainly through working with OD professionals on large-scale projects and through attending OD training sessions. For example, most of the large accounting firms have diversified into management consulting and change management.[7] In most cases, professionals in these related fields do not subscribe fully to traditional OD values, nor do they have extensive OD training and experience. Rather, they have formal training and experience in their respective specialties, such as industrial relations, management consulting, information systems, health care, and work design. They are OD practitioners in the sense that they apply their special competence within an OD-like process, typically by engaging OD professionals and managers to design and implement change programs. They also practice OD when they apply their OD competence to their own specialties, thus spreading an OD perspective into such areas as compensation practices, work design, labor relations, and planning and strategy.

Third, the term OD practitioner applies to the increasing number of managers and administrators who have gained competence in OD and who apply it to their own work areas. Studies and recent articles argue that OD applied by managers rather than OD professionals is growing rapidly.[8] They suggest that the faster pace of change affecting organizations today is highlighting the centrality of the manager in managing change. Consequently, OD must become a general management skill. Along those lines, Kanter studied a growing number of firms, such as General Electric, Hewlett-Packard, and 3M, where managers and employees have become "change masters."[9] They have gained the expertise to introduce change and innovation into the organization.

In practice, the distinctions among the three sets of OD practitioners are blurring. A growing number of managers have transferred, either temporarily or permanently, into the OD profession. For example, companies such as Procter & Gamble have trained and rotated managers into full-time OD roles so that they can gain skills and experience needed for higher-level management positions. Also, it is increasingly common to find managers using their experience in OD to become external consultants. More OD practitioners are gaining professional competence in related specialties, such as business process reengineering, reward systems, and organization design. Conversely, many specialists in those related areas are achieving professional competence in OD. Cross-training and integration are producing a more comprehensive and complex kind of OD practitioner, one with a greater diversity of values, skills, and experience than a traditional practitioner.

A SHORT HISTORY OF ORGANIZATION DEVELOPMENT

A brief history of OD will help clarify the evolution of the term as well as some of the problems and confusion that have surrounded it. As currently practiced, OD emerged from five major backgrounds or stems, as shown in Figure 1.1. The first was the growth of the National Training Laboratories (NTL) and the development of training groups, otherwise known as sensitivity training or T-groups. The second stem of OD was the classic work on action research conducted by social scientists interested in applying research to managing change. An important feature of action research was a technique known as survey feedback. Kurt Lewin, a prolific theorist, researcher, and practitioner in group dynamics and social change, was instrumental in the development of T-groups, survey feedback, and action research. His work led to the creation of OD and still serves as a major source of its concepts and methods. The third stem reflects the work of Rensis Likert and represents the application of participative management to organization structure and design. The fourth background is the approach focusing on productivity and the quality of work life. The fifth stem of OD, and the most recent influence on current practice, involves strategic change and organization transformation.

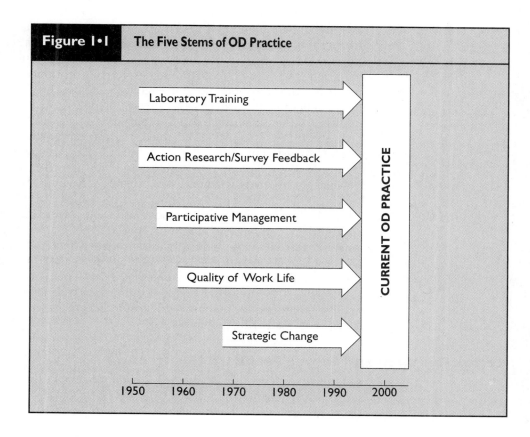

Figure 1•1   **The Five Stems of OD Practice**

Laboratory Training Background

This stem of OD pioneered laboratory training, or the T-group—a small, unstructured group in which participants learn from their own interactions and evolving dynamics about such issues as interpersonal relations, personal growth, leadership, and group dynamics. Essentially, laboratory training began in the summer of 1946, when Kurt Lewin and his staff at the Research Center for Group Dynamics at the Massachusetts Institute of Technology (MIT) were asked by the Connecticut Inter-racial Commission and the Committee on Community Interrelations of the American Jewish Congress for help in research on training community leaders. A workshop was developed, and the community leaders were brought together to learn about leadership and to discuss problems. At the end of each day, the researchers discussed privately what behaviors and group dynamics they had observed. The community leaders asked permission to sit in on these feedback sessions. Reluctant at first, the researchers finally agreed. Thus, the first T-group was formed in which people reacted to data about their own behavior. The researchers drew two conclusions about this first T-group experiment: (1) feedback about group interaction was a rich learning experience, and (2) the process of "group building" had potential for learning that could be transferred to "back-home" situations.[10]

As a result of this experience, the Office of Naval Research and the National Education Association provided financial backing to form the National Training Laboratories, and Gould Academy in Bethel, Maine, was selected as a site for further work (since then, Bethel has played an important part in NTL). The first Basic Skill Groups were offered in the summer of 1947. The program was so successful that the Carnegie Foundation provided support for programs in 1948 and 1949. This led to a permanent program for NTL within the National Education Association.

A new phenomenon arose in 1950. An attempt was made to have T-groups in the morning and cognitive-skill groups (A-groups) in the afternoon. However, the staff found that the high level of carry-over from the morning sessions turned the afternoon A-groups into T-groups, despite the resistance of the afternoon staff members, who were committed to cognitive-skill development. This was the beginning of a decade of learning experimentation and frustration, especially in the attempt to transfer skills learned in the T-group setting to the "back-home" situation.

In the 1950s, three trends emerged: (1) the emergence of regional laboratories, (2) the expansion of summer program sessions to year-round sessions, and (3) the expansion of the T-group into business and industry, with NTL members becoming increasingly involved with industry programs. Notable among these industry efforts was the pioneering work of Douglas McGregor at Union Carbide, of Herbert Shepard and Robert Blake at Esso Standard Oil (now Exxon), and of McGregor and Richard Beckhard at General Mills. Applications of T-group methods at these three companies spawned the term "organization development" and, equally important, led corporate personnel and industrial relations specialists to expand their roles to offer internal consulting services to managers.[11]

Applying T-group techniques to organizations gradually became known as *team building*—a process for helping work groups become more effective in accomplishing tasks and satisfying member needs.

Action Research and Survey Feedback Background

Kurt Lewin also was involved in the second movement that led to OD's emergence as a practical field of social science. This second background refers to the processes of action research and survey feedback. The action research contribution began in the

1940s with studies conducted by social scientists John Collier, Kurt Lewin, and William Whyte. They discovered that research needed to be closely linked to action if organization members were to use it to manage change. A collaborative effort was initiated between organization members and social scientists to collect research data about an organization's functioning, to analyze it for causes of problems, and to devise and implement solutions. After implementation, further data were collected to assess the results, and the cycle of data collection and action often continued. The results of action research were twofold: members of organizations were able to use research on themselves to guide action and change, and social scientists were able to study that process to derive new knowledge that could be used elsewhere.

Among the pioneering action research studies was the work of Lewin and his students at the Harwood Manufacturing Company[12] and the classic research by Lester Coch and John French on overcoming resistance to change.[13] The latter study led to the development of participative management as a means of getting employees involved in planning and managing change. Other notable action research contributions included Whyte and Edith Hamilton's famous study of Chicago's Tremont Hotel[14] and Collier's efforts to apply action research techniques to improving race relations when he was commissioner of Indian affairs from 1933 to 1945.[15] These studies did much to establish action research as integral to organization change. Today, it is the backbone of most OD applications.

A key component of most action research studies was the systematic collection of survey data that was fed back to the client organization. Following Lewin's death in 1947, his Research Center for Group Dynamics at MIT moved to Michigan and joined with the Survey Research Center as part of the Institute for Social Research. The institute was headed by Rensis Likert, a pioneer in developing scientific approaches to attitude surveys. Likert's doctoral dissertation at Columbia University, "A Technique for the Measurement of Attitudes," was the classic study in which he developed the widely used, five-point "Likert Scale."[16]

In an early study by the institute, Likert and Floyd Mann administered a companywide survey of management and employee attitudes at Detroit Edison.[17] Over a two-year period beginning in 1948, three sets of data were developed: (1) the viewpoints of eight thousand nonsupervisory employees about their supervisors, promotion opportunities, and work satisfaction with fellow employees; (2) similar reactions from first- and second-line supervisors; and (3) information from higher levels of management.

The feedback process that evolved was an "interlocking chain of conferences." The major findings of the survey were first reported to the top management and then transmitted throughout the organization. The feedback sessions were conducted in task groups, with supervisors and their immediate subordinates discussing the data together. Although there was little substantial research evidence, the researchers intuitively felt that this was a powerful process for change.

In 1950, eight accounting departments asked for a repeat of the survey, thus generating a new cycle of feedback meetings. In four departments, feedback approaches were used, but the method varied, with two of the remaining departments receiving feedback only at the departmental level. Because of changes in key personnel, nothing was done in two departments.

A third follow-up study indicated that more significant and positive changes, such as job satisfaction, had occurred in the departments receiving feedback than in the two departments that did not participate. From those findings, Likert and Mann derived several conclusions about the effects of survey feedback on organization change. This led to extensive applications of survey-feedback methods in a variety of settings. The common pattern of data collection, data feedback, action planning, implementation, and follow-up data collection in both action research and survey feedback can be seen in these examples.

Participative Management Background

The intellectual and practical advances from the laboratory training stem and the action research/survey-feedback stem were followed closely by the belief that a human relations approach represented a one-best-way to manage organizations. This belief was exemplified in research that associated Likert's Participative Management (System 4) style with organizational effectiveness.[18] This framework characterized organizations as having one of four types of management systems:[19]

- *Exploitive authoritative* systems (System 1) exhibit an autocratic, top-down approach to leadership. Employee motivation is based on punishment and occasional rewards. Communication is primarily downward, and there is little lateral interaction or teamwork. Decision making and control reside primarily at the top of the organization. System 1 results in mediocre performance.

- *Benevolent authoritative* systems (System 2) are similar to System 1, except that management is more paternalistic. Employees are allowed a little more interaction, communication, and decision making but within boundaries defined by management.

- *Consultative* systems (System 3) increase employee interaction, communication, and decision making. Although employees are consulted about problems and decisions, management still makes the final decisions. Productivity is good, and employees are moderately satisfied with the organization.

- *Participative group* systems (System 4) are almost the opposite of System 1. Designed around group methods of decision making and supervision, this system fosters high degrees of member involvement and participation. Work groups are highly involved in setting goals, making decisions, improving methods, and appraising results. Communication occurs both laterally and vertically, and decisions are linked throughout the organization by overlapping group membership. System 4 achieves high levels of productivity, quality, and member satisfaction.[20]

Likert applied System 4 management to organizations using a survey-feedback process. The intervention generally started with organization members completing the *Profile of Organizational Characteristics*.[21] The survey asked members for their opinions about both the present and ideal conditions of six organizational features: leadership, motivation, communication, decisions, goals, and control. In the second stage, the data were fed back to different work groups within the organization. Group members examined the discrepancy between their present situation and their ideal, generally using System 4 as the ideal benchmark, and generated action plans to move the organization toward System 4 conditions.

Productivity and Quality-of-Work-Life Background

The contribution of the productivity and quality-of-work-life (QWL) background to OD can be described in two phases. The first phase is described by the original projects developed in Europe in the 1950s and their emergence in the United States during the 1960s. Based on the research of Eric Trist and his colleagues at the Tavistock Institute of Human Relations in London, early practitioners in Great Britain, Ireland, Norway, and Sweden developed work designs aimed at better integrating technology and people.[22] These QWL programs generally involved joint participation by unions and management in the design of work and resulted in work designs giving employees high levels of discretion, task variety, and feedback about results. Perhaps the most distinguishing characteristic of these QWL programs was the development of self-managing work groups as a new form of work design. These groups were composed of multiskilled workers who were given the necessary autonomy and information to design and manage their own task performances.

As these programs migrated to America, a variety of concepts and techniques were adopted and the approach tended to be more mixed than in European practice. For example, two definitions of QWL emerged during its initial development.[23] QWL was first defined in terms of people's reaction to work, particularly individual outcomes related to job satisfaction and mental health. Using this definition, QWL focused primarily on the personal consequences of the work experience and how to improve work to satisfy personal needs.

A second definition of QWL defined it as an approach or method.[24] People defined QWL in terms of specific techniques and approaches used for improving work.[25] It was viewed as synonymous with methods such as job enrichment, self-managed teams, and labor–management committees. This technique orientation derived mainly from the growing publicity surrounding QWL projects, such as the General Motors–United Auto Workers project at Tarrytown and the Gaines Pet Food plant project. These pioneering projects drew attention to specific approaches for improving work.

The excitement and popularity of this first phase of QWL in the United States lasted until the mid-1970s, when other, more pressing issues, such as inflation and energy costs, diverted national attention. However, starting in 1979, a second phase of QWL activity emerged. A major factor contributing to the resurgence of QWL was growing international competition faced by the United States in markets at home and abroad. It became increasingly clear that the relatively low cost and high quality of foreign-made goods resulted partially from the management practices used abroad, especially in Japan. Books extolling the virtues of Japanese management, such as Ouchi's *Theory Z*,[26] made bestseller lists.

As a result, QWL programs expanded beyond their initial focus on work design to include other features of the workplace that can affect employee productivity and satisfaction, such as reward systems, work flows, management styles, and the physical work environment. This expanded focus resulted in larger-scale and longer-term projects than had the early job enrichment programs and shifted attention beyond the individual worker to work groups and the larger work context. Equally important, it added the critical dimension of organizational efficiency to what had been up to that time a primary concern for the human dimension.

At one point, the productivity and QWL approach became so popular that it was called an ideological movement. This was particularly evident in the spread of quality circles within many companies. Popularized in Japan, *quality circles* are groups of employees trained in problem-solving methods who meet regularly to resolve work-environment, productivity, and quality-control concerns and to develop more efficient ways of working. At the same time, many of the QWL programs started in the early 1970s were achieving success. Highly visible corporations, such as General Motors, Ford, and Honeywell, and unions, such as the United Automobile Workers, the Oil, Chemical, and Atomic Workers, the Communications

Workers of America, and the Steelworkers, were more willing to publicize their QWL efforts. In 1980, for example, more than eighteen hundred people attended an international QWL conference in Toronto, Canada. Unlike previous conferences, which were dominated by academics, the presenters at Toronto were mainly managers, workers, and unionists from private and public corporations.

Today, this second phase of QWL activity continues primarily under the banner of "employee involvement," rather than of QWL. For many OD practitioners, the term "EI," more than the name QWL, signifies the growing emphasis on how employees can contribute more to running the organization so it can be more flexible, productive, and competitive. Recently, the term "employee empowerment" has been used interchangeably with the term EI, the former suggesting the power inherent in moving decision making downward in the organization.[27] "Employee empowerment" may be too restrictive, however. Because it draws attention to the power aspects of these interventions, it may lead practitioners to neglect other important elements needed for success, such as information, skills, and rewards. Consequently, EI seems a broader and less restrictive banner than does employee empowerment for these approaches to organizational improvement.

Finally, the productivity and QWL approach has gained new momentum by joining forces with the total quality movement advocated by W. Edwards Deming[28] and Joseph Juran.[29] In this approach, the organization is viewed as a set of processes that can be linked to the quality of products and services, modeled through statistical techniques and improved continuously.[30] Quality efforts at Ford, Motorola, and Xerox, along with federal government support through the establishment of the Malcolm Baldrige National Quality Award, have popularized this strategy of organization development.

Strategic Change Background

The strategic change background is a recent influence on OD's evolution. As organizations and their technological, political, and social environments have become more complex and more uncertain, the scale and intricacies of organizational change have increased. This trend has produced the need for a strategic perspective from OD and encouraged planned change processes at the organization level.[31]

Strategic change involves improving the alignment among an organization's environment, strategy, and organization design.[32] Strategic change interventions include efforts to improve both the organization's relationship to its environment and the fit between its technical, political, and cultural systems.[33] The need for strategic change is usually triggered by some major disruption to the organization, such as the lifting of regulatory requirements, a technological breakthrough, or a new chief executive officer coming in from outside the organization.[34]

One of the first applications of strategic change was Richard Beckhard's use of *open systems planning*.[35] He proposed that an organization's environment and its strategy could be described and analyzed. Based on the organization's core mission, the differences between what the environment demanded and how the organization responded could be reduced and performance improved. Since then, change agents have proposed a variety of large-scale or strategic change models,[36] each of which recognizes that strategic change involves multiple levels of the organization and a change in its culture, is often driven from the top by powerful executives, and has important effects on performance.

The strategic change background has significantly influenced OD practice. For example, implementing strategic change requires OD practitioners to be familiar with competitive strategy, finance, and marketing, as well as team building, action research, and survey feedback. Together, these skills have improved OD's relevance to organizations and their managers.

OVERVIEW OF THE BOOK

This book presents the process and practice of organization development in a logical flow, as shown in Figure 1.2. Part 1 comprises two chapters. This chapter has described the history of OD and those who perform the work. Chapter 2 discusses the nature of planned change, describes models of the process, and provides a critique of those models.

Part 2 is composed of five chapters that describe the process of organization development. Chapter 3 characterizes the first activity in this process—entering an

Figure 1•2	Overview of the Book

Part 1: Overview of Organization Development

General Introduction to Organization Development
(Chapter 1)

The Nature of Planned Change
(Chapter 2)

Part 2: The Process of Organization Development

Entering and Contracting
(Chapter 3)

Diagnosing Organizations,
Groups, and Jobs
(Chapter 4)

Collecting, Analyzing,
and Feeding Back
Diagnostic Information
(Chapter 5)

Designing Interventions
(Chapter 6)

Leading and Managing Change
(Chapter 7)

Part 3: Organization Development Interventions

Human Process
Interventions
(Chapter 8)

Restructuring
Organizations
(Chapter 9)

Employee
Involvement
(Chapter 10)

Work Design
(Chapter 11)

Human Resources
Management
Interventions
(Chapter 12)

Organization and
Environment
Relationships
(Chapter 13)

Organization
Transformation
(Chapter 14)

Part 4: The Future of Organization Development

Organization Development in
Global Settings
(Chapter 15)

Future Directions in
Organization Development
(Chapter 16)

organizational system and contracting with it for organization development work. The next two chapters describe the content and process of diagnosis, the second major OD activity. Chapter 4 presents models used to diagnose organizations, groups, and jobs. Chapter 5 discusses the processes associated with diagnosis. This involves helping the organization understand its current functioning and discover areas for improvement. Chapter 6 addresses OD's third activity: planning and implementing change. In that chapter we identify major kinds of interventions and introduce the specific approaches to planned change that make up the next part of the book. Chapter 7 discusses the process of leading and managing change, including activities associated with evaluating and institutionalizing OD interventions.

Part 3 presents the major interventions used in OD today. Chapter 8 is concerned with human process interventions aimed at the social processes occurring within organizations, including process consultation, team building, and large-group interventions. Chapter 9 through 11 review technostructural interventions aimed at organization structure and at better integrating people and technology, and describe such interventions as the alternative methods of organizing work activities, downsizing and reengineering the organization, improving employee involvement, and work design. Chapter 12 presents human resources management interventions directed at integrating people into the organization. These interventions, including performance management, career development, and workforce diversity, traditionally are associated with the personnel function in the organization and increasingly have become a part of OD activities. Finally, Chapters 13 and 14 describe strategic interventions that focus on organizing the firm's resources to gain a competitive advantage in the business environment. These change programs, which generally are managed from the top of the organization and take considerable amounts of time, effort, and resources, include integrated strategic change, transorganizational development, mergers and acquisitions, culture change, self-designing organizations, and organization learning and knowledge management.

Part 4 addresses the future of OD and consists of two chapters. Chapter 15 describes the practice of OD in worldwide settings. OD is becoming increasingly international, and in organizations operating outside of the United States it requires modification of the interventions to fit a country's cultural context. In worldwide organizations, OD is aimed at improving the internal alignment of strategy, structure, and process to achieve global objectives. Finally, the practice of OD in global social change organizations promotes sustainable development and enhances human potential in emerging countries. Chapter 16 examines the future of OD, including the trends affecting the field and the prospects for its influence on organization effectiveness.

■ SUMMARY

This chapter introduced OD as a planned change discipline concerned with applying behavioral science knowledge and practice to help organizations achieve greater effectiveness. Managers and staff specialists must work with and through people to perform their jobs, and OD can help them form effective relationships with others. Organizations are faced with rapidly accelerating change, and OD can help them cope with the consequences of change. The concept of OD has multiple meanings. The definition given here integrates earlier definitions and offers a clear focus for the text. The history of OD reveals its five roots: laboratory training, action research and survey feedback, participative management, productivity and quality of work life, and strategic change. The current practice of OD goes far beyond its humanistic origins by incorporating concepts from organization strategy and structure that complement the early emphasis on social processes. The continued growth in the number and diversity of OD approaches, practitioners, and involved organizations attests to the health of the discipline and offers a favorable prospect for the future.

■ NOTES

1. R. Marshak, "Reclaiming the Heart of OD: Putting People Back into Organizations" (keynote address to the National OD Network Conference, Orlando, Fl., 6 October 1996).

2. T. Peters, *Liberation Management: Necessary Disorganization for the Nanosecond Nineties* (New York: Alfred A. Knopf, 1992); J. Kotter, *Leading Change* (Boston: Harvard Business School Press, 1996); S. Brown and K. Eisenhardt, *Competing on the Edge* (Boston: Harvard Business School Press, 1998); M. Wheatley, *Leadership and the New Science* (San Francisco: Berrett-Koehler, 1999); W. Joyce, *Megachange* (New York: Free Press, 1999).

3. T. Stewart, "Welcome to the Revolution," *Fortune* (13 December 1993): 66–80; C. Farrell, "The New Economic Era," *Business Week* (18 November 1994).

4. M. Anderson, ed., *Fast Cycle Organization Development* (Cincinnati: South-Western College Publishing, 2000).

5. A. Church and W. Burke, "Practitioner Attitudes about the Field of Organization Development," in *Research in Organizational Change and Development,* eds. W. Pasmore and R. Woodman (Greenwich, Conn.: JAI Press, 1995).

6. C. Worley, D. Hitchin, and W. Ross, *Integrated Strategic Change* (Reading, Mass.: Addison-Wesley, 1996).

7. R. Henkoff, "Inside Anderson's Army of Advice," *Fortune* (4 October 1993).

8. M. Beer and E. Walton, "Organization Change and Development," *Annual Review of Psychology* 38 (1987): 229–72; S. Sherman, "Wanted: Company Change Agents," *Fortune* (11 December 1999): 197–98.

9. R. Kanter, *The Change Masters* (New York: Simon & Schuster, 1983).

10. L. Bradford, "Biography of an Institution," *Journal of Applied Behavioral Science* 3 (1967): 127; A. Marrow, "Events Leading to the Establishment of the National Training Laboratories," *Journal of Applied Behavioral Science* 3 (1967): 145–50.

11. W. French, "The Emergence and Early History of Organization Development with Reference to Influences upon and Interactions among Some of the Key Actors," in *Contemporary Organization Development: Current Thinking and Applications,* ed. D. Warrick (Glenview, Ill.: Scott, Foresman, 1985): 12–27.

12. A. Marrow, D. Bowers, and S. Seashore, *Management by Participation* (New York: Harper & Row, 1967).

13. L. Coch and J. French, "Overcoming Resistance to Change," *Human Relations* 1 (1948): 512–32.

14. W. Whyte and E. Hamilton, *Action Research for Management* (Homewood, Ill.: Irwin-Dorsey, 1964).

15. J. Collier, "United States Indian Administration as a Laboratory of Ethnic Relations," *Social Research* 12 (May 1945): 275–76.

16. French, "Emergence and Early History," 19–20.

17. F. Mann, "Studying and Creating Change," in *The Planning of Change: Readings in the Applied Behavioral Sciences,* eds. W. Bennis, K. Benne, and R. Chin (New York: Holt, Rinehart, & Winston, 1962): 605–15.

18. R. Likert, *The Human Organization* (New York: McGraw-Hill, 1967); S. Seashore and D. Bowers, "Durability of Organizational Change," *American Psychologist* 25 (1970): 227–33; D. Mosley, "System Four Revisited: Some New Insights," *Organization Development Journal* 5 (Spring 1987): 19–24.

19. Likert, *Human Organization.*

20. Ibid.

21. W. Dowling, "System 4 Builds Performance and Profits," *Organizational Dynamics* 3 (1975): 23–38.

22. A. Rice, *Productivity and Social Organization: The Ahmedabad Experiment* (London: Tavistock Publications, 1958); E. Trist and K. Bamforth, "Some Social and Psychological Consequences of the Longwall Method of Coal-Getting," *Human Relations* 4 (January 1951): 1–38; P. Gyllenhamer, *People at Work* (Reading, Mass.: Addison-Wesley, 1977); E. Thorsrud, B. Sorensen, and B. Gustavsen, "Sociotechnical Approach to Industrial Democracy in Norway," in *Handbook of Work Organization and Society,* ed. R. Dubin (Chicago: Rand McNally, 1976): 648–87; *Work in America: Report of a Special Task Force to the Secretary of Health, Education, and Welfare* (Cambridge: MIT Press, 1973); L. Davis

and A. Cherns, eds., *The Quality of Working Life*, 2 vols. (New York: Free Press, 1975).

23. D. Nadler and E. Lawler III, "Quality of Work Life: Perspectives and Directions" (working paper, Center for Effective Organizations, University of Southern California, Los Angeles, 1982); L. Davis, "Enhancing the Quality of Work Life: Developments in the United States," *International Labour Review* 116 (July-August 1977): 53–65; L. Davis, "Job Design and Productivity: A New Approach," *Personnel* 33 (1957): 418–30.

24. Ibid.

25. R. Ford, "Job Enrichment Lessons from AT&T," *Harvard Business Review* 51 (January-February 1973): 96–106; J. Taylor, J. Landy, M. Levine, and D. Kamath, *Quality of Working Life: An Annotated Bibliography, 1957–1972* (Center for Organizational Studies, Graduate School of Management, University of California at Los Angeles, 1972); J. Taylor, "Experiments in Work System Design: Economic and Human Results," *Personnel Review* 6 (1977): 28–37; J. Taylor, "Job Satisfaction and Quality of Working Life: A Reassessment," *Journal of Occupational Psychology* 50 (December 1977): 243–52.

26. W. Ouchi, *Theory Z* (Reading, Mass.: Addison-Wesley, 1981).

27. J. Vogt and K. Murrell, *Empowerment in Organizations* (San Diego: University Associates, 1990).

28. M. Walton, *The Deming Management Method* (New York: Dodd, Mead, 1986).

29. J. Juran, *Juran on Leadership for Quality: An Executive Handbook* (New York: Free Press, 1989).

30. "The Quality Imperative," *Business Week*, Special Issue (25 October 1991).

31. M. Jelinek and J. Litterer. "Why OD Must Become Strategic," in *Research in Organizational Change and Development*, vol. 2, eds. W. Pasmore and R. Woodman (Greenwich, Conn.: JAI Press, 1988): 135–62; P. Buller, "For Successful Strategic Change: Blend OD Practices with Strategic Management," *Organizational Dynamics* (Winter 1988): 42–55;

32. Worley, Hitchin, and Ross, *Integrated Strategic Change*; N. Rajagopalan and G. Spreitzer, "Toward a Theory of Strategic Change: A Multi-Lens Perspective and Integrative Framework," *Academy of Management Review* 22 (1997): 48–79.

33. R. Beckhard and R. Harris, *Organizational Transitions: Managing Complex Change*, 2d ed. (Reading, Mass.: Addison-Wesley, 1987); N. Tichy, *Managing Strategic Change* (New York: John Wiley & Sons, 1983); E. Schein, *Organizational Culture and Leadership* (San Francisco: Jossey-Bass, 1985); C. Lundberg, "Working with Culture," *Journal of Organization Change Management* 1 (1988): 38–47.

34. D. Miller and P. Freisen, "Momentum and Revolution in Organization Adaptation," *Academy of Management Journal* 23 (1980): 591–614; M. Tushman and E. Romanelli, "Organizational Evolution: A Metamorphosis Model of Convergence and Reorientation," in *Research in Organizational Behavior*, vol. 7, eds. L. Cummings and B. Staw (Greenwich, Conn.: JAI Press, 1985): 171–222.

35. Beckhard and Harris, *Organizational Transitions*.

36. T. Covin and R. Kilmann, "Critical Issues in Large-Scale Organization Change," *Journal of Organization Change Management* 1 (1988): 59–72; A. Mohrman, S. Mohrman, G. Ledford Jr., T. Cummings, and E. Lawler, eds., *Large-Scale Organization Change* (San Francisco: Jossey-Bass, 1989); W. Torbert, "Leading Organizational Transformation," in *Research in Organizational Change and Development*, vol. 3, eds. R. Woodman and W. Pasmore (Greenwich, Conn.: JAI Press, 1989): 83–116; J. Bartunek and M. Louis, "The Interplay of Organization Development and Organization Transformation," in *Research in Organizational Change and Development*, vol. 2, eds. W. Pasmore and R. Woodman (Greenwich, Conn.: JAI Press, 1988): 97–134; A. Levy and U. Merry, *Organizational Transformation: Approaches, Strategies, Theories* (New York: Praeger, 1986).

2 The Nature of Planned Change

The pace of global, economic, and technological development makes change an inevitable feature of organizational life. However, change that happens to an organization can be distinguished from change that is planned by its members. In this book, the term *change* will refer to planned change. Organization development is directed at bringing about planned change to increase an organization's effectiveness. It generally is initiated and implemented by managers, often with the help of an OD practitioner either from inside or outside of the organization. Organizations can use planned change to solve problems, to learn from experience, to reframe shared perceptions, to adapt to external environmental changes, to improve performance, and to influence future changes.

All approaches to OD rely on some theory about planned change. The theories describe the different stages through which planned change may be effected in organizations and explain the temporal process of applying OD methods to help organization members manage change. In this chapter, we describe and compare three major theories of organization change that have received considerable attention in the field: Lewin's change model, the action research model, and contemporary adaptations of action research. Next we present a general model of planned change that integrates the earlier models and incorporates recent conceptual advances in OD. The general model has broad applicability to many types of planned change efforts and serves to organize the chapters in this book. We then discuss different types of change and how the process can vary depending on the change situation. Finally, we present a critique of planned change and discuss the values and ethics involved in carrying out such change.

THEORIES OF PLANNED CHANGE

Conceptions of planned change have tended to focus on how change can be implemented in organizations.[1] Called "theories of changing," these frameworks describe the activities that must take place to initiate and carry out successful organizational change. In this section, we describe and compare three theories of changing: Lewin's change model, the action research model, and contemporary approaches to change. These frameworks have received widespread attention in OD and serve as the primary basis for a general model of planned change. We then present a general model of planned change that integrates these approaches and organizes the material in this book. Following that model, we describe different types of planned change. Finally, we summarize several criticisms of the planned change model.

Lewin's Change Model

One of the early fundamental models of planned change was provided by Kurt Lewin.[2] He conceived of change as modification of those forces keeping a system's behavior stable. Specifically, a particular set of behaviors at any moment in time is the result of two groups of forces—those striving to maintain the status quo and those pushing for change. When both sets of forces are about equal, current behaviors are maintained in what Lewin termed a state of "quasi-stationary equilibrium." To change that state, one can increase those forces pushing for change, decrease those forces maintaining the current state, or apply some combination of both. For example, the level of performance of a work group might be stable because group norms maintaining that level are equivalent to the supervisor's pressures for change to higher levels. This level can be increased either by changing the group norms to support higher levels of performance or by increasing supervisor pressures to produce at higher levels. Lewin suggested that modifying those forces maintaining the status quo produces less tension and resistance than increasing forces for change and consequently is a more effective change strategy.

Lewin viewed this change process as consisting of the following three steps, which are shown in Figure 2.1(A):

1. *Unfreezing.* This step usually involves reducing those forces maintaining the organization's behavior at its present level. Unfreezing is sometimes accomplished through a process of "psychological disconfirmation." By introducing information that shows discrepancies between behaviors desired by organization members and those behaviors currently exhibited, members can be motivated to engage in change activities.[3]

2. *Moving.* This step shifts the behavior of the organization, department, or individual to a new level. It involves intervening in the system to develop new behaviors, values, and attitudes through changes in organizational structures and processes.

3. *Refreezing.* This step stabilizes the organization at a new state of equilibrium. It is frequently accomplished through the use of supporting mechanisms that reinforce the new organizational state, such as organizational culture, norms, policies, and structures.

Lewin's model provides a general framework for understanding organizational change. Because the three steps of change are relatively broad, considerable effort has gone into elaborating them. For example, the planning model, developed by Lippitt, Watson, and Westley, arranges Lewin's model into seven steps: scouting, entry, diagnosis (unfreezing), planning, action (movement), stabilization and evaluation, and termination (refreezing).[4] Lewin's model remains closely identified with the field of OD, however, and is used to illustrate how other types of change can be implemented. For example, Lewin's three-step model has been used to explain how information technologies can be implemented more effectively.[5]

Action Research Model

The action research model focuses on planned change as a cyclical process in which initial research about the organization provides information to guide subsequent action. Then the results of the action are assessed to provide further information to guide further action, and so on. This iterative cycle of research and action involves considerable collaboration among organization members and OD practitioners. It places heavy emphasis on data gathering and diagnosis prior to action planning and implementation, as well as careful evaluation of results after action is taken.

Action research is traditionally aimed both at helping specific organizations to implement planned change and at developing more general knowledge that can be applied to other settings.[6] Although action research was originally developed to have this dual focus on change and knowledge, it has been adapted to OD efforts in which the major emphasis is on planned change.[7] Figure 2.1(B) shows the cyclical phases of planned change as defined by the original action research model. There are eight main steps.

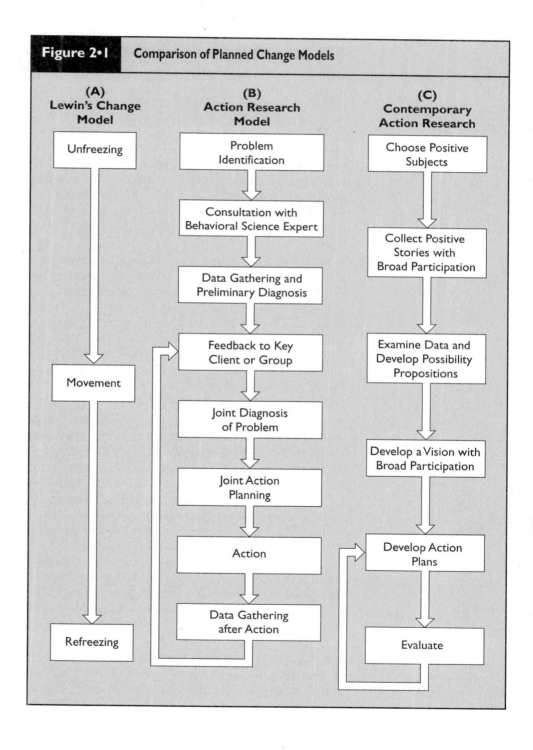

Figure 2•1   Comparison of Planned Change Models

(A) Lewin's Change Model

- Unfreezing
- Movement
- Refreezing

(B) Action Research Model

- Problem Identification
- Consultation with Behavioral Science Expert
- Data Gathering and Preliminary Diagnosis
- Feedback to Key Client or Group
- Joint Diagnosis of Problem
- Joint Action Planning
- Action
- Data Gathering after Action

(C) Contemporary Action Research

- Choose Positive Subjects
- Collect Positive Stories with Broad Participation
- Examine Data and Develop Possibility Propositions
- Develop a Vision with Broad Participation
- Develop Action Plans
- Evaluate

1. *Problem identification.* This stage usually begins when a key executive in the organization or someone with power and influence senses that the organization has one or more problems that might be solved with the help of an OD practitioner.

2. *Consultation with a behavioral science expert.* During the initial contact, the OD practitioner and the client carefully assess each other. The practitioner has his or her own normative, developmental theory or frame of reference and must be conscious of those assumptions and values.[8] Sharing them with the client from the beginning establishes an open and collaborative atmosphere.

3. *Data gathering and preliminary diagnosis.* This step is usually completed by the OD practitioner, often in conjunction with organization members. It involves gathering appropriate information and analyzing it to determine the underlying causes of organizational problems. The four basic methods of gathering data are interviews, process observation, questionnaires, and organizational performance data (unfortunately, often overlooked). One approach to diagnosis begins with observation, proceeds to a semistructured interview, and concludes with a questionnaire to measure precisely the problems identified by the earlier steps.[9] When gathering diagnostic information, OD practitioners may influence members from whom they are collecting data. In OD, "every action on the part of the . . . consultant constitutes an intervention" that will have some effect on the organization.[10]

4. *Feedback to a key client or group.* Because action research is a collaborative activity, the diagnostic data are fed back to the client, usually in a group or work-team meeting. The feedback step, in which members are given the information gathered by the OD practitioner, helps them determine the strengths and weaknesses of the organization or the department under study. The consultant provides the client with all relevant and useful data. Obviously, the practitioner will protect confidential sources of information and, at times, may even withhold data. Defining what is relevant and useful involves consideration of privacy and ethics as well as judgment about whether the group is ready for the information or if the information would make the client overly defensive.

5. *Joint diagnosis of the problem.* At this point, members discuss the feedback and explore with the OD practitioner whether they want to work on identified problems. A close interrelationship exists among data gathering, feedback, and diagnosis because the consultant summarizes the basic data from the client members and presents the data to them for validation and further diagnosis. An important point to remember, as Schein suggests, is that the action research process is very different from the doctor–patient model, in which the consultant comes in, makes a diagnosis, and prescribes a solution. Schein notes that the failure to establish a common frame of reference in the client–consultant relationship may lead to a faulty diagnosis or to a communications gap whereby the client is sometimes "unwilling to believe the diagnosis or accept the prescription." He believes "most companies have drawers full of reports by consultants, each loaded with diagnoses and recommendations which are either not understood or not accepted by the 'patient.'"[11]

6. *Joint action planning.* Next, the OD practitioner and the client members jointly agree on further actions to be taken. This is the beginning of the moving process (described in Lewin's change model), as the organization decides how best to reach a different quasi-stationary equilibrium. At this stage, the specific action to

be taken depends on the culture, technology, and environment of the organization; the diagnosis of the problem; and the time and expense of the intervention.

7. *Action.* This stage involves the actual change from one organizational state to another. It may include installing new methods and procedures, reorganizing structures and work designs, and reinforcing new behaviors. Such actions typically cannot be implemented immediately but require a transition period as the organization moves from the present to a desired future state.[12]

8. *Data gathering after action.* Because action research is a cyclical process, data must also be gathered after the action has been taken to measure and determine the effects of the action and to feed the results back to the organization. This, in turn, may lead to rediagnosis and new action.

Contemporary Adaptations of Action Research

The action research model underlies most current approaches to planned change and is often identified with the practice of OD. Recently, action research has been extended to new settings and applications, and consequently researchers and practitioners have made requisite adaptations of its basic framework.[13] The adaptations are depicted in Figure 2.1(C).

Trends in the application of action research include movement from smaller subunits of organizations to total systems and communities.[14] In those larger contexts, action research is more complex and political than in smaller settings. Therefore, the action research cycle is coordinated across multiple change processes and includes a diversity of stakeholders who have an interest in the organization. (We describe these applications more thoroughly in Chapter 14.)

Action research also is applied increasingly in international settings, particularly in developing nations in the southern hemisphere.[15] Embedded within the action research model, however, are "northern-hemisphere" assumptions about change. For example, action research traditionally views change more linearly than do Eastern cultures, and it treats the change process more collaboratively than do Latin American and African countries.[16] To achieve success in those settings, action research is tailored to fit cultural assumptions. (See "Different Types of Planned Change" below and Chapter 15.)

Finally, action research is applied increasingly to promote social change and innovation,[17] as demonstrated most clearly in community development and global social change projects.[18] Those applications are heavily value laden and seek to redress imbalances in power and resource allocations across different groups. Action researchers tend to play an activist role in the change process, which is often chaotic and conflictual. (Chapter 15 reviews global social change processes.)

In light of these general trends, action research has undergone two key adaptations. First, contemporary applications have increased substantially the degree of member involvement in the change process. That contrasts with traditional approaches to planned change, whereby consultants carried out most of the change activities, with the agreement and collaboration of management.[19] Although consultant-dominated change still persists in OD, there is a growing tendency to involve organization members in learning about their organization and about how to change it. Referred to as "participatory action research,"[20] "action learning,"[21] "action science,"[22] "self-design,"[23] or "appreciative inquiry,"[24] this approach to planned change emphasizes the need for organization members to learn firsthand about planned change if they are to gain the knowledge and skills needed to change the organization. In today's complex and changing environment, some argue that OD must go beyond solving particular problems to helping members gain the competence needed to change and improve the organization continually.[25]

In this modification of action research, the role of OD consultants is to work with members to facilitate the learning process. Both parties are "co-learners" in diagnosing the organization, designing changes, and implementing and assessing them.[26] Neither party dominates the change process. Rather, each participant brings unique information and expertise to the situation, and they combine their resources to learn how to change the organization. Consultants, for example, know how to design diagnostic instruments and OD interventions, and organization members have local knowledge about the organization and how it functions. Each participant learns from the change process. Organization members learn how to change their organization and how to refine and improve it. OD consultants learn how to facilitate complex organizational change and learning.

The second adaptation to action research is the integration of an "interpretive" or "social constructionist" approach to planned change.[27] Called "appreciative inquiry," this model proposes that words and conversations determine what is important and meaningful in organizational life. Take, for example, the work group whose daily conversations are dominated by management feedback that its costs are too high. Even if the group performs well on quality and customer satisfaction, the focus on cost problems can lead group members to believe that the group is a poor performer. Accordingly, this approach to change involves starting new conversations that drive new shared meanings of key goals, processes, and achievements. Proponents of appreciative inquiry point out that most organizational conversations are focused on poor financial results or on how the organization could be better, on the gap between where the organization is and where it wants to be, and on the problems it faces. Metaphorically, organizations are like problems to be solved and the conversations among members dwell on the organization's faults.[28]

Appreciative inquiry challenges that assumption. It suggests that the most important change an organization can make is to begin conversations about what the organization is doing right.[29] Appreciative inquiry helps organization members to understand and describe their organization when it is working at its best. That knowledge is then applied to creating a powerful and guiding image of what the organization could be. Broad involvement of organization members in creating the vision starts a new conversation about the organization's potential and creates a new focus and positive expectation. Considerable research on expectation effects supports this positive approach to planned change.[30] It suggests that people tend to act in ways that make their expectations occur: a positive vision of the organization's future energizes and directs behavior to make that expectation come about.

Planned change emphasizes member involvement and starts with which organization features to examine. For example, members can choose to look for successful male–female collaboration (as opposed to sexual discrimination), instances of customer satisfaction (as opposed to customer dissatisfaction), particularly effective work teams, or product development processes that brought new ideas to market especially fast. If the focus of inquiry is real and vital to organization members, the change process itself will take on these positive attributes. The second step involves gathering data about the "best of what is" in the organization. A broad array of organization members are involved in developing data-gathering instruments, collecting information, and analyzing it. In the third step, members examine the data to find stories, however small, that present a truly exciting and possible picture of the future. From those stories, members develop "possibility propositions"—statements that bridge the organization's current best practices with ideal possibilities for future organizing.[31] That effort redirects attention from "what is" to "what might be." In step four, relevant stakeholders are brought together to construct a vision of the future and to devise action plans for moving in that direction. The vision becomes a statement of "what should be." Finally, implementation of those plans proceeds similarly to the action and assessment phases of action research described previously. Members make changes, assess the results, make necessary adjustments, and so on as they move the organization toward the vision.

GENERAL MODEL OF PLANNED CHANGE

The three theories of planned change in organizations described above—Lewin's change model, the action research model, and contemporary adaptations of the action research model—suggest a general framework for planned change, as shown in Figure 2.2. The framework describes the four basic activities that practitioners and organization members jointly carry out in organization development. The arrows connecting the different activities in the model show the typical sequence of events, from entering and contracting, to diagnosing, to planning and implementing change, to evaluating and institutionalizing change. The lines connecting the activities emphasize that organizational change is not a straightforward, linear process but involves considerable overlap and feedback among the activities. Because the model serves to organize the remaining parts of this book, Figure 2.2 also shows which specific chapters apply to the four major change activities.

Entering and Contracting

The first set of activities in planned change concerns entering and contracting (events described in Chapter 3). Those events help managers decide whether they want to engage further in a planned change program and to commit resources to such a process. Entering an organization involves gathering initial data to understand the problems facing the organization or the positive opportunities for inquiry. Once this information is collected, the problems or opportunities are discussed with managers and other organization members to develop a contract or agreement to engage in planned change. The contract spells out future change activities, the resources that will be committed to the process, and how OD practitioners and organization members will be involved. In many cases, organizations do not get beyond

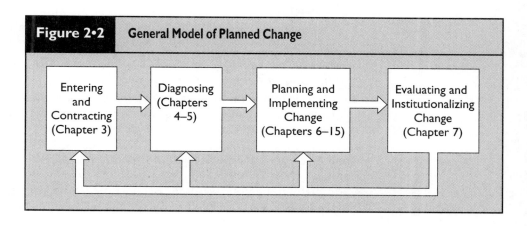

Figure 2•2   General Model of Planned Change

Entering and Contracting (Chapter 3) → Diagnosing (Chapters 4–5) → Planning and Implementing Change (Chapters 6–15) → Evaluating and Institutionalizing Change (Chapter 7)

this early stage of planned change because disagreements about the need for change surface, resource constraints are encountered, or other methods for change appear more feasible. When OD is used in nontraditional and international settings, the entering and contracting process must be sensitive to the context in which the change is taking place.

Diagnosing

In this stage of planned change, the client system is carefully studied. Diagnosis can focus on understanding organizational problems, including their causes and consequences, or on identifying the organization's positive attributes. The diagnostic process is one of the most important activities in OD. It includes choosing an appropriate model for understanding the organization and gathering, analyzing, and feeding back information to managers and organization members about the problems or opportunities that exist.

Diagnostic models for analyzing problems (described in Chapter 4) explore three levels of activities. Organization issues represent the most complex level of analysis and involve the total system. Group-level issues are associated with department and group effectiveness. Individual-level issues involve the way jobs are designed.

Gathering, analyzing, and feeding back data are the central change activities in diagnosis. Chapter 5 describes how data can be gathered through interviews, observations, survey instruments, or such archival sources as meeting minutes and organization charts. It also explains how data can be reviewed and analyzed. We also describe the process of feeding back diagnostic data. Organization members, often in collaboration with an OD practitioner, jointly discuss the data and their implications for change.

Planning and Implementing Change

In this stage, organization members and practitioners jointly plan and implement OD interventions. They design interventions to achieve the organization's vision or goals and make action plans to implement them. There are several criteria for designing interventions, including the organization's readiness for change, its current change capability, its culture and power distributions, and the change agent's skills and abilities (discussed in Chapter 6). Depending on the outcomes of diagnosis, there are four major types of interventions in OD:

1. Human process interventions at the individual, group, and total system levels (Chapter 8)
2. Interventions that modify and integrate an organization's structure, technology, and member employees (Chapters 9 through 11)
3. Human resources interventions that address member performance, career planning, and workforce diversity (Chapter 12)
4. Strategic interventions that involve managing the organization's relationship to its external environment and the internal structure and process necessary to support a business strategy (Chapters 13 and 14).

Chapter 15 presents specialized information for carrying out OD in international settings.

Implementing interventions is concerned with leading and managing the change process. As discussed in Chapter 7, it includes motivating change, creating a desired future vision of the organization, developing political support, managing the transition toward the vision, and sustaining momentum for change.

Evaluating and Institutionalizing Change

The final stage in planned change involves evaluating the effects of the intervention and managing the institutionalization of successful processes. (Those two activities are described in Chapter 7.) Feedback to organization members about the intervention's results provides information about whether the changes should be continued, modified, or suspended. Institutionalizing successful changes involves reinforcing them through feedback, rewards, and training.

DIFFERENT TYPES OF PLANNED CHANGE

The general model of planned change describes how the OD process typically unfolds in organizations. In actual practice, the different phases are not nearly as orderly as the model implies. OD practitioners tend to modify or adjust the stages to fit the needs of the situation. Steps in planned change may be implemented in a variety of ways, depending on the client's needs and goals, the change agent's skills and values, and the organization's context. Thus, planned change can vary enormously from one situation to another.

To understand the differences better, planned change can be contrasted across situations on three key dimensions: the magnitude of organizational change, the degree to which the client system is organized, and whether the setting is domestic or international.

Magnitude of Change

Planned change efforts can be characterized as falling along a continuum ranging from incremental changes that involve fine-tuning the organization to quantum changes that entail fundamentally altering how it operates.[32] Incremental changes tend to involve limited dimensions and levels of the organization, such as the decision-making processes of work groups. They occur within the context of the organization's existing business strategy, structure, and culture and are aimed at improving the status quo. Quantum changes, on the other hand, are directed at significantly altering how the organization operates. They tend to involve several organizational dimensions, including structure, culture, reward systems, information processes, and work design. They also involve changing multiple levels of the organization, from top-level management through departments and work groups to individual jobs.

Planned change traditionally has been applied in situations involving incremental change. Organizations in the 1960s and 1970s were concerned mainly with fine-tuning their bureaucratic structures by resolving many of the social problems that emerged with increasing size and complexity. In those situations, planned change involves a relatively bounded set of problem-solving activities. OD practitioners typically are contracted by managers to help solve specific problems in particular organizational systems, such as poor communication among members of a work team or low customer satisfaction scores in a department store. Diagnostic and change activities tend to be limited to the defined issues, although additional problems may be uncovered and may need to be addressed. Similarly, the change process tends to focus on those organizational systems having specific problems, and it generally terminates when the problems are resolved. Of course, the change agent may contract to help solve additional problems.

In recent years, OD has been concerned increasingly with quantum change. As described in Chapter 1, the greater competitiveness and uncertainty of today's environment have led a growing number of organizations to alter drastically the way in which they operate. In such situations, planned change is more complex, extensive, and long term than when applied to incremental change.[33] Because quantum change involves most features and levels of the organization, it is typically driven from the top, where corporate strategy and values are set. Change agents help senior managers create a vision of a desired future organization and energize movement in that direction. They also help executives develop structures for managing the transition from the present to the future organization and may include, for example, a variety of overlapping steering committees and redesign teams. Staff experts also may redesign many features of the firm, such as performance measures, rewards, planning processes, work designs, and information systems.

Because of the complexity and extensiveness of quantum change, OD professionals often work in teams comprising members with different yet complementary areas of expertise. The consulting relationship persists over relatively long time periods and includes a great deal of renegotiation and experimentation among consultants and managers. The boundaries of the change effort are more uncertain and diffuse than in incremental change, thus making diagnosis and change seem more like discovery than like problem solving. (We describe complex strategic and transformational types of change in more detail in Chapters 13 and 14.)

It is important to emphasize that quantum change may or may not be developmental in nature. Organizations may drastically alter their strategic direction and way of operating without significantly developing their capacity to solve problems and to achieve both high performance and quality of work life. For example, firms simply may change their marketing mix, dropping or adding products, services, or customers; they may downsize drastically by cutting out marginal businesses and laying off managers and workers; or they may tighten managerial and financial controls and attempt to squeeze more out of the labor force. On the other hand, organizations may undertake quantum change from a developmental perspective. They may seek to make themselves more competitive by developing their human resources; by getting managers and employees more involved in problem solving and innovation; and by promoting flexibility and direct, open communication. That OD approach to quantum change is particularly relevant in today's rapidly changing and competitive environment. To succeed in this setting, firms such as General Electric, Kimberly-Clark, ABB, Hewlett-Packard, and Motorola are transforming themselves from control-oriented bureaucracies to high-involvement organizations capable of changing and improving themselves continually.

Degree of Organization

Planned change efforts also can vary depending on the degree to which the organization or client system is organized. In overorganized situations, such as in highly mechanistic, bureaucratic organizations, various dimensions such as leadership styles, job designs, organization structure, and policies and procedures are too rigid and overly defined for effective task performance. Communication between management and employees typically is suppressed, conflicts are avoided, and employees are apathetic. In underorganized organizations, on the other hand, there is too little constraint or regulation for effective task performance. Leadership, structure, job design, and policy are poorly defined and fail to control task behaviors effectively. Communication is fragmented, job responsibilities are ambiguous, and employees' energies are dissipated because they lack direction. Underorganized situations typically are found in such areas as product development, project management, and community development, where relationships among diverse groups and participants must be coordinated around complex, uncertain tasks.

In overorganized situations, where much of OD practice historically has taken place, planned change generally is aimed at loosening constraints on behavior. Changes in leadership, job design, structure, and other features are designed to liberate suppressed energy, to increase the flow of relevant information between employees and managers, and to promote effective conflict resolution. The typical steps of planned change—entry, diagnosis, intervention, and evaluation—are intended to penetrate a relatively closed organization or department and make it increasingly open to self-diagnosis and revitalization. The relationship between the OD practitioner and the management team attempts to model this loosening process. The consultant shares leadership of the change process with management, encourages open communications and confrontation of conflict, and maintains flexibility in relating to the organization.

When applied to organizations facing problems in being underorganized, planned change is aimed at increasing organization by clarifying leadership roles, structuring communication between managers and employees, and specifying job and departmental responsibilities. These activities require a modification of the traditional phases of planned change and include the following four steps:[34]

1. *Identification.* This step identifies the relevant people or groups who need to be involved in the change program. In many underorganized situations, people and departments can be so disconnected that there is ambiguity about who should be included in the problem-solving process. For example, when managers of different departments have only limited interaction with each other, they may disagree or be confused about which departments should be involved in developing a new product or service.

2. *Convention.* In this step the relevant people or departments in the company are brought together to begin organizing for task performance. For example, department managers might be asked to attend a series of organizing meetings to discuss the division of labor and the coordination required to introduce a new product.

3. *Organization.* Different organizing mechanisms are created to structure the newly required interactions among people and departments. This might include creating new leadership positions, establishing communication channels, and specifying appropriate plans and policies.

4. *Evaluation.* In this final step the outcomes of the organization step are assessed. The evaluation might signal the need for adjustments in the organizing process or for further identification, convention, and organization activities.

In carrying out these four steps of planned change in underorganized situations, the relationship between the OD practitioner and the client system attempts to reinforce the organizing process. The consultant develops a well-defined leadership role, which might be autocratic during the early stages of the change program. Similarly, the consulting relationship is clearly defined and tightly specified. In effect, the interaction between the consultant and the client system supports the larger process of bringing order to the situation.

Domestic vs. International Settings

Planned change efforts traditionally have been applied in North American and European settings but increasingly are used outside of those cultures. Developed in western societies, the action research model reflects the underlying values and assumptions of these cultural settings, including equality, involvement, and short-term time horizons. Under such conditions, the action research model works quite well. In other societies, however, a very different set of cultural values and assumptions may operate and make the application of OD problematic. For example, the cultures of most Asian countries are more hierarchical and status conscious, are less open to discussing personal issues, more concerned with saving "face," and have a longer time horizon for results. Even when the consultant is aware of the cultural norms and values that permeate the society, those cultural differences make the traditional action research steps more difficult to implement, especially for a North American or European OD practitioner.

The cultural values that guide OD practice in the United States, for example, include a tolerance for ambiguity, equality among people, individuality, and achievement motives. An OD process that encourages openness among individuals, high levels of participation, and actions that promote increased effectiveness are viewed favorably. The OD practitioner is also assumed to hold those values and to model them in the conduct of planned change. Most reported cases of OD involve western-based organizations using practitioners trained in the traditional model and raised and experienced in western society.

When OD is applied outside of the North American or European context (and sometimes even within those settings), the action research process must be adapted to fit the cultural context. For example, the diagnostic phase, which is aimed at understanding the current drivers of organization effectiveness, can be modified in a variety of ways. Diagnosis can involve many organization members or include only senior managers; be directed from the top, conducted by an outside consultant, or performed by internal consultants; or involve face-to-face interviews or organization documents. Each step in the general model of planned change must be carefully mapped against the cultural context.

Conducting OD in international settings is highly stressful on OD practitioners. To be successful, they must develop a keen awareness of their own cultural biases, be open to seeing a variety of issues from another perspective, be fluent in the values and assumptions of the host country, and understand the economic and political context of business there. Most OD practitioners are not able to meet all of those criteria and partner with a "cultural guide," often a member of the client organization, to help navigate the cultural, operational, and political nuances of change in that society.

CRITIQUE OF PLANNED CHANGE

Despite their continued refinement, the models and practice of planned change are still in a formative stage of development, and there is considerable room for improvement. Critics of OD have pointed out several problems with the way planned change has been conceptualized and practiced. First, planned change generally is described as a rationally controlled, orderly process. Critics have argued that although this view may be comforting, it is seriously misleading.[35] They point out that planned change has a more chaotic quality, often involving shifting goals, discontinuous activities, surprising events, and unexpected combinations of changes. For example, managers often initiate changes without clear plans that clarify their strategies and goals. As change unfolds, new stakeholders may emerge and demand modifications reflecting previously unknown or unvoiced needs. These emergent conditions make planned change a far more disorderly and dynamic process than customarily is portrayed, and conceptions need to capture this reality.

Second, the relationship between planned change and organizational performance and effectiveness is not well understood. OD traditionally has had problems assessing whether interventions are producing observed results. The complexity of the change situation, the lack of sophisticated analyses, and the long time periods for producing results all have contributed to weak evaluation of OD efforts. Moreover, managers often have accounted for OD efforts with post hoc testimonials, reports of possible future benefits, and calls to support OD as the right thing to do. In the absence of rigorous assessment and measurement, it is difficult to make resource allocation decisions about change programs and to know which interventions are most effective in certain situations.

Third, a growing number of OD practitioners have acquired skills in a specific technique, such as team building, total quality management, large-group interventions, or gain sharing, and have chosen to specialize in that method. Although such specialization may be necessary given the complex array of techniques that make up modern OD, it can lead to myopia. Some practitioners favor particular techniques and ignore other OD strategies that might be more appropriate. Because they tend to interpret organizational problems as requiring the favored technique, it is not unusual to see consultants pushing such methods as diversity training, reengineering, organization learning, or self-managing work teams as solutions to most organizational problems.

Fourth, effective change depends on a careful diagnosis of how the organization is functioning. Diagnosis identifies the underlying causes of organizational problems, such as poor product quality and employee dissatisfaction. It requires both time and money and some organizations are not willing to make the necessary investment. They rely on preconceptions about what the problem is and then hire consultants with skills appropriate to solve it. Managers may think, for example, that work design is the problem so they hire an expert in job enrichment to implement a change program. If the problem is caused instead by another factor such as poor reward practices, job enrichment is an inappropriate approach. Careful diagnosis can help the consultant and client avoid such mistakes.

Finally, in situations requiring complex organizational changes, planned change is a long-term process that calls for considerable innovation and learning on site. It requires a good deal of time and commitment and a willingness to modify and refine changes as the circumstances dictate. Some organizations demand more rapid solutions to their problems and seek "quick fixes" from experts. Unfortunately, some OD consultants are more than willing to provide quick solutions.[36] They sell prepackaged programs for organizations to adopt. These programs appeal to managers because typically they include an explicit recipe to be followed, standard training materials, and clear time and cost boundaries. The quick fixes do not easily gain wide organizational support and commitment, and they seldom produce the positive results that have been advertised.

VALUES AND ETHICS IN OD

Values and ethics have played an important role in organization development from its beginning, and here we will first outline the values basis of the field. Ethical issues in OD are concerned with how practitioners behave in their helping relationship with organization members. Inherent in any helping relationship is the potential for misconduct and client abuse. OD practitioners may let personal values stand in the way of good practices or they may use the power inherent in their professional role to abuse organization members, often unintentionally.

Values in Organization Development

Traditionally, OD professionals have promoted a set of values under a humanistic framework, including a concern for inquiry and science, democracy, and being helpful.[37] They have sought to build trust and collaboration; to create an open, problem-solving climate; and to increase the self-control of organization members. More recently, OD practitioners have extended those humanistic values to include a concern for improving organizational effectiveness (for example, to increase productivity or to reduce turnover) and performance (for example, to increase profitability). They have shown an increasing desire to optimize both human benefits and production objectives.[38]

The joint values of humanizing organizations and improving their effectiveness have received widespread support in the OD profession as well as increasing encouragement from managers, employees, and union officials. Indeed, it would be difficult not to support those joint concerns. But in practice OD professionals face serious challenges in simultaneously pursuing greater humanism and organizational effectiveness.[39] More practitioners are experiencing situations in which there is conflict between employees' needs for greater meaning and the organization's need for more effective and efficient use of its resources. For example, expensive capital equipment may run most efficiently if it is highly programmed and routinized, but people may not derive satisfaction from working with such technology. Should efficiency be maximized at the expense of people's satisfaction? Can technology be changed to make it more humanly satisfying while remaining efficient? What compromises are possible? How do these tradeoffs shift when they are applied in different social cultures? These are the value dilemmas often faced when we try to optimize both human benefits and organizational effectiveness.

In addition to value issues within organizations, OD practitioners are dealing more and more with value conflicts with powerful outside groups. Organizations are open systems and exist within increasingly turbulent environments. For example, hospitals are facing complex and changing task environments. This has led to a proliferation of external stakeholders with interests in the organization's functioning, including patients, suppliers, medical groups, insurance companies, employers, the government, stockholders, unions, the press, and various interest groups. Those external groups often have different and competing values for judging the organization's effectiveness. For example, stockholders may judge the firm in terms of earnings per share, the government in terms of compliance with equal employment opportunity legislation, patients in terms of quality of care, and ecology groups in terms of hazardous waste disposal. Because organizations must rely on these external groups for resources and legitimacy, they cannot simply ignore these competing values. They must respond to them somehow and try to reconcile the different interests.

Ethical Dilemmas in Organization Development

To its credit, the field of OD always has shown concern for the ethical conduct of its practitioners. There have been several articles and symposia about ethics in OD.[40] Furthermore, statements of ethics governing OD practice have been sponsored by the Organization Development Institute,[41] the American Society for Training & Development,[42] and a consortium of professional OD associations. The consortium has sponsored an ethical code derived from a large-scale project conducted at the Center for the Study of Ethics in the Professions at the Illinois Institute of Technology. The project's purposes included preparing critical incidents describing ethical dilemmas and using that material for preprofessional and continuing education in OD, providing an empirical basis for a statement of values and ethics for OD professionals, and initiating a process for making the ethics of OD practice explicit on a continuing basis.[43] The ethical guidelines from this project appear in the appendix to this chapter.

Although adherence to statements of ethics helps prevent the occurrence of ethical problems, OD practitioners still can encounter ethical dilemmas. Figure 2.3 is a process model that explains how ethical dilemmas can occur in OD. The antecedent conditions include an OD practitioner and a client system with different goals, values, needs, skills, and abilities. During the entry and contracting phase these differences may or may not be addressed and clarified. If the contracting process is incomplete, the subsequent intervention process or role episode is subject to role conflict and role ambiguity. Neither the client nor the OD practitioner is clear about respective responsibilities. Each party is pursuing different goals, and each is using different skills and values to achieve those goals. The role conflict and ambiguity may produce five types of ethical dilemmas: misrepresentation, misuse of data, coercion, value and goal conflict, and technical ineptness.

- *Misrepresentation.* This dilemma occurs when OD practitioners claim that an intervention will produce results that are unreasonable for the change program or the situation. The client can contribute to the problem by portraying inaccurate goals and needs. In either case, one or both parties is operating under false

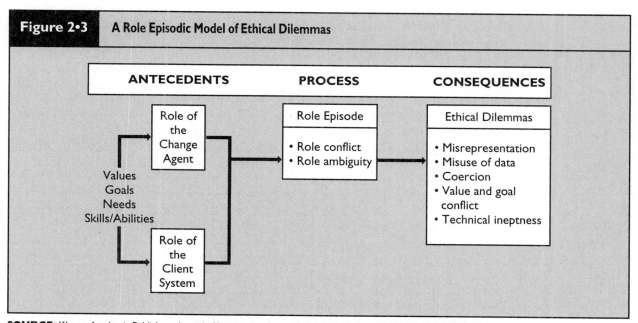

Figure 2•3   A Role Episodic Model of Ethical Dilemmas

SOURCE: Kluwer Academic Publishers, *Journal of Business Ethics,* 11 (1992), page 665, "Ethical Dilemmas in Organization Development: A Cross-Cultural Analysis," L. White and M. Rhodeback, Figure 1. © 1992, Kluwer. With kind permission from Kluwer Academic Publishers.

pretenses and an ethical dilemma exists. Misrepresentation is likely to occur in the entering and contracting phases of planned change when the initial consulting relationship is being established. To prevent misrepresentation, OD practitioners need to gain clarity about the goals of the change effort and to explore openly with the client its expected effects, its relevance to the client system, and the practitioner's competence in executing the intervention.

- *Misuse of data.* This occurs when information gathered during the OD process is used punitively. Large amounts of information are invariably obtained during the entry and diagnostic phases of OD. Although most OD practitioners value openness and trust, it is important that they be aware of how such data are going to be used. It is a human tendency to use data to enhance a power position. Openness is one thing, but leaking inappropriate information can be harmful to individuals and to the organization. It is easy for a consultant, under the guise of obtaining information, to gather data about whether a particular manager is good or bad. When, how, or if this information can be used is an ethical dilemma not easily resolved. To minimize misuse of data, practitioners should reach agreement up front with organization members about how data collected during the change process will be used. This agreement should be reviewed periodically in light of changing circumstances.

- *Coercion.* This ethical dilemma occurs when organization members are forced to participate in an OD intervention. It also can pose ethical dilemmas for the helping relationship between OD practitioners and organization members. Inherent in any helping relationship are possibilities for excessive manipulation and dependency, two facets of coercion. Kelman pointed out that behavior change "inevitably involves some degree of manipulation and control, and at least an implicit imposition of the change agent's values on the client or the person he [or she] is influencing."[44] This places the practitioner on two horns of a dilemma: (1) any attempt to change is in itself a change and thereby a manipulation, no matter how slight, and (2) there exists no formula or method to structure a change situation so that such manipulation can be totally absent. To attack the first aspect of the dilemma, Kelman stressed freedom of choice, seeing any action that limits freedom of choice as being ethically ambiguous or worse. To address the second aspect, Kelman argued that the OD practitioner must remain keenly aware of her or his own value system and alert to the possibility that those values are being imposed on a client. In other words, an effective way to resolve this dilemma is to make the change effort as open as possible, with the free consent and knowledge of the people involved.

The second facet of coercion that can pose ethical dilemmas for the helping relationship involves dependency. Helping relationships invariably create dependency between those who need help and those who provide it.[45] A major goal in OD is to lessen clients' dependency on consultants by helping clients gain the knowledge and skills to address organizational problems and manage change themselves. In some cases, however, achieving independence from OD practitioners can result in clients being either counterdependent or overdependent, especially in the early stages of the relationship. To resolve dependency issues, consultants can openly and explicitly discuss with the client how to handle the dependency problem, especially what the client and consultant expect of one another. Another approach is to focus on problem finding. Usually, the client is looking for a solution to a perceived problem. The consultant can redirect the energy to improved joint diagnosis so that both are working on problem identification and problem solving. Such action moves the energy of the client away from dependency. Finally, dependency can be reduced by changing the client's expectation from being helped or controlled by the practitioner to a greater focus on the need to manage the problem. Such a refocusing can reinforce the understanding that the consultant is working for the client and offering assistance that is at the client's discretion.

- *Value and goal conflict.* This ethical conflict occurs when the purpose of the change effort is not clear or when the client and the practitioner disagree over how to achieve the goals. The important practical issue for OD consultants is whether it is justifiable to withhold services unilaterally from an organization that does not agree with their values or methods. OD pioneer Gordon Lippitt suggested that the real question is the following: assuming that some kind of change is going to occur anyway, doesn't the consultant have a responsibility to try to guide the change in the most constructive fashion possible?[46] That question may be of greater importance and relevance to an internal consultant or to a consultant who already has an ongoing relationship with the client.

  Argyris takes an even stronger stand, maintaining that the responsibilities of professional OD practitioners to clients are comparable to those of lawyers or physicians, who, in principle, may not refuse to perform their services. He suggests that the very least the consultant can do is to provide "first aid" to the organization, as long as the assistance does not compromise the consultant's values.[47]

- *Technical ineptness.* This final ethical dilemma occurs when OD practitioners try to implement interventions for which they are not skilled or when the client attempts a change for which it is not ready. Critical to the success of any OD program is the selection of an appropriate intervention, which depends, in turn, on careful diagnosis of the organization. Selecting an intervention is closely related to the practitioner's own values, skills, and abilities. In solving organizational problems, many OD consultants emphasize a favorite intervention or technique, such as team building, total quality management, or self-managed teams. They let their own values and beliefs dictate the change method.[48] Technical ineptness dilemmas also can occur when interventions do not align with the ability of the organization to implement them. Again, careful diagnosis can reveal the extent to which the organization is ready to make a change and possesses the skills and knowledge to implement it.

■ SUMMARY

Theories of planned change describe the activities necessary to modify strategies, structures, and processes to increase an organization's effectiveness. Lewin's change model, the action research model, and more recent adaptations of action research offer different views of the phases through which planned change occurs in organizations. Lewin's change model views planned change as a three-step process of unfreezing, movement, and refreezing. The action research model focuses on planned change as a cyclical process involving joint activities between organization members and OD practitioners. Recent trends in action research include movement from smaller to larger systems, from domestic to international applications, and from organizational issues to social change. Those trends have led to two key adaptations of action research: increased involvement of participants in the change process and a more appreciative approach to organizational change.

These theories can be integrated into a general model of planned change that includes entering and contracting, diagnosing, planning and implementing, and evaluating and institutionalizing. The general model has broad applicability to planned change. Although the planned change models describe general stages of how the OD process unfolds, there are different types of change depending on the magnitude of the change, the degree to which the client system is organized, and whether the change is being conducted in a domestic or international setting. Critics of OD have pointed out several problems with the way planned change has been conceptualized and practiced.

This chapter also discussed the values and ethics associated with OD practitioners. Traditional values promoting trust, collaboration, and openness recently have been supplemented with concerns for improving organizational effectiveness and productivity. Ethical issues in OD involve how practitioners perform their helping role with clients. OD always has shown a concern for the ethical conduct of practitioners, and several ethical codes for practice have been developed by the various professional OD associations. Ethical dilemmas in OD arise around the following issues: misrepresentation, misuse of data, coercion, value and goal conflict, and technical ineptness.

■ NOTES

1. W. Bennis, *Changing Organizations* (New York: McGraw-Hill, 1966); J. Porras and P. Robertson, "Organization Development Theory: A Typology and Evaluation," in *Research in Organizational Change and Development*, vol. 1, eds. R. Woodman and W. Pasmore (Greenwich, Conn.: JAI Press, 1987): 1–57.

2. K. Lewin, *Field Theory in Social Science* (New York: Harper & Row, 1951).

3. E. Schein, *Process Consultation*, vols. 1 and 2 (Reading, Mass.: Addison-Wesley, 1987).

4. R. Lippitt, J. Watson, and B. Westley, *The Dynamics of Planned Change* (New York: Harcourt, Brace and World, 1958).

5. R. Benjamin and E. Levinson, "A Framework for Managing IT-Enabled Change," *Sloan Management Review* (Summer 1993): 23–33.

6. A. Shani and G. Bushe, "Visionary Action Research: A Consultation Process Perspective," *Consultation* 6 (Spring 1987): 3–19; G. Sussman and R. Evered, "An Assessment of the Scientific Merit of Action Research," *Administrative Science Quarterly* 12 (1978): 582–603.

7. W. French, "Organization Development: Objectives, Assumptions, and Strategies," *California Management Review* 12 (1969): 23–34; A. Frohman, M. Sashkin, and M. Kavanagh, "Action Research as Applied to Organization Development," *Organization and Administrative Sciences* 7

(1976): 129–42; E. Schein, *Organizational Psychology*, 3d ed. (Englewood Cliffs, N.J.: Prentice Hall, 1980).

8. N. Tichy, "Agents of Planned Change: Congruence of Values, Cognitions, and Actions," *Administrative Science Quarterly* 19 (1974): 163–82.

9. M. Beer, "The Technology of Organization Development," in *Handbook of Industrial and Organizational Psychology*, ed. M. Dunnette (Chicago: Rand McNally, 1976): 945.

10. E. Schein, *Process Consultation: Its Role in Organization Development* (Reading, Mass.: Addison-Wesley, 1969): 98.

11. Ibid, 6.

12. R. Beckhard and R. Harris, *Organizational Transitions*, 2d ed. (Reading, Mass.: Addison-Wesley, 1987).

13. M. Elden and R. Chisholm, "Emerging Varieties of Action Research: Introduction to the Special Issue," *Human Relations* 46, 2 (1993): 121–42.

14. G. Ledford and S. Mohrman, "Self-Design for High Involvement," *Human Relations* 46 (1993): 143–68; B. B. Bunker and B. Alban, "The Large Group Intervention—A New Social Innovation?" *Journal of Applied Behavioral Science* 28, 4 (1992): 473–80.

15. R. Marshak, "Lewin Meets Confucius: A Re-view of the OD Model of Change," *Journal of Applied Behavioral Science* 29, 4 (1993): 393–415; K. Murrell, "Evaluation as Action Research: The Case of the Management Development Institute in Gambia, West Africa," *International*

Journal of Public Administration 16, 3 (1993): 341–56; J. Preston and L. DuToit, "Endemic Violence in South Africa: An OD Solution Applied to Two Educational Settings," *International Journal of Public Administration* 16 (1993): 1767–91.

16. D. Brown, "Participatory Action Research for Social Change: Collective Reflections with Asian Nongovernmental Development Organizations," *Human Relations* 46, 2 (1993): 208–27.

17. D. Cooperrider and S. Srivastva, "Appreciative Inquiry in Organizational Life," in *Research in Organizational Change and Development*, vol. 1, eds. R. Woodman and W. Pasmore (Greenwich, Conn.: JAI Press, 1987): 129–70.

18. D. Cooperrider and W. Pasmore, "Global Social Change: A New Agenda for Social Science?" *Human Relations* 44, 10 (1991): 1037–55.

19. W. Burke, *Organization Development: A Normative View* (Reading, Mass.: Addison-Wesley, 1987).

20. D. Greenwood, W. Whyte, and I. Harkavy, "Participatory Action Research as Process and as Goal," *Human Relations* 46, 2 (1993): 175–92.

21. G. Morgan and R. Ramirez, "Action Learning: A Holographic Metaphor for Guiding Social Change," *Human Relations* 37 (1984): 1–28.

22. C. Argyris, R. Putnam, and D. Smith, *Action Science* (San Francisco: Jossey-Bass, 1985).

23. S. Mohrman and T. Cummings, *Self-Designing Organizations: Learning How to Create High Performance* (Reading, Mass.: Addison-Wesley, 1989).

24. Cooperrider and Srivastva, "Appreciative Inquiry"; S. Hammond and C. Royal, *Lessons from the Field: Applying Appreciative Inquiry* (Plano, Tex.: Practical Press).

25. P. Senge, *The Fifth Discipline* (New York: Doubleday, 1990).

26. M. Weisbord, *Productive Workplaces* (San Francisco: Jossey-Bass, 1987).

27. K. Gergen, "The Social Constructionist Movement in Modern Psychology," *American Psychologist* 40 (1985): 266–75; L. Isabella, "Evolving Interpretations as Change Unfolds: How Managers Construe Key Organizational Events," *Academy of Management Journal* 33 (1990): 7–41; D. Cooperrider, "Positive Image, Positive Action: The Affirmative Basis for Organizing," in *Appreciative Management and Leadership,* eds. S. Srivastva, D. Cooperrider, and Associates (San Francisco: Jossey-Bass, 1990); D. Cooperrider (lecture notes, presentation to the MSOD Chi Class, Monterey, Calif., October 1995); F. Barrett, G. Thomas, and S.

Hocevar, "The Central Role of Discourse in Large-Scale Change: A Social Constructionist Perspective," *Journal of Applied Behavioral Science* 31 (1995): 352–72; D. Cooperrider, F. Barrett, and S. Srivastva, "Social Construction and Appreciative Inquiry: A Journey in Organization Theory," in *Management and Organization: Relational Alternatives to Individualism,* eds. D. Hosking, P. Dachler, and K. Gergen (Aldershot, U.K.: Avebury Press, 1995).

28. F. Barrett and D. Cooperrider, "Generative Metaphor Intervention: A New Approach for Working with Systems Divided by Conflict and Caught in Defensive Perception," *Journal of Applied Behavioral Science* 26 (1990): 219–39.

29. Cooperrider and Srivastva, "Appreciative Inquiry."

30. D. Eden, "Creating Expectation Effects in OD: Applying Self-Fulfilling Prophecy," in *Research in Organizational Change and Development*, vol. 2, eds. W. Pasmore and R. Woodman (Greenwich, Conn.: JAI Press, 1988); D. Eden, "OD and Self-Fulfilling Prophesy: Boosting Productivity by Raising Expectations," *Journal of Applied Behavioral Science* 22 (1986): 1–13; Cooperrider, "Positive Image."

31. Barrett and Cooperrider, "Generative Metaphor Intervention."

32. D. Nadler, "Organizational Frame-Bending: Types of Change in the Complex Organization," in *Corporate Transformation,* eds. R. Kilmann and T. Covin (San Francisco: Jossey-Bass, 1988): 66–83; P. Watzlawick, J. Weakland, and R. Fisch, *Change* (New York: W. W. Norton, 1974); R. Golembiewski, K. Billingsley, and S. Yeager, "Measuring Change and Persistence in Human Affairs: Types of Change Generated by OD Designs," *Journal of Applied Behavioral Science* 12 (1975): 133–57; A. Meyer, G. Brooks, and J. Goes, "Environmental Jolts and Industry Revolutions: Organizational Responses to Discontinuous Change," *Strategic Management Journal* 11 (1990): 93–110.

33. A. Mohrman, G. Ledford Jr., S. Mohrman, E. Lawler III, and T. Cummings, *Large-Scale Organization Change* (San Francisco: Jossey-Bass, 1989).

34. L. D. Brown, "Planned Change in Underorganized Systems," in *Systems Theory for Organization Development*, ed. T. Cummings (Chichester, England: John Wiley & Sons, 1980): 181–203.

35. T. Cummings, S. Mohrman, A. Mohrman, and G. Ledford, "Organization Design for the Future: A Collaborative Research Approach," in *Doing Research That Is Useful for Theory and Practice,* eds. E. Lawler III, A. Mohrman, S. Mohrman, G. Ledford, and T. Cummings (San Francisco: Jossey-Bass, 1985): 275–305.

36. C. Worley and R. Patchett, "Myth and Hope Meet Reality: The Fallacy of and Opportunities for Reducing Cycle Time in Strategic Change," in *Fast Cycle Organization Development*, ed. M. Anderson (Cincinnati: South-Western College Publishing, 2000).

37. P. Hanson and B. Lubin, *Answers to Questions Most Frequently Asked about Organization Development* (Newbury Park, Calif.: Sage Publications, 1995).

38. A. Church and W. Burke, "Practitioner Attitudes about the Field of Organization Development," in *Research in Organizational Change and Development*, eds. W. Pasmore and R. Woodman (Greenwich, Conn.: JAI Press, 1995).

39. D. Jamieson and B. Tannenbaum, *The Heart and Mind of the Practitioner: Enduring Values and Perspectives for the Practice of Change* (San Francisico: Jossey-Bass, in press).

40. D. Warrick and H. Kelman, "Ethical Issues in Social Intervention," in *Processes and Phenomena of Social Change*, ed. G. Zaltman (New York: John Wiley & Sons, 1973): 377–449; R. Walton, "Ethical Issues in the Practice of Organization Development" (working paper no. 1840, Harvard University Graduate School of Business Administration, 1973); D. Bowen, "Value Dilemmas in Organization Development," *Journal of Applied Behavioral Science* 13 (1977): 545–55; L. Greiner and R. Metzger, *Consulting to Management* (Englewood Cliffs, N.J.: Prentice Hall, 1983): 311–25; L. White and K. Wooten, "Ethical Dilemmas in Various Stages of Organization Development," *Academy of Management Review* 8 (1963): 690–97; K. Scalzo, "When Ethics and Consulting Collide" (unpublished Master's Thesis, Pepperdine University, Graziadio School of Business and Management, Culver City, Calif., 1994); L.

White and M. Rhodeback, "Ethical Dilemmas in Organization Development: A Cross-Cultural Analysis," *Journal of Business Ethics* 11, 9 (1992): 663–70; S. DeVogel, R. Sullivan, G. McLean, and W. Rothwell, "Ethics in OD," in *Practicing Organization Development*, eds. W. Rothwell, R. Sullivan, and G. McLean (San Diego: Pfeiffer, 1995).

41. OD Institute, *International Registry of O.D. Professionals and O.D. Handbook* (Cleveland: OD Institute, 1992).

42. *Who's Who in Training and Development* (Alexandria, Va: American Society for Training & Development, 1992).

43. W. Gellerman, M. Frankel, and R. Ladenson, *Values and Ethics in Organization and Human System Development: Responding to Dilemmas in Professional Life* (San Francisco: Jossey-Bass, 1990).

44. H. Kelman, "Manipulation of Human Behavior: An Ethical Dilemma for the Social Scientist," in *The Planning of Change*, 2d ed., eds. W. Bennis, K. Benne, and R. Chin (New York: Holt, Rinehart, & Winston, 1969): 584.

45. E. Schein, Process Consultation Revisited (Reading, Mass.: Addison-Wesley, 1999); R. Beckhard, "The Dependency Dilemma," *Consultants' Communique* 6 (July-September 1978): 1–3.

46. G. Lippitt, *Organization Renewal* (Englewood Cliffs, N.J.: Prentice Hall, 1969).

47. C. Argyris, "Explorations in Consulting–Client Relationships," *Human Organizations* 20 (Fall 1961): 121–33.

48. J. Slocum Jr., "Does Cognitive Style Affect Diagnosis and Intervention Strategies?" *Group and Organization Studies* 3 (June 1978): 199–210.

■ APPENDIX

Ethical Guidelines for an Organization Development/Human Systems Development (OD/HSD) Professional

Sponsored by the Human Systems Development Consortium (HSDC), a significant integrative effort by Bill Gellermann has been under way to develop "A Statement of Values and Ethics for Professionals in Organization and Human System Development." HSDC is an informal collection of the leaders of most of the professional associations related to the application of the behavioral and social sciences. A series of drafts based on extensive contributions, comments, and discussions involving many professionals and organizations has led to the following version of this statement.

As an OD/HSD Professional, I commit to supporting and acting in accordance with the following guidelines:

I. Responsibility for Professional Development and Competence

A. Accept responsibility for the consequences of my acts and make every effort to ensure that my services are properly used.

B. Recognize the limits of my competence, culture, and experience in providing services and using techniques; neither seek nor accept assignments outside those limits without clear understanding by the client when exploration at the edge of my competence is reasonable; refer client to other professionals when appropriate.

C. Strive to attain and maintain a professional level of competence in the field, including

　1. broad knowledge of theory and practice in

　　a. applied behavioral science generally.
　　b. management, administration, organizational behavior, and system behavior specifically.
　　c. multicultural issues including issues of color and gender.
　　d. other relevant fields of knowledge and practice.

　2. ability to

　　a. relate effectively with individuals and groups.
　　b. relate effectively to the dynamics of large, complex systems.
　　c. provide consultation using theory and methods of the applied behavioral sciences.
　　d. articulate theory and direct its application, including creation of learning experiences for individuals, small and large groups, and for whole systems.

D. Strive continually for self-knowledge and personal growth; be aware that "what is in me" (my perceptions of myself in my world) and "what is outside me" (the realities that exist apart from me) are not the same; be aware that my values, beliefs, and aspirations can both limit and empower me and that they are primary determinants of my perceptions, my behavior, and my personal and professional effectiveness.

E. Recognize my own personal needs and desires and deal with them responsibly in the performance of my professional roles.

F. Obtain consultation from OD/HSD professionals who are native to and aware of the specific cultures within which I work when those cultures are different from my own.

II. Responsibility to Clients and Significant Others

A. Serve the short- and long-term welfare, interests, and development of the client system and all its stakeholders; maintain balance in the timing, pace, and magnitude of planned change so as to support a mutually beneficial relationship between the system and its environment.

B. Discuss candidly and fully goals, costs, risks, limitations, and anticipated outcomes of any program or other professional relationship under consideration; seek to avoid automatic confirmation of predetermined conclusions, either the client's or my own; seek optimum involvement by client system members in every step of the process, including managers and workers' representatives; fully inform client system members about my role, contribution, and strategy in working with them.

C. Fully inform participants in any activity or procedure as to its sponsorship, nature, purpose, implications, and any significant risk associated with it so that they can freely choose their participation in any activity initiated by me; acknowledge that their choice may be limited with activity initiated by recognized authorities; be particularly sensitive to implications and risks when I work with people from cultures other than my own.

D. Be aware of my own personal values, my values as an OD/HSD professional, the values of my native culture, the values of the people with whom I am working, and the values of their cultures; involve the client system in making relevant cultural differences explicit and exploring the possible implications of any OD/HSD intervention for all the stakeholders involved; be prepared to make explicit my assumptions, values, and standards as an OD/HSD professional.

E. Help all stakeholders while developing OD/HSD approaches, programs, and the like, if they wish such help; for example, this could include workers' representatives as well as managers in the case of work with a business organization.

F. Work collaboratively with other internal and external consultants serving the same client system and resolve conflicts in terms of the balanced best interests of the client system and all its stakeholders; make appropriate arrangements with other internal and external consultants about how responsibilities will be shared.

G. Encourage and enable my clients to provide for themselves the services I provide rather than foster continued reliance on me; encourage, foster, and support self-education and self-development by individuals, groups, and all other human systems.

H. Cease work with a client when it is clear that the client is not benefiting or the contract has been completed; do not accept an assignment if its scope is so limited that the client will not benefit or it would involve serious conflict with the values and ethics outlined in this statement.

I. Avoid conflicts of interest.

1. Fully inform the client of my opinion about serving similar or competing organizations; be clear with myself, my clients, and other concerned stakeholders about my loyalties and responsibilities when conflicts of interest arise; keep parties informed of these conflicts; cease work with the client if the conflicts cannot be adequately resolved.

2. Seek to act impartially when involved in conflicts between parties in the client system; help them resolve their conflicts themselves, without taking

sides; if necessary to change my role from serving as impartial consultant, do so explicitly; cease work with the client, if necessary.

3. Identify and respond to any major differences in professionally relevant values or ethics between myself and my clients with the understanding that conditions may require ceasing work with the client.

4. Accept differences in the expectations and interests of different stakeholders and realize that those differences cannot be reconciled all the time.

J. Seek consultation and feedback from neutral third parties in case of conflict between myself and my client.

K. Define and protect the confidentiality of my client–professional relationships.

1. Make limits of confidentiality clear to clients/participants.

2. Reveal information accepted in confidence only to appropriate or agreed-upon recipients or authorities.

3. Use information obtained during professional work in writings, lectures, or other public forums only with prior consent or when disguised so that it is impossible from my presentations alone to identify the individuals or systems with whom I have worked.

4. Make adequate provisions for maintaining confidentiality in the storage and disposal of records; make provisions for responsibly preserving records in the event of my retirement or disability.

L. Establish mutual agreement on a contract covering services and remuneration.

1. Ensure a clear understanding of and mutual agreement on the services to be performed; do not shift from that agreement without both a clearly defined professional rationale for making the shift and the informed consent of the clients/participants; withdraw from the agreement if circumstances beyond my control prevent proper fulfillment.

2. Ensure mutual understanding and agreement by putting the contract in writing to the extent feasible, yet recognize that

a. the spirit of professional responsibility encompasses more than the letter of the contract.

b. some contracts are necessarily incomplete because complete information is not available at the outset.

c. putting the contract in writing may be neither necessary nor desirable.

3. Safeguard the best interests of the client, the profession, and the public by making sure that financial arrangements are fair and in keeping with appropriate statutes, regulations, and professional standards.

M. Provide for my own accountability by evaluating and assessing the effects of my work.

1. Make all reasonable efforts to determine if my activities have accomplished the agreed-upon goals and have not had other undesirable consequences; seek to undo any undesirable consequences, and do not attempt to cover up these situations.

2. Actively solicit and respond with an open mind to feedback regarding my work and seek to improve.

3. Develop, publish, and use assessment techniques that promote the welfare and best interests of clients/participants; guard against the misuse of assessment results.

N. Make public statements of all kinds accurately, including promotion and advertising, and give service as advertised.

1. Base public statements providing professional opinions or information on scientifically acceptable findings and techniques as much as possible, with full recognition of the limits and uncertainties of such evidence.

2. Seek to help people make informed choices when making statements as part of promotion or advertising.

3. Deliver services as advertised and do not shift without a clear professional rationale and the informed consent of the participants/clients.

III. Responsibility to the Profession

A. Act with due regard for the needs, special competencies and obligations of my colleagues in OD/HSD and other professions; respect the prerogatives and obligations of the institutions or organizations with which these other colleagues are associated.

B. Be aware of the possible impact of my public behavior upon the ability of colleagues to perform their professional work; perform professional activity in a way that will bring credit to the profession.

C. Work actively for ethical practice by individuals and organizations engaged in OD/HSD activities and, in case of questionable practice, use appropriate channels for confronting it, including

1. direct discussion when feasible.

2. joint consultation and feedback, using other professionals as third parties.

3. enforcement procedures of existing professional organizations.

4. public confrontation.

D. Contribute to continuing professional development by

1. supporting the development of other professionals, including mentoring with less experienced professionals.

2. contributing ideas, methods, findings, and other useful information to the body of OD/HSD knowledge and skill.

E. Promote the sharing of OD/HSD knowledge and skill by various means including

1. granting use of my copyrighted material as freely as possible, subject to a minimum of conditions, including a reasonable price defined on the basis of professional as well as commercial values.

2. giving credit for the ideas and products of others.

IV. Social Responsibility

A. Strive for the preservation and protection of fundamental human rights and the promotion of social justice.

B. Be aware that I bear a heavy social responsibility because my recommendations and professional actions may alter the lives and well-being of individuals within my client systems, the systems themselves, and the larger systems of which they are subsystems.

C. Contribute knowledge, skill, and other resources in support of organizations, programs, and activities that seek to improve human welfare; be prepared to accept clients who do not have sufficient resources to pay my full fees at reduced fees or no charge.

D. Respect the cultures of the organization, community, country, or other human system within which I work (including the cultures' traditions, values, and moral and ethical expectations and their implications), yet recognize and constructively confront the counterproductive aspects of those cultures whenever feasible; be sensitive to cross-cultural differences and their implications; be aware of the cultural filters which bias my view of the world.

E. Recognize that accepting this statement as a guide for my behavior involves holding myself to a standard that may be more exacting than the laws of any country in which I practice.

F. Contribute to the quality of life in human society at large; work toward and support a culture based on mutual respect for each other's rights as human beings; encourage the development of love, trust, openness, mutual responsibility, authentic and harmonious relationships, empowerment, participation, and involvement in a spirit of freedom and self-discipline as elements of this culture.

G. Engage in self-generated or collaborative endeavor to develop means for helping across cultures.

H. Serve the welfare of all the people of Earth, all living things, and their environment.

The Process of Organization Development

2

3. Entering and Contracting

The planned change process described in Chapter 2 generally starts when one or more key managers or administrators somehow sense that their organization, department, or group could be improved or has problems that could be alleviated through organization development. The organization might be successful yet have room for improvement. It might be facing impending environmental conditions that necessitate a change in how it operates. The organization could be experiencing particular problems, such as poor product quality, high rates of absenteeism, or dysfunctional conflicts among departments. Conversely, the problems might appear more diffuse and consist simply of feelings that the organization should be "more innovative," "more competitive," or "more effective."

Entering and contracting are the initial steps in the OD process. They involve defining in a preliminary manner the organization's problems or opportunities for development and establishing a collaborative relationship between the OD practitioner and members of the client system about how to work on those issues. Entering and contracting set the initial parameters for carrying out the subsequent phases of OD: diagnosing the organization, planning and implementing changes, and evaluating and institutionalizing them. They help to define what issues will be addressed by those activities, who will carry them out, and how they will be accomplished.

Entering and contracting can vary in complexity and formality depending on the situation. In those cases where the manager of a work group or department serves as his or her own OD practitioner, entering and contracting typically involve the manager and group members meeting to discuss what issues to work on and how they will accomplish that jointly. Here, entering and contracting are relatively simple and informal. They involve all relevant members directly in the process without a great number of formal procedures. In situations where managers and administrators are considering the use of professional OD practitioners, either from inside or from outside the organization, entering and contracting tend to be more complex and formal.[1] OD practitioners may need to collect preliminary information to help define the problematic or development issues. They may need to meet with representatives of the client organization rather than with the total membership; they may need to formalize their respective roles and how the change process will unfold.

This chapter first discusses the activities and content-oriented issues involved in entering into and contracting for an OD initiative. Major attention will be directed at complex processes involving OD professionals and client organizations. Similar entering and contracting issues, however, need to be addressed in even the simplest OD efforts where managers serve as OD practitioners for their own work units. Unless there is clarity and agreement about what issues to work on, who will address them, and how that will be accomplished, subsequent stages of the OD process are likely to be confusing and ineffective. The chapter concludes with a discussion of the interpersonal process issues involved in entering and contracting for OD work.

ENTERING INTO AN OD RELATIONSHIP

An OD process generally starts when a member of an organization or unit contacts an OD practitioner about potential help in addressing an organizational issue.[2] The organization member may be a manager, staff specialist, or some other key participant, and the practitioner may be an OD professional from inside or outside of the organization. Determining whether the two parties should enter into an OD relationship typically involves clarifying the nature of the organization's current functioning and the issue(s) to be addressed, the relevant client system for that issue, and the appropriateness of the particular OD practitioner.[3] In helping assess these issues, the OD practitioner may need to collect preliminary data about the organization. Similarly, the organization may need to gather information about the practitioner's competence and experience.[4] This knowledge will help both parties determine whether they should proceed to develop a contract for working together.

This section describes the following activities involved in entering an OD relationship: clarifying the organizational issue, determining the relevant client, and selecting the appropriate OD practitioner.

Clarifying the Organizational Issue

When seeking help from OD practitioners, organizations typically start with a *presenting problem*—the issue that has caused them to consider an OD process. It may be specific (decreased market share, increased absenteeism) or general ("we're growing too fast," "we need to prepare for rapid changes"). The presenting problem often has an implied or stated solution. For example, managers may believe that because members of their teams are in conflict, team building is the obvious answer. They may even state the presenting problem in the form of a solution: "We need some team building."

In many cases, however, the presenting problem is only a symptom of an underlying problem. For example, conflict among members of a team may result from several deeper causes, including ineffective reward systems, personality differences, inappropriate structure, and poor leadership. The issue facing the organization or department must be clarified early in the OD process so that subsequent diagnostic and intervention activities are focused correctly.[5]

Gaining a clearer perspective on the organizational issue may require collecting preliminary data.[6] OD practitioners often examine company records and interview a few key members to gain an introductory understanding of the organization, its context, and the nature of the presenting problem. Those data are gathered in a relatively short period of time, typically over a few hours to one or two days. They are intended to provide enough rudimentary knowledge of the organizational issue to enable the two parties to make informed choices about proceeding with the contracting process.

The diagnostic phase of OD involves a far more extensive assessment of the problematic or development issue than occurs during the entering and contracting stage. The diagnosis also might discover other issues that need to be addressed, or it might lead to redefining the initial issue that was identified during the entering and contracting stage. This is a prime example of the emergent nature of the OD process, where things may change as new information is gathered and new events occur.

Determining the Relevant Client

A second activity in entering an OD relationship is to define who is the relevant client for addressing the organizational issue.[7] Generally, the relevant client includes those organization members who can directly impact the change issue, whether it is solving a particular problem or improving an already successful organization or department. Unless these members are identified and included in the entering and contracting process, they may withhold their support for and commitment to the OD process. In trying to improve the productivity of a unionized manufacturing plant, for example, the relevant client may need to include union officials as well as managers and staff personnel. It is not unusual for an OD project to fail because the relevant client was inappropriately defined.

Determining the relevant client can vary in complexity depending on the situation. In those cases where the organizational issue can be addressed in a specific organization unit, client definition is relatively straightforward. Members of that unit constitute the relevant client. They or their representatives must be included in the entering and contracting process. For example, if a manager asked for help in improving the decision-making process of his or her team, the manager and team members would be the relevant client. Unless they are actively involved in choosing an OD practitioner and defining the subsequent change process, there is little likelihood that OD will improve team decision making.

Determining the relevant client is more complex when the organizational issue cannot readily be addressed in a single organization unit. Here, it may be necessary to expand the definition of the client to include members from multiple units, from different hierarchical levels, and even from outside of the organization. For example, the manager of a production department may seek help in resolving conflicts between his or her unit and other departments in the organization. The relevant client would extend beyond the boundaries of the production department because that department alone cannot resolve the issue. The client might include members from all departments involved in the conflict as well as the executive to whom all of the departments report. If that interdepartmental conflict also involved key suppliers and customers from outside of the firm, the relevant client might include members of those groups.

In such complex situations, OD practitioners need to gather additional information about the organization to determine the relevant client, generally as part of the preliminary data collection that typically occurs when clarifying the issue to be addressed. When examining company records or interviewing personnel, practitioners can seek to identify the key members and organizational units that need to be involved. For example, they can ask organization members such questions as Who can directly impact the organizational issue? Who has a vested interest in it? Who has the power to approve or reject the OD effort? Answers to those questions can help determine who is the relevant client for the entering and contracting stage, although the client may change during the later stages of the OD process as new data are gathered and changes occur. If so, participants may have to return to and modify this initial stage of the OD effort.

Selecting an OD Practitioner

The last activity involved in entering an OD relationship is selecting an OD practitioner who has the expertise and experience to work with members on the organizational issue. Unfortunately, little systematic advice is available on how to choose a competent OD professional, whether from inside or outside of the organization.

Perhaps the best criteria for selecting, evaluating, and developing OD practitioners are those suggested by the late Gordon Lippitt, a pioneering practitioner in the field.[8] Lippitt listed areas that managers should consider before selecting a practitioner, including the ability of the consultant to form sound interpersonal relationships, the degree of focus on the problem, the skills of the practitioner relative to the problem, the extent that the consultant clearly informs the client as to his or her role and contribution, and whether the practitioner belongs to a professional association. References from other clients are highly important. A client may not like the consultant's work, but it is critical to know the reasons for both pleasure and displeasure. One important consideration is whether the consultant approaches the organization with openness and an insistence on diagnosis or whether the practitioner appears to have a fixed program that is applicable to almost any organization.

Certainly, OD consulting is as much a *person* specialization as it is a *task* specialization. The OD professional needs not only a repertoire of technical skills but also the personality and interpersonal competence to use himself or herself as an instrument of change. Regardless of technical training, the consultant must be able to maintain a boundary position, coordinating among various units and departments and mixing disciplines, theories, technology, and research findings in an organic rather than a mechanical way. The practitioner is potentially the most important OD technology available.

Thus, in selecting an OD practitioner, perhaps the most important issue is the fundamental question, How effective has the person been in the past, with what kinds of organizations, using what kinds of techniques? In other words, references must be checked. Interpersonal relationships are tremendously important, but even con artists have excellent interpersonal relationships and skills.

The burden of choosing an effective OD practitioner should not rest entirely with the client organization.[9] Consultants also bear a heavy responsibility for seeking an appropriate match between their skills and knowledge and what the organization or department needs. Few managers are sophisticated enough to detect or to understand subtle differences in expertise among OD professionals, and they often do not understand the difference between intervention specialties. Thus, practitioners should help educate potential clients, being explicit about their strengths and weaknesses and about their range of competence. If OD professionals realize that a good match does not exist, they should inform managers and help them find more suitable help.

DEVELOPING A CONTRACT

The activities of entering an OD relationship are a necessary prelude to developing an OD contract. They define the major focus for contracting, including the relevant parties. Contracting is a natural extension of the entering process and clarifies how the OD process will proceed. It typically establishes the expectations of the parties, the time and resources that will be expended, and the ground rules under which the parties will operate.

The goal of contracting is to make a good decision about how to carry out the OD process.[10] It can be relatively informal and involve only a verbal agreement between the client and OD practitioner. A team leader with OD skills, for example, may voice his or her concerns to members about how the team is functioning. After some discussion, they might agree to devote one hour of future meeting time to diagnosing the team with the help of the leader. Here, entering and contracting are done together informally. In other cases, contracting can be more protracted and result in a formal document. That typically occurs when organizations employ outside OD practitioners. Government agencies, for example, generally have procurement regulations that apply to contracting with outside consultants.[11]

Regardless of the level of formality, all OD processes require some form of explicit contracting that results in either a verbal or a written agreement. Such contracting clarifies the client's and the practitioner's expectations about how the OD process will take place. Unless there is mutual understanding and agreement about the process, there is considerable risk that someone's expectations will be unfilled.[12] That can lead to reduced commitment and support, to misplaced action, or to premature termination of the process.

The contracting step in OD generally addresses three key areas:[13] what each party expects to gain from the OD process, the time and resources that will be devoted to it, and the ground rules for working together.

Mutual Expectations

This part of the contracting process focuses on the expectations of the client and the OD practitioner. The client states the services and outcomes to be provided by the OD practitioner and describes what the organization expects from the process and the consultant. Clients usually can describe the desired outcomes, such as decreased turnover or higher job satisfaction. Encouraging them to state their wants in the form of outcomes, working relationships, and personal accomplishments can facilitate the development of a good contract.[14]

The OD practitioner also should state what he or she expects to gain from the OD process. This can include opportunities to try new interventions, report the results to other potential clients, and receive appropriate compensation or recognition.

Time and Resources

To accomplish change, the organization and the OD practitioner must commit time and resources to the effort. Each must be clear about how much energy and how many resources will be dedicated to the change process. Failure to make explicit the necessary requirements of a change process can quickly ruin an OD effort. For example, a client may clearly state that the assignment involves diagnosing the causes of poor productivity in a work group. However, the client may expect the practitioner to complete the assignment without talking to the workers. Typically, clients want to know how much time will be necessary to complete the assignment, who needs to be involved, how much it will cost, and so on.

Block has suggested that resources can be divided into two parts.[15] *Essential requirements* are things that are absolutely necessary if the change process is to be successful. From the practitioner's perspective, they can include access to key people or information, enough time to do the job, and commitment from certain people. The organization's essential requirements might include a speedy diagnosis or assurances that the project will be conducted at the lowest price. Being clear about the constraints on carrying out the assignment will facilitate the contracting process and improve the chances for success. *Desirable requirements* are those things that would be nice to have but are not absolutely necessary, such as access to special resources and written rather than verbal reports.

Ground Rules

The final part of the contracting process involves specifying how the client and the OD practitioner will work together. The parameters established may include such issues as confidentiality, if and how the OD practitioner will become involved in personal or interpersonal issues, how to terminate the relationship, and whether the practitioner is supposed to make expert recommendations or help the manager make decisions. For internal consultants, organizational politics make it especially important to clarify issues of how to handle sensitive information and how to deliver "bad news."[16] Such process issues are as important as the needed substantive changes. Failure to address the concerns may mean that the client or the practitioner has inappropriate assumptions about how the process will unfold.

PERSONAL PROCESS ISSUES IN ENTERING AND CONTRACTING

The prior discussion on entering and contracting addressed the activities and content-oriented issues associated with beginning an OD project. In this final section, we discuss the interpersonal issues an OD practitioner must be aware of to produce a successful agreement. In most cases, the client's expectations, resources, and working relationship requirements will not fit perfectly with the OD practitioner's essential and desirable requirements. Negotiating the differences to improve the likelihood of success can be intra- and interpersonally challenging.

Entering and contracting are the first exchanges between a client and an OD practitioner. Establishing a healthy relationship at the outset makes it more likely that the client's desired outcomes will be achieved and that the OD practitioner will be able to improve the organization's capacity to manage change in the future. In this initial stage, both parties are facing a considerable amount of uncertainty and ambiguity. On the one hand, the client is likely to feel exposed, inadequate, or vulnerable. The organization's current effectiveness and the request for help may seem to the client like an admission that they are incapable of solving the problem or providing the leadership necessary to achieve a set of results. Moreover, they are entering into a relationship where they may feel unable to control the activities of the OD practitioner. As a result, they feel vulnerable because of their dependency on the practitioner to provide assistance. Consciously or unconsciously, feelings of exposure, inadequacy, or vulnerability may lead the client to resist coming to closure on the contract. The OD practitioner must be alert to the signs of resistance, such as asking for extraordinary amounts of detail, and be able to address them skillfully.

On the other hand, the OD practitioner may have feelings of empathy, unworthiness, and dependency. The practitioner may overidentify with the client's issues and want to be so helpful that she or he agrees to unreasonable deadlines or inadequate resources. The practitioner's desire to be seen as competent and worthy may lead to an agreement on a project for which the practitioner has few skills or experience. Finally, in response to reasonable client requests, the practitioner may challenge the client's motivation and become defensive.

Actually coming to agreement during the contracting phase can be difficult and intense. A number of complex emotional and psychological issues are in play, and OD practitioners must be mindful of their own as well as the client's perspectives. Attending to those issues as well as to the content of the contract will help increase the likelihood of success.

■ SUMMARY

The entering and contracting processes constitute the initial activities of the OD process. They set the parameters for the phases of planned change that follow: diagnosing, planning and implementing change, and evaluating and institutionalizing it.

Organizational entry involves clarifying the organizational issue or presenting problem, determining the relevant client, and selecting an OD practitioner. Developing an OD contract focuses on making a good decision about whether to proceed and allows both the client and the OD practitioner to clarify expectations about how the change process will unfold. Contracting involves setting mutual expectations, negotiating time and resources, and developing ground rules for working together.

■ NOTES

1. M. Lacey, "Internal Consulting: Perspectives on the Process of Planned Change," *Journal of Organization Change Management* 8, 3 (1995): 75–84; J. Geirland and M. Maniker-Leiter, "Five Lessons for Internal Organization Development Consultants," *OD Practitioner* 27 (1995): 44–48.

2. P. Block, *Flawless Consulting: A Guide to Getting Your Expertise Used,* 2d ed. (San Francisco: Jossey-Bass, 1999); C. Margerison, "Consulting Activities in Organizational Change," *Journal of Organizational Change Management* 1 (1988): 60–67; R. Harrison, "Choosing the Depth of Organizational Intervention," *Journal of Applied Behavioral Science* 6 (1970): 182–202.

3. M. Beer, *Organization Change and Development: A Systems View* (Santa Monica, Calif.: Goodyear, 1980); G. Lippitt and R. Lippitt, *The Consulting Process in Action,* 2d ed. (San Diego: University Associates, 1986).

4. L. Greiner and R. Metzger, *Consulting to Management* (Englewood Cliffs, N.J.: Prentice Hall, 1983): 251–58; Beer, *Organization Change and Development,* 81–83.

5. Block, *Flawless Consulting.*

6. D. Jamieson, "Start-up," in *Practicing Organization Development,* eds. W. Rothwell, R. Sullivan, and G. McLean (San Diego: Pfeiffer, 1995); J. Fordyce and R. Weil, *Managing WITH People,* 2d ed. (Reading, Mass.: Addison-Wesley, 1979).

7. Beer, *Organization Change and Development;* Fordyce and Weil, *Managing WITH People.*

8. G. Lippitt, "Criteria for Selecting, Evaluating, and Developing Consultants," *Training and Development Journal* 28 (August 1972): 10–15.

9. Greiner and Metzger, *Consulting to Management.*

10. Block, *Flawless Consulting;* Beer, *Organization Change and Development.*

11. T. Cody, *Management Consulting: A Game Without Chips* (Fitzwilliam, N.H.: Kennedy and Kennedy, 1986): 108–16; H. Holtz, *How to Succeed as an Independent Consultant,* 2d ed. (New York: John Wiley & Sons, 1988): 145–61.

12. G. Bellman, *The Consultant's Calling* (San Francisco: Jossey-Bass, 1990).

13. M. Weisbord, "The Organization Development Contract," *Organization Development Practitioner* 5 (1973): 1–4; M. Weisbord, "The Organization Contract Revisited," *Consultation* 4 (Winter 1985): 305–15; D. Nadler, *Feedback and Organization Development: Using Data-Based Methods* (Reading, Mass.: Addison-Wesley, 1977): 110–14.

14. Block, *Flawless Consulting.*

15. Ibid.

16. Lacey, "Internal Consulting."

4.

Diagnosing Organizations, Groups, and Jobs

Entry and contracting processes can result in a need to understand a whole system or some part, process, or feature of the organization. To diagnose an organization, OD practitioners and organization members need to have an idea about what information to collect and analyze. Choices about what to look for invariably depend on how organizations are perceived. Such perceptions can vary from intuitive hunches to scientific explanations of how organizations function. Conceptual frameworks that people use to understand organizations are referred to as *diagnostic models*.[1] They describe the relationships among different features of the organization, its context, and its effectiveness. As a result, diagnostic models point out what areas to examine and what questions to ask in assessing how an organization is functioning.

However, all models represent simplifications of reality and therefore choose certain features as critical. Focusing attention on those features, often to the exclusion of others, can result in a biased diagnosis. For example, a diagnostic model that relates team effectiveness to the handling of interpersonal conflict would lead an OD practitioner to ask questions about relationships among members, decision-making processes, and conflict resolution methods. Although relevant, those questions ignore other group issues such as the composition of skills and knowledge, the complexity of the tasks performed by the group, and member interdependencies. Thus, diagnostic models must be chosen carefully to address the organization's presenting problems as well as to ensure comprehensiveness.

Potential diagnostic models are everywhere. Any collection of concepts and relationships that attempts to represent a system or explain its effectiveness can potentially qualify as a diagnostic model. Major sources of diagnostic models in OD are the thousands of articles and books that discuss, describe, and analyze how organizations function. They provide information about how and why certain organizational systems, processes, or functions are effective. The studies often concern a specific facet of organizational behavior, such as employee stress, leadership, motivation, problem solving, group dynamics, job design, and career development. They also can involve the larger organization and its context, including the environment, strategy, structure, and culture. Diagnostic models can be derived from that information by noting the dimensions or variables that are associated with organizational effectiveness.

Another source of diagnostic models is OD practitioners' experience in organizations. That field knowledge is a wealth of practical information about how organizations operate. Unfortunately, only a small part of that vast experience has been translated into diagnostic models that represent the professional judgments of people with years of experience in organizational diagnosis. The models generally link diagnosis with specific organizational processes, such as group problem solving, employee motivation, or communication between managers and employees. The models list specific questions for diagnosing such processes.

This chapter presents a general framework for diagnosing organizations rather than trying to cover the range of OD diagnostic models. It first describes the open-systems model, a theory that underlies most diagnostic models. The chapter then discusses an integrated diagnostic model that addresses organization-, group-, and job-level issues. Specific concepts at each level of analysis are discussed. (Additional diagnostic models that are linked to specific OD interventions are presented in Chapters 8 through 15.)

OPEN-SYSTEMS MODEL

This section introduces systems theory, a set of concepts and relationships describing the properties and behaviors of things called *systems*—organizations, groups, and people, for example. Systems are viewed as unitary wholes composed of parts or subsystems; the system serves to integrate the parts into a functioning unit. For example, organization systems are composed of departments such as sales, operations, and finance. The organization serves to coordinate behaviors of its departments so that they function together in service of a goal or strategy. The general diagnostic model based on systems theory that underlies most of OD is called the *open-systems model.*

Organizations as Open Systems

Systems can vary in how open they are to their outside environments. *Open systems,* such as organizations and people, exchange information and resources with their environments. They cannot completely control their own behavior and are influenced in part by external forces. Organizations, for example, are affected by such environmental conditions as the availability of raw material, customer demands, and government regulations. Understanding how these external forces affect the organization can help explain some of its internal behavior.

Open systems display a hierarchical ordering. Each higher level of system comprises lower-level systems: systems at the level of society comprise organizations, organizations comprise groups (departments), and groups comprise individuals. Although systems at different levels vary in many ways—in size and complexity, for example—they have a number of common characteristics by virtue of being open systems, and those properties can be applied to systems at any level. The following key properties of open systems are described below: inputs, transformations, and outputs; boundaries; feedback; equifinality; and alignment.

Inputs, Transformations, and Outputs

Any organizational system is composed of three related parts: inputs, transformations, and outputs, as shown in Figure 4.1. *Inputs* consist of human or other resources, such as information, energy, and materials, coming into the system. Inputs are acquired from the system's external environment. For example, a manufacturing organization acquires raw materials from an outside supplier. Similarly, a hospital nursing unit acquires information concerning a patient's condition from the attending physician. In each case, the system (organization or nursing unit) obtains resources (raw materials or information) from its external environment.

Transformations are the processes of converting inputs into outputs. In organizations, a production or operations function composed of both social and technological components generally carries out transformations. The social component consists of people and their work relationships, whereas the technological component

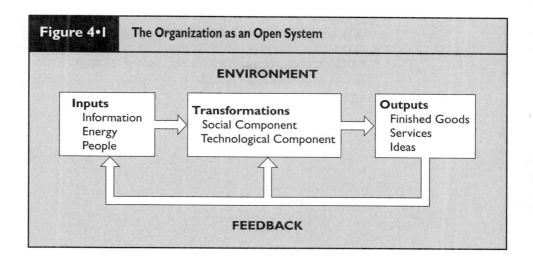

Figure 4•1   The Organization as an Open System

ENVIRONMENT

Inputs
Information
Energy
People

Transformations
Social Component
Technological Component

Outputs
Finished Goods
Services
Ideas

FEEDBACK

involves tools, techniques, and methods of production or service delivery. Organizations have developed elaborate mechanisms for transforming incoming resources into goods and services. Banks, for example, transform deposits into mortgage loans and interest income. Schools attempt to transform students into more educated people. Transformation processes also can take place at the group and individual levels. For example, research and development departments can transform the latest scientific advances into new product ideas.

Outputs are the results of what is transformed by the system and sent to the environment. Thus, inputs that have been transformed represent outputs ready to leave the system. Group health insurance companies receive premiums, healthy and unhealthy individuals, and medical bills, transform them through physician visits and record keeping, and export treated patients and payments to hospitals and physicians.

Boundaries

The idea of boundaries helps to distinguish between systems and environments. Closed systems have relatively rigid and impenetrable boundaries, whereas open systems have far more permeable borders. Boundaries—the borders, or limits, of the system—are seen easily in many biological and mechanical systems. Defining the boundaries of social systems is more difficult because there is a continuous inflow and outflow through them. For example, where are the organizational boundaries in this case? When a fire alarm sounds in Malmo, Sweden, a firefighter puts the address of the fire into a computer terminal. A moment later, the terminal gives out a description of potential hazards at the address. The computer storing the information is in Cleveland, Ohio. The emergence of the information superhighway and worldwide information networks will continue to challenge the notion of boundaries in open systems.

The definition of a *boundary* is somewhat arbitrary because a social system has multiple subsystems and the boundary line for one subsystem may not be the same as that for a different subsystem. As with the system itself, arbitrary boundaries may have to be assigned to any social organization, depending on the variable to be stressed. The boundaries used for studying or analyzing leadership, for instance, may be quite different from those used to study intergroup dynamics.

Just as systems can be considered relatively open or closed, the permeability of boundaries also varies from fixed to diffuse. The boundaries of a community's police force are probably far more rigid and sharply defined than those of the community's political parties. Conflict over boundaries is always a potential problem within an organization, just as it is in the world outside the organization.

Feedback

As shown in Figure 4.1, *feedback* is information regarding the actual performance or the results of the system. Not all such information is feedback, however. Only information used to control the future functioning of the system is considered feedback. Feedback can be used to maintain the system in a steady state (for example, keeping an assembly line running at a certain speed) or to help the organization adapt to changing circumstances. McDonald's, for example, has strict feedback processes to ensure that a meal in one outlet is as similar as possible to a meal in any other outlet. On the other hand, a salesperson in the field may report that sales are not going well and may insist on some organizational change to improve sales. A market research study may lead the marketing department to recommend a change to the organization's advertising campaign.

Equifinality

In closed systems, a direct cause-and-effect relationship exists between the initial condition and the final state of the system: when a computer's "on" switch is pushed, the system powers up. Biological and social systems, however, operate quite differently. The idea of *equifinality* suggests that similar results may be achieved with different initial conditions and in many different ways. This concept suggests that a manager can use varying degrees of inputs into the organization and can transform them in a variety of ways to obtain satisfactory outputs. Thus, the function of management is not to seek a single rigid solution but rather to develop a variety of satisfactory options. Systems and contingency theories suggest that there is no universal best way to design an organization. Organizations and departments providing routine services, such as AT&T's and MCI WorldCom's long-distance phone services could be designed quite differently and still achieve the same result. Similarly, customer service functions at major retailers, software manufacturers, or airlines could be designed according to similar principles.

Alignment

A system's overall effectiveness is determined by the extent to which the different parts are aligned with each other. This alignment or fit concerns the relationships between inputs and transformations, between transformations and outputs, and among the subsystems of the transformation process. Diagnosticians who view the relationships among the various parts of a system as a whole are taking what is referred to as a *systemic* perspective.

Alignment refers to a characteristic of the relationship between two or more parts. It represents the extent to which the features, operations, and characteristics of one system support the effectiveness of another system. Just as the teeth in two wheels of a watch must mesh perfectly for the watch to keep time, so do the parts of an organization need to mesh for it to be effective. For example, General Electric attempts to achieve its goals through a strategy of diversification, and a divisional structure is used to support that strategy. A functional structure would not be a good fit with the strategy because it is more efficient for one division to focus on one product line than for one manufacturing department to try to make many different products. The systemic perspective suggests that diagnosis is the search for misfits among the various parts and subsystems of an organization.

DIAGNOSING ORGANIZATIONAL SYSTEMS

When viewed as open systems, organizations can be diagnosed at three levels. The highest level is the overall organization and includes the design of the company's strategy, structure, and processes. Large organization units, such as divisions, subsidiaries, or strategic business units, also can be diagnosed at that level. The next-lowest level is the group or department, which includes group design and devices for structuring interactions among members such as norms and work schedules. The lowest level is the individual position or job. This includes ways in which jobs are designed to elicit required task behaviors.

Diagnosis can occur at all three organizational levels, or it may be limited to issues occurring at a particular level. The key to effective diagnosis is to know what to look for at each level as well as how the levels affect each other.[2] For example, diagnosing a work group requires knowledge of the variables important for group functioning and how the larger organization design affects the group. In fact, a basic understanding of organization-level issues is important in almost any diagnosis because they serve as critical inputs to understanding groups and individuals.

Figure 4.2 presents a comprehensive model for diagnosing these different organizational systems. For each level, it shows: (1) the inputs that the system has to work with, (2) the key design components of the transformation subsystem, and (3) the system's outputs.

The relationships shown in Figure 4.2 illustrate how each organization level affects the lower levels. The larger environment is an input to organization design. Organization design is an input to group design, which in turn serves as an input to job design. These cross-level relationships emphasize that organizational levels must fit with each other if the organization is to operate effectively. For example, organization structure must fit with and support group task design, which in turn must fit with individual job design.

Organization-Level Diagnosis

The organization level of analysis is the broadest systems perspective typically taken in diagnostic activities. The model shown in Figure 4.2(A) is similar to other popular organization-level diagnostic models. These include Weisbord's six-box model,[3] Nadler and Tushman's congruency model,[4] Galbraith's star model,[5] and Kotter's organization dynamics model.[6] Figure 4.2(A) proposes that an organization's transformation processes, or design components, represent the way the organization positions and organizes itself within an environment (inputs) to achieve specific outputs. The combination of design component elements is called a *strategic orientation*.[7]

Inputs

To understand how a total organization functions, it is necessary to examine particular inputs, design components, and the alignment of the two sets of dimensions. Figure 4.2 shows that two key inputs affect the way an organization designs its strategic orientation: the general environment and industry structure.

The *general environment* represents the external elements and forces that can affect the attainment of organization objectives.[8] It can be described in terms of the amount of uncertainty present in social, technological, economic, ecological, and political forces. The more uncertainty there is in how the environment will affect the organization, the more difficult it is to design an effective strategic orientation. For example, the technological environment in the watch industry has been highly uncertain over time. The Swiss, who build precision watches with highly skilled craftspeople, were caught off guard by the mass production and distribution technology of Timex in the 1960s. Similarly, many watch manufacturers were surprised by and failed to take advantage of digital technology. Similarly, the increased incidence of AIDS in the workplace (social environment) and the passage of the

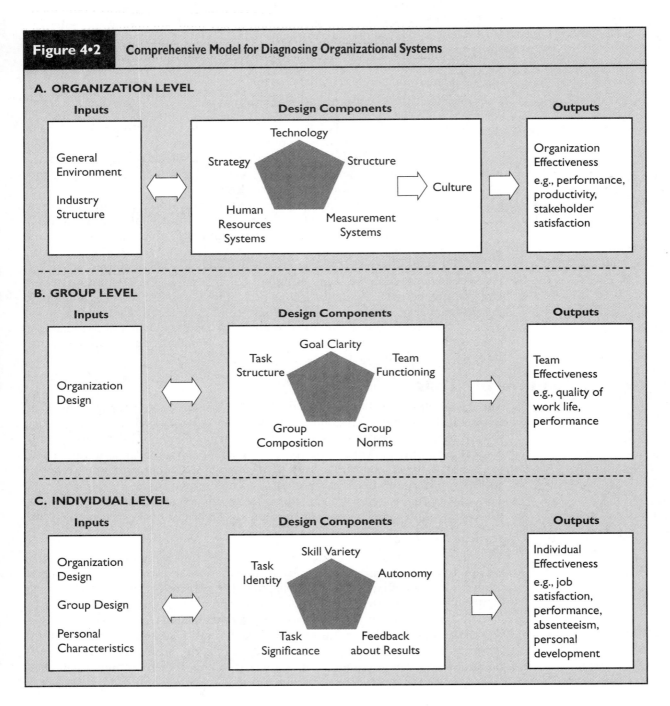

Figure 4•2   Comprehensive Model for Diagnosing Organizational Systems

A. ORGANIZATION LEVEL

Inputs

General Environment

Industry Structure

Design Components

Technology

Strategy

Structure

Human Resources Systems

Measurement Systems

Culture

Outputs

Organization Effectiveness

e.g., performance, productivity, stakeholder satisfaction

B. GROUP LEVEL

Inputs

Organization Design

Design Components

Goal Clarity

Task Structure

Team Functioning

Group Composition

Group Norms

Outputs

Team Effectiveness

e.g., quality of work life, performance

C. INDIVIDUAL LEVEL

Inputs

Organization Design

Group Design

Personal Characteristics

Design Components

Skill Variety

Task Identity

Autonomy

Task Significance

Feedback about Results

Outputs

Individual Effectiveness

e.g., job satisfaction, performance, absenteeism, personal development

Americans with Disabilities Act (political environment) have forced changes in the strategic orientations of organizations.

An organization's *industry structure* or *task environment* is another important input into strategic orientation. As defined by Michael Porter, an organization's task environment consists of five forces: supplier power, buyer power, threats of substitutes, threats of entry, and rivalry among competitors.[9] First, strategic orientations must be sensitive to powerful suppliers who can increase prices (and therefore lower profits) or force the organization to pay more attention to the supplier's needs than to the organization's needs. For example, unions represent powerful suppliers of labor that can affect the costs of any organization within an industry. Second, strategic orientations must be sensitive to powerful buyers. Airplane purchasers, such as American Airlines or country governments, can force Airbus Industrie or Boeing to lower prices or appoint the planes in particular ways. Third, strategic orientations must be sensitive to the threat of new firms entering into competition. Profits in the restaurant business tend to be low because of the ease of starting a new restaurant. Fourth, strategic orientations must be sensitive to the threat of new products or services that can replace existing offerings. Ice cream producers must carefully monitor their costs and prices because it is easy for a consumer to purchase frozen yogurt or other types of desserts instead. Finally, strategic orientations must be sensitive to rivalry among existing competitors. If many organizations are competing for the same customers, for example, then the strategic orientation must monitor product offerings, costs, and structures carefully if the organization is to survive and prosper. Together, these forces play an important role in determining the success of an organization, whether it is a manufacturing or service firm, a nonprofit organization, or a government agency.

General environments and industry structures describe the input content. In addition to understanding what inputs are available, the inputs must be understood for their rate of change and complexity.[10] An organization's general environment or industry structure can be characterized along a *dynamic–static continuum*. Dynamic environments change rapidly and unpredictably and suggest that the organization adopt a flexible strategic orientation. Dynamic environments are relatively high in uncertainty. The *complexity* of the environment refers to the number of important elements in the general environment and industry structure. For example, software development organizations face dynamic and complex environments. Not only do technologies, regulations, customers, and suppliers change rapidly, but all of them are important to the firm's survival. On the other hand, manufacturers of glass jars face more stable and less complex environments.

Design Components

Figure 4.2(A) shows that a strategic orientation is composed of five major design components—strategy, technology, structure, measurement systems, and human resources systems—and an intermediate output—culture. Effective organizations align their design components to each other and to the environment.

A *strategy* represents the way an organization uses its resources (human, economic, or technical) to gain and sustain a competitive advantage.[11] It can be described by the organization's mission, goals and objectives, strategic intent, and functional policies. A mission statement describes the long-term purpose of the organization, the range of products or services offered, the markets to be served, and the social needs served by the organization's existence. Goals and objectives are statements that provide explicit direction, set organization priorities, provide guidelines for management decisions, and serve as the cornerstone for organizing activities, designing jobs, and setting standards of achievement. Goals and objectives should set a target of achievement (such as 50-percent gross margins, an average employee satisfaction score of four on a five-point scale, or some level of productivity); provide a means or system for measuring achievement; and provide a deadline or timeframe for accomplishment.[12] A strategic intent is a succinct label that describes how the organization intends to achieve its goals and objectives. For example, an organization can achieve goals through differentiation of its product or service, by achieving the lowest costs in the industry, or by growth. Finally, functional policies are the methods, procedures, rules, or administrative practices that guide decision making and convert plans into actions. In the semiconductor business, for example, Intel has a policy of allocating about 30 percent of revenues to research and development to maintain its lead in microprocessors production.[13]

Technology is concerned with the way an organization converts inputs into products and services. It represents the core of the transformation function and includes production methods, work flow, and equipment. Automobile companies traditionally have used an assembly-line technology to build cars and trucks. Two features of the technological core have been shown to influence other design components: interdependence and uncertainty.[14] *Technical interdependence* involves ways in which the different parts of a technological system are related. High interdependence requires considerable coordination among tasks, such as might occur when departments must work together to bring out a new product. *Technical uncertainty* refers to the amount of information processing and decision making required during task performance. Generally, when tasks require high amounts of information processing and decision making, they are difficult to plan and routinize. The technology of car manufacturing is relatively certain and moderately interdependent. As a result, automobile manufacturers can specify in advance the behaviors workers should perform and how their work should be coordinated.

The *structural system* describes how attention and resources are focused on task accomplishment. It represents the basic organizing mode chosen to (1) divide the overall work of an organization into subunits that can assign tasks to individuals or groups and (2) coordinate these subunits for completion of the overall work.[15] Structure, therefore, needs to be closely aligned with the organization's technology.

Two ways of determining how an organization divides work are to examine its formal structure or to examine its level of differentiation and integration. Formal structures divide work by function (accounting, sales, or production), by product or service (Chevrolet, Buick, or Pontiac), or by some combination of both (a matrix composed of functional departments and product groupings). These are described in more detail in Chapter 9. The second way to describe how work is divided is to specify the amount of differentiation and integration there is in a structure. Applied to the total organization, differentiation refers to the degree of similarity or difference in the design of two or more subunits or departments.[16] In a highly differentiated organization, there are major differences in design among the departments. Some departments are highly formalized with many rules and regulations, others have few rules and regulations, and still others are moderately formal or flexible.

The way an organization coordinates the work across subunits is called *integration*. Integration can be achieved in a variety of ways—for example, by using plans and schedules; using budgets; assigning special roles, such as project managers, liaison positions, or integrators; or creating cross-departmental task forces and teams. The amount of integration required in a structure is a function of (1) the amount of uncertainty in the environment, (2) the level of differentiation in the structure, and (3) the amount of interdependence among departments. As uncertainty, differentiation, and interdependence increase, more sophisticated integration devices are required.

Measurement systems are methods of gathering, assessing, and disseminating information on the activities of groups and individuals in organizations. Such data tell how well the organization is performing and are used to detect and control deviations from goals. Closely related to structural integration, measurement systems monitor organizational operations and feed data about work activities to managers and members so that they can better understand current performance and coordinate work. Effective information and control systems clearly are linked to strategic objectives; provide accurate, understandable, and timely information; are accepted as legitimate by organization members; and produce benefits in excess of their cost.

Human resources systems include mechanisms for selecting, developing, appraising, and rewarding organization members. These influence the mix of skills, personalities, and behaviors of organization members. The strategy and technology provide important information about the skills and knowledge required if the organization is to be successful. Appraisal processes identify whether those skills and knowledge are being applied to the work, and reward systems complete the cycle by recognizing performance that contributes to goal achievement. Reward systems may be tied to measurement systems so that rewards are allocated on the basis of measured results. (Specific human resources systems, such as rewards and career development, are discussed in Chapter 12.)

Organization culture is the final design component. It represents the basic assumptions, values, and norms shared by organization members.[17] Those cultural elements are generally taken for granted and serve to guide members' perceptions, thoughts, and actions. For example, McDonald's culture emphasizes efficiency, speed, and consistency. It orients employees to company goals and suggests the kinds of behaviors necessary for success. In Figure 4.2(A), culture is shown as an intermediate output from the five other design components because it represents both an outcome and a constraint. It is an outcome of the organization's history and environment as well as of prior choices made about the strategy, technology, structure, measurement systems, and human resources systems.[18] It is also a constraint in that it is more difficult to change than the other components. In that sense it can either hinder or facilitate change. In diagnosis, the interest is in understanding the current culture well enough to determine its alignment with the other design factors. Such information may partly explain current outcomes, such as performance or effectiveness. (Culture is discussed in more detail in Chapter 14.)

Outputs

The outputs of a strategic orientation can be classified into three components. First, organization performance refers to financial outputs such as profits, return on investment, and earnings per share. For nonprofit and government agencies, performance often refers to the extent to which costs were lowered or budgets met. Second, productivity concerns internal measurements of efficiency such as sales per employee, waste, error rates, quality, or units produced per hour. Third, stakeholder satisfaction reflects how well the organization has met the expectations of different groups. Customer satisfaction can be measured in terms of market share or focus-group data; employee satisfaction can be measured in terms of an opinion survey; investor satisfaction can be measured in terms of stock price.

Alignment

The effectiveness of an organization's current strategic orientation requires knowledge of the above information to determine the alignment among the different elements.

1. Does the organization's strategic orientation fit with the inputs?
2. Do the design components fit with each other?

For example, if the elements of the external environment (inputs) are fairly similar in their degree of certainty, then an effective organization structure (design factor) should have a low degree of differentiation. Its departments should be designed similarly because each faces similar environmental demands. On the other hand, if the environment is complex and each element presents different amounts of uncertainty, a more differentiated structure is warranted. Chevron Oil Company's regulatory, ecological, technological, and social environments differ greatly in their amount of uncertainty. The regulatory environment is relatively slow paced and detail oriented. Accordingly, the regulatory affairs function within Chevron is formal and bound by protocol. In the technological environment, on the other hand, new methods for discovering, refining, and distributing oil and oil products are changing at a rapid pace. Those departments are much more flexible and adaptive, very different from the regulatory affairs function.

Analysis

Application 4.1 describes the Nike organization and provides an opportunity to perform the following organization-level analysis.[19] Organization-level dimensions and relationships may be applied to diagnose this example. A useful starting point is to ask how well the organization is currently functioning. Examination of the organization's outputs yields measures of market share, financial performance, and stakeholder satisfaction. Nike's string of solid annual increases over six years was followed by real or predicted declines. Discovering the underlying causes of these problems begins with an assessment of the inputs and strategic orientation and then proceeds to an evaluation of the alignments among the different parts. In diagnosing the inputs, these two questions are important:

1. *What is the company's general environment?* Nike's environment is uncertain and complex. Technologically, Nike is dependent on the latest breakthroughs in shoe design and materials to keep its high-performance image. Socially and politically, Nike's international manufacturing and marketing operations require that it be aware of a variety of stakeholder demands from several countries, cultures, and governments, including the U.S. government, which might view Nike's foreign manufacturing strategy with some concern about U.S. jobs. Other stakeholders are pressuring Nike for changes to its human resources practices.

2. *What is the company's industry structure?* Nike's industry is highly competitive and places considerable pressure on profits. First, the threat of entry is high. It is not difficult or expensive to enter the athletic shoe market. Many shoe manufacturers could easily offer an athletic shoe if they wanted. The threat of substitute products is also high. Nike's image and franchise depend on people wanting to be athletic. If fitness trends were to change, then other footwear could easily fill the need. This possibility clearly exists because Nike's marketing has sensationalized professional athletes and sports, rather than emphasizing fitness for the average person. The bargaining power of suppliers, such as providers of labor, shoe

APPLICATION 4•1   Nike's Strategic Orientation

In 1993, Nike was the leader in domestic-brand athletic footwear with more than 30 percent market share. It also produced sports apparel, hiking boots, and upscale men's shoes. But after six years of solid growth, international sales were falling, sales of basketball shoes were down, and the firm's stock price had dropped 41 percent since November 1992. Analysts were projecting declines in both total revenues and profits for the next fiscal year. In addition, Nike had been the focus of attack from several stakeholder groups. Organized labor believed that Nike exploited foreign labor; the African-American sector noted the lack of diversity in Nike's workforce; and the general public was growing tired of sensationalizing athletes.

Nike's traditional strategy was built around high-performance, innovative athletic shoes, aggressive marketing, and low-cost manufacturing. Using input from athletes, Nike developed a strong competence in producing high-quality athletic shoes, first for running, then for basketball and other sports. By contracting with well-known and outspoken athletes to endorse its products, a Nike image of renegade excellence and high performance emerged. Other consumers who wanted to associate with the Nike image could do so by purchasing its shoes. Thus, a large market of "weekend warriors," people pursuing a more active lifestyle, serious runners, and anyone wanting to project a more athletic image became potential customers. Nike contracted with low-cost, foreign manufacturing plants to produce its shoes.

An athletic shoe retailer places orders with Nike representatives, who are not employees of Nike but contract with Nike to sell its shoes, for delivery in six to eight months. The Futures program, as it is called, offers the retailer 10 percent off the wholesale price for making these advanced orders. The orders are then compiled and production scheduled with one of Nike's Asian manufacturing partners. Nike doesn't actually make shoes. Instead, it develops contract relationships with Taiwanese, Korean, Japanese, and other low-cost sources. On-site Nike employees guarantee that the shoes meet the Nike standards of quality.

Nike's culture is distinctive. The organization, built by athletes for athletes, is very entrepreneurial, and the "Just Do It" marketing campaign aptly describes the way things are done at Nike. As one senior executive put it, "It's fine to develop structures and plans and policies, if they are viewed, and used, as tools. But it is so easy for them to become substitutes for good thinking, alibis for not taking responsibility, reasons to not become involved. And then we'd no longer be Nike."

What emerged, by the mid-1980s, was a way of working that involved setting direction, dividing up the work, pulling things together, and providing rewards.

Although Phil Knight, founder and chairman of Nike, sets the general direction for Nike, he rarely sets clear goals. For example, Knight views Nike as a growth company. The athletic drive pushes employees to achieve bigger sales and put more shoes on more feet than anyone else. Others are concerned that the decision to go public in the early 1980s has produced pressures for profitability that sometimes work against growth. Implementation of the general direction depends on people being tuned into the day-to-day operations. "You tune into what other people are doing, and if you're receptive, you start to see the need for something to be done," Knight says.

Nike changed from a functional organization in 1985 to a product division structure in 1987. In addition, 1993 brought additional structural change. The new president, Tom Clark, was busy implementing stronger communication and collaboration among manufacturing, marketing, and sales. This description, however, belies the informality of the organization. In essence, the aim of the Nike structure is to fit the pieces together in ways that best meet the needs of the product, the customers, and the market.

In pulling things together, Nike relies on meetings as the primary method for coordination. The word "meeting" connotes more formality than is intended. Meetings, which occur at all levels and all parts of the organization, range from an informal gathering in the hallway, to a three-day off-site event, to formal reviews of a product line. Membership in a meeting is equally fluid, with the people who need to be involved invited and those who don't, not invited. Although more formal systems have emerged over the years, their use is often localized to the people or groups who invented them and is met with resistance by others. Thus, with the exception of the Futures program, there is little in the way of formal information systems.

Finally, Knight favors an annual performance review system with annual pay increases tied to performance. In fact, the system is fairly unstructured; some managers take time to do the reviews well and others do not. Although no formal compensation policy exists, most employees and managers believe that Nike is a "great place to work." For the majority of people there, rewards come in the form of growth opportunities, autonomy, and responsibility. ∎

materials, and manufacturing, is generally low because the resources are readily available and there are many sources. The bargaining power of buyers is moderate. At the high-performance end, buyers are willing to pay more for high quality, whereas at the casual end, price is important and the purchasing power of large accounts can bid down Nike's price. Finally, rivalry among firms is severe. A number of international and domestic competitors exist, such as Reebok, Adidas, New Balance, Puma, Converse, and Tiger. Many of them have adopted marketing and promotion tactics similar to Nike's and are competing for the same customers. Thus, the likelihood of new competition, the threat of new substitute products, and the rivalry among existing competitors are the primary forces creating uncertainty in the environment and squeezing profits in the athletic shoe industry.

The following questions are important in assessing Nike's strategic orientation:

1. *What is the company's strategy?* Nike's strategy is clear on some points and nebulous on others. First, although the company has no formal mission statement, it has a clear sense about its initial purpose in producing high-quality, high-performance athletic footwear. That focus has blurred somewhat as Nike has ventured into apparel, hiking boots, and casual shoes. Its goals also are nebulous because Phil Knight does not set specific goals, only general direction. The tension between growth and profits is a potential source of problems for the organization. On the other hand, its strategic intent is fairly clear. It is attempting to achieve its growth and profitability goals by offering a differentiated product—a high quality, high-performance shoe. Informal policies dominate the Nike organization.

2. *What are the company's technology, structure, measurement systems, and human resources systems?* First, the technology of Nike is moderately uncertain and interdependent. For example, developing high-quality, state-of-the-art shoes is uncertain, but there is no evidence that research and development is tightly linked to production. In addition, the Futures program creates low interdependence between manufacturing and distribution, both of which are fairly routine processes. Second, Nike's product division structure appears moderately differentiated, but the new president's emphasis on communication and coordination suggests that it is not highly integrated. Moreover, although Nike appears to have a divisional structure, its contract relationships with manufacturing plants and sales representatives give it a fluid, network-like structure. Third, human resources and measurement systems are underdeveloped. There is no compensation policy, for example, and formal control systems are generally resisted. The one exception to this is the Futures program that tracks orders (which are really advance revenues).

3. *What is Nike's culture?* Finally, Nike's culture is a dominant feature of the organization design. The organization appears driven by typical athletic norms of winning, competition, achievement, and performance.

Now that the organization inputs, design components, and outputs have been assessed, it is time to ask the crucial question about how well they fit together. The first concern is the fit between the inputs and the strategic orientation. The complex and uncertain environment fits well with Nike's focus on differentiation and a generally flexible organization design. That explains its incredible success during the 1970s, 1980s, and into the 1990s. The alignment between its strategic orientation and its environment appears sound.

The second concern is the alignment of the design components. With respect to strategy, the individual elements of Nike's strategy are not aligned. It clearly intends to differentiate its product by serving the high-end athlete with high-performance shoes. However, this small group of athletes may have trouble communicating its needs to a large, diversified organization. Growth goals and a diversified mission obviously do not align with Nike's differentiation intent. The market for higher priced and more specialized athletic shoes is much smaller than the market for low-priced tennis shoes and limits the growth potential of sales. That hypothesis is supported by the lack of clear goals in general and policies that support neither growth nor profitability. However, there appears to be a good fit between strategy and the other design components. The differentiated strategic intent requires technologies, structures, and systems that focus on creating new ideas in products, marketing, and manufacturing. The flexible structure, informal systems, and driving culture would seem well suited for that purpose.

The technology appears well supported and aligned with the structure. Product development, market development, and manufacturing development are inherently unprogrammable tasks that require flexibility and adaptability from the organization. Although a product structure overlays most of Nike's activities, the structure is not rigid, and there appears to be a willingness to create structure as necessary to complete a task. In addition, the Futures program is important for two reasons. First, it reduces uncertainty from the market by getting retailers to take the risk that a shoe will not do well. For the retailer, this risk is mitigated by Nike's tremendous reputation and marketing clout. Second, knowing in advance what will be ordered provides Nike with the ability to schedule production and distribution far in advance. This is a powerful device for integrating Nike's activities. Finally, the lack of a formal human resources system supports the fluid and flexible design, but it creates problems in that there is no direction for hiring and development, a point noted by the various stakeholders at the beginning of the application.

Obviously, any discussion of Nike's organization design has to recognize the powerful role its culture plays. More than any design component, the culture promotes coordination of a variety of tasks, serves as a method for socializing and developing people, and establishes methods for moving information around the organization. Clearly, any change effort at Nike will have to acknowledge this role and design an intervention accordingly. The strong culture will either sabotage or facilitate change depending on how the change process aligns with the culture's impact on individual behavior.

Based on this diagnosis of the Nike organization, at least two intervention possibilities are suggested. First, in collaboration with the client, the OD practitioner could suggest increasing Nike's clarity about its strategy. In this intervention, the practitioner would want to avoid talking about formalizing Nike's strategy because the culture would resist such an attempt. However, there are some clear advantages to be gained from a clearer sense of Nike's future, its businesses, and the relationships among them. Second, Nike could focus on increasing the integration and coordination of its structure, measurement systems, and human resources systems. Although the culture provides a considerable amount of social control, the lack of any human resources systems and the relatively underdeveloped integration mechanisms suggest that finding ways to coordinate activities without increasing formalization would be a value-added intervention.

Group-Level Diagnosis

Figure 4.2 shows the inputs, design components, outputs, and relational fits for group-level diagnosis.[20] The model is similar to other popular group-level diagnostic models, such as Hackman and Morris's task group design model,[21] McCaskey's framework for analyzing groups,[22] and Ledford, Lawler, and Mohrman's participation group design model.[23]

Inputs

Organization design is clearly the major input to group design. It consists of the design components characterizing the larger organization within which the group is embedded: technology, structure, measurement systems, and human resources systems, as well as organization culture. Technology can determine the characteristics of the group's task; structural systems can specify the level of coordination required among groups. The human resources and measurement systems, such as performance appraisal and reward systems, play an important role in determining team functioning.[24] For example, individually based performance appraisal and reward systems tend to interfere with team functioning because members may be more concerned with maximizing their individual performance to the detriment of team performance. Collecting information about the group's organization design context can greatly improve the accuracy of diagnosis.

Design Components

Figure 4.2(B) shows that groups have five major components: goal clarity, task structure, group composition, group functioning, and performance norms.

Goal clarity involves how well the group understands its objectives. In general, goals should be moderately challenging; there should be a method for measuring, monitoring, and feeding back information about goal achievement; and the goals should be clearly understood by all members.

Task structure is concerned with how the group's work is designed. Task structures can vary along two key dimensions: coordination of members' efforts and regulation of their task behaviors.[25] The coordination dimension involves the degree to which group tasks are structured to promote effective interaction among group members. Coordination is important in groups performing interdependent tasks, such as surgical teams and problem-solving groups. It is relatively unimportant, however, in groups composed of members who perform independent tasks, such as a group of telephone operators or salespeople. The regulation dimension involves the degree to which members can control their own task behaviors and be relatively free from external controls such as supervision, plans, and programs. Self-regulation generally occurs when members can decide on such issues as task assignments, work methods, production goals, and membership. (Interventions for designing group task structure are discussed in Chapter 11.)

Composition concerns the membership of groups. Members can differ on a number of dimensions having relevance to group behavior. Demographic variables, such as age, education, experience, and skills and abilities, can affect how people behave and relate to each other in groups. Demographics can determine whether the group is composed of people having task-relevant skills and knowledge, including interpersonal skills. People's internal needs also can influence group behaviors. Individual differences in social needs can determine whether group membership is likely to be satisfying or stressful.[26]

Group functioning is the underlying basis of group life. How members relate to each other is important in work groups because the quality of relationships can affect task performance. In some groups, for example, interpersonal competition and conflict among members result in their providing little support and help for each other. Conversely, groups may become too concerned about sharing good feelings and support and spend too little time on task performance. In organization development, considerable effort has been invested to help work group members develop healthy interpersonal relations, including an ability and a willingness to share feelings and perceptions about members' behaviors so that interpersonal problems and task difficulties can be worked through and resolved.[27] Group functioning therefore involves task-related activities, such as giving and seeking information and elaborating, coordinating, and evaluating activities; and the group-maintenance function, which is directed toward holding the group together as a cohesive team and includes encouraging, harmonizing, compromising, setting standards, and observing.[28] (Interpersonal interventions are discussed in Chapter 8.)

Performance norms are member beliefs about how the group should perform its task and include acceptable levels of performance.[29] Norms derive from interactions among members and serve as guides to group behavior. Once members agree on performance norms, either implicitly or explicitly, then members routinely perform tasks according to those norms. For example, members of problem-solving groups often decide early in the life of the group that decisions will be made through voting; voting then becomes a routine part of group task behavior. (Interventions aimed at helping groups develop appropriate performance norms are discussed in Chapter 8.)

Outputs

Group effectiveness has two dimensions: performance and quality of work life. Performance is measured in terms of the group's ability to control or reduce costs, increase productivity, or improve quality. This is a "hard" measure of effectiveness. In addition, effectiveness is indicated by the group member's quality of work life. It concerns work satisfaction, team cohesion, and organizational commitment.

Alignment

The diagnostic model in Figure 4.2(B) shows that group design components must fit inputs if groups are to be effective in terms of performance and the quality of work life. Research suggests the following fits between the inputs and design dimensions:

1. Group design should be congruent with the larger organization design. Organization structures with low differentiation and high integration should have work groups that are composed of highly skilled and experienced members performing highly interdependent tasks. Organizations with differentiated structures and formalized human resources and information systems should spawn groups that have clear, quantitative goals and support standardized behaviors. Although there is little direct research on these fits, the underlying rationale is that congruence between organization and group designs supports overall integration within the company. When group designs are not compatible with organization designs, groups often conflict with the organization.[30] They may develop norms that run counter to organizational effectiveness, such as occurs in groups supportive of horseplay, goldbricking, and other counterproductive behaviors.

2. When the organization's technology results in interdependent tasks, coordination among members should be promoted by task structures, composition, performance norms, and group functioning. Conversely, when technology permits

independent tasks, the design components should promote individual task performance.[31] For example, when coordination is needed, task structure might physically locate related tasks together; composition might include members with similar interpersonal skills and social needs; performance norms would support task-relevant interactions; and healthy interpersonal relationships would be developed.

3. When the technology is relatively uncertain and requires high amounts of information processing and decision making, group task structure, composition, performance norms, and group functioning should promote self-regulation. Members should have the necessary freedom, information, and skills to assign members to tasks, to decide on production methods, and to set performance goals.[32] When technology is relatively certain, group designs should promote standardization of behavior, and groups should be externally controlled by supervisors, schedules, and plans.[33] For example, when self-regulation is needed, task structure might be relatively flexible and allow the interchange of members across group tasks; composition might include members with multiple skills, interpersonal competencies, and social needs; performance norms would support complex problem solving; and efforts would be made to develop healthy interpersonal relations.

Analysis

Application 4.2 presents an example of applying group-level diagnosis to a top-management team engaged in problem solving.

The group is having a series of ineffective problem-solving meetings. Members report a backlog of unresolved issues, poor use of meeting time, lack of follow-through and decision implementation, and a general dissatisfaction with the team meetings. Examining group inputs and design components and how the two fit can help explain the causes of those group problems.

The key issue in diagnosing group inputs is the design of the larger organization within which the group is embedded. The Ortiv Glass Corporation's design is relatively differentiated. Each plant is allowed to set up its own organization design. Similarly, although no specific data are given, the company's technology, structure, measurement systems, human resources systems, and culture appear to promote flexible and innovative behaviors at the plant level. Indeed, freedom to innovate in the manufacturing plants is probably an outgrowth of the firm's OD activities and participative culture.

In the case of decision-making groups such as this one, organization design also affects the nature of the issues that are worked on. The team meetings appear to be devoted to problems affecting all of the functional departments. This suggests that the problems entail high interdependence among the functions; consequently, high coordination among members is needed to resolve them. The team meetings also seem to include many issues that are complex and not easily solved, so there is probably a relatively high amount of uncertainty in the technology or work process. The causes of the problems or acceptable solutions are not readily available. Members must process considerable information during problem solving, especially when there are different perceptions and opinions about the issues.

Diagnosis of the team's design components answers the following questions:

1. *How clear are the group's goals?* The team's goals seem relatively clear: they are to solve problems. There appears to be no clear agreement, however, on the specific problems to be addressed. As a result, members come late because they have "more pressing" problems needing attention.

APPLICATION 4•2   Top-Management Team at Ortiv Glass Corporation

The Ortiv Glass Corporation produces and markets plate glass for use primarily in the construction and automotive industries. The multiplant company has been involved in OD for several years and actively supports participative management practices and employee-involvement programs. Ortiv's organization design is relatively organic, and the manufacturing plants are given freedom and encouragement to develop their own organization designs and approaches to participative management. It recently put together a problem-solving group made up of the top-management team at its newest plant.

The team consisted of the plant manager and the managers of the five functional departments reporting to him: engineering (maintenance), administration, human resources, production, and quality control. In recruiting managers for the new plant, the company selected people with good technical skills and experience in their respective functions. It also chose people with some managerial experience and a desire to solve problems collaboratively, a hallmark of participative management. The team was relatively new, and members had been working together for only about five months.

The team met formally for two hours each week to share pertinent information and to deal with plantwide issues affecting all of the departments, such as safety procedures, interdepartmental relations, and personnel practices. Members described these meetings as informative but often chaotic in terms of decision making. The meetings typically started late as members straggled in at different times. The latecomers generally offered excuses about more pressing problems occurring elsewhere in the plant. Once started, the meetings were often interrupted by "urgent" phone messages for various members, including the plant manager, and in most cases the recipient would leave the meeting hurriedly to respond to the call.

The group had problems arriving at clear decisions on particular issues. Discussions often rambled from topic to topic, and members tended to postpone the resolution of problems to future meetings. This led to a backlog of unresolved issues, and meetings often lasted far beyond the two-hour limit. When group decisions were made, members often reported problems in their implementation. Members typically failed to follow through on agreements, and there was often confusion about what had actually been agreed upon. Everyone expressed dissatisfaction with the team meetings and their results.

Relationships among team members were cordial yet somewhat strained, especially when the team was dealing with complex issues in which members had varying opinions and interests. Although the plant manager publicly stated that he wanted to hear all sides of the issues, he often interrupted the discussion or attempted to change the topic when members openly disagreed in their views of the problem. This interruption was typically followed by an awkward silence in the group. In many instances when a solution to a pressing problem did not appear forthcoming, members either moved on to another issue or they informally voted on proposed options, letting majority rule decide the outcome. Members rarely discussed the need to move on or vote; rather, these behaviors emerged informally over time and became acceptable ways of dealing with difficult issues. ■

2. *What is the group's task structure?* The team's task structure includes face-to-face interaction during the weekly meetings. That structure allows members from different functional departments to come together physically to share information and to solve problems mutually affecting them. It facilitates coordination of problem solving among the departments in the plant. The structure also seems to provide team members with the freedom necessary to regulate their task behaviors in the meetings. They can adjust their behaviors and interactions to suit the flow of the discussion and problem-solving process.

3. *What is the composition of the group?* The team is composed of the plant manager and managers of five functional departments. All members appear to have task-relevant skills and experience, both in their respective functions and in their managerial roles. They also seem to be interested in solving problems collaboratively. That shared interest suggests that members have job-related social needs and should feel relatively comfortable in group problem-solving situations.

4. ***What are the group's performance norms?*** Group norms cannot be observed directly but must be inferred from group behaviors. The norms involve member beliefs about how the group should perform its task, including acceptable levels of performance. A useful way to describe norms is to list specific behaviors that complete the sentences "A good group member should. . . ." and "It's okay to. . . ." Examination of the team's problem-solving behaviors suggests the following performance norms are operating in the example:

- "It's okay to come late to team meetings."
- "It's okay to interrupt meetings with phone messages."
- "It's okay to leave meetings to respond to phone messages."
- "It's okay to hold meetings longer than two hours."
- "A good group member should not openly disagree with others' views."
- "It's okay to vote on decisions."
- "A good group member should be cordial to other members."
- "It's okay to postpone solutions to immediate problems."
- "It's okay not to follow through on previous agreements."

5. ***What is the nature of team functioning in the group?*** The case strongly suggests that interpersonal relations are not healthy on the management team. Members do not seem to confront differences openly. Indeed, the plant manager purposely intervenes when conflicts emerge. Members feel dissatisfied with the meetings, but they spend little time talking about those feelings. Relationships are strained, but members fail to examine the underlying causes.

The problems facing the team can now be explained by assessing how well the group design fits the inputs. The larger organization design of Ortiv is relatively differentiated and promotes flexibility and innovation in its manufacturing plants. The firm supports participative management, and the team meetings can be seen as an attempt to implement that approach at the new plant. Although it is too early to tell whether the team will succeed, there does not appear to be significant incongruity between the larger organization design and what the team is trying to do. Of course, team problem solving may continue to be ineffective, and the team might revert to a more autocratic approach to decision making. In such a case, a serious mismatch between the plant management team and the larger company would exist, and conflict between the two would likely result.

The team's issues are highly interdependent and often uncertain, and meetings are intended to resolve plantwide problems affecting the various functional departments. Those problems are generally complex and require the members to process a great deal of information and create innovative solutions. The team's task structure and composition appear to fit the nature of team issues. The face-to-face meetings help to coordinate problem solving among the department managers, and except for the interpersonal skills, members seem to have the necessary task-relevant skills and experience to drive the problem-solving process. There appears, however, to be a conflict in the priority between the problems to be solved by the team and the problems faced by individual managers.

More important, the key difficulty seems to be a mismatch between the team's performance norms and interpersonal relations and the demands of the problem-solving task. Complex, interdependent problems require performance norms that support sharing of diverse and often conflicting kinds of information. The norms must encourage members to generate novel solutions and to assess the relevance of problem-solving strategies in light of new issues. Members need to address explicitly how they are using their knowledge and skills and how they are weighing and combining members' individual contributions.

In our example, the team's performance norms fail to support complex problem solving; rather, they promote a problem-solving method that is often superficial, haphazard, and subject to external disruptions. Members' interpersonal relationships reinforce adherence to the ineffective norms. Members do not confront personal differences or dissatisfactions with the group process. They fail to examine the very norms contributing to their problems. In this case, diagnosis suggests the need for group interventions aimed at improving performance norms and developing healthy interpersonal relations.

Individual-Level Diagnosis

The lowest level of organizational diagnosis is the individual job or position. An organization consists of numerous groups; a group, in turn, is composed of several individual jobs. This section discusses the inputs, design components, and relational fits for diagnosing jobs. The model shown in Figure 4.2(C) is similar to other popular job diagnostic frameworks, such as Hackman and Oldham's job diagnostic survey and Herzberg's job enrichment model.[34]

Inputs

Three major inputs affect job design: organization design, group design, and the personal characteristics of jobholders.

Organization design is concerned with the larger organization within which the individual job is the smallest unit. Organization design is a key part of the larger context surrounding jobs. Technology, structure, measurement systems, human resources systems, and culture can have a powerful impact on the way jobs are designed and on people's experiences in jobs. For example, company reward systems can orient employees to particular job behaviors and influence whether people see job performance as fairly rewarded. In general, technology characterized by relatively uncertain tasks and low interdependency is likely to support job designs allowing employees flexibility and discretion in performing tasks. Conversely, low-uncertainty work systems are likely to promote standardized job designs requiring routinized task behaviors.[35]

Group design concerns the larger group or department containing the individual job. Like organization design, group design is an essential part of the job context. Group task structure, goal clarity, composition, performance norms, and group functioning serve as inputs to job design. They typically have a more immediate impact on jobs than do the larger, organization-design components. For example, group task structure can determine how individual jobs are grouped together—as in groups requiring coordination among jobs or in ones comprising collections of independent jobs. Group composition can influence the kinds of people who are available to fill jobs. Group performance norms can affect the kinds of job designs that are considered acceptable, including the level of jobholders' performances. Goal clarity helps members to prioritize work, and group functioning can affect how powerfully the group influences job behaviors. When members maintain close relationships and the group is cohesive, group norms are more likely to be enforced and followed.[36]

Personal characteristics of individuals occupying jobs include their age, education, experience, and skills and abilities. All of these can affect job performance as well as how people react to job designs. Individual needs and expectations also can affect employee job responses. For example, individual differences in growth need—the need for self-direction, learning, and personal accomplishment—can determine how much people are motivated and satisfied by jobs with high levels of skill variety, autonomy, and feedback about results.[37] Similarly, work motivation can be influenced by people's expectations that they can perform a job well and that good job performance will result in valued outcomes.[38]

Design Components

Figure 4.2(C) shows that individual jobs have five key dimensions: skill variety, task identity, task significance, autonomy, and feedback about results.[39]

Skill variety identifies the degree to which a job requires a range of activities and abilities to perform the work. Assembly-line jobs, for example, generally have limited skill variety because employees perform a small number of repetitive activities. Most professional jobs, on the other hand, include a great deal of skill variety because people engage in diverse activities and employ several different skills in performing their work.

Task identity measures the degree to which a job requires the completion of a relatively whole, identifiable piece of work. Skilled craftspeople, such as tool-and-die makers and carpenters, generally have jobs with high levels of task identity. They are able to see a job through from beginning to end. Assembly-line jobs involve only a limited piece of work and score low on task identity.

Task significance identifies the degree to which a job has a significant impact on other people's lives. Custodial jobs in a hospital are likely to have more task significance than similar jobs in a toy factory because hospital custodians are likely to see their jobs as affecting someone else's health and welfare.

Autonomy indicates the degree to which a job provides freedom and discretion in scheduling the work and determining work methods. Assembly-line jobs generally have little autonomy: the work pace is scheduled, and people perform preprogrammed tasks. College teaching positions have more autonomy: professors usually can determine how a course is taught, even though they may have limited say over class scheduling.

Feedback about results involves the degree to which a job provides employees with direct and clear information about the effectiveness of task performance. Assembly-line jobs often provide high levels of feedback about results, whereas college professors must often contend with indirect and ambiguous feedback about how they are performing in the classroom.

Those five job dimensions can be combined into an overall measure of job enrichment. Enriched jobs have high levels of skill variety, task identity, task significance, autonomy, and feedback about results. They provide opportunities for self-direction, learning, and personal accomplishment at work. Many people find enriched jobs internally motivating and satisfying. (Job enrichment is discussed more fully in Chapter 11.)

Alignment

The diagnostic model in Figure 4.2(C) suggests that job design must fit job inputs to produce effective job outputs, such as high quality and quantity of individual performance, low absenteeism, and high job satisfaction. Research reveals the following fits between job inputs and job design:

1. Job design should be congruent with the larger organization and group designs within which the job is embedded.[40] Both the organization and the group serve as a powerful context for individual jobs or positions. They tend to support and reinforce particular job designs. Highly differentiated and integrated organizations and groups that permit members to self-regulate their behavior fit enriched

jobs. These larger organizations and groups promote autonomy, flexibility, and innovation at the individual job level. Conversely, bureaucratic organizations and groups relying on external controls are congruent with job designs scoring low on the five key dimensions. Both organizations and groups reinforce standardized, routine jobs. As suggested earlier, congruence across different levels of organization design promotes integration of the organization, group, and job levels. Whenever the levels do not fit each other, conflict is likely to emerge.

2. Job design should fit the personal characteristics of the jobholders if they are to perform effectively and derive satisfaction from work. Generally, enriched jobs fit people with strong growth needs.[40] These people derive satisfaction and accomplishment from performing jobs involving skill variety, autonomy, and feedback about results. Enriched jobs also fit people possessing moderate to high levels of task-relevant skills, abilities, and knowledge. Enriched jobs generally require complex information processing and decision making; people must have comparable skills and abilities to perform effectively. Jobs scoring low on the five job dimensions generally fit people with rudimentary skills and abilities and with low growth needs. Simpler, more routinized jobs requiring limited skills and experience fit better with people who place a low value on opportunities for self-direction and learning. In addition, because people can grow through education, training, and experience, job design must be monitored and adjusted from time to time.

Analysis

Application 4.3 presents an example of applying individual-level diagnosis to job design. The plant discussed there seemed to have problems implementing new, more enriched job designs. Production was below expectations, and employee absenteeism and turnover were higher than average. Employees were complaining that the jobs were less challenging than expected and that management failed to follow through on promised opportunities for decision making. Examination of inputs and job design features and how the two fit can help explain the causes of these problems.

Diagnosis of individual-level inputs answers the following questions:

1. *What is the design of the larger organization within which the individual jobs are embedded?* Although the example says little about the new plant design, a number of inferences are possible. Management at the new plant was trying to design more enriched jobs than were provided at Mot's older plants. This suggests that the culture of the plant was supportive of employee involvement, at least during the initial design and start-up stages. At the organization level, there seemed little need for flexible and innovative responses; consequently, the plant design is likely to have been more formal and bureaucratic than innovative and integrated. The market for surgical sutures was stable and production methods routinized, with changes in technology or scheduling rare.

2. *What is the design of the group containing the individual jobs?* Individual jobs were grouped together according to the type of suture produced. Although people spent most of their time working on individual jobs—either swaging, inspecting, or handwinding—they did meet weekly to share information and to solve common problems. Interaction during task performance seemed limited because of highly scheduled work flow. However, some interaction between the swaging and inspection jobs did occur because inspectors handed unacceptable sutures back to swagers to be redone.

APPLICATION 4•3   Job Design at Mot Surgical Corporation

Mot Surgical Corporation is a subsidiary of a large pharmaceutical company that produces drugs and related medical products. Mot specializes in surgical sutures and has three manufacturing plants. At the time of the case in 1980, Mot's parent corporation had supported employee involvement for several years. It had encouraged its subsidiaries to increase employee participation and to design meaningful jobs. The newest plant in the southwestern United States was seen as a potential site to enrich jobs that at Mot's older plants had been routinized for years.

Traditionally, the jobs involved in producing surgical sutures were divided according to the three main stages of production. First, the job of swager involved attaching a surgical needle to a filament made of a catgut or synthetic fiber. The needle and filament were placed in a press, and the press joined the two together. The swaging activities were of a short time cycle, highly standardized, and repetitive; workers sat at individual presses turning out dozens of finished sutures per hour. Second, the job of inspector involved examining the finished swaging product for defects. Product quality was especially important because the condition of sutures can affect the outcome of surgery. Inspectors took samples of swaging product and visibly examined them. The job took extreme concentration because defects were difficult to detect. Inspectors passed poor-quality work back to relevant swagers and passed good product on to the next production stage. Third, the job of handwinder involved taking acceptable swaging product and winding it by hand into a figure eight for packaging. Like swaging, handwinding activities were highly routinized and repetitive; handwinders sat at individual workstations and wound literally thousands of figure eights per hour.

The activities surrounding the suture jobs were also highly programmed and scheduled. The market for surgical sutures was relatively stable. Production runs were long and scheduled well in advance, and changes in schedule were rare. Similarly, the production methods associated with swaging, inspection, and handwinding were highly programmed, and technical changes in production were infrequent. The primary goal of management was the production of large quantities of acceptable product.

Before hiring in the new plant began, the three suture jobs were placed into discrete groups according to the specific type of suture produced. People in each product group were to be trained in all three jobs. Members would stay on a job for a specified period of time and then rotate to another job. Performance of the swaging and handwinding jobs also included some minor setup, inspection, and scheduling activities.

Weekly meetings also were planned so that employees could share information, solve common problems, and make work-related decisions. The new, more enriched jobs were expected to result in high productivity and quality of work life.

Mot made great efforts to recruit people who were likely to respond favorably to enriched jobs. Newspaper advertisements and job interviews explicitly mentioned the enriched nature of the new jobs and the promise that employees would be involved in decision making. Potential recruits were shown the new plant setup and asked about their desire to learn new things and to be involved in decision making. Initially, about thirty people were hired and trained in the new job; additional employees were assimilated into the plant over the next few months. The training program was oriented to learning the swaging, inspection, and handwinding jobs and to gaining problem-solving skills.

As training progressed and the plant gradually started production, several unexpected problems emerged. First, employees found it difficult to rotate among the different jobs without a considerable loss of production. The swaging, inspection, and handwinding tasks involved entirely different kinds of manual dexterity and mental concentration. Each time people switched from one job to another, much relearning and practice were necessary to achieve a normal level of production. The net result of this rotation was lower-than-expected productivity. When this problem persisted, workers were urged to stay on one particular job.

A second problem concerned employee participation in decision making. During the early stages of the plant startup, workers had ample opportunities for decision making. They were involved in solving certain break-in problems and deciding on housekeeping, personnel, and operating issues. They were undergoing training and had time to devote to problem solving without heavy pressures for production. Over time, however, plant operations became more routine and predictable, and there was less need for employee decision making. Moreover, increased pressures for production cut into the limited time devoted to decision making.

A third problem involved employee behaviors and attitudes. After six months of operation, employee absenteeism and turnover were higher than the local industry average. People complained that the job was more routine and boring than they had expected. They felt that management had sold them a bill of goods about opportunities for decision making. These behaviors and attitudes were especially prevalent among those who were hired first and had participated in the initial recruiting and startup. ■

3. *What are the personal characteristics of jobholders?* People were recruited for the new plant because of their desire for enriched jobs and participation in decision making. This suggests that employees likely had strong growth needs. Moreover, the recruiting process explicitly promoted enriched jobs and employee decision making, and thus employees were also likely to have strong expectations about such job characteristics.

Diagnosis of individual jobs involves the following job dimensions:

1. *How much skill variety is included in the jobs?* The individual jobs in the new plant seemed to have low to moderate amounts of skill variety. Although some additional set-up, inspection, and scheduling activities were added to the swaging and handwinding jobs, these jobs primarily involved a limited set of repetitive activities. The inspection job included a bit more skill variety—gathering samples of product, examining them for defects, recording results, and either passing the product to handwinders or back to swagers for redoing. The job rotation scheme was an attempt to enhance skill variety by giving employees a greater number of tasks across the different jobs. Unfortunately, because people had problems maintaining high levels of production when they rotated jobs, they were urged to stay on one job.

2. *How much task identity do the jobs contain?* The jobs seemed to include moderate amounts of task identity. Each job produced a small yet identifiable piece of work. The swagers, in attaching a needle to a filament, produced a completed suture. Inspectors performed most of the activities needed to ensure product quality. The handwinders, in preparing sutures for packaging, probably had the lowest task identity. The grouping of the three jobs into discrete product groups was an attempt to increase task identity because employees could see how the three jobs fit together to produce a suture ready for packaging.

3. *How much task significance is involved in the jobs?* All three jobs seemed to score high on this feature. Surgical sutures are an integral part of surgery, and the jobs contributed to helping physicians heal people and save lives.

4. *How much autonomy is included in the jobs?* The jobs appeared to contain almost no freedom in either work schedules or work methods. Each job was highly routinized. The little autonomy there was in making decisions at the weekly meetings had decreased over time. Increased pressures for production also reduced the opportunities for decision making.

5. *How much feedback about results do the jobs contain?* Employees were provided with direct and clear information about their performances. The swagers and handwinders did minor inspection tasks, and the former received continual feedback from inspectors about the quality of their swaging.

When the job characteristics are examined together, the jobs appear to contain moderate levels of enrichment. Feedback about results and task significance are fairly high; task identity is moderate; skill variety and autonomy are low to moderate. Over time, however, the level of enrichment dropped because skill variety and autonomy were decreased. Indeed, the jobs in the new plant came to resemble those in Mot's older plants.

Mot's problems with reduced performance and employee withdrawal and dissatisfaction can be explained by assessing how well the job designs fit the inputs. The new plant design seems only partially to fit the job designs. The plant seems more formal and certain than flexible and innovative, and this fits well with jobs consisting of limited amounts of autonomy and skill variety. The plant programmed production rigidly, and the job designs reflect this standardization. The organization culture of promoting quality of work life seems to conflict with the way the jobs were designed, however. Initial attempts to rotate jobs and to involve employees in decision making gave way to more traditional job designs. Over time, pressures for production and fewer opportunities for decision making displaced the initial focus on quality of work life. The plant's espoused culture was incongruent with the way jobs finally developed. This incongruity was especially troublesome for the initial recruits who were led to expect a more enriched work life.

The various product groups seem to fit well with the job designs. The groups' task structures promoted only limited interaction among jobholders, and this was consistent with the individualized nature of each job. Moreover, the reduced emphasis on group decision making was congruent with jobs that have become more routine and scheduled over time.

The technology of producing sutures is highly certain and includes limited interdependence among the different tasks. Tasks that are certain require little information processing and decision making. Routinized jobs fit such tasks, and the jobs in the plant gradually became routinized to fit the high level of technical certainty. The plant's initial attempts to enrich jobs in a situation of high technical certainty seem misguided. Indeed, job rotation disrupted the routine, repetitive nature of the tasks and resulted in poor performance. The limited technical interdependence seems to fit the individualized focus of the job designs. Again, attempts at group problem solving and decision making probably provided more member interaction than was technically needed. The meetings might have contributed to lowered productivity by reducing time for individual performance.

Employee withdrawal and dissatisfaction seem directly related to a mismatch between the job designs and people's growth needs. People with strong growth needs like enriched jobs allowing self-direction, challenge, and learning. Although the initial job designs were intended to provide such opportunities, the resulting designs were routine and boring. Employees could not satisfy their needs by performing such jobs, and worse yet, they felt betrayed by a company that had promised enriched jobs.

Examination of the fits between the job designs and the inputs suggests an intervention dilemma in this case. Should the plant continue to maintain the fit between technology and job design and risk alienating or losing many of its initial recruits? If so, interventions probably should be aimed at changing the plant's espoused culture and recruiting and training practices. Alternatively, should the plant attempt to bring about a better fit between its current employees and job design and risk lowered or more costly production? If so, interventions should probably be aimed at job enrichment and at reducing pressures for production from the parent corporation. (Interventions for matching people, technology, and job design are discussed in Chapter 11.)

■ SUMMARY

This chapter presented background information for diagnosing organizations, groups, and individual jobs. Diagnosis is based on conceptual frameworks about how organizations function. Such diagnostic models serve as road maps by identifying areas to examine and questions to ask in determining how an organization or department is operating.

The comprehensive model presented here views organizations as open systems. The organization serves to coordinate the behaviors of its departments. It is open to exchanges with the larger environment and is influenced by external forces. As open systems, organizations are hierarchically ordered; that is, they are composed of groups, which in turn are composed of individual jobs. Organizations also display five key systems properties: inputs, transformations, and outputs; boundaries; feedback; equifinality; and alignment.

An organization-level diagnostic model consists of environmental inputs; a set of design components called a strategic orientation; and a variety of outputs, such as performance, productivity, and stakeholder satisfaction. Diagnosis involves understanding each of the parts in the model and then assessing how the elements of the strategic orientation align with each other and with the inputs. Organization effectiveness is likely to be high when there is good alignment.

Group diagnostic models take the organization's design as the primary input; examine goal clarity, task structure, group composition, performance norms, and group functioning as the key design components; and list group performance and member quality of work life as the outputs. As with any open-systems model, the alignment of these parts is the key to understanding effectiveness.

At the individual job level, organization design, group design, and personal characteristics of individuals occupying jobs are the salient inputs. Individual jobs have five key dimensions: skill variety, task significance, task identity, autonomy, and feedback that work together to produce outputs of work satisfaction and work quality.

■ NOTES

1. D. Nadler, "Role of Models in Organizational Assessment," in *Organizational Assessment*, eds. E. Lawler III, D. Nadler, and C. Cammann (New York: John Wiley & Sons, 1980): 119–31; R. Keidel, *Seeing Organizational Patterns* (San Francisco: Berrett-Koehler, 1995); M. Harrison, *Diagnosing Organizations*, 2d ed. (Thousand Oaks, Calif.: Sage Publications, 1994).

2. D. Coghlan, "Organization Development through Interlevel Dynamics, *International Journal of Organizational Analysis* 2 (1994): 264–79.

3. M. Weisbord, "Organizational Diagnosis: Six Places to Look for Trouble with or without a Theory," *Group and Organizational Studies* 1 (1976): 430–37.

4. D. Nadler and M. Tushman, "A Diagnostic Model for Organization Behavior," in *Perspectives on Behavior in Organizations*, eds. J. Hackman, E. Lawler III, and L. Porter (New York: McGraw-Hill, 1977): 85–100.

5. J. Galbraith, *Competing with Flexible Lateral Organizations*, 2d ed. (Reading, Mass.: Addison-Wesley, 1994).

6. J. Kotter, *Organizational Dynamics: Diagnosis and Intervention* (Reading, Mass.: Addison-Wesley, 1978).

7. M. Tushman and E. Romanelli, "Organization Evolu-

tion: A Metamorphosis Model of Convergence and Reorientation," in *Research in Organizational Behavior*, vol. 7, eds. L. Cummings and B. Staw (Greenwich, Conn.: JAI Press, 1985); C. Worley, D. Hitchin, and W. Ross, *Integrated Strategic Change: How OD Builds Competitive Advantage* (Reading, Mass.: Addison-Wesley, 1996).

8. F. Emery and E. Trist, "The Causal Texture of Organizational Environments," *Human Relations* 18 (1965): 21–32; H. Aldrich, *Organizations and Environments* (Englewood Cliffs, N.J.: Prentice Hall, 1979).

9. M. Porter, *Competitive Strategy* (New York: Free Press, 1980).

10. Emery and Trist, "Causal Texture"; Aldrich, *Organizations and Environments*.

11. M. Porter, *Competitive Advantage* (New York: Free Press, 1985); C. Hill and G. Jones, *Strategic Management*, 3d ed. (Boston: Houghton Mifflin, 1995).

12. C. Hofer and D. Schendel, *Strategy Formulation: Analytical Concepts* (St. Paul, Minn.: West Publishing, 1978).

13. R. Hoff, "Inside Intel," *Business Week* (1 June 1992): 86–94.

14. J. Thompson, *Organizations in Action* (New York:

McGraw-Hill, 1967); D. Gerwin, "Relationships between Structure and Technology," in Handbook of Organizational Design, vol. 2, eds. P. Nystrom and W. Starbuck (Oxford: Oxford University Press, 1981): 3–38.

15. J. Galbraith, *Organization Design* (Reading, Mass.: Addison-Wesley, 1977); D. Robey and C. Sales, *Designing Organizations*, 4th ed. (Homewood, Ill.: Irwin, 1994).

16. P. Lawrence and J. Lorsch, *Organization and Environment* (Cambridge: Harvard University Press, 1967).

17. V. Sathe, "Implications of Corporate Culture: A Manager's Guide to Acting," *Organizational Dynamics* (Autumn 1983): 5–23; E. Schein, *Organizational Culture and Leadership*, 2d ed. (San Francisco: Jossey-Bass, 1990).

18. E. Abrahamson and C. Fombrun, "Macrocultures: Determinants and Consequences," *Academy of Management Review* 19 (1994): 728–56.

19. Adapted from material in G. Willigan, "High-Performance Marketing: An Interview with Nike's Phil Knight," *Harvard Business Review* (July-August, 1992); D. Yang and M. Oneal, "Can Nike Just Do It?" *Business Week* (18 April 1994): 86–90; D. Rikert and C. Christensen, *Nike (A)* 9-395-025 (Boston: Harvard Business School, 1984); D. Rikert and C. Christensen, *Nike (B)* 9-385-027 (Boston: Harvard Business School, 1984).

20. S. Cohen, "Designing Effective Self-Managing Work Teams," in *Advances in Interdisciplinary Studies of Work Teams*, vol. 1, ed. M. Beyerlein (Greenwich, Conn.: JAI Press, 1995).

21. J. Hackman and C. Morris, "Group Tasks, Group Interaction Process, and Group Performance Effectiveness: A Review and Proposed Integration," in *Advances in Experimental Social Psychology*, vol. 9, ed. L. Berkowitz (New York: Academic Press, 1975): 45–99; J. Hackman, ed., *Groups That Work (and Those That Don't): Creating Conditions for Effective Teamwork* (San Francisco: Jossey-Bass, 1989).

22. M. McCaskey, "Framework for Analyzing Work Groups," *Harvard Business School Case 9-480-009* (Boston: Harvard Business School, 1997).

23. G. Ledford, E. Lawler, and S. Mohrman, "The Quality Circle and Its Variations," in *Productivity in Organizations: New Perspectives from Industrial and Organizational Psychology*, eds. J. Campbell, R. Campbell, and Associates (San Francisco: Jossey-Bass, 1988): 255–94.

24. D. Ancona and D. Caldwell, "Bridging the Boundary: External Activity and Performance in Organizational Teams," *Administrative Science Quarterly* 37 (1992): 634–65; Cohen, "Self-Managing Work Teams"; S. Mohrman, S.

Cohen, and A. Mohrman, *Designing Team-Based Organizations* (San Francisco: Jossey-Bass, 1995).

25. G. Susman, *Autonomy at Work* (New York: Praeger, 1976); T. Cummings, "Self-Regulating Work Groups: A Socio-Technical Synthesis," *Academy of Management Review* 3 (1978): 625–34; J. Slocum and H. Sims, "A Typology for Integrating Technology, Organization, and Job Design," *Human Relations* 33 (1980): 193–212.

26. J. R. Hackman and G. Oldham, *Work Redesign* (Reading, Mass.: Addison-Wesley, 1980).

27. E. Schein, *Process Consultation*, vols. I–II (Reading, Mass.: Addison-Wesley, 1987).

28. W. Dyer, *Team Building*, 3d ed. (Reading, Mass.: Addison-Wesley, 1994).

29. Hackman and Morris, "Group Tasks"; T. Cummings, "Designing Effective Work Groups," in *Handbook of Organizational Design*, vol. 2, eds. P. Nystrom and W. Starbuck (Oxford, U.K.: Oxford University Press, 1981): 250–71.

30. Cummings, "Effective Work Groups."

31. Susman, *Autonomy at Work;* Cummings, "Self-Regulating Work Groups"; Slocum and Sims, "Typology."

32. Cummings, "Self-Regulating Work Groups"; Slocum and Sims, "Typology."

33. Ibid.

34. Hackman and Oldham, *Work Redesign;* F. Herzberg, "One More Time: How Do You Motivate Employees?" *Harvard Business Review* 46 (1968): 53–62.

35. J. Pierce, R. Dunham, and R. Blackburn, "Social Systems Structure, Job Design, and Growth Need Strength: A Test of a Congruence Model," *Academy of Management Journal* 22 (1979): 223–40.

36. Susman, *Autonomy at Work;* Cummings, "Self-Regulating Work Groups"; Slocum and Sims, "Typology."

37. Hackman and Oldham, *Work Redesign;* Pierce, Dunham, and Blackburn, "Social Systems Structure."

38. E. Lawler III, *Motivation in Work Organizations* (Monterey, Calif.: Brooks/Cole, 1973).

39. Hackman and Oldham, *Work Redesign.*

40. Pierce, Dunham, and Blackburn, "Social Systems Structure"; Susman, *Autonomy at Work;* Cummings, "Self-Regulating Work Groups"; Slocum and Sims, "Typology."

41. Hackman and Oldham, *Work Redesign;* Pierce, Dunham, and Blackburn, "Social Systems Structure."

5. Collecting, Analyzing, and Feeding Back Diagnostic Information

Organization development is vitally dependent on effective diagnosis to assess how the organization is functioning and to choose an appropriate change intervention. The quality of the information gathered, therefore, is an important part of the OD process. In this chapter, we discuss several key issues associated with collecting, analyzing, and feeding back diagnostic data. The first step involves establishing an effective relationship between the OD practitioner and those from whom data will be collected and then choosing methods for collecting data. Next, data analysis organizes and examines the information to make clear the underlying causes of an organizational problem or to identify areas for future development. The final step in the cyclical OD process is the feedback of data to the client system. The overall process of data collection, analysis, and feedback is shown in Figure 5.1. The chapter ends with a description of the survey feedback process, a widely used method for collecting, analyzing, and feeding back diagnostic data.

THE DIAGNOSTIC RELATIONSHIP

In most cases of planned change, OD practitioners play an active role in gathering data from organization members for diagnostic purposes. For example, they might interview members of a work team about causes of conflict among members; they might survey employees at a large industrial plant about factors contributing to poor product quality. Before collecting diagnostic information, practitioners need to establish a relationship with those who will provide and subsequently use it. Because the nature of that relationship affects the quality and usefulness of the data collected, it is vital that OD practitioners clarify for organization members who they are, why the data are being collected, what the data gathering will involve, and

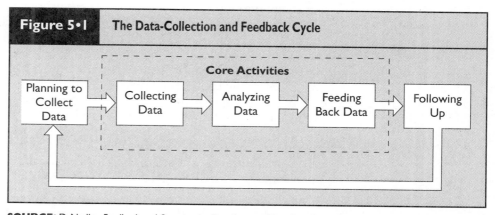

Figure 5•1	The Data-Collection and Feedback Cycle

Core Activities

Planning to Collect Data → Collecting Data → Analyzing Data → Feeding Back Data → Following Up

SOURCE: D. Nadler, *Feedback and Organization Development: Using Data-Based Methods*, page 43. © 1977 by Addison-Wesley Publishing Co., Inc. Reprinted by permission of Addison Wesley Longman.

how the data will be used.[1] That information can help allay people's natural fears that the data might be used against them and gain members' participation and support, which are essential to developing successful interventions.

Establishing the diagnostic relationship between the consultant and relevant organization members is similar to forming a contract. It is meant to clarify expectations and to specify the conditions of the relationship. In those cases where members have been directly involved in the entering and contracting process described in Chapter 3, the diagnostic contract typically will be part of the initial contracting step. In situations where data will be collected from members who have not been directly involved in entering and contracting, however, OD practitioners will need to establish a diagnostic contract as a prelude to diagnosis. The answers to the following questions provide the substance of the diagnostic contract:[2]

1. *Who am I?* The answer to this question introduces the OD practitioner to the organization, particularly to those members who do not know the consultant and yet will be asked to provide diagnostic data.

2. *Why am I here, and what am I doing?* These answers are aimed at defining the goals of the diagnosis and data-gathering activities. The consultant needs to present the objectives of the action research process and to describe how the diagnostic activities fit into the overall developmental strategy.

3. *Whom do I work for?* This answer clarifies who has hired the consultant, whether it be a manager, a group of managers, or a group of employees and managers. One way to build trust and support for the diagnosis is to have those people directly involved in establishing the diagnostic contract. Thus, for example, if the consultant works for a joint labor–management committee, representatives from both sides of that group could help the consultant build the proper relationship with those from whom data will be gathered.

4. *What do I want from you, and why?* Here, the consultant needs to specify how much time and effort people will need to give to provide valid data and subsequently to work with these data in solving problems. Because some people may not want to participate in the diagnosis, it is important to specify that such involvement is voluntary.

5. *How will I protect your confidentiality?* This answer addresses member concerns about who will see their responses and in what form. This is especially critical when employees are asked to provide information about their attitudes or perceptions. OD practitioners can either ensure confidentiality or state that full participation in the change process requires open information sharing. In the first case, employees frequently are concerned about privacy and the possibility of being punished for their responses. To alleviate concern and to increase the likelihood of obtaining honest responses, the consultant may need to assure employees of the confidentiality of their information, perhaps through explicit guarantees of response anonymity. In the second case, full involvement of the participants in their own diagnosis may be a vital ingredient of the change process. If sensitive issues arise, assurances of confidentiality can co-opt the OD practitioner and thwart meaningful diagnosis. The consultant is bound to keep confidential the issues that are most critical for the group or organization to understand.[3] OD practitioners must think carefully about how they want to handle confidentiality issues.

6. *Who will have access to the data?* Respondents typically want to know whether they will have access to their data and who else in the organization will have

similar access. The OD practitioner needs to clarify access issues and, in most cases, should agree to provide respondents with their own results. Indeed, the collaborative nature of diagnosis means that organization members will work with their own data to discover causes of problems and to devise relevant interventions.

7. *What's in it for you?* This answer is aimed at providing organization members with a clear delineation of the benefits they can expect from the diagnosis. This usually entails describing the feedback process and how they can use the data to improve the organization.

8. *Can I be trusted?* The diagnostic relationship ultimately rests on the trust established between the consultant and those providing the data. An open and honest exchange of information depends on such trust, and the practitioner should provide ample time and face-to-face contact during the contracting process to build this trust. This requires the consultant to listen actively and discuss openly all questions raised by participants.

Careful attention to establishing the diagnostic relationship helps to promote the three goals of data collection.[4] The first and most immediate objective is to obtain valid information about organizational functioning. Building a data-collection contract can ensure that organization members provide honest, reliable, and complete information.

Data collection also can rally energy for constructive organizational change. A good diagnostic relationship helps organization members start thinking about issues that concern them, and it creates expectations that change is possible. When members trust the consultant, they are likely to participate in the diagnostic process and to generate energy and commitment for organizational change.

Finally, data collection helps develop the collaborative relationship necessary for effecting organizational change. The diagnostic stage of action research is probably the first time that most organization members meet the OD practitioner, and it can be the basis for building a longer-term relationship. The data-collection contract and subsequent data-gathering and feedback activities provide members with opportunities for seeing the consultant in action and for knowing her or him personally. If the consultant can show employees that she or he is trustworthy, is willing to work with them, and is able to help improve the organization, then the data-collection process will contribute to the longer-term collaborative relationship so necessary for carrying out organizational changes.

METHODS FOR COLLECTING DATA

The four major techniques for gathering diagnostic data are questionnaires, interviews, observations, and unobtrusive measures. Table 5.1 briefly compares the methods and lists their major advantages and problems. No single method can fully measure the kinds of variables important to OD because each has certain strengths and weaknesses.[5] For example, perceptual measures, such as questionnaires and surveys, are open to self-report biases, such as respondents' tendency to give socially desirable answers rather than honest opinions. Observations, on the other hand, are susceptible to observer biases, such as seeing what one wants to see rather than what is really there. Because of the biases inherent in any data-collection method, we recommend that more than one method be used when collecting diagnostic data. If data from the different methods are compared and found to be consistent, it is likely that the variables are being measured validly. For example, questionnaire

Table 5•1	A Comparison of Different Methods of Data Collection	
METHOD	**MAJOR ADVANTAGES**	**MAJOR POTENTIAL PROBLEMS**
Questionnaires	1. Responses can be quantified and easily summarized 2. Easy to use with large samples 3. Relatively inexpensive 4. Can obtain large volume of data	1. Nonempathy 2. Predetermined questions/missing issues 3. Overinterpretation of data 4. Response bias
Interviews	1. Adaptive—allows data collection on a range of possible subjects 2. Source of "rich" data 3. Empathic 4. Process of interviewing can build rapport	1. Expense 2. Bias in interviewer responses 3. Coding and interpretation difficulties 4. Self-report bias
Observations	1. Collects data on behavior, rather than reports of behavior 2. Real time, not retrospective 3. Adaptive	1. Coding and interpretation difficulties 2. Sampling inconsistencies 3. Observer bias and questionable reliability 4. Expense
Unobtrusive measures	1. Nonreactive—no response bias 2. High face validity 3. Easily quantified	1. Access and retrieval difficulties 2. Validity concerns 3. Coding and interpretation difficulties

SOURCE: D. Nadler, *Feedback and Organization Development: Using Data-Based Methods*, page 119. © 1977 by Addison-Wesley Publishing Co., Inc. Reprinted by permission of Addison Wesley Longman.

measures of job discretion could be supplemented with observations of the number and kinds of decisions employees are making. If the two kinds of data support one another, job discretion is probably being accurately assessed. If the two kinds of data conflict, then the validity of the measures should be examined further—perhaps by using a third method, such as interviews.

Questionnaires

One of the most efficient ways to collect data is through *questionnaires*. Because they typically contain fixed-response queries about various features of an organization, these paper-and-pencil measures can be administered to large numbers of people simultaneously. Also, they can be analyzed quickly, especially with the use of computers, thus permitting quantitative comparison and evaluation. As a result, data can easily be fed back to employees. Numerous basic resource books on survey methodology and questionnaire development are available.[6]

Questionnaires can vary in scope, some measuring selected aspects of organizations and others assessing more comprehensive organizational characteristics. They also can vary in the extent to which they are either standardized or tailored to a specific organization. Standardized instruments generally are based on an explicit model of organization, group, or individual effectiveness and contain a predetermined set of questions that have been developed and refined over time.

Several research organizations have been highly instrumental in developing and refining surveys. The Institute for Social Research at the University of Michigan (http://www.isr.umich.edu) and the Center for Effective Organizations at the University of Southern California (http://www.marshall.usc.edu/ceo) are two prominent examples. Two of the institute's most popular measures of organizational dimensions are the *Survey of Organizations* and the *Michigan Organizational Assessment Questionnaire*. Few other instruments are supported by such substantial reliability and validity data.[7] Other examples of packaged instruments include Weisbord's *Organizational Diagnostic Questionnaire*, Dyer's *Team Development Survey*, and Hackman and Oldham's *Job Diagnostic Survey*.[8] In fact, so many questionnaires are available that rarely would an organization have to create a totally new one. However, because every organization has unique problems and special jargon for referring to them, almost any standardized instrument will need to have organization-specific additions, modifications, or omissions.

Customized questionnaires, on the other hand, are tailored to the needs of a particular client. Typically, they include questions composed by consultants or organization members, receive limited use, and do not undergo longer-term development. They can be combined with standardized instruments to provide valid and reliable data focused toward the particular issues facing an organization.

Questionnaires, however, have a number of drawbacks that need to be taken into account in choosing whether to employ them for data collection. First, responses are limited to the questions asked in the instrument. They provide little opportunity to probe for additional data or to ask for points of clarification. Second, questionnaires tend to be impersonal, and employees may not be willing to provide honest answers. Third, questionnaires often elicit response biases, such as the tendency to answer questions in a socially acceptable manner. This makes it difficult to draw valid conclusions from employees' self-reports.

Interviews

A second important measurement technique is the *individual* or *group interview*. Interviews are probably the most widely used technique for collecting data in OD. They permit the interviewer to ask the respondent direct questions. Further probing and clarification is, therefore, possible as the interview proceeds. This flexibility is invaluable for gaining private views and feelings about the organization and for exploring new issues that emerge during the interview.

Interviews may be highly structured, resembling questionnaires, or highly unstructured, starting with general questions that allow the respondent to lead the way. Structured interviews typically derive from a conceptual model of organization functioning; the model guides the types of questions that are asked. For example, a structured interview based on the organization-level design components identified in Chapter 4 would ask managers specific questions about organization structure, measurement systems, human resources systems, and organization culture.

Unstructured interviews are more general and include broad questions about organizational functioning, such as:

- What are the major goals or objectives of the organization or department?
- How does the organization currently perform with respect to these purposes?
- What are the strengths and weaknesses of the organization or department?
- What barriers stand in the way of good performance?

Although interviewing typically involves one-to-one interaction between an OD practitioner and an employee, it can be carried out in a group context. Group interviews save time and allow people to build on others' responses. A major drawback, however, is that group settings may inhibit some people from responding freely.

Interviews are an effective method for collecting data in OD. They are adaptive, allowing the interviewer to modify questions and to probe emergent issues during the interview process. They also permit the interviewer to develop an empathetic relationship with employees, frequently resulting in frank disclosure of pertinent information.

A major drawback of interviews is the amount of time required to conduct and analyze them. Interviews can consume a great deal of time, especially if interviewers take full advantage of the opportunity to hear respondents out and change their questions accordingly. Personal biases also can distort the data. Like questionnaires, interviews are subject to the self-report biases of respondents and, perhaps more important, to the biases of the interviewer. For example, the nature of the questions and the interactions between the interviewer and the respondent may discourage or encourage certain kinds of responses. These problems suggest that interviewing takes considerable skill to gather valid data. Interviewers must be able to understand their own biases, to listen and establish empathy with respondents, and to change questions to pursue issues that develop during the course of the interview.

Observations

One of the more direct ways of collecting data is simply to *observe* organizational behaviors in their functional settings. The OD practitioner may do this by walking casually through a work area and looking around or by simply counting the occurrences of specific kinds of behaviors (for example, the number of times a phone call is answered after three rings in a service department). Observation can range from complete participant observation, in which the OD practitioner becomes a member of the group under study, to more detached observation, in which the observer is clearly not part of the group or situation itself and may use film, videotape, and other methods to record behaviors.

Observations have a number of advantages. They are free of the biases inherent in self-report data. They put the practitioner directly in touch with the behaviors in question, without having to rely on others' perceptions. Observations also involve real-time data, describing behavior occurring in the present rather than the past. This avoids the distortions that invariably arise when people are asked to recollect their behaviors. Finally, observations are adaptive in that the consultant can modify what he or she chooses to observe, depending on the circumstances.

Among the problems with observations are difficulties interpreting the meaning underlying the observations. Practitioners may need to devise a coding scheme to make sense out of observations, and this can be expensive, take time, and introduce biases into the data. Because the observer is the data-collection instrument, personal bias and subjectivity can distort the data unless the observer is trained and skilled in knowing what to look for; how, where, and when to observe; and how to record data systematically. Another problem concerns sampling: observers not only must decide which people to observe; they also must choose the time periods, territory, and events in which to make those observations. Failure to attend to these sampling issues can result in highly biased samples of observational data.

When used correctly, observations provide insightful data about organization and group functioning, intervention success, and performance. For example, observations are particularly helpful in diagnosing the interpersonal relations of members of work groups. As discussed in Chapter 4, interpersonal relationships are a key component of work groups; observing member interactions in a group setting can provide direct information about the nature of those relationships.

Unobtrusive Measures

Unobtrusive data are not collected directly from respondents but from secondary sources, such as company records and archives. These data generally are available in organizations and include records of absenteeism or tardiness; grievances; quantity and quality of production or service; financial performance; meeting minutes; and correspondence with key customers, suppliers, or governmental agencies.

Unobtrusive measures are especially helpful in diagnosing the organization, group, and individual outputs presented in Chapter 4. At the organization level, for example, market share and return on investment usually can be obtained from company reports. Similarly, organizations typically measure the quantity and quality of the outputs of work groups and individual employees. Unobtrusive measures also can help to diagnose organization-level design components—structure, work systems, control systems, and human resources systems. A company's organization chart, for example, can provide useful information about organization structure. Information about control systems usually can be obtained by examining the firm's management information system, operating procedures, and accounting practices. Data about human resources systems often are included in a company's personnel manual.

Unobtrusive measures provide a relatively objective view of organizational functioning. They are free from respondent and consultant biases and are perceived as being "real" by many organization members. Moreover, unobtrusive measures tend to be quantified and reported at periodic intervals, permitting statistical analysis of behaviors occurring over time. Examining monthly absenteeism rates, for example, might reveal trends in employee withdrawal behavior.

The major problems with unobtrusive measures occur in collecting such information and drawing valid conclusions from it. Company records may not include data in a form that is usable by the consultant. If, for example, individual performance data are needed, the consultant may find that many firms only record production information at the group or departmental level. Unobtrusive data also may have their own built-in biases. Changes in accounting procedures and in methods of recording data are common in organizations, and such changes can affect company records independently of what is actually happening in the organization. For example, observed changes in productivity over time might be caused by modifications in methods of recording production rather than by actual changes in organizational functioning.

Despite these drawbacks, unobtrusive data serve as a valuable adjunct to other diagnostic measures, such as interviews and questionnaires. Archival data can be used in preliminary diagnosis, identifying those organizational units with absenteeism, grievance, or production problems. Then, interviews might be conducted or observations made in those units to discover the underlying causes of the problems. Conversely, unobtrusive data can be used to crosscheck other forms of information. For example, if questionnaires reveal that employees in a department are dissatisfied with their jobs, company records might show whether that discontent is manifested in heightened withdrawal behaviors, in lowered quality of work, or in similar counterproductive behaviors.

TECHNIQUES FOR ANALYZING DATA

Once diagnostic data have been collected, they must be analyzed and summarized for feedback to the client system. Data analysis techniques fall into two broad classes: qualitative and quantitative. Qualitative techniques generally are easier to use because they do not rely on numerical data. That fact also makes them easier to understand and interpret. Quantitative techniques, on the other hand, can provide more accurate readings of the organizational problem.

Qualitative Tools

Of the several methods for summarizing diagnostic data in qualitative terms, two of the most important are content analysis and force-field analysis.

Content Analysis

A popular technique for assessing qualitative data, especially interview data, is *content analysis,* which attempts to summarize comments into meaningful categories. When done well, a content analysis can reduce hundreds of interview comments into a few themes that effectively summarize the issues or attitudes of a group of respondents. The process of content analysis can be quite formal, and specialized references describe this technique in detail.[9] In general, however, the process can be broken down into three major steps. First, responses to a particular question are read to gain familiarity with the range of comments made and to determine whether some answers are occurring over and over again. Second, based on this sampling of comments, themes are generated that capture recurring comments. Themes consolidate different responses that say essentially the same thing. For example, in answering the question "What do you like most about your job?" different respondents might list their co-workers, their supervisors, the new machinery, and a good supply of tools. The first two answers concern the social aspects of work, and the second two address the resources available for doing the work. Third, the respondents' answers to a question are then placed into one of the categories. The categories with the most responses represent those themes that are most often mentioned.

Force-Field Analysis

A second method for analyzing qualitative data in OD derives from Kurt Lewin's three-step model of change. Called *force-field analysis,* this method organizes information pertaining to organizational change into two major categories: forces for change and forces for maintaining the status quo or resisting change.[10] Using data collected through interviews, observation, or unobtrusive measures, the first step in conducting a force-field analysis is to develop a list of all the forces promoting change and all those resisting it. Then, based either on the OD practitioner's personal belief or perhaps on input from several members of the client organization, a determination is made of which of the positive and which of the negative forces are most powerful. One can either rank the order or rate the strength of the different forces.

Figure 5.2 illustrates a force-field analysis of the performance of a work group. The arrows represent the forces, and the length of the arrows corresponds to the strength of the forces. The information could have been collected in a group interview in which members were asked to list those factors maintaining the current level of group performance and those factors pushing for a higher level. Members also could have been asked to judge the strength of each force, with the average judgment shown by the length of the arrows.

This analysis reveals two strong forces pushing for higher performance: pressures from the supervisor of the group and competition from other work groups performing similar work. These forces for change are offset by two strong forces for maintaining the status quo: group norms supporting present levels of performance

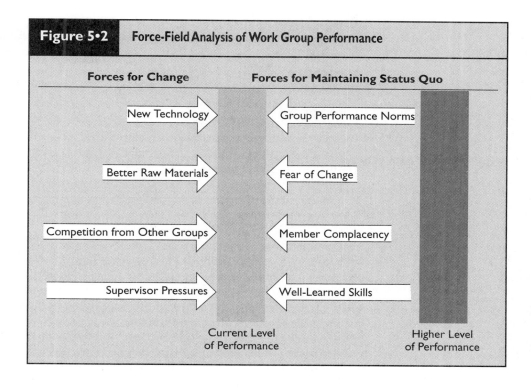

Figure 5•2   Force-Field Analysis of Work Group Performance

Forces for Change   Forces for Maintaining Status Quo

New Technology   Group Performance Norms

Better Raw Materials   Fear of Change

Competition from Other Groups   Member Complacency

Supervisor Pressures   Well-Learned Skills

Current Level
of Performance

Higher Level
of Performance

and well-learned skills that are resistant to change. According to Lewin, efforts to change to a higher level of group performance, shown by the darker band in Figure 5.2, should focus on reducing the forces maintaining the status quo. This might entail changing the group's performance norms and helping members to learn new skills. The reduction of forces maintaining the status quo is likely to result in organizational change with little of the tension or conflict typically accompanying change caused by increasing the forces for change.

Quantitative Tools

Methods for analyzing quantitative data range from simple descriptive statistics of items or scales from standard instruments to more sophisticated, multivariate analysis of the underlying instrument properties and relationships among measured variables.[11] The most common quantitative tools are means, standard deviations, frequency distributions, scattergrams, correlation coefficients, and difference tests. These measures are routinely produced by most statistical computer software packages. Therefore, mathematical calculations are not discussed here.

Means, Standard Deviations, and Frequency Distributions

One of the most economical and straightforward ways to summarize quantitative data is to compute a *mean* and *standard deviation* for each item or variable measured. These represent the respondents' average score and the spread or variability of the responses, respectively. These two numbers easily can be compared across different measures or subgroups. For example, Table 5.2 shows the means and standard deviations for six questions asked of one hundred employees concerning the value of different kinds of organizational rewards. Based on the five-point scale ranging from one (very low value) to five (very high value), the data suggest that challenging

Table 5•2	Descriptive Statistics of Value of Organizational Rewards	
ORGANIZATIONAL REWARDS	**MEAN**	**STANDARD DEVIATION**
Challenging work	4.6	0.76
Respect from peers	4.4	0.81
Pay	4.0	0.71
Praise from supervisor	4.0	1.55
Promotion	3.3	0.95
Fringe benefits	2.7	1.14

Number of respondents = 100.
I = very low value; 5 = very high value.

work and respect from peers are the two most highly valued rewards. Monetary rewards, such as pay and fringe benefits, are not as highly valued.

But the mean can be a misleading statistic. It only describes the average value and thus provides no information on the distribution of the responses. Different patterns of responses can produce the same mean score. Therefore, it is important to use the standard deviation along with the frequency distribution to gain a clearer understanding of the data. The *frequency distribution* is a graphical method for displaying data that shows the number of times a particular response was given. For example, the data in Table 5.2 suggest that both pay and praise from the supervisor are equally valued with a mean of 4.0. However, the standard deviations for these two measures are very different at 0.71 and 1.55, respectively. Table 5.3 shows the

Table 5•3	Frequency Distributions of Responses to "Pay" and "Praise from Supervisor" Items	
Pay (Mean = 4.0)		
RESPONSE	**NUMBER CHECKING EACH RESPONSE**	**GRAPH***
(1) Very low value	0	
(2) Low value	0	
(3) Moderate value	25	XXXXX
(4) High value	50	XXXXXXXXXX
(5) Very high value	25	XXXXX
Praise from Supervisor (Mean = 4.0)		
RESPONSE	**NUMBER CHECKING EACH RESPONSE**	**GRAPH***
(1) Very low value	15	XXX
(2) Low value	10	XX
(3) Moderate value	0	
(4) High value	10	XX
(5) Very high value	60	XXXXXXXXXXXX

*Each X = five people checking the response.

frequency distributions of the responses to the questions about pay and praise from the supervisor. Employees' responses to the value of pay are distributed toward the higher end of the scale, with no one rating it of low or very low value. In contrast, responses about the value of praise from the supervisor fall into two distinct groupings: twenty-five employees felt that supervisor praise has a low or very low value, whereas seventy-five people rated it high or very high. Although both rewards have the same mean value, their standard deviations and frequency distributions suggest different interpretations of the data.

In general, when the standard deviation for a set of data is high, there is considerable disagreement over the issue posed by the question. If the standard deviation is small, the data are similar on a particular measure. In the example described above, there is disagreement over the value of supervisory praise (some people think it is important but others do not), but there is fairly good agreement that pay is a reward with high value.

Scattergrams and Correlation Coefficients

In addition to describing data, quantitative techniques also permit OD consultants to make inferences about the relationships between variables. Scattergrams and correlation coefficients are measures of the strength of a relationship between two variables. For example, suppose the problem being faced by an organization is increased conflict between the manufacturing department and the engineering design department. During the data-collection phase, information about the number of conflicts and change orders per month over the past year is collected. The data are shown in Table 5.4 and plotted in a scattergram in Figure 5.3.

A *scattergram* is a diagram that visually displays the relationship between two variables. It is constructed by locating each case (person or event) at the intersection of its value for each of the two variables being compared. For example, in the month of August, there were eight change orders and three conflicts, whose intersection is shown on Figure 5.3 as an X.

Three basic patterns can emerge from a scattergram, as shown in Figure 5.4. The first pattern is called a positive relationship because as the values of x increase, so do the values of y. The second pattern is called a negative relationship because as

Table 5•4	Relationship Between Change Orders and Conflicts	
MONTH	**NUMBER OF CHANGE ORDERS**	**NUMBER OF CONFLICTS**
April	5	2
May	12	4
June	14	3
July	6	2
August	8	3
September	20	5
October	10	2
November	2	1
December	15	4
January	8	3
February	18	4
March	10	5

the values of *x* increase, the values of *y* decrease. Finally, there is the "shotgun" pattern wherein no relationship between the two variables is apparent. In the example shown in Figure 5.3, an apparently strong positive relationship exists between the number of change orders and the number of conflicts between the engineering design department and the manufacturing department. This suggests that change orders may contribute to the observed conflict between the two departments.

The *correlation coefficient* is simply a number that summarizes data in a scattergram. Its value ranges between +1.0 and −1.0. A correlation coefficient of +1.0

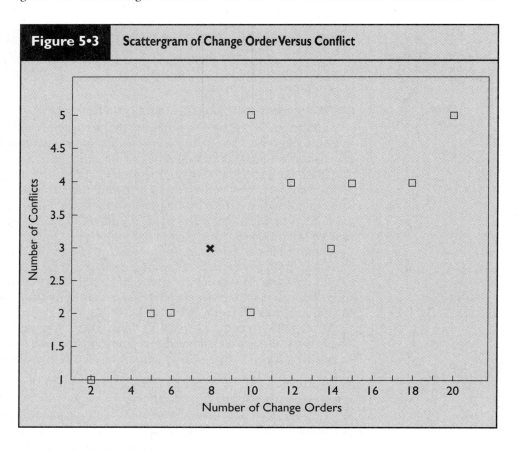

Figure 5•3   Scattergram of Change Order Versus Conflict

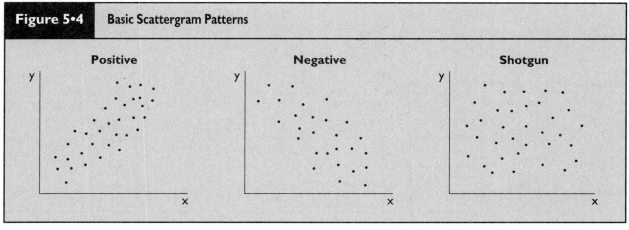

Figure 5•4   Basic Scattergram Patterns

means that there is a perfect, positive relationship between two variables, whereas a correlation of −1.0 signifies a perfectly negative relationship. A correlation of 0 implies a "shotgun" scattergram where there is no relationship between two variables.

Difference Tests

The final technique for analyzing quantitative data is the *difference test*. It can be used to compare a sample group against some standard or norm to determine whether the group is above or below that standard. It also can be used to determine whether two samples are significantly different from each other. In the first case, such comparisons provide a broader context for understanding the meaning of diagnostic data. They serve as a "basis for determining 'how good is good or how bad is bad.'"[12] Many standardized questionnaires have standardized scores based on the responses of large groups of people. It is critical, however, to choose a comparison group that is similar to the organization being diagnosed. For example, if one hundred engineers take a standardized attitude survey, it makes little sense to compare their scores against standard scores representing married males from across the country. On the other hand, if industry-specific data are available, a comparison of sales per employee (as a measure of productivity) against the industry average would be valid and useful.

The second use of difference tests involves assessing whether two (or more) groups differ from one another on a particular variable, such as job satisfaction or absenteeism. For example, job satisfaction differences between an accounting department and a sales department can be determined with this tool. Given that each group took the same questionnaire, their means and standard deviations can be used to compute a difference score (t-score or z-score) indicating whether the two groups are statistically different. The larger the difference score relative to the sample size and standard deviation for each group, the more likely that one group is more satisfied than the other.

Difference tests also can be used to determine whether a group has changed its score on job satisfaction or some other variable over time. The same questionnaire can be given to the same group at two points in time. Based on the group's means and standard deviations at each point in time, a difference score can be calculated. The larger the score, the more likely that the group actually changed its job satisfaction level.

The calculation of difference scores can be very helpful for diagnosis but requires the OD practitioner to make certain assumptions about how the data were collected. These assumptions are discussed in most standard statistical texts, and OD practitioners should consult them before calculating difference scores for purposes of diagnosis or evaluation.[13]

FEEDING BACK DIAGNOSTIC INFORMATION

Perhaps the most important step in the diagnostic process is feeding back diagnostic information to the client organization. Although the data may have been collected with the client's help, the OD practitioner usually is responsible for organizing and presenting them to the client. Properly analyzed and meaningful data can have an impact on organizational change only if organization members can use the information to devise appropriate action plans. A key objective of the feedback process is to be sure that the client has ownership of the data.

As shown in Figure 5.5, the success of data feedback depends largely on its ability to arouse organizational action and to direct energy toward organizational problem solving. Whether feedback helps to energize the organization depends on the

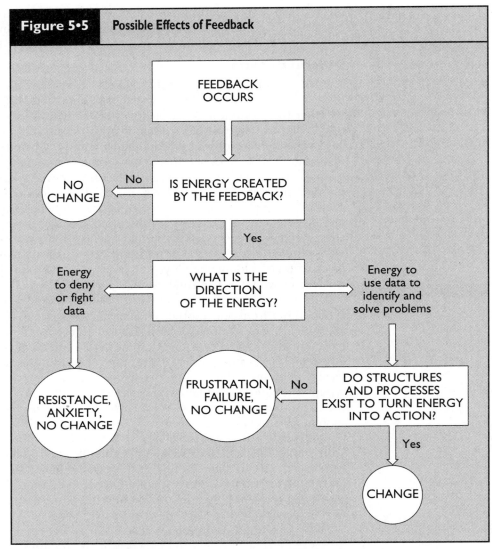

Figure 5•5   Possible Effects of Feedback

FEEDBACK OCCURS

NO CHANGE ← No — IS ENERGY CREATED BY THE FEEDBACK?

Yes

Energy to deny or fight data ← WHAT IS THE DIRECTION OF THE ENERGY? → Energy to use data to identify and solve problems

RESISTANCE, ANXIETY, NO CHANGE

FRUSTRATION, FAILURE, NO CHANGE ← No — DO STRUCTURES AND PROCESSES EXIST TO TURN ENERGY INTO ACTION?

Yes

CHANGE

SOURCE: D. Nadler, *Feedback and Organization Development: Using Data-Based Methods,* page 146. © 1977 by Addison-Wesley Publishing Co., Inc. Reprinted by permission of Addison Wesley Longman.

content of the feedback data and on the *process* by which they are fed back to organization members.

Determining the Content of the Feedback

In the course of diagnosing the organization, a large amount of data is collected. In fact, there is often more information than the client needs or could interpret in a realistic period of time. If too many data are fed back, the client may decide that changing is impossible. Therefore, OD practitioners need to summarize the data in ways that enable clients to understand the information and draw action implications from it. The techniques for data analysis described above can inform this task. Additional criteria for determining the content of diagnostic feedback are described below.

Several characteristics of effective feedback data have been described in the literature.[14] They include the following nine properties:

1. *Relevant.* Organization members are likely to use feedback data for problem solving when they find the information meaningful. Including managers and employees in the initial data-collection activities can increase the relevance of the data.

2. *Understandable.* Data must be presented to organization members in a form that is readily interpreted. Statistical data, for example, can be made understandable through the use of graphs and charts.

3. *Descriptive.* Feedback data need to be linked to real organizational behaviors if they are to arouse and direct energy. The use of examples and detailed illustrations can help employees gain a better feel for the data.

4. *Verifiable.* Feedback data should be valid and accurate if they are to guide action. Thus, the information should allow organization members to verify whether the findings really describe the organization. For example, questionnaire data might include information about the sample of respondents as well as frequency distributions for each item or measure. Such information can help members verify whether the feedback data accurately represent organizational events or attitudes.

5. *Timely.* Data should be fed back to members as quickly as possible after being collected and analyzed. This will help ensure that the information is still valid and is linked to members' motivations to examine it.

6. *Limited.* Because people can easily become overloaded with too much information, feedback data should be limited to what employees can realistically process at one time.

7. *Significant.* Feedback should be limited to those problems that organization members can do something about because it will energize them and help direct their efforts toward realistic changes.

8. *Comparative.* Feedback data can be ambiguous without some benchmark as a reference. Whenever possible, data from comparative groups should be provided to give organization members a better idea of how their group fits into a broader context.

9. *Unfinalized.* Feedback is primarily a stimulus for action and thus should spur further diagnosis and problem solving. Members should be encouraged, for example, to use the data as a starting point for more in-depth discussion of organizational issues.

Characteristics of the Feedback Process

In addition to providing effective feedback data, it is equally important to attend to the process by which that information is fed back to people. Typically, data are provided to organization members in a meeting or series of meetings. Feedback meetings provide a forum for discussing the data, drawing relevant conclusions, and devising preliminary action plans. Because the data might include sensitive material and evaluations about organization members' behaviors, people may come to the meeting with considerable anxiety and fear about receiving the feedback. This anxiety can result in defensive behaviors aimed at denying the information or providing rationales. More positively, people can be stimulated by the feedback and the hope that desired changes will result from the feedback meeting.

Because people are likely to come to feedback meetings with anxiety, fear, and hope, OD practitioners need to manage the feedback process so that constructive discussion and problem solving occur. The most important objective of the feedback process is to ensure that organization members *own* the data. Ownership is the opposite of resistance to change and refers to people's willingness to take responsibility for the data, their meaning, and the consequences of using them to devise a change strategy.[15] If the feedback session results in organization members rejecting the data as invalid or useless, then the motivation to change is lost and members will have difficulty engaging in a meaningful process of change.

Ownership of the feedback data is facilitated by the following five features of successful feedback processes:[16]

1. *Motivation to work with the data.* People need to feel that working with the feedback data will have beneficial outcomes. This may require explicit sanction and support from powerful groups so that people feel free to raise issues and to identify concerns during the feedback sessions. If people have little motivation to work with the data or feel that there is little chance to use the data for change, then the information will not be owned by the client system.

2. *Structure for the meeting.* Feedback meetings need some structure or they may degenerate into chaos or aimless discussion. An agenda or outline and a discussion leader usually can provide the necessary direction. If the meeting is not kept on track, especially when the data are negative, ownership can be lost in conversations that become too general. When this happens, the energy gained from dealing directly with the problem is lost.

3. *Appropriate attendance.* Generally, people who have common problems and can benefit from working together should be included in the feedback meeting. This may involve a fully intact work team or groups comprising members from different functional areas or hierarchical levels. Without proper representation in the meeting, ownership of the data is lost because participants cannot address the problem(s) suggested by the feedback.

4. *Appropriate power.* It is important to clarify the power possessed by the group. Members need to know on which issues they can make necessary changes, on which they can only recommend changes, and over which they have no control. Unless there are clear boundaries, members are likely to have some hesitation about using the feedback data for generating action plans. Moreover, if the group has no power to make changes, the feedback meeting will become an empty exercise rather than a real problem-solving session. Without the power to address change, there will be little ownership of the data.

5. *Process help.* People in feedback meetings require assistance in working together as a group. When the data are negative, there is a natural tendency to resist the implications, deflect the conversation onto safer subjects, and the like. An OD practitioner with group process skills can help members stay focused on the subject and improve feedback discussion, problem solving, and ownership.

When combined with effective feedback data, these features of successful feedback meetings enhance member ownership of the data. They help ensure that organization members fully discuss the implications of the diagnostic information and that their conclusions are directed toward relevant and feasible organizational changes.

SURVEY FEEDBACK

Survey feedback is used widely in OD. It enables practitioners to collect diagnostic data from a large number of organization members and to feed that information back to them for purposes of problem solving. Survey feedback involves collecting data from an organization or department through the use of a questionnaire or survey. The data are analyzed, fed back to organization members, and used by them to diagnose the organization and to develop interventions to improve it. Because questionnaires often are used in organization diagnosis, particularly in OD efforts involving large numbers of participants, and because it is a powerful intervention in its own right, survey feedback is discussed here as a special case of data feedback.

As discussed in Chapter 1, survey feedback is a major technique in the history and development of OD. Originally, this intervention included only data from questionnaires about members' attitudes. However, attitudinal data can be supplemented with interview data and more objective measures, such as productivity, turnover, and absenteeism.[17] Another trend has been to combine survey feedback with other OD interventions, including work design, structural change, large-group interventions, and intergroup relations. These change methods are the outcome of the planning and implementation phase following from survey feedback and are described fully in Chapters 8 through 14.

Application Stages

Survey feedback generally involves the following five steps:[18]

1. ***Members of the organization, including those at the top, are involved in preliminary planning of the survey.*** In this step, all parties must be clear about the level of analysis (organization, department, or small group) and the objectives of the survey. Because most surveys derive from a model about organizational or group functioning, organization members must, in effect, approve that diagnostic framework. This is an important initial step in gaining ownership of the data and in ensuring that the right problems and issues are addressed by the survey.

   Once the objectives are determined, the organization can use one of the standardized questionnaires described earlier, or it can develop its own survey instrument. If the survey is developed internally, pretesting the questionnaire is essential to ensure that it has been constructed properly. In either case, the survey items need to reflect the objectives established for the survey and the diagnostic issues being addressed.

2. ***The survey instrument is administered to all members of the organization or department.*** That breadth of data collection is ideal, but it may be necessary to administer the instrument to a sample of members because of cost or time constraints. If so, the size of the sample should be as large as possible to improve the motivational basis for participation in the feedback sessions.

3. ***The OD consultant usually analyzes the survey data, tabulates the results, suggests approaches to diagnosis, and trains client members to lead the feedback process.***

4. *Data feedback usually begins at the top of the organization and cascades downward to groups reporting to managers at successively lower levels.* This waterfall approach ensures that all groups at all organizational levels involved in the survey receive appropriate feedback. Most often, members of each organization group at each level discuss and deal with *only* that portion of the data involving their particular group. They, in turn, prepare to introduce data to groups at the next lower organizational level if appropriate.

   Data feedback also can occur in a "bottom-up" approach. Initially, the data for specific work groups or departments are fed back and action items are proposed. At this point, the group addresses problems and issues within its control. The group notes any issues that are beyond its authority and suggests actions. That information is combined with information from groups reporting to the same manager, and the combined data are fed back to the managers who review the data and the recommended actions. Problems that can be solved at this level are addressed. In turn, their analyses and suggestions regarding problems of a broader nature are combined, and feedback and action sessions proceed up the hierarchy. In such a way, the people who most likely will carry out recommended action get the first chance to propose suggestions.

5. *Feedback meetings provide an opportunity to work with the data.* At each meeting, members discuss and interpret their data, diagnose problem areas, and develop action plans. OD practitioners can play an important role during these meetings,[19] facilitating group discussion to produce accurate understanding, focusing the group on its strengths and weaknesses, and helping to develop effective action plans.

■ SUMMARY

Organization development is vitally dependent on organization diagnosis: the process of collecting information that will be shared with the client in jointly assessing how the organization is functioning and determining the most beneficial change intervention. This chapter has described the key issues involved in the process of diagnosis: collecting, analyzing, and feeding back diagnostic data. Because diagnosis is an important step that occurs frequently in the planned change process, a working familiarity with these techniques is essential. Methods of data collection include questionnaires, interviews, observation, and unobtrusive measures. Methods of analysis include qualitative techniques, such as content and force-field analysis, and quantitative techniques, such as the determination of mean, standard deviation, correlation coefficient, as well as difference tests.

Data feedback is concerned with identifying the content of the data to be fed back and designing a feedback process that ensures ownership of the data. Feeding back data is a central activity in almost any OD program. If members own the data, they will be motivated to solve organizational problems. A special application of the data-collection and feedback process is called survey feedback. It is one of the most accepted processes in organization development. Survey feedback highlights the importance of contracting appropriately with the client system, establishing relevant categories for data collection, and feeding back the data as necessary steps for diagnosing organizational problems and developing interventions for resolving them.

■ NOTES

1. S. Mohrman, T. Cummings, and E. Lawler III, "Creating Useful Knowledge with Organizations: Relationship and Process Issues," in *Producing Useful Knowledge for Organizations*, eds. R. Kilmann and K. Thomas (New York: Praeger, 1983): 613–24; C. Argyris, R. Putnam, and D. Smith, eds., *Action Science* (San Francisco: Jossey-Bass, 1985); E. Lawler III, A. Mohrman, S. Mohrman, G. Ledford Jr., and T. Cummings, *Doing Research That Is Useful for Theory and Practice* (San Francisco: Jossey-Bass, 1985).

2. D. Nadler, *Feedback and Organization Development: Using Data-Based Methods* (Reading, Mass.: Addison-Wesley, 1977): 110–14.

3. W. Nielsen, N. Nykodym, and D. Brown, "Ethics and Organizational Change," *Asia Pacific Journal of Human Resources* 29 (1991).

4. Nadler, *Feedback,* pp. 105–7.

5. W. Wymer and J. Carsten, "Alternative Ways to Gather Opinion," *HR Magazine* (April 1992): 71–78.

6. Examples of basic resource books on survey methodology include L. Rea, R. Parker, and A. Shrader, *Designing and Conducting Survey Research: A Comprehensive Guide* (San Francisco: Jossey Bass, 1997); S. Seashore, E. Lawler III, P. Mirvis, and C. Cammann, *Assessing Organizational Change* (New York: Wiley Interscience, 1983); J. Van Mannen and J. Dabbs, *Varieties of Qualitative Research* (Beverly Hills, Calif.: Sage Publications, 1983); E. Lawler III, D. Nadler, and C. Cammann, *Organizational Assessment: Perspectives on the Measurement of Organizational Behavior and the Quality of Worklife* (New York: Wiley-Interscience, 1980); Nadler, *Feedback;* S. Sudman and N. Bradburn, *Asking Questions* (San Francisco: Jossey-Bass, 1983).

7. J. Taylor and D. Bowers, *Survey of Organizations: A Machine Scored Standardized Questionnaire Instrument* (Ann Arbor: Institute for Social Research, University of Michigan, 1972); C. Cammann, M. Fichman, G. Jenkins, and J. Klesh, "Assessing the Attitudes and Perceptions of Organizational Members," in *Assessing Organizational Change: A Guide to Methods, Measures, and Practices,* eds. S. Seashore, E. Lawler III, P. Mirvis, and C. Cammann (New York: Wiley Interscience, 1983): 71–138.

8. M. Weisbord, "Organizational Diagnosis: Six Places to Look for Trouble with or without a Theory," *Group and Organization Studies* 1 (1976): 430–37; R. Preziosi, "Organizational Diagnosis Questionnaire," in *The 1980 Handbook for Group Facilitators,* ed. J. Pfeiffer (San Diego: University Associates, 1980); W. Dyer, *Team Building: Issues and Alternatives* (Reading, Mass.: Addison-Wesley, 1977); J. Hackman and G. Oldham, *Work Redesign* (Reading, Mass.: Addison-Wesley, 1980).

9. B. Berelson, "Content Analysis," *Handbook of Social Psychology,* ed. G. Lindzey (Reading, Mass.: Addison-Wesley, 1954); K. Krippendorf, *Content Analysis: An Introduction to Its Methodology* (Thousand Oaks, Calif.: Sage Publications, 1980); W. Weber, *Basic Content Analysis* (Thousand Oaks, Calif.: Sage Publications, 1990).

10. K. Lewin, *Field Theory in Social Science* (New York: Harper and Row, 1951).

11. More sophisticated methods of quantitative analysis are found in the following sources: W. Hays, *Statistics* (New York: Holt, Rinehart, & Winston, 1963); J. Nunnally and I. Bernstein, *Psychometric Theory,* 3d ed. (New York: McGraw-Hill, 1994); F. Kerlinger, *Foundations of Behavioral Research,* 2d ed. (New York: Holt, Rinehart, & Winston, 1973); J. Cohen and P. Cohen, *Applied Multiple Regression/Correlation Analysis for the Behavioral Sciences,* 2d ed. (Hillsdale, N.J.: Lawrence Erlbaum Associates, 1983); E. Pedhazur, *Multiple Regression in Behavioral Research* (New York: Harcourt Brace, 1997).

12. A. Armenakis and H. Field, "The Development of Organizational Diagnostic Norms: An Application of Client Involvement," *Consultation* 6 (Spring 1987): 20–31.

13. Cohen and Cohen, *Applied Multiple Regression.*

14. Mohrman, Cummings, and Lawler, "Creating Useful Knowledge."

15. C. Argyris, *Intervention Theory and Method: A Behavioral Science View* (Reading, Mass.: Addison-Wesley, 1970); P. Block, *Flawless Consulting: A Guide to Getting Your Expertise Used,* 2d ed. (San Francisco: Jossey-Bass, 1999).

16. Nadler, *Feedback,* pp. 156–58.

17. D. Nadler, P. Mirvis, and C. Cammann, "The Ongoing Feedback System: Experimenting with a New Managerial Tool," *Organizational Dynamics* 4 (Spring 1976): 63–80.

18. F. Mann, "Studying and Creating Change," in *The Planning of Change,* eds. W. Bennis, K. Benne, and R. Chin (New York: Holt, Rinehart, & Winston, 1964): 605–15; Nadler, *Feedback;* J. Wiley, "Making the Most of Survey Feedback as a Strategy for Organization Development," *OD Practitioner* 23 (1991): 1–5; A. Church, A. Margiloff, and C. Coruzzi, "Using Surveys for Change: An Applied

Example in a Pharmaceuticals Organization," *Leadership and Organization Development Journal* 16 (1995): 3–12; J. Folkman and J. Zenger, *Employee Surveys That Make a Difference: Using Customized Feedback Tools to Transform Your Organization* (New York: Executive Excellence, 1999).

19. G. Ledford and C. Worley, "Some Guidelines for Effective Survey Feedback" (working paper, Center for Effective Organizations, University of Southern California, Los Angeles, 1987).

6. Designing Interventions

An organization development intervention is a sequence of activities, actions, and events intended to help an organization improve its performance and effectiveness. Intervention design, or action planning, derives from careful diagnosis and is meant to resolve specific problems and to improve particular areas of organizational functioning identified in the diagnosis. OD interventions vary from standardized programs that have been developed and used in many organizations to relatively unique programs tailored to a specific organization or department.

This chapter describes criteria that define effective OD interventions and then identifies contingencies that guide successful intervention design. Finally, the various types of OD interventions presented in this book are reviewed.

WHAT ARE EFFECTIVE INTERVENTIONS?

The term "intervention" refers to a set of sequenced planned actions or events intended to help an organization increase its effectiveness. Interventions purposely disrupt the status quo; they are deliberate attempts to change an organization or subunit toward a different and more effective state. In OD, three major criteria define an effective intervention: (1) the extent to which it fits the needs of the organization, (2) the degree to which it is based on causal knowledge of intended outcomes, and (3) the extent to which it transfers change-management competence to organization members.

The first criterion concerns the extent to which the intervention is relevant to the organization and its members. Effective interventions are based on valid information about the organization's functioning; they provide organization members with opportunities to make free and informed choices; and they gain members' internal commitment to those choices.[1]

Valid information is the result of an accurate diagnosis of the organization's functioning. It must reflect fairly what organization members perceive and feel about their primary concerns and issues. *Free and informed choice* suggests that members are actively involved in making decisions about the changes that will affect them. It means that they can choose not to participate and that interventions will not be imposed on them. *Internal commitment* means that organization members accept ownership of the intervention and take responsibility for implementing it. If interventions are to result in meaningful changes, management, staff, and other relevant members must be committed to carrying them out.

The second criterion of an effective intervention involves knowledge of outcomes. Because interventions are intended to produce specific results, they must be based on valid knowledge that those outcomes actually can be produced. Otherwise there is no scientific basis for designing an effective OD intervention. Unfortunately, and in contrast to other applied disciplines such as medicine and engineering, knowledge of intervention effects is in a rudimentary stage of development in OD. Much of the evaluation research lacks sufficient rigor to make strong causal inferences about the success or failure of change programs. (Chapter 7 discusses how to evaluate OD programs.) Moreover, few attempts have been made to examine the comparative effects of different OD techniques. All of these factors make it difficult to know whether one method is more effective than another.

Despite these problems, more attempts are being made to assess systematically the strengths and weaknesses of OD interventions and to compare the impact of different techniques on organization effectiveness.[2] Many of the OD interventions that will be discussed here in Chapters 8 through 15 have been subjected to evaluative research, which is explored in the appropriate chapters along with respective change programs.

The third criterion of an effective intervention involves the extent to which it enhances the organization's capacity to manage change. The values underlying OD suggest that organization members should be better able to carry out planned change activities on their own following an intervention. They should gain knowledge and skill in managing change from active participation in designing and implementing the intervention. Competence in change management is essential in today's environment, where technological, social, economic, and political changes are rapid and persistent.

HOW TO DESIGN EFFECTIVE INTERVENTIONS

Designing OD interventions requires paying careful attention to the needs and dynamics of the change situation and crafting a change program that will be consistent with the previously described criteria of effective interventions. Current knowledge of OD interventions provides only general prescriptions for change. There is scant precise information or research about how to design interventions or how they can be expected to interact with organizational conditions to achieve specific results.[3] Moreover, because the ability to implement most OD interventions is highly dependent on the skills and knowledge of the change agent, the design of an intervention will depend to some extent on the expertise of the practitioner.

Two major sets of contingencies that can affect intervention success have been discussed in the OD literature: those having to do with the change situation (including the practitioner) and those related to the target of change. Both kinds of contingencies need to be considered in designing interventions.

Contingencies Related to the Change Situation

Researchers have identified a number of contingencies present in the change situation that can affect intervention success. These include individual differences among organization members (for example, needs for autonomy), organizational factors (for example, management style and technical uncertainty), and dimensions of the change process itself (for example, degree of top-management support). Unless these factors are taken into account in designing an intervention, it will have little impact on organizational functioning or, worse, it may produce negative results. For example, to resolve motivational problems among blue-collar workers in an oil refinery, it is important to know whether interventions intended to improve motivation (for example, job enrichment) will succeed with the kinds of people who work there. In many cases, knowledge of these contingencies results in modifying or adjusting the change program to fit the setting. In applying a reward-system intervention to an organization, the changes might have to be modified depending on whether the firm wants to reinforce individual or team performance.

Although knowledge of contingencies is still at a rudimentary stage of development in OD, researchers have discovered several situational factors that can affect intervention success.[4] These factors include contingencies for many of the interventions reviewed in this book, and they will be discussed in respective chapters describing the change programs. More generic contingencies that apply to all OD interventions are presented below. They include the following situational factors that must be considered in designing any intervention: the organization's readiness for change, its change capability, its cultural context, and the change agent's skills and abilities.

Readiness for Change

Intervention success depends heavily on the organization being ready for planned change. Indicators of readiness for change include sensitivity to pressures for change, dissatisfaction with the status quo, availability of resources to support change, and commitment of significant management time. When such conditions are present, interventions can be designed to address the organizational issues uncovered during diagnosis. When readiness for change is low, however, interventions need to focus first on increasing the organization's willingness to change.[5]

Capability to Change

Managing planned change requires particular knowledge and skills (as outlined in Chapter 7), including the ability to motivate change, to lead change, to develop political support, to manage the transition, and to sustain momentum. If organization members do not have these capabilities, then a preliminary training intervention may be needed before members can engage meaningfully in intervention design.

Cultural Context

The national culture within which the organization is embedded can exert a powerful influence on members' reactions to change, so intervention design must account for the cultural values and assumptions held by organization members. Interventions may have to be modified to fit the local culture, particularly when OD practices developed in one culture are applied to organizations in another culture.[6] For example, a team-building intervention designed for top managers at an American firm may need to be modified when applied to the company's foreign subsidiaries. (Chapter 15 will describe the cultural values of different countries and show how interventions can be modified to fit different cultural contexts.)

Capabilities of the Change Agent

Many failures in OD result when change agents apply interventions beyond their competence. In designing interventions, OD practitioners should assess their experience and expertise against the requirements needed to implement the intervention effectively. When a mismatch is discovered, practitioners can explore whether the intervention can be modified to fit their talents better, whether another intervention more suited to their skills can satisfy the organization's needs, or whether they should enlist the assistance of another change agent who can guide the process more effectively. The ethical guidelines under which OD practitioners operate require full disclosure of the applicability of their knowledge and expertise to the client situation. Practitioners are expected to intervene within their capabilities or to recommend someone more suited to the client's needs.

Contingencies Related to the Target of Change

OD interventions seek to change specific features or parts of organizations. These targets of change are the main focus of interventions, and researchers have identified two key contingencies related to change targets that can affect intervention success: the organizational issues that the intervention is intended to resolve and the level of organizational system at which the intervention is expected to have a primary impact.

Organizational Issues

Organizations need to address certain issues to operate effectively. Figure 6.1 lists these issues along with the OD interventions that are intended to resolve them. (The parts and chapters of this book that describe the specific interventions also are identified in the figure.) It shows the following four interrelated issues that are key targets of OD interventions:

1. *Strategic issues.* Organizations need to decide what products or services they will provide and the markets in which they will compete, as well as how to relate to their environments and how to transform themselves to keep pace with changing conditions. These strategic issues are among the most critical facing organizations in today's changing and highly competitive environments. OD methods aimed at these issues are called strategic interventions. The methods are among the most recent additions to OD and include integrated strategic change, mergers and acquisitions, transorganizational development, and organization learning.

2. *Technology and structure issues.* Organizations must decide how to divide work into departments and then how to coordinate among those departments to support strategic directions. They also must make decisions about how to deliver products or services and how to link people to tasks. OD methods for dealing with these structural and technological issues are called technostructural interventions and include OD activities relating to organization design, employee involvement, and work design.

3. *Human resources issues.* These issues are concerned with attracting competent people to the organization, setting goals for them, appraising and rewarding their performance, and ensuring that they develop their careers and manage stress. OD techniques aimed at these issues are called human resources management interventions.

4. *Human process issues.* These issues have to do with social processes occurring among organization members, such as communication, decision making, leadership, and group dynamics. OD methods focusing on these kinds of issues are called human process interventions; included among them are some of the most common OD techniques, such as conflict resolution and team building.

Consistent with system theory as described in Chapter 4, these organizational issues are interrelated and need to be integrated with each other. The double-headed arrows connecting the different issues in Figure 6.1 represent the fits or linkages among them. Organizations need to match answers to one set of questions with answers to other sets of questions to achieve high levels of effectiveness. For example, decisions about gaining competitive advantage need to fit with choices about organization structure, setting goals for and rewarding people, communication, and problem solving.

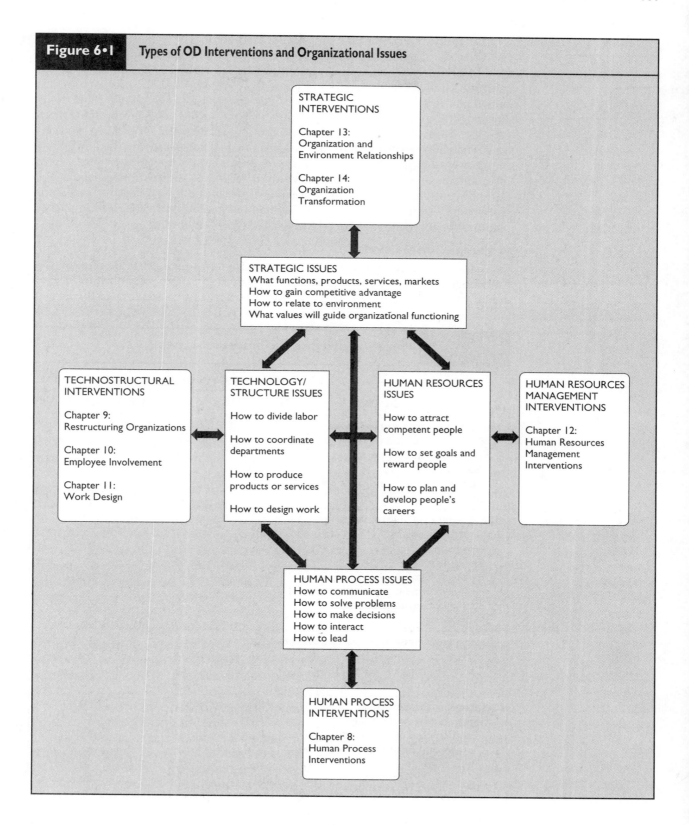

Figure 6·1   Types of OD Interventions and Organizational Issues

The interventions presented in this book are intended to resolve these different concerns. As shown in Figure 6.1, particular OD interventions apply to specific issues. Thus, intervention design must create change methods appropriate to the organizational issues identified in diagnosis. Moreover, because the organizational issues are themselves linked together, OD interventions similarly need to be integrated with one another. For example, a goal-setting intervention that tries to establish motivating goals may need to be integrated with supporting interventions, such as a reward system that links pay to goal achievement. The key point is to think systemically. Interventions aimed at one kind of organizational issue will invariably have repercussions on other kinds of issues. Careful thinking about how OD interventions affect the different kinds of issues and how different change programs might be integrated to bring about a broader and more coherent impact on organizational functioning are critical to effective intervention.

Organizational Levels

In addition to facing interrelated issues, organizations function at different levels—individual, group, organization, and transorganization. Thus, organizational levels are targets of change in OD. Table 6.1 lists OD interventions in terms of the level of

Table 6·1	Types of Interventions and Organizational Levels		
TYPE OF OD PROCESS	**INDIVIDUAL**	**Primary Organizational Level Affected** **GROUP**	**ORGANIZATION**
Human process interventions			
Process consultation		X	
Third-party intervention	X	X	
Team building		X	
Conflict resolution intervention	X	X	X
Large-group interventions			X
Technostructural interventions			
Structural design			X
Downsizing			X
Reengineering		X	X
Parallel structures		X	X
High-involvement organizations	X	X	X
Total quality management		X	X
Work design	X	X	
Human resources management interventions			
Performance management	X	X	X
Career planning and development	X		
Managing workforce diversity	X	X	
Strategic interventions			
Integrated strategic change			X
Transorganizational development			X
Mergers and acquisitions integration			X
Culture change			X
Self-designing organizations		X	X
Organization learning and knowledge management		X	X

organization that they primarily affect. For example, some technostructural interventions affect mainly individuals and groups (for example, work design), whereas others impact primarily the total organization (for example, structural design).

It is important to emphasize that only the primary level affected by the intervention is identified in Table 6.1. Many OD interventions also have a secondary impact on the other levels. For example, structural design affects mainly the organization level but can have an indirect effect on groups and individuals because it sets the broad parameters for designing work groups and individual jobs. Again, practitioners need to think systemically. They must design interventions to apply to specific organizational levels, address the possibility of cross-level effects, and perhaps integrate interventions affecting different levels to achieve overall success.[7] For example, an intervention to create self-managed work teams may need to be linked to organization-level changes in measurement and reward systems to promote team-based work.

OVERVIEW OF INTERVENTIONS

The OD interventions discussed in Part 3 of this book are described briefly below. They represent the major organizational change methods used in OD today.

Human Process Interventions

Chapter 8 of the book presents interventions focusing on people within organizations and the processes through which they accomplish organizational goals. Human process interventions derive mainly from the disciplines of psychology and social psychology and the applied fields of group dynamics and human relations. Practitioners applying these interventions generally value human fulfillment and expect that organizational effectiveness follows from improved functioning of people and organizational processes.[8] Many of these interventions, such as intergroup conflict resolution, are closely associated with the history of OD. The following four interventions are described:

1. *Process consultation.* This intervention focuses on interpersonal relations and social dynamics occurring in work groups. Typically, a process consultant helps group members diagnose group functioning and devise appropriate solutions to process problems, such as dysfunctional conflict, poor communication, and ineffective norms. The aim is to help members gain the skills and understanding necessary to identify and solve problems themselves.

2. *Team building.* This intervention helps work groups become more effective in accomplishing tasks. Like process consultation, team building helps members diagnose group processes and devise solutions to problems. It goes beyond group processes, however, to include examination of the group's task, member roles, and strategies for performing tasks. The consultant also may function as a resource person offering expertise related to the group's task.

3. *Conflict resolution interventions.* These interventions focus on resolving differences among people or organizational units. Interpersonal conflict resolution is a form of process consultation aimed at dysfunctional relationships among two or more people. The intergroup conflict resolution model involves a consultant helping two or more groups understand the causes of the conflict and choose appropriate solutions.

4. *Large-group interventions.* These interventions involve getting a broad variety of stakeholders into a large meeting to clarify important values, to develop new ways of working, to articulate a new vision for the organization, or to solve pressing organizational problems. Such meetings are powerful tools for creating awareness of organizational problems and opportunities and for specifying valued directions for future action.

Technostructural Interventions

Chapters 9 through 11 of the book present interventions focusing on an organization's technology (for example, task methods and job design) and structure (for example, division of labor and hierarchy). These change methods are receiving increasing attention in OD, especially in light of current concerns about productivity and organizational effectiveness. They include approaches to employee involvement, as well as methods for designing organizations, groups, and jobs. Technostructural interventions are rooted in the disciplines of engineering, sociology, and psychology and in the applied fields of sociotechnical systems and organization design. Practitioners generally stress both productivity and human fulfillment and expect that organization effectiveness will result from appropriate work designs and organization structures.[9]

In Chapter 9, we discuss the following three technostructural interventions concerned with restructuring organizations:

1. *Structural design.* This change process concerns the organization's division of labor—how to specialize task performances. Interventions aimed at structural design include moving from more traditional ways of dividing the organization's overall work (such as functional, self-contained–unit, and matrix structures) to more integrative and flexible forms (such as process-based and network-based structures). Diagnostic guidelines exist to determine which structure is appropriate for particular organizational environments, technologies, and conditions.

2. *Downsizing.* This intervention reduces costs and bureaucracy by decreasing the size of the organization through personnel layoffs, organization redesign, and outsourcing. Each of these downsizing methods must be planned with a clear understanding of the organization's strategy.

3. *Reengineering.* This recent intervention radically redesigns the organization's core work processes to create tighter linkage and coordination among the different tasks. This work-flow integration results in faster, more responsive task performance. Reengineering often is accomplished with new information technology that permits employees to control and coordinate work processes more effectively. Reengineering often fails if it ignores basic principles and processes of OD.

Chapter 10 is concerned with *employee involvement* (EI). This broad category of interventions is aimed at improving employee well-being and organizational effectiveness. It generally attempts to move knowledge, power, information, and rewards downward in the organization. EI includes parallel structures (such as cooperative union–management projects and quality circles), high-involvement plants, and total quality management.

Chapter 11 discusses *work design.* These change programs are concerned with designing work for work groups and individual jobs. The intervention includes engineering, motivational, and sociotechnical systems approaches that produce traditionally designed jobs and work groups; enriched jobs that provide employees with greater task variety, autonomy, and feedback about results; and self-managing teams that can govern their own task behaviors with limited external control.

Human Resources Management Interventions

Chapter 12 focuses on personnel practices used to integrate people into organizations. These practices include performance management (goal setting, performance appraisal, and reward systems), career planning, and diversity interventions—change methods that traditionally have been associated with the personnel function in organizations. In recent years, interest has grown in integrating human resources management with OD. Human resources management interventions are rooted in the disciplines of economics and labor relations and in the applied personnel practices of wages and compensation, employee selection and placement, performance appraisal, and career development. Practitioners in this area typically focus on the people in organizations, believing that organizational effectiveness results from improved practices for integrating employees into organizations. The following change programs are discussed:

1. *Performance management.* This change program helps individuals and groups set clear and challenging goals; systematically assesses work-related achievements, strengths, and weaknesses; and recognizes and rewards goal achievement. It improves organization effectiveness by establishing a better fit between personal and organizational objectives. Managers and subordinates periodically meet to plan work, review accomplishments, solve problems in achieving goals, and reward performance.

2. *Career planning and development.* This intervention helps people choose organizations and career paths and attain career objectives. It generally focuses on managers and professional staff and is seen as a way of improving the quality of their work life.

3. *Managing workforce diversity.* This change program makes human resources practices more responsive to a variety of individual needs. Important trends, such as the increasing number of women, ethnic minorities, and physically and mentally challenged people in the workforce, require a more flexible set of policies and practices.

Strategic Interventions

Chapters 13 and 14 present interventions that link the internal functioning of the organization to the larger environment and transform the organization to keep pace with changing conditions. These change programs are among the newest additions to OD. They are implemented organizationwide and bring about a fit between business strategy, structure, culture, and the larger environment. The interventions derive from the disciplines of strategic management, organization theory, open-systems theory, and cultural anthropology.

In Chapter 13, we discuss the following three major interventions for managing organization and environment relationships:

1. *Integrated strategic change.* This comprehensive OD intervention describes how planned change can make a value-added contribution to strategic management. It argues that business strategies and organizational systems must be

changed together in response to external and internal disruptions. A strategic change plan helps members manage the transition between a current strategy and organization design and the desired future strategic orientation.

2. *Transorganizational development.* This intervention helps organizations enter into alliances, partnerships, and joint ventures to perform tasks or solve problems that are too complex for single organizations to resolve. It helps organizations recognize the need for partnerships and develop appropriate structures for implementing them.

3. *Merger and acquisition integration.* This intervention describes how OD practitioners can assist two or more organizations to form a new entity. Addressing key strategic, leadership, and cultural issues prior to the legal and financial transaction helps to smooth operational integration.

Chapter 14 presents three major interventions for transforming organizations:

1. *Culture change.* This intervention helps organizations develop cultures (behaviors, values, beliefs, and norms) appropriate to their strategies and environments. It focuses on developing a strong organization culture to keep organization members pulling in the same direction.

2. *Self-designing organizations.* This change program helps organizations gain the capacity to alter themselves fundamentally. It is a highly participative process involving multiple stakeholders in setting strategic directions and designing and implementing appropriate structures and processes. Organizations learn how to design and implement their own strategic changes.

3. *Organization learning and knowledge management.* This intervention describes two interrelated change processes: organization learning (OL), which seeks to enhance an organization's capability to acquire and develop new knowledge, and knowledge management (KM), which focuses on how that knowledge can be organized and used to improve organization performance. These interventions move the organization beyond solving existing problems so as to become capable of continuous improvement.

■ SUMMARY

This chapter presented an overview of interventions currently used in OD. An intervention is a set of planned activities intended to help an organization improve its performance and effectiveness. Effective interventions are designed to fit the needs of the organization, are based on causal knowledge of intended outcomes, and transfer competence to manage change to organization members.

Intervention design involves understanding situational contingencies such as individual differences among organization members and dimensions of the change process itself. Four key organizational factors—readiness for change, capability to change, cultural context, and the capabilities of the change agent—affect the design and implementation of almost any intervention.

Furthermore, OD interventions seek to change specific features or parts of organizations. These targets of change can be classified based on the organizational issues that the intervention is intended to resolve and the level of organizational system at which the intervention is expected to have a primary impact. Four types of OD interventions are addressed in this book: (1) human process programs aimed at people within organizations and their interaction processes; (2) technostructural methods directed at organization technology and structures for linking people and technology; (3) human resources management interventions focused at integrating people into the organization successfully; and (4) strategic programs targeted at how the organization uses its resources to gain a competitive advantage in the larger environment. For each type of intervention, specific change programs at different organization levels are discussed in Chapters 8 through 14 of this book.

■ NOTES

1. C. Argyris, *Intervention Theory and Method: A Behavioral Science View* (Reading, Mass.: Addison-Wesley, 1970).

2. T. Cummings, E. Molloy, and R. Glen, "A Methodological Critique of 58 Selected Work Experiments," *Human Relations* 30 (1977): 675–708; T. Cummings, E. Molloy, and R. Glen, "Intervention Strategies for Improving Productivity and the Quality of Work Life," *Organizational Dynamics* 4 (Summer 1975): 59–60; J. Porras and P. O. Berg, "The Impact of Organization Development," *Academy of Management Review* 3 (1978): 249–66; J. Nicholas, "The Comparative Impact of Organization Development Interventions on Hard Criteria Measures," *Academy of Management Review* 7 (1982): 531–42; R. Golembiewski, C. Proehl, and D. Sink, "Estimating the Success of OD Applications," *Training and Development Journal* 72 (April 1982): 86–95.

3. D. Warrick, "Action Planning," in *Practicing Organization Development*, eds. W. Rothwell, R. Sullivan, and G. McClean (San Diego: Pfeiffer, 1995).

4. Nicholas, "Comparative Impact"; J. Porras and P. Robertson, "Organization Development Theory: A Typology and Evaluation," in *Research in Organizational Change and Development*, vol. 1, eds. R. Woodman and W. Pasmore (Greenwich, Conn.: JAI Press, 1987): 1–57.

5. T. Stewart, "Rate Your Readiness for Change," *Fortune* (7 February 1994): 106–10.

6. G. Hofstede, *Culture's Consequences* (Beverly Hills, Calif.: Sage, 1980); K. Johnson, "Estimating National Culture and O.D. Values," in *Global and International Organization Development*, eds. P. Sorensen Jr., T. Head, K. Johnson, et al. (Champaign, Ill.: Stipes, 1995): 266–81.

7. D. Coghlan, "Rediscovering Organizational Levels for OD Interventions," *Organization Development Journal* 13 (1995): 19–27.

8. F. Friedlander and L. D. Brown, "Organization Development," *Annual Review of Psychology* 25 (1974): 313–41.

9. E. Lawler III, *The Ultimate Advantage* (San Francisco: Jossey-Bass, 1992).

7. Leading and Managing Change

After diagnosis reveals the causes of problems or opportunities for development, organization members begin planning and subsequently implementing the changes necessary to improve organization effectiveness and performance. A large part of OD is concerned with interventions for improving organizations. The previous chapter discussed the design of interventions and introduced the major ones currently used in OD. Chapters 8 through 14 describe those interventions in detail. This chapter addresses the key activities associated with leading and managing organizational change for successful implementation. (Activities applicable to specific kinds of changes are examined in the intervention chapters.)

The OD literature has directed considerable attention to effective change management. The diversity of practical advice for managing change can be organized into six major activities, as shown in Figure 7.1. The tasks contribute to effective change management and are listed roughly in the order in which they typically are performed. Each activity represents a key element in change leadership.[1] The first task involves *motivating change* and includes creating a readiness for change among organization members and helping them address resistance to change. The second activity is concerned with *creating a vision* that provides a purpose and reason for change and describes the desired future state. The third task involves *developing political support* for change, and the fourth activity is concerned with *managing the transition* from the current state to the desired future state. The fifth task involves *sustaining and institutionalizing change,* and the sixth activity is concerned with *evaluating change.*

Each of the activities shown in Figure 7.1 is important for managing change. Although little research has been conducted on their relative contributions, organizational leaders must give careful attention to each activity when planning and implementing organizational change. Unless people are motivated and committed to change, unfreezing the status quo will be extremely difficult. In the absence of vision, change is likely to be disorganized and diffuse. Without the support of powerful individuals and groups, change may be blocked and possibly sabotaged. Unless the transition process is managed carefully, the organization will have difficulty functioning while it moves from the current state to the future state. Without efforts to sustain momentum and institutionalize the changes, the organization will have problems realizing the expected benefits. Unless the changes and their outcomes are evaluated, the organization will not know if it should continue to support the changes or modify them. Thus, all six activities must be managed effectively if organizational change is to be successful.

In the following sections of this chapter, we discuss more fully each of these change activities, directing attention to how the activities contribute to planning and implementing organizational change.

MOTIVATING CHANGE

Organizational change involves moving from the known to the unknown. Because the future is uncertain and may adversely affect people's competencies, worth, and coping abilities, organization members generally do not support change unless

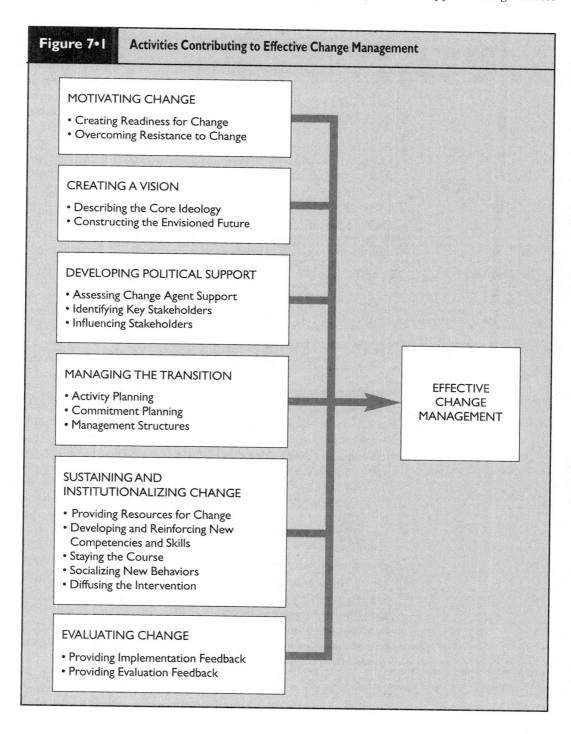

| Figure 7•1 | Activities Contributing to Effective Change Management |

MOTIVATING CHANGE

• Creating Readiness for Change
• Overcoming Resistance to Change

CREATING A VISION

• Describing the Core Ideology
• Constructing the Envisioned Future

DEVELOPING POLITICAL SUPPORT

• Assessing Change Agent Support
• Identifying Key Stakeholders
• Influencing Stakeholders

MANAGING THE TRANSITION

• Activity Planning
• Commitment Planning
• Management Structures

SUSTAINING AND INSTITUTIONALIZING CHANGE

• Providing Resources for Change
• Developing and Reinforcing New Competencies and Skills
• Staying the Course
• Socializing New Behaviors
• Diffusing the Intervention

EVALUATING CHANGE

• Providing Implementation Feedback
• Providing Evaluation Feedback

EFFECTIVE CHANGE MANAGEMENT

compelling reasons convince them to do so. Similarly, organizations tend to be heavily invested in the status quo, and they resist changing it in the face of uncertain future benefits. Consequently, a key issue in planning for action is how to motivate commitment to organizational change. As shown in Figure 7.1, this requires attention to two related tasks: creating readiness for change and overcoming resistance to change.

Creating Readiness for Change

One of the more fundamental axioms of OD is that people's readiness for change depends on creating a felt need for change. This involves making people so dissatisfied with the status quo that they are motivated to try new work processes, technologies, or ways of behaving. Creating such dissatisfaction can be difficult, as anyone knows who has tried to lose weight, stop smoking, or change some other habitual behavior. Generally, people and organizations need to experience deep levels of hurt before they seriously will undertake meaningful change. For example, IBM, GM, and Sears experienced threats to their survival before they undertook significant change programs. The following three methods can help generate sufficient dissatisfaction to produce change:

1. *Sensitize organizations to pressures for change.* Innumerable pressures for change operate both externally and internally to organizations. As described in Chapter 1, modern organizations face unprecedented environmental pressures to change themselves, including heavy foreign competition, rapidly changing technology, and the draw of global markets. Internal pressures to change include new leadership, poor product quality, high production costs, and excessive employee absenteeism and turnover. Before these pressures can serve as triggers for change, however, organizations must be sensitive to them. The pressures must pass beyond an organization's threshold of awareness if managers are to respond to them. Many organizations, such as Kodak, Apple, Polaroid, and Jenny Craig, set their thresholds of awareness too high and neglected pressures for change until those pressures reached disastrous levels.[2] Organizations can make themselves more sensitive to pressures for change by encouraging leaders to surround themselves with devil's advocates;[3] by cultivating external networks that comprise people or organizations with different perspectives and views; by visiting other organizations to gain exposure to new ideas and methods; and by using external standards of performance, such as competitors' progress or benchmarks,[4] rather than the organization's own past standards of performance. At Wesley Long Community Hospital, in Greensboro, North Carolina, for example, managers visited the Ritz-Carlton Hotel, Marconi Commerce Systems' high-involvement plant, and other hospitals known for high quality to gain insights about revitalizing their own organization.

2. *Reveal discrepancies between current and desired states.* In this approach to generating a felt need for change, information about the organization's current functioning is gathered and compared with desired states of operation. (See "Creating a Vision" later in this chapter for more information about desired future states.) These desired states may include organizational goals and standards, as well as a general vision of a more desirable future state.[5] Significant discrepancies between actual and ideal states can motivate organization members to initiate corrective changes, particularly when members are committed to achieving those ideals. A major goal of diagnosis, as described in Chapters 4 and 5, is to

provide members with feedback about current organizational functioning so that the information can be compared with goals or with desired future states. Such feedback can energize action to improve the organization. At Waste Management, Sunbeam, and Banker's Trust, for example, financial statements had reached the point at which it was painfully obvious that drastic renewal was needed.[6]

3. ***Convey credible positive expectations for the change.*** Organization members invariably have expectations about the results of organizational changes. The contemporary approaches to planned change described in Chapter 2 suggest that these expectations can play an important role in generating motivation for change.[7] The expectations can serve as a self-fulfilling prophecy, leading members to invest energy in change programs that they expect will succeed. When members expect success, they are likely to develop greater commitment to the change process and to direct more energy into the constructive behaviors needed to implement it.[8] The key to achieving these positive effects is to communicate realistic, positive expectations about the organizational changes. Organization members also can be taught about the benefits of positive expectations and be encouraged to set credible positive expectations for the change program.

Overcoming Resistance to Change

Change can generate deep resistance in people and in organizations, thus making it difficult, if not impossible, to implement organizational improvements.[9] At a personal level, change can arouse considerable anxiety about letting go of the known and moving to an uncertain future. People may be unsure whether their existing skills and contributions will be valued in the future, or have significant questions about whether they can learn to function effectively and to achieve benefits in the new situation. At the organization level, resistance to change can come from three sources.[10] *Technical resistance* comes from the habit of following common procedures and the consideration of the sunk costs of resources invested in the status quo. *Political resistance* can arise when organizational changes threaten powerful stakeholders, such as top executive or staff personnel, or call into question the past decisions of leaders. Organization change often implies a different allocation of already scarce resources, such as capital, training budgets, and good people. Finally, *cultural resistance* takes the form of systems and procedures that reinforce the status quo, promoting conformity to existing values, norms, and assumptions about how things should operate.

There are at least three major strategies for dealing with resistance to change:[11]

1. ***Empathy and support.*** A first step in overcoming resistance is to learn how people are experiencing change. This strategy can identify people who are having trouble accepting the changes, the nature of their resistance, and possible ways to overcome it, but it requires a great deal of empathy and support. It demands a willingness to suspend judgment and see the situation from another's perspective, a process called *active listening*. When people feel that those people who are responsible for managing change are genuinely interested in their feelings and perceptions, they are likely to be less defensive and more willing to share their concerns and fears. This more open relationship not only provides useful information about resistance but also helps establish the basis for the kind of joint problem solving needed to overcome barriers to change.

2. *Communication.* People resist change when they are uncertain about its consequences. Lack of adequate information fuels rumors and gossip and adds to the anxiety generally associated with change. Effective communication about changes and their likely results can reduce this speculation and allay unfounded fears. It can help members realistically prepare for change.

However, communication is also one of the most frustrating aspects of managing change. Organization members constantly receive data about current operations and future plans as well as informal rumors about people, changes, and politics. Managers and OD practitioners must think seriously about how to break through this stream of information. One strategy is to make change information more salient by communicating through a new or different channel. If most information is delivered through memos and emails, then change information can be sent through meetings and presentations. Another method that can be effective during large-scale change is to substitute change information for normal operating information deliberately. This sends a message that changing one's activities is a critical part of a member's job.

3. *Participation and involvement.* One of the oldest and most effective strategies for overcoming resistance is to involve organization members directly in planning and implementing change. Participation can lead both to designing high-quality changes and to overcoming resistance to implementing them.[12] Members can provide a diversity of information and ideas, which can contribute to making the innovations effective and appropriate to the situation. They also can identify pitfalls and barriers to implementation. Involvement in planning the changes increases the likelihood that members' interests and needs will be accounted for during the intervention. Consequently, participants will be committed to implementing the changes because doing so will suit their interests and meet their needs. Moreover, for people having strong needs for involvement, the act of participation itself can be motivating, leading to greater effort to make the changes work.[13]

CREATING A VISION

The second activity in leading and managing change involves creating a vision of what members want the organization to look like or become. It is one of the most popular yet least understood practices in management.[14] Generally, a vision describes the core values and purpose that guide the organization as well as an envisioned future toward which change is directed. It provides a valued direction for designing, implementing, and assessing organizational changes. The vision also can energize commitment to change by providing members with a common goal and a compelling rationale for why change is necessary and worth the effort. However, if the vision is seen as impossible or promotes changes that the organization cannot implement, it actually can depress member motivation. For example, George Bush's unfulfilled "thousand points of light" vision was emotionally appealing, but it was too vague and contained little inherent benefit. In contrast, John Kennedy's vision of "putting a man on the moon and returning him safely to the earth" was just beyond engineering and technical feasibility. In the context of the 1960s, it was bold, alluring, and vivid; it provided not only a purpose but a valued direction as well.[15] Recent research suggests that corporations with carefully crafted visions can significantly outperform the stock market over long periods of time.[16]

Creating a vision is considered a key element in most leadership frameworks.[17] Organization or subunit leaders are responsible for effectiveness, and they must take an active role in describing a desired future and energizing commitment to it. In many cases, leaders encourage participation in developing the vision to gain wider input and support. For example, they involve subordinates and others who have a stake in the changes. The popular media frequently offer accounts of executives who have helped to mobilize and direct organizational change, including Nobuhiko Kawamoto of Honda and Jack Welch at General Electric. Describing a desired future is no less important for people leading change in small departments and work groups than for senior executives. At lower organizational levels, there are ample opportunities to involve employees directly in the visioning process.

Developing a vision is heavily driven by people's values and preferences for what the organization should look like and how it should function. The envisioned future represents people's ideals, fantasies, or dreams of what they would like the organization to look like or become. Unfortunately, dreaming about the future is discouraged in most organizations[18] because it requires creative and intuitive thought processes that tend to conflict with the rational, analytical methods prevalent there. Consequently, leaders may need to create special conditions in which to describe a desired future such as off-site workshops or exercises that stimulate creative thinking.

Research by Collins and Porras suggests that compelling visions are composed of two parts: (1) a relatively stable core ideology that describes the organization's core values and purpose, and (2) an envisioned future with bold goals and a vivid description of the desired future state that reflects the specific change under consideration.[19]

Describing the Core Ideology

The fundamental basis of a vision for change is the organization's core ideology. It describes the organization's core values and purpose and is relatively stable over time. *Core values* typically include three to five basic principles or beliefs that have stood the test of time and best represent what the organization stands for. Although the vision ultimately describes a desired future, it must acknowledge the organization's historical roots, the intrinsically meaningful core values and principles that have guided and will guide the organization over time. Core values are not "espoused values"; they are the "values in use" that actually inform members what is important in the organization. The retailer Nordstrom, for example, has clear values around the importance of customer service; toymaker Lego has distinct values around the importance of families; and the Disney companies have explicit values around wholesomeness and imagination. These values define the true nature of these firms and cannot be separated from them. Thus, core values are not determined or designed; they are discovered and described through a process of inquiry.

Members can spend considerable time and energy discovering their organization's core values through long discussions about organizational history, key events, founder's beliefs, the work people actually do, and the "glue" that holds the organization together.[20] In many cases, organizations want the core values to be something they are not. For example, many U.S. firms want "teamwork" to be a core value despite strong cultural norms and organizational practices that reward individuality.

The organization's *core purpose* is its reason for being, the idealistic motivation that brings people to work each day. A core purpose is not a strategy. Purpose describes why the organization exists; strategy describes how an objective will be achieved. Organizations often create a slogan or metaphor that captures the real reason they are in business. For example, part of Disneyland's return to prominence in the late 1980s and 1990s was guided by the essential purpose of "creating a place where people can feel like kids again." Similarly, Apple's original vision of "changing the way people do their work" described well the benefits the organization was providing to its customers and society at large. Many Apple employees previously had experienced the drudgery of a boring job, an uninspired boss, or an alienating workplace, and it was alluring to be part of a company that was changing work into something more challenging, creative, or satisfying.

The real power of an organization's core ideology is its stability over time and the way it can help the organization change itself. Core values and purpose provide guidelines for the strategic choices that will work and can be implemented versus those that will not work because they contradict the real nature of the organization's identity. An envisioned future can be compelling and emotionally powerful to members only if it aligns with and supports the organization's core values and purpose.

Constructing the Envisioned Future

The core ideology provides the context for the envisioned future. Unlike core values and purpose, which are stable aspects of the organization and must be discovered, the envisioned future is specific to the change project at hand and must be created. The envisioned future varies in complexity and scope depending on the changes being considered. A relatively simple upgrading of a work group's word-processing software requires a less complex envisioned future than the transformation of a government bureaucracy.

The envisioned future typically includes the following elements that can be communicated to organization members:[21]

1. *Bold and valued outcomes.* Descriptions of envisioned futures often include specific performance and human outcomes that the organization or unit would like to achieve. These valued outcomes can serve as goals for the change process and standards for assessing progress. For example, BHAGs (Big, Hairy, Audacious Goals) are clear, tangible, energizing targets that serve as rallying points for organization action. They can challenge members to meet clear target levels of sales growth or customer satisfaction, to overcome key competitors, to achieve role-model status in the industry, or to transform the organization in some meaningful way. For example, in 1990 Wal-Mart Stores made a statement of intent "to become a $125 billion company by the year 2000." (Net sales in 1999 exceeded $137.6 billion.) Following the downsizing of the U.S. military budget, Rockwell proposed the following bold outcome for its change efforts: "Transform this company from a defense contractor into the best diversified high-technology company in the world."

2. *Desired future state.* This element of the envisioned future specifies, in vivid detail, what the organization should look like to achieve bold and valued outcomes. It is a passionate and engaging statement intended to draw organization members into the future. The organizational features described in the statement help define a desired future state toward which change activities should move. This aspect of the visioning process is exciting and compelling. It seeks to create a word picture that is emotionally powerful to members and motivates them to change.

DEVELOPING POLITICAL SUPPORT

From a political perspective, organizations can be seen as loosely structured coalitions of individuals and groups having different preferences and interests.[22] For example, shop-floor workers may want secure, high-paying jobs, and top executives may be interested in diversifying the organization into new businesses. The marketing department might be interested in developing new products and markets, and the production department may want to manufacture standard products in the most efficient way. These different groups or coalitions compete with one another for scarce resources and influence. They act to preserve or enhance their self-interests while managing to arrive at a sufficient balance of power to sustain commitment to the organization and achieve overall effectiveness.

Given this political view, attempts to change the organization may threaten the balance of power among groups, thus resulting in political conflicts and struggles.[23] Individuals and groups will be concerned with how the changes affect their own power and influence, and they will act accordingly. Some groups will become less powerful; others will gain influence. Those whose power is threatened by the change will act defensively and seek to preserve the status quo. For example, they may try to present compelling evidence that change is unnecessary or that only minor modifications are needed. On the other hand, those participants who will gain power from the changes will push heavily for them, perhaps bringing in seemingly impartial consultants to legitimize the need for change. Consequently, significant organizational changes are frequently accompanied by conflicting interests, distorted information, and political turmoil.

Methods for managing the political dynamics of organizational change are relatively recent additions to OD. Traditionally, OD has neglected political issues mainly because its humanistic roots promoted collaboration and power sharing among individuals and groups.[24] Today, change agents are paying increased attention to power and political activity, particularly as they engage in strategic change involving most parts and features of organizations. Some practitioners are concerned, however, about whether power and OD are compatible. A growing number of advocates suggest that OD practitioners can use power in positive ways.[25] They can build their own power base to gain access to other power holders within the organization. Without such access, those who influence or make decisions may not have the advantage of an OD perspective. OD practitioners can use power strategies that are open and aboveboard to get those in power to consider OD applications. They can facilitate processes for examining the uses of power in organizations and help power holders devise more creative and positive strategies than political bargaining, deceit, and the like. They can help power holders confront the need for change and can help ensure that the interests and concerns of those with less power are considered. Although OD professionals can use power constructively in organizations, they probably will continue to be ambivalent and tense about whether such uses promote OD values and ethics or whether they represent the destructive, negative side of power. That tension seems healthy, and we hope that it will guide the wise use of power in OD.

Assessing Change Agent Power

The first task is to evaluate the change agent's own sources of power. This agent may be the leader of the organization or department undergoing change, or he or she may be the OD consultant if professional help is being used. By assessing their own power base, change agents can determine how to use it to influence others to support changes. They also can identify areas in which they need to enhance their sources of power.

Greiner and Schein, in the first OD book written entirely from a power perspective, identified three key sources of personal power in organizations (in addition to one's formal position): knowledge, personality, and others' support.[26] Knowledge bases of power include having expertise that is valued by others and controlling important information. OD professionals typically gain power through their expertise in organizational change. Personality sources of power can derive from change agents' charisma, reputation, and professional credibility. Charismatic leaders can inspire devotion and enthusiasm for change from subordinates. OD consultants with strong reputations and professional credibility can wield considerable power during organizational change. Others' support can contribute to individual power by providing access to information and resource networks. Others also may use their power on behalf of the change agent. For example, leaders in organizational units undergoing change can call on their informal networks for resources and support, and encourage subordinates to exercise power in support of the change.

Identifying Key Stakeholders

Having assessed their own power bases, change agents can identify powerful individuals and groups with an interest in the changes, such as staff groups, unions, departmental managers, and top-level executives. These key stakeholders can thwart or support change, and it is important to gain broad-based support to minimize the risk that a single interest group will block the changes. Identifying key stakeholders can start with the simple question "Who stands to gain or to lose from the changes?" Once stakeholders are identified, creating a map of their influence may be useful.[27] The map could show relationships among the stakeholders in terms of who influences whom and what the stakes are for each party. This would provide change agents with information about which people and groups need to be influenced to accept and support the changes.

Influencing Stakeholders

This activity involves gaining the support of key stakeholders to motivate a critical mass for change. There are at least three major strategies for using power to influence others in OD: playing it straight, using social networks, and going around the formal system.[28] Figure 7.2 links these strategies to the individual sources of power discussed above.

The strategy of playing it straight is very consistent with an OD perspective, and thus it is the most widely used power strategy in OD. It involves determining the needs of particular stakeholders and presenting information about how the changes can benefit them. This relatively straightforward approach is based on the premise that information and knowledge can persuade people about the need and direction for change. The success of this strategy relies heavily on the change agent's knowledge base. He or she must have the expertise and information to persuade stakeholders that the changes are a logical way to meet their needs. For example, a change agent might present diagnostic data, such as company reports on productivity and absenteeism or surveys of members' perceptions of problems, to generate a felt need for change among specific stakeholders. Other persuasive evidence might include educational material and expert testimony, such as case studies and research reports, demonstrating how organizational changes can address pertinent issues.

The second power strategy, using social networks, is more foreign to OD and includes forming alliances and coalitions with other powerful individuals and groups, dealing directly with key decision makers, and using formal and informal contacts to gain information. In this strategy, change agents attempt to use their social

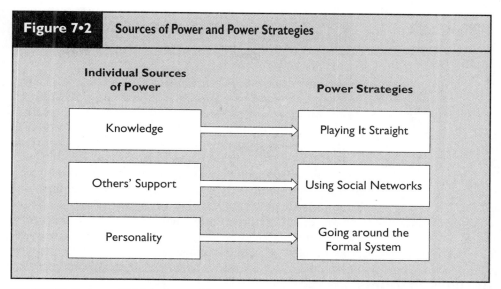

Figure 7·2   Sources of Power and Power Strategies

Individual Sources of Power

Power Strategies

Knowledge → Playing It Straight

Others' Support → Using Social Networks

Personality → Going around the Formal System

SOURCE: L. Greiner and V. Schein, *Power and Organization Development: Mobilizing Power to Implement Change,* page 52. © 1988 by Addison-Wesley Publishing Co., Inc. Reprinted by permission of Addison Wesley Longman.

relationships to gain support for changes. As shown in Figure 7.2, they use the individual power base of others' support to gain the resources, commitment, and political momentum needed to implement change. This social networking might include, for example, meeting with other powerful groups and forming alliances to support specific changes. This would likely involve ensuring that the interests of the different parties—labor and management, for example—are considered in the change process. Many union and management quality-of-work-life efforts involve forming such alliances. This strategy also might include using informal contacts to discover key roadblocks to change and to gain access to major decision makers who need to sanction the changes.

The power strategy of going around the formal system is probably least used in OD and involves purposely circumventing organizational structures and procedures to get the changes made. Existing organizational arrangements can be roadblocks to change, and working around the barriers may be more expedient and effective than taking the time and energy to remove them. As shown in Figure 7.2, this strategy relies on a strong personality base of power. The change agent's charisma, reputation, or professional credibility lend legitimacy to going around the system and can reduce the likelihood of negative reprisals. For example, managers with reputations as winners often can bend the rules to implement organizational changes. Their judgment is trusted by those whose support they need to enact the changes. This power strategy is relatively easy to abuse, however, and OD practitioners should consider carefully the ethical issues and possible unintended consequences of circumventing formal policies and practices.

MANAGING THE TRANSITION

Implementing organizational change involves moving from the existing organization state to the desired future state. Such movement does not occur immediately but, as shown in Figure 7.3, instead requires a transition state during which the

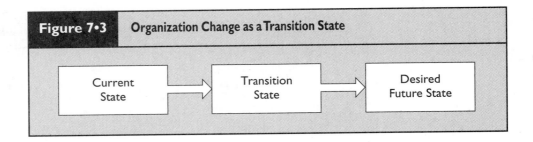

Figure 7•3   Organization Change as a Transition State

| Current State | → | Transition State | → | Desired Future State |

organization learns how to implement the conditions needed to reach the desired future. Beckhard and Harris pointed out that the transition state may be quite different from the present state of the organization and consequently may require special management structures and activities.[29] They identified three major activities and structures to facilitate organizational transition: activity planning, commitment planning, and change-management structures.

Activity Planning

This involves making a road map for change, citing specific activities and events that must occur if the transition is to be successful. Activity planning should clearly identify, temporally orient, and integrate discrete change tasks and should link these tasks to the organization's change goals and priorities. Activity planning also should gain top-management approval, be cost effective, and remain adaptable as feedback is received during the change process.

An important feature of activity planning is that visions and desired future states can be quite general when compared with the realities of implementing change. As a result, it may be necessary to supplement them with midpoint goals as part of the activity plan.[30] Such goals represent desirable organizational conditions between the current state and the desired future state. For example, if the organization is implementing continuous improvement processes, an important midpoint goal can be the establishment of a certain number of improvement teams focused on understanding and controlling key work processes. Midpoint goals are clearer and more detailed than desired future states, and thus they provide more concrete and manageable steps and benchmarks for change. Activity plans can use midpoint goals to provide members with the direction and security they need to work toward the desired future.

Commitment Planning

This activity involves identifying key people and groups whose commitment is needed for change to occur and formulating a strategy for gaining their support. Although commitment planning is generally a part of developing political support, discussed above, specific plans for identifying key stakeholders and obtaining their commitment to change need to be made early in the change process.

Change-Management Structures

Because organizational transitions tend to be ambiguous and to need direction, special structures for managing the change process need to be created. These management structures should include people who have the power to mobilize resources to promote change, the respect of the existing leadership and change advocates, and the interpersonal and political skills to guide the change process. Alternative management structures include the following:[31]

- The chief executive or head person manages the change effort.
- A project manager temporarily is assigned to coordinate the transition.
- The formal organization manages the change effort in addition to supervising normal operations.
- Representatives of the major constituencies involved in the change jointly manage the project.
- Natural leaders who have the confidence and trust of large numbers of affected employees are selected to manage the transition.
- A cross section of people representing different organizational functions and levels manages the change.
- A "kitchen cabinet" representing people whom the chief executive consults with and confides in manages the change effort.

SUSTAINING AND INSTITUTIONALIZING CHANGE

Once organizational changes are under way, explicit attention must be directed to sustaining energy and commitment for implementing them. The initial excitement and activity of changing often dissipate in the face of the practical problems of trying to learn new ways of operating. A strong tendency exists among organization members to return to what is learned and well known unless they receive sustained support and reinforcement for carrying the changes through to completion. In addition, attention should be directed at institutionalizing the changes—making them a permanent part of the organization's normal functioning. To the extent that changes persist, they can be said to be *institutionalized*.[32] Such changes are not dependent on any one person but exist as a part of the organization's culture. This means that numerous others share norms about the appropriateness of the changes.

How planned changes are sustained and institutionalized has not received much attention in the OD literature. Rapidly changing environments have led to admonitions from consultants and practitioners to "change constantly," to "change before you have to," and "if it's not broke, fix it anyway." Such a context has challenged the utility of the institutionalization concept. Why try to make change permanent, given that it may require changing again soon? Those admonitions, however, also have resulted in institutionalization concepts being applied in new ways. Change itself has become the focus of institutionalization. Total quality management, organization learning, integrated strategic change, and self-design interventions all are aimed at enhancing the organization's capability for change.[33] In this vein, processes of institutionalization take on increased utility.

The following five activities can help to sustain momentum and institutionalize change: providing resources for change, developing and reinforcing new competencies and skills, staying the course, socializing new behaviors, and diffusing the intervention.

Providing Resources for Change

Implementing organization change generally requires additional financial and human resources, particularly if the organization continues day-to-day operations while trying to change itself. These extra resources are needed for such change activities as training, consultation, data collection and feedback, and special meetings. Extra resources also are helpful to provide a buffer as performance drops during the transition period. Organizations can underestimate seriously the need for special resources devoted to the change process. Significant organizational change invariably requires considerable management time and energy, as well as the help of consultants. A separate "change budget" that exists along with capital and operating budgets can earmark the resources needed for training members in how to behave differently and for assessing progress and making necessary modifications in the change program.[34] Unless these extra resources are planned for and provided, meaningful change is less likely to occur.

Providing resources also includes building a support system for change agents. Organization change can be difficult and filled with tension for both participants and change agents.[35] Change agents often must support members emotionally, but they receive little support themselves. To help them cope with the resulting tension and isolation, change agents may need to create their own support systems. The people in these support systems can offer emotional grounding and serve as sounding boards for ideas and problems. For example, OD professionals often use trusted colleagues as "shadow consultants" to help them think through difficult client issues and to offer conceptual and emotional support. Similarly, an increasing number of companies, such as Intel, Procter & Gamble, TRW, and Texas Instruments, are forming internal networks of change agents to provide mutual learning and support.

Developing and Reinforcing New Competencies and Skills

Organizational changes frequently demand new knowledge, skills, and behaviors from organization members. In many cases, the changes cannot be implemented unless members gain new competencies. For example, employee-involvement programs often require managers to learn new leadership styles and new approaches to problem solving. Change agents must ensure that such learning occurs. They need to provide multiple learning opportunities, such as traditional training programs, on-the-job counseling and coaching, and experiential simulations. Ford's new CEO, Jacques Nasser, is supporting the organization's efforts to increase the speed of decision making through a concerted emphasis on "teaching." Through small-group discussions of strategy, providing all employees with a computer, assignments to develop new ideas, and 360-degree feedback, Ford managers are learning new skills and a new mindset to support the organization's need for faster decision making.[36]

In organizations, people generally do those things that bring them rewards. Consequently, one of the most effective ways to sustain momentum for change is to reinforce the new behaviors needed to implement the changes. This can be accomplished by linking formal rewards directly to the desired behaviors. For example, Integra Financial encouraged more teamwork by designing a rewards and recognition program in which the best team players got both financial rewards and management attention, and a variety of behaviors aimed at promoting self-interest were directly discouraged.[37] (Chapter 12 discusses several reward-system interventions.) In addition, desired behaviors can be reinforced more frequently through informal recognition, encouragement, and praise. Perhaps equally important are the intrinsic rewards that people can experience through early success in the change effort. Achieving identifiable early successes can make participants feel good about themselves and their behaviors, and thus reinforce the drive to change.

Staying the Course

Change requires time, and many of the expected financial and organizational benefits from change lag behind its implementation. If the organization changes again too quickly or abandons the change before it is fully implemented, the desired results may never materialize. There are two primary reasons that managers do not keep a steady focus on change implementation. First, many managers fail to anticipate the decline in performance, productivity, or satisfaction as change is implemented. Organization members need time to practice, develop, and learn new behaviors; they do not abandon old ways of doing things and adopt a new set of behaviors overnight. Moreover, change activities, such as training, extra meetings, and consulting assistance, are extra expenses added onto current operating expenditures. There should be little surprise, therefore, that effectiveness declines before it gets better. However, perfectly good change projects often are abandoned when questions are raised about short-term performance declines. Patience and trust in the diagnosis and intervention design work are necessary.

Second, many managers do not keep focused on a change because they want to implement the next big idea that comes along. When organizations change before they have to in response to the latest management fad, a "flavor-of-the-month" cynicism can develop. As a result, organization members provide only token support to a change under the (accurate) notion that the current change won't last. Successful organizational change requires persistent leadership that does not waiver unnecessarily.

Socializing New Behaviors

This activity involves the transmission of information about beliefs, preferences, norms, and values with respect to the intervention. Because implementing OD interventions generally involves considerable learning and experimentation, a continual process of socialization is needed to promote persistence of the change program. Organization members must focus attention on the evolving nature of the intervention and its ongoing meaning, and communicate this information to other employees, especially new members. Transmitting information about the intervention helps bring new members onboard and enables participants to reaffirm the beliefs, norms, and values underlying the interventions.[38] For example, employee involvement programs often include initial transmission of information about the intervention, as well as retraining of existing participants and training of new members. These processes promote program persistence as both new behaviors are learned and new members are introduced.

Diffusing the Intervention

This action transfers interventions from one system to another. Diffusion facilitates institutionalization by providing a wider organizational base to support the new behaviors. Many interventions fail to persist because they run counter to the values and norms of the larger organization. Rather than support the intervention, the larger organization rejects the changes and often puts pressure on the change target to revert to old behaviors. Diffusing the intervention to other organizational units reduces this counterimplementation strategy, and locks in behaviors by providing normative consensus from other parts of the organization. Moreover, the act of transmitting institutionalized behaviors to other systems reinforces commitment to the changes.

EVALUATING CHANGE

This last activity of leading and managing change involves assessing organization development interventions to discover whether they have been implemented as intended and, if so, whether they are having desired results.[39] Managers investing resources in OD efforts increasingly are being held accountable for results—being asked to justify the expenditures in terms of hard, bottom-line outcomes. More and more, managers are asking for rigorous assessment of OD interventions and are using the results to make important resource allocation decisions about OD, such as whether to continue to support the change program, to modify or alter it, or to terminate it and try something else. There are two distinct types of OD evaluation—one intended to guide the implementation of interventions and another to assess their overall impact.

Most discussions and applications of OD evaluation imply that evaluation is something done after intervention. It is typically argued that once the intervention is implemented, it should be evaluated to discover whether it is producing intended effects. For example, it might be expected that a job enrichment program would lead to higher employee satisfaction and performance. After implementing job enrichment, evaluation would involve assessing whether these positive results indeed did occur.

This after-implementation view of evaluation is only partially correct. It assumes that interventions have been implemented as intended and that the key purpose of evaluation is to assess their effects. In many, if not most, organization development programs, however, implementing interventions cannot be taken for granted.[40] Most OD interventions require significant changes in people's behaviors and ways of thinking about organizations, but they typically offer only broad prescriptions for how such changes are to occur. For example, job enrichment (see Chapter 9) calls for adding discretion, variety, and meaningful feedback to people's jobs. Implementing such changes requires considerable learning and experimentation as employees and managers discover how to translate these general prescriptions into specific behaviors and procedures. This learning process involves much trial and error and needs to be guided by information about whether behaviors and procedures are being changed as intended.[41] Consequently, we should expand our view of evaluation to include both *during-implementation* assessment of whether interventions are actually being implemented and *after-implementation* evaluation of whether they are producing expected results.

Both kinds of evaluation provide organization members with feedback about interventions. Evaluation aimed at guiding implementation may be called *implementation feedback,* and assessment intended to discover intervention outcomes may be called *evaluation feedback.*[42] Figure 7.4 shows how the two kinds of feedback fit with the diagnostic and intervention stages of OD. The application of OD to a particular organization starts with a thorough diagnosis of the situation (Chapters 4 and 5), which helps identify particular organizational problems or areas for improvement, as well as likely causes underlying them. Next, from an array of possible interventions (Chapters 8 through 12), one or some set is chosen as a means of improving the organization. The choice is based on knowledge linking interventions to diagnosis (Chapter 6) and the steps of change management described above.

In most cases, the chosen intervention provides only general guidelines for organizational change, leaving managers and employees with the task of translating those guidelines into specific behaviors and procedures. Implementation feedback guides this process by supplying data about the different features of the intervention itself and data about the immediate effects of the intervention. These data, collected

Figure 7•4	Implementation and Evaluation Feedback

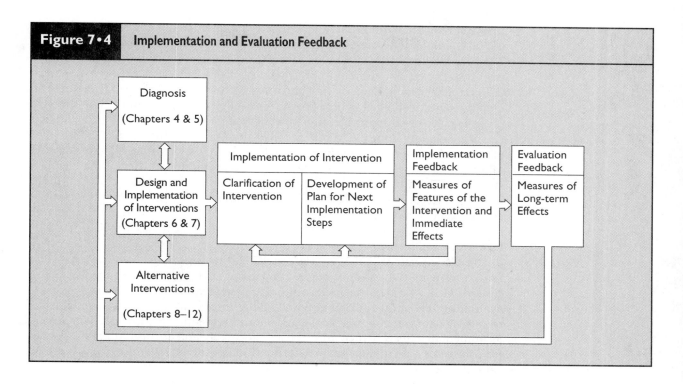

repeatedly and at short intervals, provide a series of snapshots about how the intervention is progressing. Organization members can use this information, first, to gain a clearer understanding of the intervention (the kinds of behaviors and procedures required to implement it) and, second, to plan for the next implementation steps. This feedback cycle might proceed for several rounds, with each round providing members with knowledge about the intervention and ideas for the next stage of implementation.

Once implementation feedback informs organization members that the intervention is sufficiently in place, evaluation feedback begins. In contrast to implementation feedback, it is concerned with the overall impact of the intervention and with whether resources should continue to be allocated to it or to other possible interventions. Evaluation feedback takes longer to gather and interpret than does implementation feedback. It typically includes a broad array of outcome measures, such as performance, job satisfaction, absenteeism, and turnover. Negative results on these measures tell members either that the initial diagnosis was seriously flawed or that the wrong intervention was chosen. Such feedback might prompt additional diagnosis and a search for a more effective intervention. Positive results, on the other hand, tell members that the intervention produced expected outcomes and might prompt a search for ways to institutionalize the changes, making them a permanent part of the organization's normal functioning.

■ SUMMARY

In this chapter, we described five kinds of activities that change agents must carry out when planning and implementing changes. The first activity is motivating change, which involves creating a readiness for change among organization members and overcoming their resistance. The second activity concerns creating a vision that builds on an organization's core ideology. It describes an envisioned future that includes a bold and valued outcome and a vividly described desired future state. The core ideology and envisioned future articulate a compelling reason for implementing change. The third task for change agents is developing political support for the changes. Change agents first must assess their own sources of power, then identify key stakeholders whose support is needed for change and devise strategies for gaining their support. The fourth activity concerns managing the transition of the organization from its current state to the desired future state. This requires planning a road map for the change activities, as well as planning how to gain commitment for the changes. It also may involve creating special change-management structures. The fifth change task is sustaining and institutionalizing change. This includes providing resources for the change program, creating a support system for change agents, developing new competencies and skills, reinforcing the new behaviors required to implement the changes, staying the course, socializing new behaviors, and diffusing the intervention.

We also discussed issues associated with evaluating change, addressing evaluation in terms of two kinds of necessary feedback: implementation feedback, concerned with whether the intervention is being implemented as intended, and evaluation feedback, indicating whether the intervention is producing expected results. The former comprises collected data about features of the intervention and its immediate effects, which are fed back repeatedly and at short intervals. The latter comprises data about the long-term effects of the intervention, which are fed back at long intervals.

■ NOTES

1. J. Conger, G. Spreitzer, and E. Lawler, *The Leader's Change Handbook* (San Francisco: Jossey-Bass, 1999).

2. N. Tichy and M. Devanna, *The Transformational Leader* (New York: John Wiley & Sons, 1986); A. Armenakis, S. Harris, and K. Mossholder, "Creating Readiness for Organizational Change," *Human Relations* 46 (1993): 681–704.

3. R. Cosier and C. Schwenk, "Agreement and Thinking Alike: Ingredients for Poor Decisions," *Academy of Management Executive* 4 (1990): 69–74.

4. S. Walleck, D. O'Halloran, and C. Leader, "Benchmarking World-Class Performance," *McKinsey Quarterly* 1 (1991).

5. W. Burke, *Organization Development: A Normative View* (Reading, Mass.: Addison-Wesley, 1987); J. Collins and J. Porras, *Built to Last* (New York: Harper Business, 1994).

6. R. Charan and G. Colvin, "Why CEOs Fail," *Fortune* (21 June 1999): 69–78.

7. D. Eden, "OD and Self-Fulfilling Prophesy: Boosting Productivity by Raising Expectations," *Journal of Applied Behavioral Science* 22 (1986): 1–13; D. Cooperrider, "Positive Image, Positive Action: The Affirmative Basis of Organizing," in *Appreciative Management and Leadership: The*

Power of Positive Thought and Actions in Organizations, eds. S. Srivastva, D. Cooperrider, and associates (San Francisco: Jossey-Bass, 1990).

8. Eden, "OD and Self-Fulfilling Prophesy," p. 8.

9. J. Kotter and L. Schlesinger, "Choosing Strategies for Change," *Harvard Business Review* 57 (1979): 106–14; P. Block, *Flawless Consulting: A Guide to Getting Your Expertise Used* (Austin, Tex.: Learning Concepts, 1981); P. Strebel, "Why Do Employees Resist Change?" *Harvard Business Review* (May-June 1996): 86–93.

10. N. Tichy, "Revolutionize Your Company," *Fortune* (13 December 1993): 114–18.

11. D. Kirkpatrick, ed., *How to Manage Change Effectively* (San Francisco: Jossey-Bass, 1985).

12. V. Vroom and P. Yetton, *Leadership and Decision Making* (Pittsburgh: University of Pittsburgh Press, 1973).

13. T. Cummings and E. Molloy, *Strategies for Improving Productivity and the Quality of Work Life* (New York: Praeger, 1977).

14. Collins and Porras, *Built to Last*; T. Stewart, "A Refreshing Change: Vision Statements That Make Sense," *Fortune*

(30 September 1996): 195–96; T. Stewart, "Why Value Statements Don't Work," *Fortune* (10 June 1996): 137–38.

15. P. Senge, *The Fifth Discipline* (New York: Doubleday, 1990).

16. Collins and Porras, *Built to Last.*

17. J. Kotter, *Leading Change* (Boston: Harvard Business School Press, 1994); W. Bennis and B. Nanus, *Leadership* (New York: Harper & Row, 1985); J. O'Toole, *Leading Change: Overcoming the Ideology of Comfort and the Tyranny of Custom* (San Francisco: Jossey-Bass, 1995); F. Hesselbein, M. Goldsmith, R. Beckhard, eds., *The Leader of the Future* (San Francisco: Jossey-Bass, 1995).

18. Tichy and Devanna, *Transformational Leader.*

19. Collins and Porras, *Built to Last.*

20. T. Stewart, "Company Values That Add Value," *Fortune* (8 July 1996): 145–47; J. Pearce II and F. David, "Corporate Mission Statements: The Bottom Line," *Academy of Management Executive* 1 (1987): 109–15.

21. Collins and Porras, *Built to Last.*

22. J. Pfeffer, *Power in Organizations* (New York: Pitman, 1982).

23. D. Nadler, "The Effective Management of Change," in *Handbook of Organizational Behavior,* ed. J. Lorsch (Englewood Cliffs, N.J.: Prentice Hall, 1987): 358–69.

24. C. Alderfer, "Organization Development," *Annual Review of Psychology* 28 (1977): 197–223.

25. T. Bateman, "Organizational Change and the Politics of Success," *Group and Organization Studies* 5 (June 1980): 198–209; A. Cobb and N. Margulies, "Organization Development: A Political Perspective," *Academy of Management Review* 6 (1981): 49–59; A. Cobb, "Political Diagnosis: Applications in Organization Development," *Academy of Management Review* 11 (1986): 482–96; L. Greiner and V. Schein, *Power and Organization Development: Mobilizing Power to Implement Change* (Reading, Mass.: Addison-Wesley, 1988); D. Buchanan and R. Badham, "Politics and Organizational Change: The Lived Experience," *Human Relations* 52 (1999): 609–11.

26. Greiner and Schein, *Power and Organization Development.*

27. Nadler, "Effective Management"; R. Beckhard and W. Pritchard, *Changing the Essence* (San Francisco: Jossey-Bass, 1991).

28. Greiner and Schein, *Power and Organization Development.*

29. R. Beckhard and R. Harris, *Organizational Transitions: Managing Complex Change,* 2d ed. (Reading, Mass.: Addison-Wesley, 1987).

30. Ibid.

31. Ibid.

32. P. Goodman and J. Dean, "Creating Long-Term Organizational Change," in *Change in Organizations,* ed. P. Goodman (San Francisco: Jossey-Bass, 1982): 226–79; G. Ledford, "The Persistence of Planned Organizational Change: A Process Theory Perspective" (Ph.D. diss., University of Michigan, 1984).

33. D. Ciampa, *Total Quality: A User's Guide for Implementation* (Reading, Mass.: Addison-Wesley, 1992); Senge, *Fifth Discipline;* T. Cummings and S. Mohrman, "Self-Designing Organizations: Towards Implementing Quality-of-Work-Life Innovations," in *Research in Organizational Change and Development,* vol. 1, eds. R. Woodman and W. Pasmore (Greenwich, Conn.: JAI Press, 1987): 275–310; C. Worley, D. Hitchin, and W. Ross, *Integrated Strategic Change: How OD Helps to Build Competitive Advantage* (Reading, Mass.: Addison-Wesley, 1996).

34. Worley, Hitchin, and Ross, *Integrated Strategic Change.*

35. M. Beer, *Organization Change and Development: A Systems View* (Santa Monica, Calif.: Goodyear, 1980).

36. S. Wetlaufer, "Driving Change: An Interview with Ford Motor Company's Jacques Nasser," *Harvard Business Review* (March-April 1999): 76–88.

37. A. Fisher, "Making Change Stick," *Fortune* (17 April 1995): 121–31.

38. L. Zucker, "The Role of Institutionalization in Cultural Persistence," *American Sociological Review* 42 (1977): 726–43.

39. P. Goodman, *Assessing Organizational Change: The Rushton Quality of Work Experiment* (New York: John Wiley, 1979); A. Van de Ven and D. Ferry, eds., *Measuring and Assessing Organizations* (New York: John Wiley, 1985); E. Lawler III, D. Nadler, and C. Cammann, eds., *Organizational Assessment: Perspectives on the Measurement of Organizational Behavior and Quality of Work Life* (New York: John Wiley, 1980); A. Van de Ven and W. Joyce, eds., *Perspectives on Organizational Design and Behavior* (New York: John Wiley, 1981); S. Seashore, E. Lawler III, P. Mirvis, and C. Cammann, eds., *Assessing Organizational Change: A Guide to Methods, Measures, and Practices* (New York: John Wiley, 1983); B. Macy and P. Mirvis, "Organizational Change Efforts: Methodologies for Assessing Organizational Effectiveness and Program Costs Versus Benefits," *Evaluation*

Review 6 (1982): 301–72; D. Miller, *Handbook of Research Design and Social Measurement* (Thousand Oaks, Calif.: Sage Publications, 1991); N. Denzin and Y. Lincoln, eds., *Handbook of Qualitative Research* (Thousand Oaks, Calif.: Sage Publications, 1994); C. Selltiz, M. Jahoda, M. Deutsch, and S. Cook, *Research Methods in Social Relations,* rev. ed. (New York: Holt, Rinehart, & Winston, 1966): 385–440.

40. Cummings and Molloy, *Strategies for Improving Productivity;* J. Whitfield, W. Anthony, and K. Kacmar, "Evaluation of Team-Based Management: A Case Study," *Journal of Organizational Change Management* 8, 2 (1995): 17–28.

41. S. Mohrman and T. Cummings, "Implementing Quality-of-Work-Life Programs by Managers," in *The NTL Manager's Handbook,* eds. R. Ritvo and A. Sargent (Arlington, Va.: NTL Institute, 1983): 320–28; Cummings and Mohrman, "Self-Designing Organizations."

42. T. Cummings, "Institutionalizing Quality-of-Work-Life Programs: The Case for Self-Design" (paper delivered at the annual meeting of the Academy of Management, Dallas, Tex., August 1983).

Organization Development Interventions

3

8. Human Process Interventions

This chapter discusses change programs relating to interpersonal relations, group dynamics, and organization-level processes. These change programs include some of the earliest interventions in OD as well as some of the newest. All of them attempt to improve people's working relationships with one another. Four key human process interventions are presented in this chapter: process consultation, team building, conflict resolution, and large-group interventions. Team building is aimed both at helping a team perform its tasks better and at satisfying individual needs. Conflict resolution assists organizational members in resolving interpersonal as well as intergroup conflicts. Large-group interventions allow a variety of stakeholders to come together to develop new ways of looking at problems, to articulate a new vision for the organization, to solve cross-functional problems, or to devise a new organizational strategy.

PROCESS CONSULTATION

Process consultation (PC) is a general framework for carrying out helping relationships.[1] It is oriented to helping managers, employees, and groups assess and improve *processes,* such as communication, interpersonal relations, decision making, and task performance. Schein argues that effective consultants and managers should be good helpers, aiding others in getting things done and in achieving the goals they have set.[2] Thus, PC is more a philosophy than a set of techniques aimed at performing this helping relationship. The philosophy ensures that those who are receiving the help own their problems, gain the skills and expertise to diagnose them, and solve them themselves. Thus, it is an approach to helping people and groups help themselves.

Schein defines process consultation as "the creation of a relationship that permits the client to perceive, understand, and act on the process events that occur in [her/his] internal and external environment in order to improve the situation as defined by the client."[3] The process consultant does not offer expert help in the form of solutions to problems, as in the doctor–patient model. Rather, the process consultant works to develop relationships, observes groups and people in action, helps them diagnose the way they are carrying out tasks, and helps them learn how to be more effective.

Principles of Process Consultation

PC follows closely the phases of planned change described in Chapter 2: entering, defining the relationship, selecting an approach, gathering data and making a diagnosis, intervening, reducing the involvement, and terminating the relationship. When used in process consultation, however, these stages are not so clear-cut. As a philosophy of helping in relationships, Schein proposes ten principles to guide the process consultant's actions.[4]

1. *Always try to be helpful.* Process consultants must be mindful of their intentions, and each interaction must be oriented toward being helpful.

2. *Always stay in touch with the current reality.* Each interaction should produce diagnostic information about the current situation. It includes data about the client's opinions, beliefs, and emotions; the system's current functioning; and the practitioner's reactions, thoughts, and feelings.

3. *Access your ignorance.* An important source of information about current reality is the practitioner's understanding of what is known, what is assumed, and what is not known. Process consultants must use themselves as instruments of change.

4. *Everything you do is an intervention.* Any interaction in a consultative relationship generates information as well as consequences. Simply conducting preliminary interviews with group members, for example, can raise members' awareness of a situation and help them see it in a new light.

5. *The client owns the problem and the solution.* This is a key principle in all OD practice. Practitioners help clients solve their own problems and learn to manage future change.

6. *Go with the flow.* When process consultants access their own ignorance, they often realize that there is much about the client system and its culture that they do not know. Thus, practitioners must work to understand the client's motivations and perceptions.

7. *Timing is crucial.* Observations, comments, questions, and other interventions intended to be helpful may work in some circumstances and fail in others. Process consultants must be vigilant to occasions when the client is open (or not open) to suggestions.

8. *Be constructively opportunistic with confrontive interventions.* Although process consultants must be willing to go with the flow, they also must be willing to take appropriate risks. From time to time and in their best judgment, practitioners must learn to take advantage of "teachable moments." A well-crafted process observation or piece of feedback can provide a group or individual with great insight into their behavior.

9. *Everything is information; errors will always occur and are the prime source for learning.* Process consultants never can know fully the client's reality and invariably will make mistakes. The consequences of these mistakes, the unexpected and surprising reactions, are important data that must be used in the ongoing development of the relationship.

10. *When in doubt, share the problem.* The default intervention in a helping relationship is to model openness by sharing the dilemma of what to do next.

Interpersonal and Group Processes

Process consultation deals primarily with five important interpersonal and group processes: communications, the functional roles of group members, the ways in which the group solves problems and makes decisions, group norms development, and the use of leadership and authority.

Communications

One of the process consultant's areas of interest is the nature and style of communication: who talks to whom, for how long, and how often. One method for describing group communication is to keep a time log of how often and to whom people talk. For example, at an hour-long meeting conducted by a manager, the longest anyone other than the manager got to speak was one minute, and that minute was allotted to the assistant manager. Rather than telling the manager that he is cutting people off, the consultant can give descriptive feedback by citing the number of times others tried to talk and the amount of time they were given. The consultant must make certain that the feedback is descriptive and not evaluative (good or bad), unless the individual or group is ready for evaluative feedback.

By keeping a time log, the consultant also can note who talks and who interrupts. Frequently, certain people are perceived as being quiet when in fact they have tried to say something and have been interrupted. Such interruptions are one of the most effective ways of reducing communications and decreasing participation in a meeting.

Body language and other nonverbal behavior also can be a highly informative method for understanding communication processes.[5] For example, at another meeting conducted by a manager, the animated discussion at the start of the meeting was interrupted by the second-in-command, who said, "This is a problem-solving meeting, not a gripe session." As the manager continued to talk, the fourteen other members present assumed expressions of concentration. Within twenty-five minutes, all of them had folded their arms and were leaning backward, a sure sign that they were blocking out or shutting off the message. Within ten seconds of the manager's subsequent statement, "We are interested in getting your ideas," those present unfolded their arms and began to lean forward, a clear nonverbal sign that they were involved once again.

Functional Roles of Group Members

The process consultant must be keenly aware of the different roles individual members take on in a group. Both upon entering and while remaining in a group, the individual must determine a self-identity, influence, and power that will satisfy personal needs while working to accomplish group goals. Preoccupation with individual needs or power struggles can reduce the effectiveness of a group severely, and unless the individual can expose and share those personal needs to some degree, the group is unlikely to be productive. Therefore, the process consultant must help the group confront and work through these needs. Emotions are facts, but frequently they are regarded as side issues to be avoided. Whenever an individual, usually the leader, says to the group, "Let's stick with the facts," it can be a sign that the emotional needs of group members are not being satisfied and, indeed, are being disregarded as irrelevant.

Two other functions need to be performed if a group is to be effective: (1) task-related activities, such as giving and seeking information and elaborating, coordinating, and evaluating activities; and (2) group-maintenance actions, directed toward holding the group together as a cohesive team, including encouraging, harmonizing, compromising, setting standards, and observing. Most ineffective groups perform little group maintenance, and this is a primary reason for bringing in a process consultant.

The process consultant can help by suggesting that some part of each meeting be reserved for examining these functions and periodically assessing the feelings of the group's members. As Schein points out, however, the basic purpose of the process consultant is not to take on the role of expert but to help the group share in its own diagnosis and do a better job in learning to diagnose its own processes: "It is important that the process consultant encourage the group not only to allocate time for diagnosis but to take the lead itself in trying to articulate and understand its own processes."[6] Otherwise, the group may default and become dependent on the supposed expert. In short, the consultant's role is to make comments and to assist with diagnosis, but the emphasis should be on facilitating the group's understanding and articulation of its own processes.

Group Problem Solving and Decision Making

To be effective, a group must be able to identify problems, examine alternatives, and make decisions. The first part of this process is the most important. Groups often fail to distinguish between problems (either task-related or interpersonal) and symptoms. Once the group identifies the problem, a process consultant can help the group analyze its approach, restrain the group from reacting too quickly and making a premature diagnosis, or suggest additional options.

For example, a consultant was asked to process a group's actions during a three-hour meeting that had been taped. The tapes revealed that premature rejection of a suggestion had severely retarded the group's process. After one member's suggestion at the beginning of the meeting was quickly rejected by the manager, he repeated his suggestion several times in the next hour. Each time his suggestion was rejected quickly. During the second hour, this member became quite negative, opposing most of the other ideas offered. Finally, toward the end of the second hour, he brought up his proposal again. At that time, it was thoroughly discussed and then rejected for reasons that the member accepted.

During the third hour, this person was one of the most productive members of the group, offering constructive and worthwhile ideas, suggestions, and recommendations. In addition, he was able to integrate the comments of others, to modify them, and to come up with useful, integrated new suggestions. However, it was not until his first suggestion had been thoroughly discussed (even though it was finally rejected) that he was able to become a truly constructive member of the group.

Once the problem has been identified, a decision must be made. One way of making decisions is to ignore a suggestion. For example, when one person makes a suggestion, someone else offers another before the first has been discussed. A second method is to give decision-making power to the person in authority. Sometimes decisions are made by minority rule, the leader arriving at a decision and turning for agreement to several people who will comply. Frequently, silence is regarded as consent. Decisions also can be made by majority rule, consensus, or unanimous consent.

The process consultant can help the group understand how it makes its decisions and the consequences of each decision process, as well as help diagnose which type of decision process may be the most effective in a given situation. Decision by unanimous consent or consensus, for example, may be ideal in some circumstances but too time-consuming or costly in other situations.

Group Norms and Growth

Especially if a group of people works together over a period of time, it develops group norms or standards of behavior about what is good or bad, allowed or forbidden, right or wrong. There may be an explicit norm that group members are free to express their ideas and feelings, whereas the implicit norm is that one does not contradict the ideas or suggestions of certain group members (usually the more powerful ones). The process consultant can be very helpful in assisting the group to understand and articulate its own norms and to determine whether those norms are helpful or dysfunctional. By understanding its norms and recognizing which ones are helpful, the group can grow and deal realistically with its environment, make optimum use of its own resources, and learn from its own experiences.[7]

Leadership and Authority

A process consultant needs to understand processes of leadership and how different leadership styles can help or hinder a group's functioning. In addition, the consultant can help the leader adjust her or his style to fit the situation. An important step in that process is for the leader to gain a better understanding of her or his own behavior and the group's reaction to that behavior. It also is important that the leader become aware of alternative behaviors. For example, after gaining a better understanding of her or his assumptions about human behavior, the leader may do a better job of testing and perhaps changing those assumptions.

Basic Process Interventions

For each of the five interpersonal and group processes described above, a variety of interventions may be used. In broad terms, these are aimed at making individuals and groups more effective.[8]

Individual Interventions

These interventions are designed to help people be more effective or to increase the information they have about issues or feelings that they are unaware of but that they communicate clearly to others. Before process consultants can give individual feedback, they first must observe relevant events, ask questions to understand the issues fully, and make certain that the feedback is given to the client in a usable manner. The following are guidelines[9] for effective feedback:

- The giver and receiver must have consensus on the receiver's goals.
- The giver should emphasize description and appreciation.
- The giver should be concrete and specific.
- Both giver and receiver must have constructive motives.
- The giver should not withhold negative feedback if it is relevant.
- The giver should own his or her observations, feelings, and judgments.
- Feedback should be timed to when the giver and receiver are ready.

Group Interventions

These interventions are aimed at the process, content, or structure of the group. Process interventions sensitize the group to its own internal processes and generate interest in analyzing those processes. Interventions include comments, questions, or observations about

- relationships between and among group members
- problem solving and decision making
- the identity and purpose of the group.

Content interventions help the group determine what it works on. They include comments, questions, or observations about

- group membership
- agenda setting, review, and testing procedures

- interpersonal issues
- conceptual inputs on task-related topics.

Structural interventions help the group examine the stable and recurring methods it uses to accomplish tasks. They include comments, questions, or observations about

- methods for dealing with external issues, such as inputs, resources, and customers
- methods for determining goals, developing strategies, accomplishing work, assigning responsibility, monitoring progress, and addressing problems
- relationships to authority, formal rules, and levels of intimacy.

When Is Process Consultation Appropriate?

Process consultation, a general model for helping relationships, has wide applicability in organizations. Because PC helps people and groups own their problems and diagnose and resolve them, it is most applicable in the following circumstances:[10]

1. The client has a problem but does not know its source or how to resolve it.
2. The client is unsure of what kind of help or consultation is available.
3. The nature of the problem is such that the client would benefit from involvement in its diagnosis.
4. The client is motivated by goals that the consultant can accept, and the consultant has some capacity to enter into a helping relationship directed at reaching those goals.
5. The client ultimately knows what interventions are most applicable.
6. The client is capable of learning how to assess and resolve her or his own problem.

TEAM BUILDING

Team building refers to a broad range of planned activities that help groups improve the way they accomplish tasks and help group members enhance their interpersonal and problem-solving skills. Organizations comprise many permanent and temporary groups, and team building is an effective approach to improving teamwork and task accomplishment in such environments. It can help problem-solving groups make maximum use of members' resources and contributions. It can help members develop a high level of motivation to implement group decisions. Team building also can help groups overcome specific problems, such as apathy and general lack of member interest; loss of productivity; increasing complaints within the group; confusion about assignments; low participation in meetings; lack of innovation and initiation; increasing complaints from those outside the group about the quality, timeliness, and effectiveness of services and products; and hostility or conflicts among members.

It is equally important that team building can facilitate other OD interventions, such as employee involvement, work design, restructuring, and strategic change. Those change programs typically are designed by management teams and implemented through various committees and work groups. Team building can help the groups design high-quality change programs and ensure that the programs are accepted and implemented by organization members. Indeed, most technostructural, human resources management, and strategic interventions depend on some form of team building for effective implementation.

The importance of team building is well established, and its use is expected to grow even faster in the coming years. Management teams are encountering issues of greater complexity and uncertainty, especially in such fast-growing industries as electronics, entertainment, information technology and processing, and health and financial services. Team building can provide the kind of teamwork and problem-solving skills needed to tackle such issues. As manufacturing and service technologies continue to develop—for example, just-in-time inventory systems, manufacturing cells, robotics, and service quality concepts—there is increasing pressure on organizations to implement team-based work designs. Team building can assist in the development of group goals and norms that support high productivity and quality of work life. The globalization of work and organizations implies that people from different cultures and geographic locations increasingly will interact over complex management and operational tasks. Team building is an excellent vehicle for examining cross-cultural issues and their impact on decision making and problem solving. When such groups represent the senior management of an organization, team building can help establish a coherent corporate strategy and can promote the kind of close cooperation needed to make this new form of governance effective.[11] Finally, in today's business situation, mergers and acquisitions are increasing rapidly. The success of these endeavors depends partly on getting members from different organizations to work together effectively. Team building can facilitate the formation of a unified team with common goals and procedures.

In the OD literature, team building is not clearly differentiated from process consultation. This confusion exists because most team building includes process consultation—helping the group diagnose and understand its own internal processes. However, process consultation is a more general approach to helping relationships than is team building. Team building focuses explicitly on helping groups perform tasks and solve problems more effectively. Process consultation, on the other hand, is concerned with establishing effective helping relationships in organizations. It is seen as key to effective management and consultation and can be applied to any helping relationship, from subordinate development to interpersonal relationships to group development. Thus, team building consists of process consultation plus other, more task-oriented interventions.

Team-Building Activities

A team is a group of interdependent people who share a common purpose, have common work methods, and hold each other accountable.[12] The nature of that interdependence varies, creating the following types of teams: groups reporting to the same supervisor, manager, or executive; groups involving people with common organizational goals; temporary groups formed to do a specific, one-time task; groups consisting of people whose work roles are interdependent; and groups whose members have no formal links in the organization but whose collective purpose is to achieve tasks they cannot accomplish alone. In addition, there are a number of factors that affect the outcomes of any specific team-building activity: the length of time allocated to the activity, the team's willingness to look at the way in which it operates, the length of time the team has been working together, and the team's permanence. Consequently, the results of team-building activities can range from comparatively modest changes in the team's operating mechanisms (for example, meeting more frequently or gathering agenda items from more sources) to much deeper changes (for example, modifying team members' behavior patterns or the nature and style of the group's management, or developing greater openness and trust).

In general, team-building activities can be classified as follows: (1) activities relevant to one or more individuals; (2) activities specific to the group's operation and behavior; and (3) activities affecting the group's relationship with the rest of the organization. Usually, a specific team-building activity will overlap these three categories. On occasion, a change in one area will have negative results in other areas. A very cohesive team may increase its isolation from other groups, leading to intergroup conflict or other dysfunctional results, which in turn can have a negative impact on the total organization unless the team develops sufficient diagnostic skills to recognize and deal with such results.

Activities Relevant to One or More Individuals

People come into groups and organizations with varying needs and wants for achievement, inclusion, influence, and belonging. These needs and wants can be supported and nurtured by the team's structure and process or they can be discouraged. Almost all team-building efforts result in one or more of the members gaining a better understanding of the way authority, inclusion, emotions, control, and power affect problem solving and other group processes. Such activities provide information so that people have a clearer sense of how their needs and wants can or will be supported. This information then gives group members a choice about their level of involvement, commitment, and investment in the team's functioning.

For example, in one team, the typical decision-making process included the leader having several agenda items for discussion. Each of the items, however, had a predetermined set of actions that she wanted the group to take. Most members were frustrated by their inability to influence decision making. During the team-building process, group members asked whether the boss really wanted ideas and contributions from group members. They gave specific examples of the leader's not-so-subtle manipulation to arrive at preconceived decisions and described how they felt about it. At the end of the discussion, the boss indicated her willingness to be challenged about such preconceived decisions, and the other team members expressed their increased willingness to engage in problem-solving discussions, their trust in the leader, and their ability to make the challenge without fear of reprisal.

Sometimes, the team-building process generates pressures on individual members, such as requests for higher levels of task performance. Such requests could have negative results unless accompanied by agreement for further one-to-one negotiations among team members. If these demands are made of the boss, for example, he or she may feel a loss of power and authority unless the team can agree on ways in which the boss can be kept informed about what is happening. Methods to meet these needs for control and influence without causing feelings of isolation can be explored.

Activities Oriented to the Group's Operation and Behavior

The most common focus of team building activities is behavior related to task performance and group process. In an effective team, task behavior and group process must be integrated with each other as well as with the needs and wants of the people making up the group. Team-building activities often begin by clarifying the team's purpose, priorities, goals, and objectives. This establishes a framework within which further work can be done. In most team-building activities, groups spend some time finding ways to improve the mechanisms that structure their approach to work. A group may discuss how a meeting agenda is created, the efficiency of key work processes, or strategies for lowering costs. In addition, groups often examine their communications patterns and determine ways in which they can be improved. Frequently, this leads to dropping some communications patterns and establishing new ones that are more open and conducive to problem solving in nature.

Another group operation issue is the effective use of time. To improve in this area, the group may examine its present planning mechanisms, introduce better ones, and identify ways for using its skills and knowledge more effectively. The group also may make decisions about reorganizing and redistributing the workload. As the group develops over time, it tends to become more aware of the need for action plans about problems or tasks as well as for better self-diagnosis about the effectiveness of its task-accomplishment processes.

Frequently, groups examine and diagnose the nature of their problem-solving techniques. Specific items usually are diagnosed in the earlier stage of team building, and as teams mature they broaden the scope of these diagnostic efforts to include areas that are more directly related to interpersonal styles and their impact on other group members. Throughout this process, group norms become clearer, and the group can provide more opportunity for members to satisfy individual needs within the group. As a result, the team is much more willing to take risks within both the team and the organization. Team members become more capable of facing difficulties and problems, not only within their own group but also within the larger organization. A spirit of openness, trust, and risk taking develops.

Activities Affecting the Group's Relationship with the Rest of the Organization

As the team gains a better understanding of itself and becomes better able to diagnose and solve its own problems, it focuses on its role within the organization. A group's relationship to the larger organizational context is an important aspect of group effectiveness.[13] As a result, the team may perceive a need to clarify its organizational role and to consider how this role can be improved or modified. Sometimes, the team may recognize a need for more collaboration with other parts of the organization and so try to establish working parties or project teams that cross the boundaries of existing teams.

As the team becomes more cohesive, it usually exerts a stronger influence on the other subsystems of the organization. Because that is one area in which team building can have negative effects, the process consultant must help the group understand its role within the organization, develop its own diagnostic skills, and examine alternative action plans so that intergroup tensions and conflicts do not expand.

Types of Team Building

Family Group Diagnostic Meeting

The family group diagnostic meeting involves the individual "family" group—where all team members report to the same supervisor, manager, or executive. This process, which has been described by a number of authors, is aimed at getting a general reading on the overall performance of the group, including current problems that should be worked on in the future.[14] This technique allows the work group to get away from the work itself to gather data about its current performance and to formulate plans for future action. Normally, the immediate supervisor of a work group discusses the concept with the process consultant, and if both agree that there is a need for such an approach, the idea is discussed with the group to obtain members' reactions.

If the reactions are favorable, the leader or process consultant may ask the group, before the meeting, to consider areas in which performance is good and areas that need improvement. Group members also may be asked to consider their work relationships with one another and with other groups in the organization. In advance of a general meeting, the consultant may interview some or all members of the work group to gather preliminary data or merely ask all of the members to think about these and similar problems. Then the group assembles for a meeting that may last one or two days.

The diagnostic data can be made public in a number of ways. One method brings the total group together for a discussion, with everyone presenting ideas to the entire group. Another approach breaks the group into smaller groups in which more intensive discussions can take place and has the subgroups report back to the larger group. A third technique has individuals pair up, discuss their ideas, and then report to the entire group. Finally, the consultant can feed back to the group his or her diagnostic findings collected before the meeting so that the total group can process the data and determine whether they are correct and relevant.

After the data have been made public, the issues identified are discussed and categorized (categories might include, for example, planning, interdepartmental scheduling, and tight resources). Next, the group begins to develop action plans. The primary objective of the family group diagnostic meeting, however, is to bring to the surface problems and issues that need to be addressed. Taking specific action usually is reserved for a later time.

The advantage of the family group diagnostic meeting is that it allows a group to participate in generating the data necessary to identify its own strengths, weaknesses, and problem areas. The use of a process consultant is helpful but not essential. A key issue, however, is making certain that the participants recognize that their primary objective is to identify problems rather than to solve them. As Beer has noted, "All the advantages of direct involvement are inherent in this model, although there may be limited openness if the group has had no previous development and a supportive climate does not exist."[15]

Family Group Team-Building Meeting

The family group team-building meeting occurs with a permanent work group, a management team, or a temporary, project-type team. It is one of the most widely used OD interventions.

The team development process involves helping the group learn to identify, diagnose, and solve problems with the help of an OD practitioner. The problems may involve the tasks or activities the group must perform, the process by which it goes about accomplishing the tasks, or interpersonal conflict between two or more team members. French and Bell have defined team development as "an inward look by the team at its own performance, behavior, and culture for the purposes of dropping out dysfunctional behaviors and strengthening functional ones."[16]

The first intervention is to gather data through the use of questionnaires or, more commonly, through interviews. The nature of the data gathered will vary, depending on the purpose of the team-building program, the consultant's knowledge about the organization and its culture, and the people involved. The consultant already may have obtained a great deal of data by sitting in as a process observer at staff and other meetings. The data gathered also will depend on what other OD efforts have taken place in the organization. By whatever method obtained, however, the data usually include information on leadership styles and behavior; goals, objectives, and decision-making processes; such variables of organizational culture as trust, communication patterns, and interpersonal relationships and processes; barriers to effective group functioning; and task and related technical problems.

Frequently, but not always, the data-gathering stage is initiated only after the manager and her or his group have agreed that team development is a process in which they wish to engage and have set a date for an off-site meeting. This sequence ensures that organization members have freedom of choice and that the data-gathering stage is conducted as close to the actual meeting as possible. The off-site meeting may last from a day and a half to a week, with the average being about three days. The meeting is held away from the organization to reduce the number of interruptions and other pressures that might inhibit the process.

At the beginning of the meeting, the consultant feeds back the information that has been collected. This information usually is categorized by major themes, and the group must establish the agenda by placing priorities on these themes. Based on his or her knowledge of the data and the group, the consultant may help in setting the agenda or may act solely as a process observer, feeding back to the group his or her observations of what the group is doing.

As Beer points out, the consultant can play several different roles during the team-development meeting.[17] One role is that of process consultant, helping the group to understand and diagnose its own group process. The consultant also may function as a resource person, offering expertise as a behavioral scientist, or as a teacher, giving information about such areas as group dynamics, conflict resolution, and leadership. However, the primary role of the consultant is to assist the group in learning to identify, diagnose, and solve its own problems.

During the meeting, the group should develop action plans for becoming more effective. Frequently, merely discussing the barriers leads to improving the effectiveness of the group. One meeting, however, is rarely enough to effect major change. Instead, a series of meetings usually is needed to ensure permanent change.

The Manager's Role in Team Building

Ultimately, the manager is responsible for group functioning, although this responsibility obviously must be shared by the group itself. Therefore, it is management's task to develop a work group that can stop regularly to analyze and diagnose its own effectiveness and work process. With the group's involvement, the manager must diagnose the group's effectiveness and take appropriate actions if the work unit shows signs of operating difficulty or stress.

Many managers, however, have not been trained to perform the data gathering, diagnosis, planning, and action necessary to maintain and improve their teams continually. Thus, the issue of who should lead a team-building session is a function of managerial capability. The initial use of a consultant usually is advisable if a manager is aware of problems, feels that she or he may be part of the problem, and believes that some positive action is needed to improve the operation of the unit, but is not sure how to go about it.

Basically, the role of the consultant is to work closely with the manager (and members of the unit) to a point at which the manager is capable of engaging in team-development activities as a regular and ongoing part of overall managerial responsibilities. Assuming that the manager wants and needs a consultant, the two should work together as a team in developing the initial program, keeping in mind that (1) the manager ultimately is responsible for all team-building activities, even though the consultant's resources are available, and (2) the goal of the consultant's presence is to help the manager learn to continue team-development processes with minimum consultant help or without the ongoing help of the consultant.

Thus, in the first stages the consultant might be much more active in data gathering, diagnosis, and action planning, particularly if a one- to three-day off-site workshop is considered. In later stages, the consultant takes a much less active role, with the manager becoming more active and serving as both manager and team developer.

CONFLICT RESOLUTION

Conflict resolution interventions focus on resolving differences among people or organizational units. Conflict is inherent in groups and organizations and can arise from a variety of sources, including differences in personality, task orientation, and perceptions among group members, as well as competition for scarce resources. It is important to emphasize that conflict is neither good nor bad per se. Conflict can enhance motivation, innovation, and productivity, and lead to greater understanding of ideas and views. On the other hand, it can prevent people from working together constructively, destroying necessary task interactions among group members. Two or more groups may become polarized, and continued conflict may result in the development of defensiveness and negative stereotypes of the other group. Consequently, conflict resolution interventions are used primarily in situations in which conflict significantly disrupts necessary task interactions and work relationships among members.

Two conflict resolution interventions—interpersonal and intergroup—are described here. Interpersonal intervention processes work to reduce or resolve differences that arise between two or more people as a result of personality, task orientation, perceptions, or competition.

Interpersonal Conflict Resolution

Interpersonal conflict interventions vary considerably depending on the kind of issues underlying the conflict. Conflict can arise over substantive issues, such as work methods, pay rates, and conditions of employment; or it can emerge from interpersonal issues, such as personality conflicts and misperceptions. When applied to substantive issues, conflict resolution interventions often involve resolving labor–management disputes through arbitration, mediation, or alternative dispute resolution processes.[18] The methods used in such substantive interventions require considerable training and expertise in law and labor relations and generally are not considered part of OD practice.

When conflict involves interpersonal issues, however, OD has developed approaches that help control and resolve it. These third-party interventions help the parties interact with each other directly, facilitating their diagnosis of the conflict and how to resolve it. That ability to facilitate conflict resolution is a basic skill in OD and applies to all of the process interventions discussed in this chapter. Consultants, for example, frequently help organization members resolve interpersonal conflicts that invariably arise during process consultation and team building.

An Episodic Model of Conflict

Interpersonal conflict often occurs in iterative, cyclical stages known as "episodes." An episodic model is shown in Figure 8.1. At times, issues underlying a conflict are latent and do not present any manifest problems for the parties. Then something triggers the conflict and brings it into the open. For example, a violent disagreement or frank confrontation can unleash conflictual behavior. Because of the negative consequences of that behavior, the unresolved disagreement usually becomes

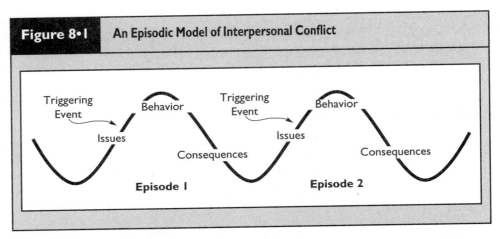

Figure 8·1   An Episodic Model of Interpersonal Conflict

SOURCE: R. G. Walton, *Managing Conflict: Interpersonal Dialogue and Third Party Roles,* page 67. © 1987 by Addison-Wesley Publishing Co., Inc. Reprinted by permission of Addison Wesley Longman.

latent again. And again, something triggers the conflict, making it overt, and so the cycle continues with the next conflict episode.

The episode model identifies four strategies for conflict resolution. The first three attempt to control the conflict, and only the last approach tries to change the basic issues underlying it.[19] The first strategy is to prevent the ignition of conflict by arriving at a clear understanding of the triggering factors and thereafter avoiding or blunting them when the symptoms occur. For example, if conflict between the research and production managers is always triggered by new product introductions, then senior management can warn them that conflict will not be tolerated during the introduction of the latest new product. However, this approach may not always be functional and merely may drive the conflict underground until it explodes. As a control strategy, however, this method may help to achieve a temporary cooling-off period.

The second control strategy is to set limits on the form of the conflict. Conflict can be constrained by informal gatherings before a formal meeting or by exploration of other options. It also can be limited by setting rules and procedures specifying the conditions under which the parties can interact. For example, a rule can be instituted that union officials can attempt to resolve grievances with management only at weekly grievance meetings.

The third control strategy is to help the parties cope differently with the consequences of the conflict. The third-party consultant may work with the people involved to devise coping techniques, such as reducing their dependence on the relationship, ventilating their feelings to friends, and developing additional sources of emotional support. These methods can reduce the costs of the conflict without resolving the underlying issues.

The fourth method is an attempt to eliminate or to resolve the basic issues causing the conflict. As Walton points out, "There is little to be said about this objective because it is the most obvious and straightforward, although it is often the most difficult to achieve."[20]

Facilitating the Conflict Resolution Process

Walton has identified a number of factors and tactical choices that can facilitate the use of the episode model in resolving the underlying causes of conflict.[21] The following ingredients can help third-party consultants achieve productive dialogue between the disputants so that they examine their differences and change their perceptions and behaviors: mutual motivation to resolve the conflict; equality of power between the parties; coordinated attempts to confront the conflict; relevant phasing of the stages of identifying differences and of searching for integrative solutions; open and clear forms of communication; and productive levels of tension and stress.

Among the tactical choices identified by Walton are those having to do with diagnosis, the context of the third-party intervention, and the role of the consultant. One of the tactics in third-party intervention is the gathering of data, usually through preliminary interviewing. Group-process observations can also be used. Data gathering provides some understanding of the nature and the type of conflict, the personality and conflict styles of the individuals involved, the issues and attendant pressures, and the participants' readiness to work together to resolve the conflict.

The context in which the intervention occurs is also important. Consideration of the neutrality of the meeting area, the formality of the setting, the appropriateness of the time for the meeting (that is, a meeting should not be started until a time has been agreed on to conclude or adjourn), and the careful selection of those who should attend the meeting are all elements of this context.

In addition, the third-party consultant must decide on an appropriate role to assume in resolving conflict. The specific tactic chosen will depend on the diagnosis of the situation. For example, facilitating dialogue of interpersonal issues might include initiating the agenda for the meeting, acting as a referee during the meeting, reflecting and restating the issues and the differing perceptions of the individuals involved, giving feedback and receiving comments on the feedback, helping the individuals diagnose the issues in the conflict, providing suggestions or recommendations, and helping the parties do a better job of diagnosing the underlying problem.

Intergroup Conflict Resolution

The intergroup conflict intervention is designed specifically to help two or more groups or departments within an organization resolve dysfunctional conflicts. Different approaches to resolving intergroup conflict form a continuum from behavioral solutions to attitudinal change solutions.[22] Behavioral methods are oriented to keeping the relevant parties physically separate and specifying the limited conditions under which interaction will occur. Little attempt is made to understand or change how members of each group see the other. Behavioral interventions seem most applicable where task interdependence between conflicting groups is relatively low and predictable. Conversely, the OD solution to intergroup conflict described below favors an attitudinal change strategy. These interventions typically require considerably more skill and time than do the behavioral solutions. Changing attitudes can be quite difficult in conflict situations, especially if the attitudes are deep-seated and form an integral part of people's personalities. Attitudinal change interventions should be reserved for those situations in which behavioral solutions might not work.

A basic strategy for improving interdepartmental or intergroup relationships is to change the perceptions (perhaps, more accurately, misperceptions) that the two groups have of each other. One formal approach for accomplishing this, originally described by Blake and his associates, consists of a ten-step procedure.[23]

1. A consultant external to the two groups obtains their agreement to work directly on improving intergroup relationships. (The use of an outside consultant

is highly recommended because without the moderating influence of such a neutral third party, it is almost impossible for the two groups to interact without becoming deadlocked and polarized in defensive positions.)

2. A time is set for the two groups to meet—preferably away from their normal work situations.

3. The consultant, together with the managers of the two groups, describes the purpose and objectives of the meeting—to develop better mutual relationships, explore the perceptions the groups have of each other, and formulate plans for improving the relationship. The two groups are presented the following or similar questions: "What qualities or attributes best describe our group?" "What qualities or attributes best describe the other group?" and "How do we think the other group will describe us?" Then, the two groups are encouraged to establish norms of openness for feedback and discussion.

4. The two groups are assigned to separate rooms and asked to write their answers to the three questions. Usually, an outside consultant works with each group to help the members become more open and to encourage them to develop lists that accurately reflect their perceptions, both of their own image and of the other group.

5. After completing their lists, the two groups reconvene. A representative from each group presents the written statements. Only the two representatives are allowed to speak. The primary objective at this stage is to make certain that the images, perceptions, and attitudes are presented as accurately as possible and to avoid the arguments that might arise if the two groups openly confronted each other. Questions, however, are allowed to ensure that both groups clearly understand the written lists. Justifications, accusations, or other statements are not permitted.

6. When it is clear that the two groups thoroughly understand the content of the lists, they separate again. By this point, a great number of misperceptions and discrepancies have been brought to light.

7. The task of the two groups (almost always with a consultant as a process observer) is to analyze and review the reasons for the discrepancies. The emphasis is on solving the problems and reducing the misperceptions. The actual or implicit question is not whether the perception of the other group is right or wrong but rather "How did these perceptions occur? What actions on the part of our group may have contributed to this set of perceptions?"

8. When the two groups have worked through the discrepancies, as well as the areas of common agreement, they meet to share both the identified discrepancies and their problem-solving approaches to those discrepancies. Because the primary focus is on the behavior underlying the perceptions, free, open discussion is encouraged between the two groups, and their joint aim is to develop an overall list of remaining and possible sources of friction and isolation.

9. The two groups are asked to develop specific plans of action for solving specific problems and for improving their relationships.

10. When the two groups have gone as far as possible in formulating action plans, at least one follow-up meeting is scheduled so that the groups can report on actions that have been implemented, identify any further problems that have emerged, and, where necessary, formulate additional action plans.

LARGE-GROUP INTERVENTIONS

Large-group interventions have been referred to variously as "search conferences," "open-space meetings," "open-systems planning," and "future searches."[24] They focus on issues that affect the whole organization or large segments of it, such as developing new products or services, responding to environmental change, or introducing new technology. The defining feature of large-group intervention is the bringing together large numbers of organization members and other stakeholders, often more than one hundred, for a two- to four-day meeting or conference. Here, conference attendees work together to identify and resolve organizationwide problems, to design new approaches to structuring and managing the firm, or to propose future directions for the organization.

Large-group interventions can vary on several dimensions, including purpose, size, length, structure, and number. The purpose of these change methods can range from solving particular organizational problems to envisioning future strategic directions. Large-group interventions have been run with groups of less than fifty to more than two thousand participants and have lasted between one and five days. Some large-group processes are relatively planned and structured; others are more informal.[25] Some interventions involve a single large-group meeting; others include a succession of meetings to accomplish systemwide change in a short period of time.[26]

Application Stages

Conducting a large-group intervention generally involves preparing for the meeting, conducting it, and following up on outcomes. These activities are described below.

Preparing for the Large-Group Meeting

A design team comprising OD practitioners and several organization members is formed to organize the event. The team generally addresses three key ingredients for successful large-group meetings: a compelling meeting theme, appropriate participants, and relevant tasks to address the theme.

1. *Compelling meeting theme.* Large-group interventions require a compelling reason or focal point for change. Although "people problems" can be an important focus, more powerful reasons for large-group efforts include managing impending mergers or reorganizations, responding to environmental threats and opportunities, or proposing radical organizational changes.[27] Whatever the focal point for change, senior leaders need to make clear to others the purpose of the large-group meeting. Ambiguity about the reason for the intervention can dissipate participants' energy and commitment to change. For example, a large-group meeting that successfully envisioned a hospital's future organization design was viewed as a failure by a few key managers who thought that the purpose was to cut costs from the hospital's budget. Their subsequent lack of support stalled the change effort.

2. *Appropriate participants.* A fundamental goal of large-group interventions is to "get the whole system in the room." This involves inviting as many people as possible who have a stake in the conference theme and who are energized and committed to conceiving and initiating change. Senior managers, suppliers, union leaders, internal and external customers, trade group representatives,

government and regulatory officials, and organization members from a variety of jobs, genders, races, and ages are potential participants.

3. *Relevant tasks to address the conference theme.* As described below, these tasks typically are assigned to several subgroups responsible for examining the theme and drawing conclusions for action. Generally, participants rely on their own experience and expertise to address systemwide issues, rather than drawing on resources from outside of the large-group meeting. This ensures that the meeting can be completed within the allotted time and that members can participate fully as important sources of information.

Conducting the Meeting

The flow of events in a large-group meeting can vary greatly, depending on its purpose and the framework adopted. Most large-group processes, however, fit within two primary frameworks: open-systems methods and open-space methods.

Open-Systems Methods. A variety of large-group approaches, such as search conferences, open-systems planning, and real-time strategic change, have their basis in open-systems methods. These approaches help organizations assess their environments systematically and develop strategic responses to them. They help organization members develop a strategic mission for relating to the environment and influencing it in favorable directions. Open-systems methods begin with a diagnosis of the existing environment and how the organization relates to it. They proceed to develop possible future environments and action plans to bring them about.[28] These steps are described below.

1. *Map the current environment surrounding the organization.* In this step, the different domains or parts of the environment are identified and prioritized. This involves listing all external groups directly interacting with the organization, such as customers, suppliers, or government agencies, and ranking them in importance. Participants then are asked to describe each domain's expectations for the organization's behavior.

2. *Assess the organization's responses to environmental expectations.* This step asks participants to describe how the organization currently addresses the environmental expectations identified in step 1.

3. *Identify the core mission of the organization.* This step helps to identify the underlying purpose or core mission of the organization, as derived from how it responds to external demands. Attention is directed at discovering the mission as it is revealed in the organization's behavior, not as it is pronounced in the organization's official statement of purpose. This is accomplished by examining the organization and environment transactions identified in steps 1 and 2 and then assessing the values that seem to underlie those interactions. These values provide clues about the actual identity or mission of the organization.

4. *Create a realistic future scenario of environmental expectations and organization responses.* This step asks members to project the organization and its environment into the near future, assuming no real changes in the organization. It asks participants to address the question, "What will happen if the organization continues to operate as it does at present?" Participant responses are combined to develop a likely organization future under the assumption of no change.

5. *Create an ideal future scenario of environmental expectations and organization responses.* Members are asked to create alternative, desirable futures. This

involves going back over steps 1, 2, and 3 and asking what members ideally would like to see happen in the near future in both the environment and the organization. People are encouraged to fantasize about desired futures without worrying about possible constraints.

6. *Compare the present with the ideal future and prepare an action plan for reducing the discrepancy.* This last step identifies specific actions that will move both the environment and the organization toward the desired future. Planning for appropriate interventions typically occurs in three timeframes: tomorrow, six months from now, and two years from now. Participants also decide on a follow-up schedule for sharing the flow of actions and updating the planning process.

Open-Space Methods. The second approach to large-group interventions is distinguished by its lack of formal structure. Open-space methods temporarily restructure or "self-organize" participants around interests and topics associated with the conference theme. They generally follow these steps:[29]

1. *Set the conditions for self-organizing.* In the first step, the OD practitioner or manager responsible for the large-group intervention sets the stage by announcing the theme of the session and the norms that will govern it. In addition, participants are informed that the meeting will consist of small-group discussions convened by the participants and addressing any topic they believe critical to the theme of the conference. Two sets of norms govern how open-space methods are applied, and although the norms may sound ambiguous, they are critical to establishing the conditions for a successful meeting.

   The first set of norms concerns the "Law of Two Feet." It encourages people to take responsibility for their own behavior; to go to meetings and discussions where they are learning, contributing, or in some way remaining interested. Moving from group to group is legitimized by the roles of "butterflies" and "bumblebees." Butterflies attract others into spontaneous conversations and, in fact, may never attend a formal meeting. Bumblebees go from group to group and sprinkle knowledge, information, or new ideas into different meetings.

   The second set of norms is labeled the "Four Principles." The first principle is "whoever comes is the right people." It is intended to free people to begin conversations with anyone at any time. It also signals that the quality of a conversation is what's most important, not who's involved. The second principle, "Whatever happens is the only thing that could have," infuses the group with responsibility, encourages participants to be flexible, and prepares them to be surprised. "Whenever it starts is the right time" is the third principle and is aimed at encouraging creativity and following the natural energy in the group. The final principle, "When it is over, it is over," allows people to move on and not feel like they have to meet for a certain time period or satisfy someone else's requirements.

2. *Create the agenda.* The second step in open-space interventions is to develop a road map for the remainder of the conference. This is accomplished by asking participants to describe a topic related to the conference theme that they have passion for and interest in discussing. This topic is written on a large piece of paper, announced to the group, and then posted on the community bulletin board where meeting topics and locations are displayed.[30] The person announcing the topic agrees to convene the meeting at the posted time and place. This process continues until everyone who wants to define a topic has been given

the chance to speak. The final activity in this step asks participants to sign up for as many of the sessions as they have interest in. The open-space meeting begins with the first scheduled sessions.

3. *Coordinate activity through information.* During an open-space session, there are two ways to coordinate activities. First, each morning and evening a community meeting is held to announce new topics that have emerged for which meeting dates and times have been assigned, or to share observations and learnings. Second, as the different meetings occur, the conveners produce one-page summaries of what happened, who attended, what subjects were discussed, and what recommendations or actions were proposed. Typically, this is done on computer in a room dedicated for this purpose. These summaries are posted near the community bulletin board in an area often labeled "newsroom." Participants are encouraged to visit the newsroom and become familiar with what other groups have been discussing. The summaries also can be printed and copied for conference participants.

Following up on Meeting Outcomes

Follow-up efforts are vital to implementing the action plans from large-scale interventions. These efforts involve communicating the results of the meeting to the rest of the organization, gaining wider commitment to the changes, and structuring the change process. In those cases where all the members of the organization were involved in the large-group meeting, implementation can proceed immediately according to the timetable included in the action plans.

■ SUMMARY

In this chapter, we presented human process interventions aimed at interpersonal relations, group dynamics, and organization processes. These change programs help people gain interpersonal skills, develop effective groups, address organization problems, and manage large-scale decision making. Process consultation is used not only as a way of helping groups become effective but also as a means whereby groups learn to diagnose and solve their own problems and continue to develop their competence and maturity. Important areas of activity include communications, roles of group members, difficulties with problem-solving and decision-making norms, and leadership and authority.

Team building is directed toward improving group effectiveness and the ways in which members of teams work together. These teams may be permanent or temporary, but their members have either common organizational aims or work activities. The general process of team building, like process consultation, tries to equip a group to handle its own ongoing problem solving. Selected aspects of team building include the family group diagnostic meeting and the family group team-building meeting. The organization confrontation meeting is a way of mobilizing resources for organizational problem solving and seems especially relevant for organizations undergoing stress. Large-group interventions are designed to focus the energy and attention of a "whole system" around organizational processes such as a vision, strategy, or culture. They are best used when the organization is about to begin a large-scale change effort or is facing a new situation.

■ NOTES

1. E. Schein, *Process Consultation Volume II: Lessons for Managers and Consultants* (Reading, Mass.: Addison-Wesley, 1987).

2. Ibid., pp. 5–17.

3. E. Schein, *Process Consultation Revisited* (Reading, Mass.: Addison-Wesley, 1998): 20.

4. Ibid.

5. J. Fast, *Body Language* (Philadelphia: Lippincott, M. Evans, 1970).

6. E. Schein, *Process Consultation: Its Role in Organization Development* (Reading, Mass.: Addison-Wesley, 1969): 44.

7. N. Clapp, "Work Group Norms: Leverage for Organizational Change, Theory and Application" (undated working paper, Block Petrella Weisbord, Plainfield, N.J.); R. Allen and S. Pilnick, "Confronting the Shadow Organization: How to Detect and Defeat Negative Norms," *Organizational Dynamics* (Spring 1973): 3–18.

8. Schein, *Process Consultation Revisited*, p. 147; J. Gibb, "Defensive Communication," *Journal of Communication* 11 (1961): 141–48.

9. Schein, *Process Consultation Revisited*, pp. 167–68; E. Schein, *Organization Culture and Leadership*, 2d ed. (San Francisco: Jossey-Bass, 1992).

10. Schein, *Process Consultation Volume II*, pp. 32–34.

11. T. Patten, *Organizational Development Through Team Building* (New York: John Wiley & Sons, 1981): 2; D. Stepchuck, "Strategies for Improving the Effectiveness of Geographically Distributed Work Teams" (unpublished Master's thesis, Pepperdine University, 1994).

12. J. Katzenbach and D. Smith, *The Wisdom of Teams* (Boston: Harvard Business School Press, 1993).

13. D. Ancona and D. Caldwell, "Bridging the Boundary: External Activity and Performance in Organizational Teams," *Administrative Science Quarterly* 37 (4, 1992): 634–65; S. Cohen, "Designing Effective Self-Managing Work Teams" (paper presented at the Theory Symposium on Self-Managed Work Teams, Denton, Tex., June 4–5, 1993).

14. M. Beer, "The Technology of Organization Development," in *Handbook of Industrial and Organizational Psychology*, ed. M. Dunnette (Chicago: Rand McNally, 1976): 937–93; W. French and C. Bell, *Organization Development: Behavioral Science Interventions for Organization Improvement* (Englewood Cliffs, N.J.: Prentice Hall, 1978).

15. Beer, "Technology of Organization Development," p. 37.

16. French and Bell, *Organization Development*, p. 115.

17. Beer, "Technology of Organization Development."

18. People interested in finding assistance might want to contact The Society of Professionals in Dispute Resolution (SPIDR) at http://www.spidr.org; D. Kolb and associates, *When Talk Works: Profiles of Mediators* (San Francisco: Jossey-Bass, 1994).

19. R. Walton, *Managing Conflict: Interpersonal Dialogue and Third-Party Roles*, 2d ed. (Reading, Mass.: Addison-Wesley, 1987).

20. Ibid., pp. 81–82.

21. Ibid., pp. 83–110.

22. E. Neilson, "Understanding and Managing Intergroup Conflict," in *Organizational Behavior and Administration*, eds. P. Lawrence, L. Barnes, and J. Lorsch (Homewood, Ill.: Richard D. Irwin, 1976): 291–305.

23. R. Blake, H. Shepard, and J. Mouton, *Managing Intergroup Conflict in Industry* (Houston, Tex.: Gulf, 1954).

24. Weisbord, *Productive Workplaces* (San Francisco: Jossey-Bass, 1987); M. Weisbord, *Discovering Common Ground* (San Francisco: Berrett-Koehler, 1993); Bunker and Alban, *Large Group Interventions* (San Francisco: Jossey-Bass, 1997); H. Owen, *Open Space Technology: A User's Guide* (Potomac, Md.: Abbott, 1992).

25. Owen, *Open Space Technology*.

26. D. Axelrod, "Getting Everyone Involved," *Journal of Applied Behavioral Science* 28 (1992): 499–509.

27. Weisbord, *Productive Workplaces*.

28. C. Krone, "Open Systems Redesign," in *Theory and Method in Organization Development: An Evolutionary Process*, ed. J. Adams (Arlington, Va.: NTL Institute for Applied Behavioral Science, 1974): 364–91; G. Jayaram, "Open Systems Planning," in *The Planning of Change*, 3d ed., eds. W. Bennis, K. Benne, R. Chin, and K. Corey (New York: Holt, Rinehart, & Winston, 1976): 275–83; R. Beckhard and R. Harris, *Organizational Transitions: Managing Complex Change*, 2d ed. (Reading, Mass.: Addison-Wesley, 1987); Cummings and Srivastva, *Management of Work*.

29. Bunker and Alban, *Large Group Interventions*; Owen, *Open Space Technology*.

30. Owen, *Open Space Technology*.

9. Restructuring Organizations

In this chapter, we begin to examine technostructural interventions—change programs focusing on the technology and structure of organizations. Increasing global competition and rapid technological and environmental changes are forcing organizations to restructure themselves from rigid bureaucracies to leaner, more flexible structures. These new forms of organizing are highly adaptive and cost efficient. They often result in fewer managers and employees and in streamlined work flows that break down functional barriers.

Interventions aimed at structural design include moving from more traditional ways of dividing the organization's overall work, such as functional, self-contained-unit, and matrix structures, to more integrative and flexible forms, such as process-based and network-based structures. Diagnostic guidelines help determine which structure is appropriate for particular organizational environments, technologies, and conditions.

Downsizing seeks to reduce costs and bureaucracy by decreasing the size of the organization. This reduction in personnel can be accomplished through layoffs, organization redesign, and outsourcing, which involves moving functions that are not part of the organization's core competence to outside contractors. Successful downsizing is closely aligned with the organization's strategy.

Reengineering radically redesigns the organization's core work processes to give tighter linkage and coordination among the different tasks. This work-flow integration results in faster, more responsive task performance. Reengineering often is accomplished with new information technology that permits employees to control and coordinate work processes more effectively.

STRUCTURAL DESIGN

Organization structure describes how the overall work of the organization is divided into subunits and how these subunits are coordinated for task completion. It is a key feature of an organization's strategic orientation.[1] Based on a contingency perspective shown in Figure 9.1, organization structures should be designed to fit with at least five factors: the environment, organization size, technology, organization strategy, and worldwide operations. Organization effectiveness depends on the extent to which its structures are responsive to these contingencies.[2]

Organizations traditionally have structured themselves into one of three forms: functional departments that are task specialized; self-contained units that are oriented to specific products, customers, or regions; or matrix structures that combine both functional specialization and self-containment. Faced with accelerating changes in competitive environments and technologies, however, organizations increasingly have redesigned their structures into more integrative and flexible forms. These more recent innovations include process-based structures that design subunits around the organization's core work processes, and network-based structures

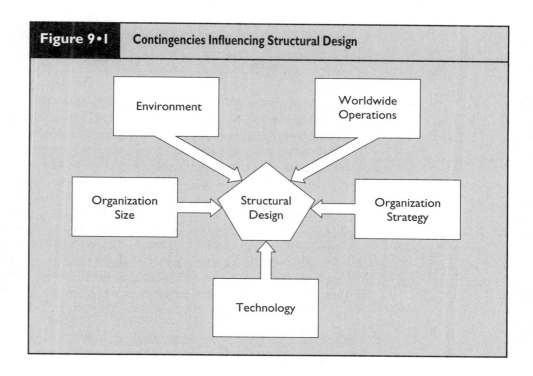

Figure 9•1   Contingencies Influencing Structural Design

that link the organization to other, interdependent organizations. The advantages, disadvantages, and contingencies of the different structures are described below.

The Functional Organization

Perhaps the most widely used organizational structure in the world today is the basic *functional structure*, depicted in Figure 9.2. The organization usually is subdivided into functional units, such as engineering, research, operations, human resources, finance, and marketing. This structure is based on early management

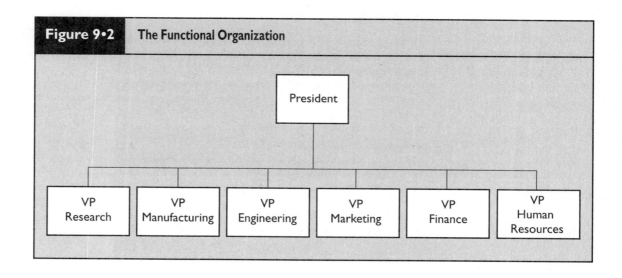

Figure 9•2   The Functional Organization

theories regarding specialization, line and staff relations, span of control, authority, and responsibility.[3] The major functional subunits are staffed by specialists in such disciplines as engineering and accounting. It is considered easier to manage specialists if they are grouped together under the same head and if the head of the department has training and experience in that particular discipline.

Table 9.1 lists the advantages and disadvantages of functional structures. On the positive side, functional structures promote specialization of skills and resources by grouping people who perform similar work and face similar problems. This grouping facilitates communication within departments and allows specialists to share their expertise. It also enhances career development within the specialty, whether it be accounting, finance, engineering, or sales. The functional structure reduces duplication of services because it makes the best use of people and resources.

On the negative side, functional structures tend to promote routine tasks with a limited orientation. Department members focus on their own tasks, rather than on the organization's total task. This can lead to conflict across functional departments when each group tries to maximize its own performance without considering the performances of other units. Coordination and scheduling among departments can be difficult when each emphasizes its own perspective. As shown in Table 9.1, the functional structure tends to work best in small- to medium-sized firms in environments that are relatively stable and certain. These organizations typically have a small number of products or services, and coordination across specialized units is

Table 9•1	Advantages, Disadvantages, and Contingencies of the Functional Form

ADVANTAGES

- Promotes skill specialization
- Reduces duplication of scarce resources and uses resources full time
- Enhances career development for specialists within large departments
- Facilitates communication and performance because superiors share expertise with their subordinates
- Exposes specialists to others within the same specialty

DISADVANTAGES

- Emphasizes routine tasks, which encourages short time horizons
- Fosters parochial perspectives by managers, which limit their capabilities for top-management positions
- Reduces communication and cooperation between departments
- Multiplies the interdepartmental dependencies, which can make coordination and scheduling difficult
- Obscures accountability for overall outcomes

CONTINGENCIES

- Stable and certain environment
- Small to medium size
- Routine technology, interdependence within functions
- Goals of efficiency and technical quality

SOURCE: Adapted by permission of the publisher from J. McCann and J. R. Galbraith, "Interdepartmental Relations," in *Handbook of Organizational Design: Remodeling Organizations and Their Environment,* eds. P. C. Nystrom and W. H. Starbuck, vol. 2 (New York: Oxford University Press, 1981): 61.

relatively easy. This structure also is best suited to routine technologies in which there is interdependence within functions, and to organizational goals emphasizing efficiency and technical quality.

The Self-Contained-Unit Organization

The *self-contained-unit structure* represents a fundamentally different way of organizing. Also known as a product or divisional structure, it was developed at about the same time by General Motors, Sears, Standard Oil of New Jersey (Exxon), and DuPont.[4] It groups organizational activities on the basis of products, services, customers, or geography. All or most of the resources necessary to accomplish a specific objective are set up as a self-contained unit headed by a product or division manager. For example, General Electric has plants that specialize in making jet engines and others that produce household appliances. Each plant manager reports to a particular division or product vice president, rather than to a manufacturing vice president. In effect, a large organization may set up smaller (sometimes temporary) special-purpose organizations, each geared to a specific product, service, customer, or region. A typical product structure is shown in Figure 9.3. It is interesting to note that the formal structure within a self-contained unit often is functional in nature.

Table 9.2 lists the advantages and disadvantages of self-contained-unit structures. These organizations recognize key interdependencies and coordinate resources toward an overall outcome. This strong outcome orientation ensures departmental accountability and promotes cohesion among those contributing to the product. These structures provide employees with opportunities for learning new skills and expanding knowledge because workers can move more easily among the different specialties contributing to the product. As a result, self-contained-unit structures are well suited for developing general managers.

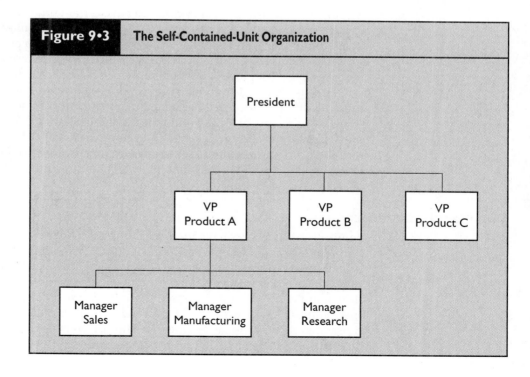

Figure 9·3   The Self-Contained-Unit Organization

Table 9•2	Advantages, Disadvantages, and Contingencies of the Self-Contained-Unit Form

ADVANTAGES

- Recognizes sources of interdepartmental dependencies
- Fosters an orientation toward overall outcomes and clients
- Allows diversification and expansion of skills and training
- Ensures accountability by departmental managers and so promotes delegation of authority and responsibility
- Heightens departmental cohesion and involvement in work

DISADVANTAGES

- May use skills and resources inefficiently
- Limits career advancement by specialists to movements out of their departments
- Impedes specialists' exposure to others within the same specialties
- Puts multiple-role demands on people and so creates stress
- May promote departmental objectives, as opposed to overall organizational objectives

CONTINGENCIES

- Unstable and uncertain environments
- Large size
- Technological interdependence across functions
- Goals of product specialization and innovation

SOURCE: Adapted by permission of the publisher from J. McCann and J. R. Galbraith, "Interdepartmental Relations," in *Handbook of Organizational Design: Remodeling Organizations and Their Environment,* eds. P. C. Nystrom and W. H. Starbuck, vol. 2 (New York: Oxford University Press, 1981): 61.

Self-contained-unit organizations do have certain problems. They may not have enough specialized work to use people's skills and abilities fully. Specialists may feel isolated from their professional colleagues and may fail to advance in their career specialty. The structures may promote allegiance to department rather than organization objectives. They also place multiple demands on people, thereby creating stress.

The self-contained-unit structure works best in conditions almost the opposite of those favoring a functional organization, as shown in Table 9.2. The organization needs to be relatively large to support the duplication of resources assigned to the units. Because each unit is designed to fit a particular niche, the structure adapts well to uncertain conditions. Self-contained units also help coordinate technical interdependencies falling across functions and are suited to goals promoting product or service specialization and innovation.

The Matrix Organization

Some OD practitioners have focused on maximizing the strengths and minimizing the weaknesses of both the functional and the self-contained-unit structures, and this effort has resulted in the *matrix organization.*[5] It superimposes the lateral structure of a product or project coordinator on the vertical functional structure, as shown in Figure 9.4. Matrix organizational designs originally evolved in the aerospace industry, where changing customer demands and technological conditions caused managers to focus on lateral relationships between functions to develop a flexible and adaptable system of resources and procedures, and to achieve a series of project objectives. Matrix organizations now are used widely in manufacturing, service, nonprofit, governmental, and professional organizations.[6]

Every matrix organization contains three unique and critical roles: the top manager, who heads and balances the dual chains of command; the matrix bosses (functional, product, or area), who share subordinates; and the two-boss managers, who report to two different matrix bosses. Each of these roles has its own unique requirements. For example, functional matrix bosses are expected to maximize their respective technical expertise within constraints posed by market realities. Two-boss managers, however, must accomplish work within the demands of supervisors who want to achieve technical sophistication on the one hand, and to meet customer expectations on the other. Thus, a matrix organization has more than its matrix structure. It also must be reinforced by matrix processes, such as performance management systems that get input from both functional and project bosses, by matrix leadership behavior that operates comfortably with lateral decision making, and by a matrix culture that fosters open conflict management and a balance of power.[7]

Matrix organizations, like all organization structures, have both advantages and disadvantages, as shown in Table 9.3. On the positive side, this structure allows multiple orientations. Specialized, functional knowledge can be applied to all projects. New products or projects can be implemented quickly by using people flexibly and by moving between product and functional orientations as circumstances demand.

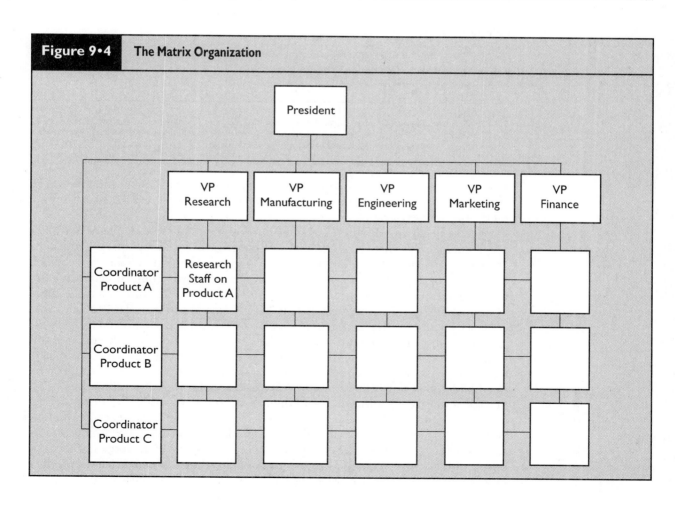

Figure 9•4   The Matrix Organization

Table 9•3	Advantages, Disadvantages, and Contingencies of the Matrix Form

ADVANTAGES

- Makes specialized, functional knowledge available to all projects
- Uses people flexibly, because departments maintain reservoirs of specialists
- Maintains consistency between different departments and projects by forcing communication between managers
- Recognizes and provides mechanisms for dealing with legitimate, multiple sources of power in the organization
- Can adapt to environmental changes by shifting emphasis between project and functional aspects

DISADVANTAGES

- Can be very difficult to introduce without a preexisting supportive management climate
- Increases role ambiguity, stress, and anxiety by assigning people to more than one department
- Without power balancing between product and functional forms, lowers overall performance
- Makes inconsistent demands, which may result in unproductive conflicts and short-term crisis management
- May reward political skills as opposed to technical skills

CONTINGENCIES

- Dual focus on unique product demands and technical specialization
- Pressure for high information processing capacity
- Pressure for shared resources

SOURCE: Adapted by permission of the publisher from J. McCann and J. R. Galbraith, "Interdepartmental Relations," in *Handbook of Organizational Design: Remodeling Organizations and Their Environment*, eds. P. C. Nystrom and W. H. Starbuck, vol. 2 (New York: Oxford University Press, 1981): 61.

Matrix organizations can maintain consistency among departments and projects by requiring communication among managers. For many people, matrix structures are motivating and exciting.

On the negative side, these organizations can be difficult to manage. To implement and maintain them requires heavy managerial costs and support. When people are assigned to more than one department, there may be role ambiguity and conflict, and overall performance may be sacrificed if there are power conflicts between functional departments and project structures. To make matrix organizations work, organization members need interpersonal and conflict management skills. People can get confused about how the matrix works, and that can lead to chaos and inefficiencies.

As shown in Table 9.3, matrix structures are appropriate under three important conditions.[8] First, there must be outside pressures for a dual focus. That is, a matrix structure works best when there are many customers with unique demands on the one hand and strong requirements for technical sophistication on the other hand. Second, a matrix organization is appropriate when the organization must process a large amount of information. Circumstances requiring such capacity are few and include the following: when external environmental demands change unpredictably and there is considerable uncertainty in decision making; when the organization produces a broad range of products or services, or offers those outputs to a large number of different markets, and there is considerable complexity in decision making; and when there is reciprocal interdependence among the tasks in the organization's technical core and there is considerable pressure on communication and coordination systems. Third, and finally, there must be pressures for shared resources. When customer demands vary greatly and technological requirements are strict, valuable human and physical resources are likely to be scarce. The matrix works well under those conditions because it facilitates the sharing of scarce resources. If any of the foregoing conditions are not met, a matrix organization is likely to fail.

Process-Based Structures

A radically new logic for structuring organizations is to form multidisciplinary teams around core processes, such as product development, order fulfillment, sales generation, and customer support.[9] As shown in Figure 9.5, *process-based structures* emphasize lateral rather than vertical relationships.[10] All functions necessary to produce a product or service are placed in a common unit usually managed by someone called a "process owner." There are few hierarchical levels, and the senior executive team is relatively small, typically consisting of the chair, the chief operating officer, and the heads of a few key support services such as strategic planning, human resources, and finance.

Process-based structures eliminate many of the hierarchical and departmental boundaries that can impede task coordination and slow decision making and task performance. They reduce the enormous costs of managing across departments and up and down the hierarchy. Process-based structures enable organizations to focus most of their resources on serving customers, both inside and outside the firm.

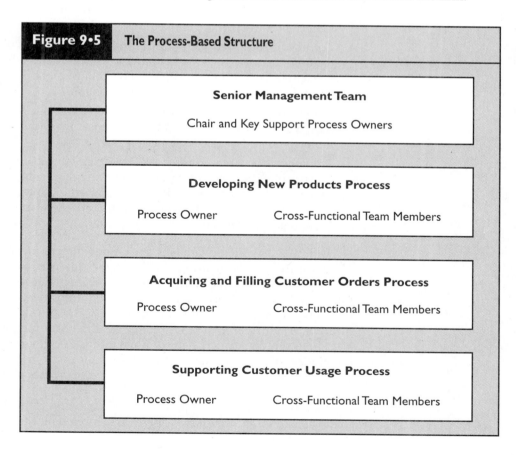

Figure 9•5   The Process-Based Structure

Senior Management Team

Chair and Key Support Process Owners

Developing New Products Process

Process Owner   Cross-Functional Team Members

Acquiring and Filling Customer Orders Process

Process Owner   Cross-Functional Team Members

Supporting Customer Usage Process

Process Owner   Cross-Functional Team Members

The use of process-based structures is growing rapidly in a variety of manufacturing and service companies. Typically referred to as "horizontal," "boundaryless," or "team-based" organizations, they are used to enhance customer service at such firms as American Express Financial Advisors, The Associates, Duke Power, 3M, Xerox, General Electric Capital Services, and the National & Provincial Building Society in the United Kingdom. Although there is no one right way to design process-based structures, the following features characterize this new form of organizing.[11]

- *Processes drive structure.* Process-based structures are organized around the three to five key processes that define the work of the organization. Rather than products or functions, processes define the structure and are governed by a "process owner." Each process has clear performance goals that drive task execution.
- *Work adds value.* To increase efficiency, process-based structures simplify and enrich work processes. Work is simplified by eliminating nonessential tasks and reducing layers of management, and it is enriched by combining tasks so that teams perform whole processes.
- *Teams are fundamental.* Teams are the key organizing feature in a process-based structure. They manage everything from task execution to strategic planning, are typically self-managing, and are responsible for goal achievement.
- *Customers define performance.* The primary goal of any team in a process-based structure is customer satisfaction. Defining customer expectations and designing team functions to meet those expectations command much of the team's attention. The organization must value this orientation as the primary path to financial performance.
- *Teams are rewarded for performance.* Appraisal systems focus on measuring team performance against customer satisfaction and other goals, and then provide real recognition for achievement. Team-based rewards are given as much, if not more, weight than is individual recognition.
- *Teams are tightly linked to suppliers and customers.* Through designated members, teams have timely and direct relationships with vendors and customers to understand and respond to emerging concerns.
- *Team members are well informed and trained.* Successful implementation of a process-based structure requires team members who can work with a broad range of information, including customer and market data, financial information, and personnel and policy matters. Team members also need problem-solving and decision-making skills and abilities to address and implement solutions.

Table 9.4 lists the advantages and disadvantages of process-based structures. The most frequently mentioned advantage is intense focus on meeting customer needs, which can result in dramatic improvements in speed, efficiency, and customer satisfaction. Process-based structures remove layers of management, and consequently information flows more quickly and accurately throughout the organization. Because process teams comprise different functional specialties, boundaries between departments are removed, thus affording organization members a broad view of the work flow and a clear line of sight between team performance and organization effectiveness. Process-based structures also are more flexible and adaptable to change than are traditional structures.

A major disadvantage of process-based structures is the difficulty of changing to this new organizational form. These structures typically require radical shifts in

Table 9•4	Advantages, Disadvantages, and Contingencies of the Process-Based Form

ADVANTAGES

- Focuses resources on customer satisfaction
- Improves speed and efficiency, often dramatically
- Adapts to environmental change rapidly
- Reduces boundaries between departments
- Increases ability to see total work flow
- Enhances employee involvement
- Lowers costs because of less overhead structure

DISADVANTAGES

- Can threaten middle managers and staff specialists
- Requires changes in command-and-control mindsets
- Duplicates scarce resources
- Requires new skills and knowledge to manage lateral relationships and teams
- May take longer to make decisions in teams
- Can be ineffective if wrong processes are identified

CONTINGENCIES

- Uncertain and changing environments
- Moderate to large size
- Nonroutine and highly interdependent technologies
- Customer-oriented goals

mindsets, skills, and managerial roles—changes that involve considerable time and resources and can be resisted by functional managers and staff specialists. Moreover, process-based structures may result in expensive duplication of scarce resources and, if teams are not skilled adequately, in slower decision making as they struggle to define and reach consensus. Finally, implementing process-based structures relies on properly identifying key processes needed to satisfy customer needs. If critical processes are misidentified or ignored altogether, performance and customer satisfaction are likely to suffer.

Table 9.4 shows that process-based structures are particularly appropriate for highly uncertain environments where customer demands and market conditions are changing rapidly. They enable organizations to manage nonroutine technologies and coordinate work flows that are highly interdependent. Process-based structures generally appear in medium- to large-sized organizations having several products or projects. They focus heavily on customer-oriented goals and are found in both domestic and global organizations.

Network-Based Structures

A *network-based structure* manages the diverse, complex, and dynamic relationships among multiple organizations or units, each specializing in a particular business function or task.[12] Some confusion over the definition of a network has been clarified recently by a typology describing four basic types of networks.[13]

- An *internal market network* exists when a single organization establishes each subunit as an independent profit center that is allowed to buy and sell services and resources from each other as well as from the external market. Asea Brown Boveri's (ABB) fifty worldwide businesses consist of twelve hundred companies organized into forty-five hundred profit centers that conduct business with each other.

- A *vertical market network* is composed of multiple organizations linked to a focal organization that coordinates the movement of resources from raw materials to end consumer. Nike, for example, has its shoes manufactured in different plants and then organizes their distribution through retail outlets.

- An *intermarket network* represents alliances among a variety of organizations in different markets and is exemplified by the Japanese *keiretsu* and the Korean *chaebol*.

- An *opportunity network* is the most advanced form of network structure. It is a temporary constellation of organizations brought together to pursue a single purpose. Once accomplished, the network disbands.

These types of networks can be distinguished from one another in terms of whether they are single or multiple organizations, single or multiple industry, and stable or temporary.[14] For example, an internal market network is a stable, single-organization, single-industry structure; an opportunity network is a temporary, multiple-organization structure that can span several different industries.

As shown in Figure 9.6, the network structure redraws organizational boundaries and links separate business units to facilitate task interaction. The essence of networks is the relationships among organizations that perform different aspects of work. In this way, organizations do the things that they do well; for example, manufacturing expertise is applied to production, and logistical expertise is applied to distribution. Network organizations use strategic alliances, joint ventures, research and development consortia, licensing agreements, and wholly owned subsidiaries to design, manufacture, and market advanced products, enter new international markets, and develop new technologies.

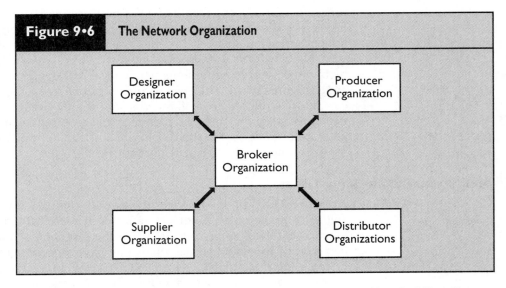

Figure 9•6   The Network Organization

Network-based structures are known by a variety of names, including sham-rock organizations and virtual, modular, or cellular corporations.[15] Less formally, they have been described as "pizza" structures, spiderwebs, starbursts, and cluster organizations. Companies such as Apple Computer, Benetton, Sun Microsystems, Liz Claiborne, MCI WorldCom, and Merck have implemented fairly sophisticated vertical market and intermarket network structures. Opportunity networks also are commonplace in the construction, fashion, and entertainment industries, as well as in the public sector.[16]

Network structures typically have the following characteristics.

- **Vertical disaggregation.** This refers to the breaking up of the organization's busi-ness functions, such as production, marketing, and distribution, into separate or-ganizations performing specialized work. In the film industry, for example, separate organizations providing transportation, cinematography, special effects, set design, music, actors, and catering all work together under a broker organiza-tion, the studio. The particular organizations making up the opportunity net-work represent an important factor in determining its success.[17] More recently, disintermediation, or the replacement of whole steps in the value chain by infor-mation technology, specifically the Internet, has fueled the development and numbers of network structures.

- **Brokers.** Networks often are managed by broker organizations that locate and assemble member organizations. The broker may play a central role and sub-contract for needed products or services, or it may specialize in linking equal partners into a network. In the construction industry, the general contractor typically assembles and manages drywall, mechanical, electrical, plumbing, and other specialties to erect a building.

- **Coordinating mechanisms.** Network organizations generally are not controlled by hierarchical arrangements or plans. Rather, coordination of the work in a network falls into three categories: informal relationships, contracts, and mar-ket mechanisms. First, coordination patterns can depend heavily on interper-sonal relationships among individuals who have a well-developed partnership. Conflicts are resolved through reciprocity; network members recognize that each likely will have to compromise at some point. Trust is built and nurtured over time by these reciprocal arrangements. Second, coordination can be achieved through formal contracts, such as ownership control, licensing arrangements, or purchase agreements. Finally, market mechanisms, such as spot payments, performance accountability, and information systems, ensure that all parties are aware of each others' activities.

Network structures have a number of advantages and disadvantages, as shown in Table 9.5.[18] They are highly flexible and adaptable to changing conditions. The ability to form partnerships with different organizations permits the creation of a "best-of-the-best" company to exploit opportunities, often global in nature. They enable each member to exploit its distinctive competence. They can accumulate and apply sufficient resources and expertise to large, complex tasks that single or-ganizations cannot perform. Perhaps most important, network organizations can have synergistic effects whereby members build on each other's strengths and com-petencies, creating a whole that exceeds the sum of its parts.

The major problems with network organizations are in managing such complex structures. Galbraith and Kazanjian describe network structures as matrix organi-zations extending beyond the boundaries of single firms but lacking the ability to

Table 9·5	Advantages, Disadvantages, and Contingencies of the Network-Based Form

ADVANTAGES

- Enables highly flexible and adaptive response to dynamic environments
- Creates a "best-of-the-best" organization to focus resources on customer and market needs
- Enables each organization to leverage a distinctive competency
- Permits rapid global expansion
- Can produce synergistic results

DISADVANTAGES

- Managing lateral relations across autonomous organizations is difficult
- Motivating members to relinquish autonomy to join the network is troublesome
- Sustaining membership and benefits can be problematic
- May give partners access to proprietary knowledge/technology

CONTINGENCIES

- Highly complex and uncertain environments
- Organizations of all sizes
- Goals of organizational specialization and innovation
- Highly uncertain technologies
- Worldwide operations

appeal to a higher authority to resolve conflicts.[19] Thus, matrix skills of managing lateral relations across organizational boundaries are critical to administering network structures. Most organizations, because they are managed hierarchically, can be expected to have difficulties managing lateral relations. Other disadvantages of network organizations include the difficulties of motivating organizations to join such structures and of sustaining commitment over time. Potential members may not want to give up their autonomy to link with other organizations and, once linked, they may have problems sustaining the benefits of joining together. This is especially true if the network consists of organizations that are not the "best of breed." Finally, joining a network may expose the organization's proprietary knowledge and skills to others.

As shown in Table 9.5, network organizations are best suited to highly complex and uncertain environments where multiple competencies and flexible responses are needed. They seem to apply to organizations of all sizes, and they deal with complex tasks or problems involving high interdependencies across organizations. Network structures fit with goals that emphasize organization specialization and innovation. They also fit well in organizations with worldwide operations.

DOWNSIZING

Downsizing refers to interventions aimed at reducing the size of the organization.[20] This typically is accomplished by decreasing the number of employees through layoffs, attrition, redeployment, or early retirement or by reducing the number of organizational units or managerial levels through divestiture, outsourcing, reorganization, or delayering. In practice, downsizing generally involves layoffs whereby a certain number or class of organization members is no longer employed by the organization. Although traditionally associated with lower-level workers, downsizing increasingly has claimed the jobs of staff specialists, middle managers, and senior executives.

An important consequence of downsizing has been the rise of the contingent workforce. These less expensive temporary or permanent part-time workers often are hired by the organizations that just laid off thousands of employees. A study by the American Management Association found that nearly a third of the 720 firms in the sample had rehired recently terminated employees as independent contractors or consultants because the downsizings had not been matched by an appropriate reduction in or redesign of the workload.[21] Overall cost reduction was achieved by replacing expensive permanent workers with a contingent workforce.

Over the past decade, most major U.S. corporations and government agencies have engaged in downsizing activities. For example, a study of more than thirty-five hundred companies found that 59 percent had fired at least 5 percent of their workers at least once between 1980 and 1994, and one-third of those companies downsized more than 15 percent of their workforce at least once.[22] In addition, 650,000 people were laid off in 1998, and more than 207,000 layoffs were announced in the first four months of 1999.[23] Other organizations have downsized through redeploying workers from one function or job to another. For example, AT&T, IBM, Boeing, Sears, and Xerox cut nearly a quarter-million jobs in 1993 and hired more than 63,000 in 1996.[24] Similarly, in 1996 IBM laid off more than 69,000 people but increased its workforce by 16,000 that same year as its demand was shifting from hardware to software and services.[25]

Downsizing is generally a response to at least four major conditions. First, it is associated increasingly with mergers and acquisitions. One in nine job cuts during 1998 were the result of the integration of two organizations.[26] Second, it can result from organization decline caused by loss of revenues and market share and by technological and industrial change. In southern California, an economy traditionally dependent on the defense industry, more than one hundred thousand jobs have been lost to relocation or elimination as that industry has contracted and consolidated. Third, downsizing can occur when organizations implement one of the new organizational structures described above. For example, creation of network-based structures often involves outsourcing to other firms work that is not essential to the organization's core competence. Fourth, downsizing can result from beliefs and social pressures that smaller is better.[27] In the United States, there is strong conviction that organizations should be leaner and more flexible. Hamel and Prahalad warned, however, that organizations must be careful that downsizing is not a symptom of "corporate anorexia."[28] Organizations may downsize for their own sake and not think about future growth. They may lose key employees who are necessary for future success, cutting into the organization's core competencies and leaving a legacy of mistrust among members. In such situations, it is questionable whether downsizing is developmental as defined in OD.

Application Stages

Successful downsizing interventions tend to proceed by the following steps:[29]

1. *Clarify the organization's strategy.* As a first step, organization leaders specify corporate strategy and communicate clearly how downsizing relates to it. They seek to inform members that downsizing is not a goal in itself, but a restructuring process for achieving strategic objectives. Leaders need to provide visible and consistent support throughout the process. They can provide opportunities

for members to voice their concerns, ask questions, and obtain counseling if necessary.

2. ***Assess downsizing options and make relevant choices.*** Once corporate strategy is clear, the full range of downsizing options can be identified and assessed. Table 9.6 describes three primary downsizing methods: workforce reduction, organization redesign, and systemic change. A specific downsizing strategy may use elements of all three approaches. *Workforce reduction* is aimed at reducing the number of employees, usually in a relatively short timeframe. It can include attrition, retirement incentives, outplacement services, and layoffs. *Organization redesign* attempts to restructure the firm to prepare it for the next stage of growth. This is a medium-term approach that can be accomplished by merging organizational units, eliminating management layers, and redesigning tasks. *Systemic change* is a longer-term option aimed at changing the culture and strategic orientation of the organization. It can involve interventions that alter the responsibilities and work behaviors of everyone in the organization and that promote continual improvement as a way of life in the firm.

Case, a manufacturer of heavy construction equipment, used a variety of methods to downsize, including eliminating money-losing product lines; narrowing the breadth of remaining product lines; bringing customers to the company headquarters to get their opinions of new product design (which surprisingly resulted in maintaining, rather than changing, certain preferred features, thus holding down redesign costs); shifting production to outside vendors; restructuring debt; and spinning off most of its 250 stores. Eventually, these changes led to closing five plants and to payroll reductions of almost 35

Table 9•6	Three Downsizing Tactics	
DOWNSIZING TACTIC	**CHARACTERISTICS**	**EXAMPLES**
Workforce reduction	Aimed at headcount reduction Short-term implementation Fosters a transition	Attrition Transfer and outplacement Retirement incentives Buyout packages Layoffs
Organization redesign	Aimed at organization change Moderate-term implementation Fosters transition and, potentially, transformation	Eliminate functions Merge units Eliminate layers Eliminate products Redesign tasks
Systemic redesign	Aimed at culture change Long-term implementation Fosters transformation	Change responsibility Involve all constituents Foster continuous improvement and innovation Simplification Downsizing: a way of life

SOURCE: K. Cameron, S. Freeman, and A. Mishra, "Best Practices in White-Collar Downsizing: Managing Contradictions," *Academy of Management Executive* 5 (1991): 62.

percent.[30] The number of jobs lost would have been much greater, however, if Case had not implemented a variety of downsizing methods.

Unfortunately, organizations often choose obvious solutions for downsizing, such as layoffs, because they can be implemented quickly. This action produces a climate of fear and defensiveness as members focus on identifying who will be separated from the organization. Examining a broad range of options and considering the entire organization rather than only certain areas can help allay fears that favoritism and politics are the bases for downsizing decisions. Moreover, participation of organization members in such decisions can have positive benefits. It can create a sense of urgency for identifying and implementing options to downsizing other than layoffs. Participation can provide members with a clearer understanding of how downsizing will proceed and can increase the likelihood that whatever choices are made are perceived as reasonable and fair.

3. *Implement the changes.* This stage involves implementing methods for reducing the size of the organization. Several practices characterize successful implementation. First, downsizing is best controlled from the top down. Many difficult decisions are required, and a broad perspective helps to overcome people's natural instincts to protect their enterprise or function. Second, identify and target specific areas of inefficiency and high cost. The morale of the organization can be hurt if areas commonly known to be redundant are left untouched. Third, link specific actions to the organization's strategy. Organization members need to be reminded consistently that restructuring activities are part of a plan to improve the organization's performance. Finally, communicate frequently using a variety of media. This keeps people informed, lowers their anxiety over the process, and makes it easier for them to focus on their work.

4. *Address the needs of survivors and those who leave.* Most downsizing eventually involves reduction in the size of the workforce, and it is important to support not only employees who remain with the organization but also those who leave. When layoffs occur, employees are generally asked to take on additional responsibilities and to learn new jobs, often with little or no increase in compensation. This added workload can be stressful, and when combined with anxiety over past layoffs and possible future ones, it can lead to what researchers have labeled the "survivor syndrome."[31] This syndrome involves a narrow set of self-absorbed and risk-averse behaviors that can threaten the organization's survival. Rather than working to ensure the organization's success, survivors often are preoccupied with whether additional layoffs will occur, with guilt over receiving pay and benefits while co-workers are struggling with termination, and with the uncertainty of career advancement.

Organizations can address these survivor concerns with communication processes that increase the amount and frequency of information provided. Communication should shift from explanations about who left or why to clarification of where the company is going, including its visions, strategies, and goals. The linkage between employees' performance and strategic success is emphasized so that remaining members feel they are valued. Organizations also can support survivors through training and development activities that prepare them for the new work they are being asked to perform. Senior management can promote greater involvement in decision making, thus reinforcing the message that people are important to the future success and growth of the organization.

Given the negative consequences typically associated with job loss, organizations have developed an array of methods to help employees who have been laid off. These include outplacement counseling, personal and family counseling, severance packages, office support for job searches, relocation services, and job retraining. Each service is intended to assist employees in their transition to another work situation.

5. ***Follow through with growth plans.*** This final stage of downsizing involves implementing an organization renewal and growth process. Failure to move quickly to implement growth plans is a key determinate of ineffective downsizing.[32] For example, a study of 1,020 human resource directors reported that only 44 percent of the companies that had downsized in the previous five years shared details of their growth plans with employees; only 34 percent told employees how they would fit into the company's new strategy.[33] Organizations must ensure that employees understand the renewal strategy and their new roles in it. Employees need credible expectations that, although the organization has been through a tough period, their renewed efforts can move it forward.

REENGINEERING

The final restructuring intervention is *reengineering*—the fundamental rethinking and radical redesign of business processes to achieve dramatic improvements in performance.[34] Reengineering transforms how organizations traditionally produce and deliver goods and services. Beginning with the Industrial Revolution, organizations have increasingly fragmented work into specialized units, each focusing on a limited part of the overall production process. Although this division of labor has enabled organizations to mass-produce standardized products and services efficiently, it can be overly complicated, difficult to manage, and slow to respond to the rapid and unpredictable changes experienced by many organizations today. Reengineering addresses these problems by breaking down specialized work units into more integrated, cross-functional work processes. This streamlines work processes and makes them faster and more flexible; consequently, they are more responsive to changes in competitive conditions, customer demands, product life cycles, and technologies.[35]

As might be expected, reengineering requires an almost revolutionary change in how organizations design their structures and their work. It addresses fundamental issues about why organizations do what they do, and why do they do it in a particular way. Reengineering identifies and questions the often unexamined assumptions underlying how organizations perform work. This effort typically results in radical changes in thinking and work methods—a shift from specialized jobs, tasks, and structures to integrated processes that deliver value to customers. Such revolutionary change differs considerably from incremental approaches to performance improvement, such as continuous improvement and total quality management (Chapter 10), which emphasize incremental changes in existing work processes. Because reengineering radically alters the status quo, it seeks to produce dramatic increases in organization performance.

In radically changing business processes, reengineering frequently takes advantage of new information technology. Modern information technologies, such as teleconferencing, expert systems, shared databases, and wireless communication, can enable organizations to reengineer. They can help organizations break out of traditional ways of thinking about work and embrace entirely new ways of producing and delivering products. At IBM Credit, for example, an integrated information system with expert systems technology enables one employee to handle all stages of the credit-delivery process. This eliminates the handoffs, delays, and errors that derived from the traditional work design, in which different employees performed sequential tasks.

Whereas new information technology can enable organizations to reengineer themselves, existing technology can thwart such efforts.[36] Many reengineering projects fail because existing information systems do not provide the data needed to operate integrated business processes. The systems do not allow interdependent departments to interface with each other; they often require new information to be entered by hand into separate computer systems before people in different work areas can access it. Given the inherent difficulty in trying to support process-based work with specialized information systems, organizations have sought to develop information technologies that are more suited to reengineered work. The most popular software system, SAP, was developed by a German company of the same name. With SAP, firms can standardize their information systems because the software processes data on a range of tasks and links it all together, thus integrating the information flow among different parts of the business. Because they believe that SAP may be the missing technological link to reengineering, many of the largest consulting firms that provide reengineering services, such as Andersen Consulting, Deloitte Touche, and PriceWaterhouseCoopers, have developed their own SAP consultants.

Reengineering also is associated with interventions having to do with downsizing, the shift from functional to process-based structures, and work design (Chapter 11). Although these interventions have different conceptual and applied backgrounds, they overlap considerably in practice. Reengineering can result in production and delivery processes that require fewer people and fewer layers of management. Conversely, downsizing may require subsequent reengineering interventions. When downsizing occurs without fundamental changes in how work is performed, the same tasks simply are being performed with a smaller number of people. Thus, expected cost savings may not be realized because lower productivity offsets lower salaries and fewer benefits.

Reengineering also can be linked to transformation of organization structures and work design. Its focus on work processes helps to break down the vertical orientation of functional and self-contained-unit organizations. The endeavor identifies and assesses core business processes and redesigns work to account for key task interdependencies running through them. That typically results in new jobs or teams that emphasize multifunctional tasks, results-oriented feedback, and employee empowerment—characteristics associated with motivational and sociotechnical approaches to work design. Regrettably, reengineering has failed to apply these approaches' attention to individual differences in people's reactions to work to its own work-design prescriptions. It advocates enriched work and teams, without consideration for the wealth of research that shows that not all people are motivated to perform such work.[37]

Application Stages

Reengineering is a relatively new intervention and is still developing applied methods. Early applications emphasized identifying which business processes to reengineer and technically assessing the work flow. More recent efforts have extended reengineering practice to address issues of managing change, such as how to deal with resistance to change and how to manage the transition to new work processes.[38] The following application steps are included in most reengineering efforts, although the order may change slightly from one situation to another.[39]

1. ***Prepare the organization.*** Reengineering begins with clarification and assessment of the organization's context, including its competitive environment, strategy, and objectives. This effort establishes the need for reengineering and the strategic direction that the process should follow. Changes in an organization's competitive environment can signal a need for radical change in how it does business. As preparation for reengineering at GTE Telephone Operations, for example, executives determined that although deregulation had begun with coin-operated telephones and long-distance service, it soon would spread to the local network. They concluded that this would present an enormous competitive challenge and that the old way of doing business, reinforced by years of regulatory protection, would seriously saddle the organization with high costs.[40]

2. ***Specify organization strategy and objectives.*** The business strategy determines the focus of reengineering and guides decisions about the business processes that are essential for strategic success. In the absence of such information, the organization may reengineer extraneous processes or ones that could be outsourced. GTE executives recognized that the keys to the firm's success in a more competitive environment were low costs and customer satisfaction. Consequently, they set dramatic goals of doubling revenues while halving costs and reducing product development time by 75 percent. Defining these objectives gave the reengineering effort a clear focus.

   A final task in this preparation step is to communicate clearly throughout the organization why reengineering is necessary and the direction it will take. GTE's communications program lasted a year and a half, and helped ensure that members understood the reasons underlying the program and the magnitude of the changes to be made. Senior executives were careful to communicate, both verbally and behaviorally, that they were fully committed to the change effort. Demonstration of such unwavering support seems necessary if organization members are to challenge their traditional thinking about how business should be conducted.

3. ***Fundamentally rethink the way work gets done.*** This step lies at the heart of reengineering and involves these activities: identifying and analyzing core business processes, defining their key performance objectives, and designing new processes. These tasks are the real work of reengineering and typically are performed by a cross-functional team who is given considerable time and resources to accomplish them.[41]

   a. ***Identify and analyze core business processes.*** Core processes are considered essential for strategic success. They include activities that transform inputs into valued outputs. Core processes typically are assessed through development of a process map that lists the different activities required to deliver an organization's products or services. GTE determined that its core processes could be characterized as "choose, use, and pay." Customers first choose a telephone carrier, then use its services, and pay for them. GTE developed a process map for these core processes that included the work flow for getting customers to choose, use, and pay for the firm's service.

      Analysis of core business processes can include assigning costs to each of the major phases of the work flow to help identify costs that may be hidden in the activities of the production process. Traditional cost-accounting systems do not store data in process terms; they identify costs according to categories of expense, such as salaries, fixed costs, and supplies.[42] This method of cost accounting can be misleading and can result in erroneous conclusions about how best to reduce costs. For example, the material control department at a Dana Corporation plant in Plymouth, Minnesota, changed from a traditional to a process-based accounting system.[43] The traditional accounting system showed that salaries and fringe benefits accounted for 82 percent of total costs—an assessment that suggested workforce downsizing was the most effective way to lower costs. The process-based accounting system revealed a different picture, however: it showed that 44 percent of the department's costs involved expediting, resolving, and reissuing orders from suppliers and customers. In other words, almost half of their costs were associated with reworking deficient orders.

Business processes also can be assessed in terms of value-added activities—the amount of value contributed to a product or service by a particular step in the process. For example, as part of its invoice collection process, Corky's Pest Control, a small service business dependent on a steady stream of cash payments, provides its customers with a self-addressed, stamped envelope. Although this adds an additional cost to each account, it more than pays for itself in customer loyalty and retention, and reduced accounts receivables and late payments handling. Conversely, organizations often engage in process activities that have little or no added value. For instance, in a Denver hospital an employee on each workshift checked a pump that circulated oxygen. Eight years earlier, the pump had failed and caused a death. Since that time, a new pump had been installed with fault-protection equipment and control sensors that no longer required the physical inspection. Yet because of habit, the checking process remained in place and drained resources that could be used more productively in other areas.

b. *Define performance objectives.* Challenging performance goals are set in this step. The highest possible level of performance for any particular process is identified, and dramatic goals are set for speed, quality, cost, or other measures of performance. These standards can derive from customer requirements or from benchmarks of the best practices of industry leaders. For example, at Andersen Windows, the demand for unique window shapes pushed the number of different products from 28,000 to more than 86,000 in 1991.[44] The pressure on the shop floor for a "batch of one" resulted in 20 percent of all shipments containing at least one order discrepancy. As part of its reengineering effort, Andersen set targets for ease of ordering, manufacturing, and delivery. Each retailer and distributor was sold an interactive, computerized version of its catalogue that allowed customers to design their own windows. The resulting design is then given a unique "license plate number" and the specifications are sent directly to the factory. By 1995, new sales had tripled at some retail locations, the number of products had increased to 188,000, and fewer than one in two hundred shipments had a discrepancy.

c. *Design new processes.* The last task in this third step of reengineering is to redesign current business processes to achieve breakthrough goals. It often starts with a clean sheet of paper and addresses the question "If we were starting this company today, what processes would we need to create a sustainable competitive advantage?" These essential processes are then designed according to the following guidelines:[45]

- Begin and end the process with the needs and wants of the customer.

- Simplify the current process by combining and eliminating steps.

- Use the "best of what is" in the current process.
- Attend to both technical and social aspects of the process.
- Do not be constrained by past practice.
- Identify the critical information required at each step in the process.
- Perform activities in their most natural order.
- Assume the work gets done right the first time.
- Listen to people who do the work.

An important activity that appears in many successful reengineering efforts is implementing "early wins" or "quick hits." Analysis of existing processes often reveals obvious redundancies and inefficiencies for which appropriate changes may be authorized immediately. These early successes can help generate and sustain momentum in the reengineering effort.

4. *Restructure the organization around the new business processes.* This last step in reengineering involves changing the organization's structure to support the new business processes. This endeavor typically results in the kinds of process-based structures that were described earlier in this chapter. An important element of this restructuring is implementing new information and measurement systems that reinforce a shift from measuring behaviors, such as absenteeism and grievances, to assessing outcomes, such as productivity, customer satisfaction, and cost savings. Moreover, information technology is one of the key drivers of reengineering because it can drastically reduce the cost and time associated with integrating and coordinating business processes.

Reengineered organizations typically have the following characteristics:[46]

- *Work units change from functional departments to process teams.* The Principal Financial Group's Individual Insurance Department was structured according to product lines, such as life, health, and auto insurance.[47] Following reengineering, the department organized around cross-functional presale teams aimed at developing and building customer relationships and postsale teams that maintained them.

- *Jobs change from simple tasks to multidimensional work.* The postsale team was responsible for a field-support process called licensing and contracting. Under the old structure, this was a sixteen-step effort that involved nine people in different departments and on different floors in Principal's home office. Following reengineering, the process consists of only six steps and involves only three people who are cross-trained to perform the various tasks.

- *People's roles change from controlled to empowered.* At Hallmark Circuits, the reengineering effort resulted not only in changed jobs and processes, but in increased employee involvement as well. Production teams meet twice daily to discuss problems; hiring decisions are made by a four-person team of employees; major equipment purchases are jointly determined by management and employees; and the manufacturing group plays a big role in deciding whether to bid on or take new jobs.[48]

- *The focus of performance measures and compensation shifts from activities to results.* Reengineered organizations routinely collect and report measures of customer satisfaction, operating costs, and productivity to all teams and then tie these measures to pay. In this way, teams and their members are rewarded for working smarter, not harder.

- *Organization structures change from hierarchical to flat.* As described earlier, the favored structure of the reengineered organization is process-based. Rather than having layers of management, the organization has empowered, cross-functional, and well-educated process teams that collect information, make decisions about task execution, and monitor their performance.
- *Managers change from supervisors to coaches; executives change from scorekeepers to leaders.* In process-based structures, the role of management and leadership changes drastically. A new set of skills is required, including facilitation, resource acquisition, information sharing, supporting, and problem solving.

■ SUMMARY

This chapter presented interventions aimed at restructuring organizations. Several basic structures, such as the functional structure, the self-contained unit, and the matrix configuration, dominate most organizations. Two newer forms, process-based and network-based structures, also were described. Each of these structures has corresponding strengths and weaknesses, and supportive conditions must be assessed when determining which structure is an appropriate fit with the organization's environment.

Two restructuring interventions were described: downsizing and reengineering. Downsizing decreases the size of the organization through workforce reduction or organizational redesign. It generally is associated with layoffs, whereby a certain number or class of organization members is no longer employed by the organization. Downsizing can contribute to organization development by focusing on the organization's strategy, using a variety of downsizing tactics, addressing the needs of all organization members, and following through with growth plans. Reengineering is the fundamental rethinking and radical redesign of business processes to achieve dramatic improvements in performance. It seeks to transform how organizations traditionally produce and deliver goods and services. A typical reengineering project prepares the organization, rethinks the way work gets done, and restructures the organization around the newly designed core processes.

■ NOTES

1. M. Tushman and E. Romanelli, "Organizational Evolution: A Metamorphosis Model of Convergence and Reorientation," in *Research in Organizational Behavior,* vol. 7, eds. L. Cummings and B. Staw (Greenwich, Conn.: JAI Press, 1985); C. Worley, D. Hitchin, and W. Ross, *Integrated Strategic Change* (Reading, Mass.: Addison-Wesley, 1996).

2. P. Lawrence and J. Lorsch, *Organization and Environment: Managing Differentiation and Integration* (Cambridge: Harvard Graduate School of Business, Administration Division of Research, 1967); J. R. Galbraith, *Organization Design* (Reading, Mass.: Addison-Wesley, 1977): 5.

3. L. Gulick and L. Urwick, eds., *Papers on the Science of Administration* (New York: Institute of Public Administration, Columbia University, 1937); M. Weber, *The Theory of Social and Economic Organization,* eds. A. Henderson and T. Parsons (Glencoe, Ill.: Free Press, 1947).

4. A. Chandler, *Strategy and Structure: Chapters in the History of the Industrial Enterprise* (Cambridge, Mass.: MIT Press, 1962).

5. S. Davis and P. Lawrence, *Matrix* (Reading, Mass.: Addison-Wesley, 1977); H. Kolodny, "Managing in a Matrix," *Business Horizons* 24 (March-April 1981): 17–35.

6. Davis and Lawrence, *Matrix.*

7. W. Joyce, "Matrix Organization: A Social Experiment," *Academy of Management Journal* 29 (1986): 536–61; C. Worley and C. Teplitz, "The Use of 'Expert Power' as an Emerging Influence Style within Successful U.S. Matrix Organizations," *Project Management Journal* (1993): 31–36.

8. Davis and Lawrence, *Matrix*.

9. J. Byrne, "The Horizontal Corporation," *Business Week* (20 December 1993): 76–81; S. Mohrman, S. Cohen, and A. Mohrman, *Designing Team-Based Organizations* (San Francisco: Jossey-Bass, 1995); R. Ashkenas, D. Ulrich, T. Jick, and S. Kerr, *The Boundaryless Organization* (San Francisco: Jossey-Bass, 1995).

10. J. Galbraith, E. Lawler, and associates, *Organizing for the Future: The New Logic for Managing Complex Organizations* (San Francisco: Jossey-Bass, 1993).

11. Byrne, "Horizontal Corporation."

12. W. Halal, "From Hierarchy to Enterprise: Internal Markets Are the New Foundation of Management," *Academy of Management Executive* 8, 4 (1994): 69–83; C. Snow, R. Miles, and H. Coleman Jr., "Managing 21st Century Network Organizations," *Organizational Dynamics* 20 (1992): 5–19; S. Tully, "The Modular Corporation," *Fortune* (8 February 1993): 106–14; R. Rycroft, "Managing Complex Networks: Key to 21st Century Innovation Success," *Research-Technology Management* (May-June 1999): 13–18.

13. R. Chisolm, *Developing Network Organizations: Learning from Theory and Practice* (Reading, Mass.: Addison-Wesley, 1998); R. Achrol, "Changes in the Theory of Interorganizational Relations in Marketing: Toward a Network Paradigm," *Journal of the Academy of Marketing Science* 25 (1997): 56–71.

14. C. Snow, "Twenty-First Century Organizations: Implications for a New Marketing Paradigm," *Journal of the Academy of Marketing Science* 25 (1997): 72–74.

15. W. Davidow and M. Malone, *The Virtual Corporation: Structuring and Revitalizing the Corporation of the 21st Century* (New York: Harper Business, 1992); J. Bryne, R. Brandt, and O. Port, "The Virtual Corporation," *Business Week* (8 February 1993): 98–102; Tully, "The Modular Corporation"; R. Keidel, "Rethinking Organizational Design," *Academy of Management Executive* 8 (1994): 12–30; C. Handy, *The Age of Unreason* (Cambridge, Mass.: Harvard Business School Press, 1989); R. Miles, C. Snow, J. Mathews, G. Miles, and H. Coleman, "Organizing in the Knowledge Age: Anticipating the Cellular Form," *Academy of Management Executive* 11 (1997): 7–20.

16. W. Powell, "Neither Market Nor Hierarchy: Network Forms of Organization," in *Research in Organizational Behavior*, vol. 12, eds. B. Staw and L. Cummings (Greenwich, Conn.: JAI Press, 1990): 295–336; M. Lawless and R. Moore, "Interorganizational Systems in Public Service Delivery: A New Application of the Dynamic Network Framework," *Human Relations* 42 (1989): 1167–84; M. Gerstein, "From Machine Bureaucracies to Networked Organizations: An Architectural Journey," in *Organizational Architecture*, eds. D. Nadler, M. Gerstein, R. Shaw, and associates (San Francisco: Jossey-Bass, 1992): 11–38.

17. D. Tapscott, *The Digital Economy* (New York: McGraw-Hill, 1996); Bryne, Brandt, and Port, "Virtual Corporation."

18. Bryne, Brandt, and Port, "Virtual Corporation"; G. Dess, A. Rasheed, K. McLaughlin, and R. Priem, "The New Corporate Architecture," *Academy of Management Executive* 9 (1995): 7–20.

19. J. Galbraith and R. Kazanjian, *Strategy Implementation: Structure, Systems and Process*, 2d ed. (St. Paul: West, 1986): 159–60.

20. W. Cascio, "Downsizing: What Do We Know? What Have We Learned?" *Academy of Management Executive* 7 (1993): 95–104.

21. J. Laabs, "Has Downsizing Missed its Mark?" *Workforce* (April 1999): 30–37.

22. J. Morris, W. Cascio, and C. Young, "Downsizing after All These Years: Questions and Answers about Who Did It, How Many Did It, and Who Benefited from It," *Organizational Dynamics* (Winter 1999): 78–87.

23. "Layoffs Continue, Despite the Strong Economy," *HR Focus* (1 September 1999): 5.

24. Laabs, "Has Downsizing Missed Its Mark?"

25. Ibid.

26. Ibid.

27. W. McKinley, C. Sanchez, and A. Schick, "Organizational Downsizing: Constraining, Cloning, Learning," *Academy of Management Executive* 9 (1995): 32–44.

28. G. Hamel and C. Prahalad, *Competing for the Future* (Cambridge, Mass: Harvard Business School Press, 1994).

29. K. Cameron, S. Freeman, and A. Mishra, "Best Practices in White-Collar Downsizing: Managing Contradictions," *Academy of Management Executive* 5 (1991): 57–73; K. Cameron, "Strategies for Successful Organizational Downsizing," *Human Resource Management* 33 (1994): 189–212; R. Marshall and L. Lyles, "Planning for a Restructured, Revitalized Organization," *Sloan Management Review* 35 (1994): 81–91; N. Polend, "Downsizing and Organization Development: An Opportunity Missed, but Not Lost" (unpublished senior project, The Union Institute, 1999).

30. K. Kelly, "Case Digs out from Way Under," *Business Week* (14 August 1995).

31. J. Brockner, "The Effects of Work Layoffs on Survivors: Research, Theory and Practice," in *Research in Organizational Behavior,* vol. 10, eds. B. M. Staw and L. L. Cummings (Greenwich, Conn.: JAI Press, 1989): 213–55; J. Byrne, "The Pain of Downsizing," *Business Week* (9 May 1994).

32. Marshall and Lyles, "Planning for a Restructured, Revitalized Organization."

33. J. E. Rogdon, "Lack of Communication Burdens Restructurings," *Wall Street Journal* (2 November 1992): B1.

34. M. Hammer and J. Champy, *Reengineering the Corporation* (New York: HarperCollins, 1993); T. Stewart, "Reengineering: The Hot New Managing Tool," *Fortune* (23 August 1993): 41–48; J. Champy, *Reengineering Management* (New York: HarperCollins, 1994).

35. R. Kaplan and L. Murdock, "Core Process Redesign," *McKinsey Quarterly* 2 (1991): 27–43.

36. Tapscott, *Digital Economy.*

37. J. Moosbruker and R. Loftin, "Business Process Redesign and Organizational Development: Enhancing Success by Removing the Barriers," *Journal of Applied Behavioral Science* (September 1998): 286–97.

38. M. Miller, "Customer Service Drives Reengineering Effort," *Personnel Journal* 73 (1994): 87–93.

39. Kaplan and Murdock, "Core Process Redesign"; R. Manganelli and M. Klein, *The Reengineering Handbook* (New York: AMACOM, 1994).

40. D. P. Allen and R. Nafius, "Dreaming and Doing: Reengineering GTE Telephone Operations," *Planning Review* (June-July 1993): 28–31.

41. J. Katzenbach and D. Smith, "The Rules for Managing Cross-Functional Reengineering Teams," *Planning Review* (March-April 1993): 12–13; A. Nahavandi and E. Aranda, "Restructuring Teams for the Re-Engineered Organization," *Academy of Management Executive* 8 (1994): 58–68.

42. M. O'Guin, *The Complete Guide to Activity Based Costing* (Englewood Cliffs, N.J.: Prentice Hall, 1991); H. Johnson and R. Kaplan, *Relevance Lost: The Rise and Fall of Management Accounting* (Cambridge, Mass.: Harvard Business School Press, 1987).

43. T. P. Pare, "A New Tool for Managing Costs," *Fortune* (14 June 1993): 124–29.

44. J. Martin, "Are You as Good as You Think You Are?" *Fortune* (30 September 1996): 142–52.

45. Hammer and Champy, *Reengineering the Corporation.*

46. Ibid.

47. C. Rohm, "The Principal Insures a Better Future by Reengineering Its Individual Insurance Deparment," *National Productivity Review* 12 (1992): 55–65.

48. R. Riggs, "Employees Re-Engineer Firm," *San Diego Union Tribune* (23 October 1993): C1–C2.

10

Employee Involvement

Faced with competitive demands for lower costs, higher performance, and greater flexibility, organizations are increasingly turning to employee involvement (EI) to enhance the participation, commitment, and productivity of their members. This chapter presents OD interventions aimed at moving decision making downward in the organization, closer to where the actual work takes place. This increased employee involvement can lead to quicker, more responsive decisions, continuous performance improvements, and greater employee flexibility, commitment, and satisfaction.

Employee involvement is a broad term that has been variously referred to as "empowerment," "participative management," "work design," "industrial democracy," and "quality of work life." It covers diverse approaches to gaining greater participation in relevant workplace decisions. Organizations, such as General Mills, AT&T, and Intel, have enhanced worker involvement through enriched forms of work; others, such as GTE and Ford, have increased participation by forming employee involvement teams that develop suggestions for improving productivity and quality; Southwest Airlines, Shell Oil, and Nucor Steel have sought greater participation through union–management cooperation on performance and quality-of-work-life issues; and still others, such as Texas Instruments, Solar Turbines, 3M, the IRS, and Motorola, have improved employee involvement by emphasizing participation in quality improvement approaches.

This chapter begins with a definition of EI and explains how it affects productivity. Next, three major EI applications are discussed: parallel structures, including cooperative union–management projects and quality circles; high-involvement organizations; and total quality management. Each application varies in the amount of power, information, knowledge and skills, and rewards that are moved downward through the organization (from least to greatest involvement).

DEFINITION OF EMPLOYEE INVOLVEMENT

Employee involvement seeks to increase members' input into decisions that affect organization performance and employee well-being.[1] It can be described in terms of four key elements that promote worker involvement:[2]

1. *Power.* This element of EI includes providing people with enough authority to make work-related decisions covering various issues such as work methods, task assignments, performance outcomes, customer service, and employee selection. The amount of power afforded employees can vary enormously, from simply asking them for input into decisions that managers subsequently make, to managers and workers jointly making decisions, to employees making decisions themselves.

2. *Information.* Timely access to relevant information is vital to making effective decisions. Organizations can promote EI by ensuring that the necessary information

flows freely to those with decision authority. This can include data about operating results, business plans, competitive conditions, new technologies and work methods, and ideas for organizational improvement.

3. *Knowledge and skills.* Employee involvement contributes to organizational effectiveness only to the extent that employees have the requisite skills and knowledge to make good decisions. Organizations can facilitate EI by providing training and development programs for improving members' knowledge and skills. Such learning can cover an array of expertise having to do with performing tasks, making decisions, solving problems, and understanding how the business operates.

4. *Rewards.* Because people generally do those things for which they are recognized, rewards can have a powerful effect on getting people involved in the organization. Meaningful opportunities for involvement can provide employees with internal rewards, such as feelings of self-worth and accomplishment. External rewards, such as pay and promotions, can reinforce EI when they are linked directly to performance outcomes that result from participation in decision making. (Reward systems are discussed more fully in Chapter 12.)

Those four elements—power, information, knowledge and skills, and rewards—contribute to EI success by determining how much employee participation in decision making is possible in organizations. The farther that all four elements are moved downward throughout the organization, the greater the employee involvement. Furthermore, because the four elements of EI are interdependent, they must be changed together to obtain positive results. For example, if organization members are given more power and authority to make decisions but do not have the information or knowledge and skill to make good decisions, then the value of involvement is likely to be negligible. Similarly, increasing employees' power, information, and knowledge and skills but not linking rewards to the performance consequences of changes gives members little incentive to improve organizational performance. The EI methods that will be described in this chapter vary in how much involvement is afforded employees. Parallel structures, such as union–management cooperative efforts and quality circles, are limited in the degree that the four elements of EI are moved downward in the organization; high-involvement organizations and total quality management provide far greater opportunities for involvement.

How Employee Involvement Affects Productivity

An assumption underlying much of the EI literature is that such interventions will lead to higher productivity. Although this premise has been based mainly on anecdotal evidence and a good deal of speculation, there is now a growing body of research findings to support that linkage.[3] Studies have found a consistent relationship between EI practices and such productivity measures as financial performance, customer satisfaction, labor hours, and waste rates.

Attempts to explain this positive linkage traditionally have followed the idea that giving people more involvement in work decisions raises their job satisfaction and, in turn, their productivity. There is growing evidence that this satisfaction-causes-productivity premise is too simplistic and sometimes wrong.

A more realistic explanation for how EI interventions can affect productivity is shown in Figure 10.1. EI practices, such as participation in workplace decisions,

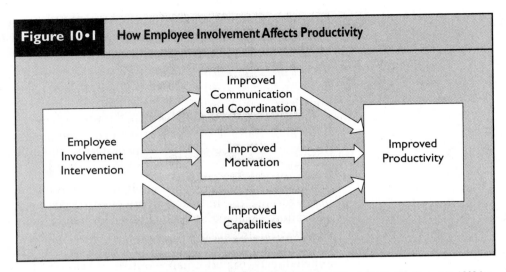

Figure 10•1 How Employee Involvement Affects Productivity

can improve productivity in at least three ways.[4] First, such interventions can improve communication and coordination among employees and organizational departments, and help integrate the different jobs or departments that contribute to an overall task.

Second, EI interventions can improve employee motivation, particularly when they satisfy important individual needs. Motivation is translated into improved performance when people have the necessary skills and knowledge to perform well and when the technology and work situation allow people to affect productivity. For example, some jobs are so rigidly controlled and specified that individual motivation can have little impact on productivity.

Third, EI practices can improve the capabilities of employees, thus enabling them to perform better. For example, attempts to increase employee participation in decision making generally include skill training in group problem solving and communication.

Figure 10.2 shows the secondary effects of EI. These practices increase employee well-being and satisfaction by providing a better work environment and a more fulfilling job. Improved productivity also can increase satisfaction, particularly when it leads to greater rewards. Increased employee satisfaction, deriving from EI interventions and increased productivity, ultimately can have a still greater impact on productivity by attracting good employees to join and remain with the organization.

In sum, EI interventions are expected to increase productivity by improving communication and coordination, employee motivation, and individual capabilities. They also can influence productivity by means of the secondary effects of increased employee well-being and satisfaction. Although a growing body of research supports these relationships,[5] there is considerable debate over the strength of the association between EI and productivity.[6] Recent data support the conclusion that relatively modest levels of EI produce moderate improvements in performance and satisfaction and that higher levels of EI produce correspondingly higher levels of performance.[7]

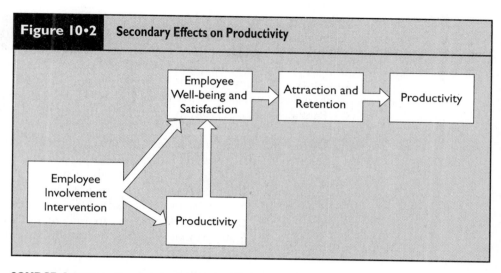

Figure 10•2 | **Secondary Effects on Productivity**

PARALLEL STRUCTURES

Parallel structures involve members in resolving ill-defined, complex problems and build adaptability into bureaucratic organizations.[8] Also known as "collateral structures," "dualistic structures," or "shadow structures,"[9] parallel structures operate in conjunction with the formal organization. They provide members with an alternative setting in which to address problems and to propose innovative solutions free from the formal organization structure and culture. Consequently, norms and procedures for working in parallel structures are entirely different from those of the formal organization.

Parallel structure interventions include cooperative union–management projects and quality circles. *Cooperative union–management projects* are one of the oldest EI applications of parallel structures. They are associated with the original quality-of-work-life (QWL) movement and its focus on workplace change, although more recent approaches have broadened that focus to include productivity improvement.[10] Their distinguishing feature is the involvement of labor unions in all phases of the intervention.

Quality circles, or "employee involvement teams" as they are often called in the United States, consist of small groups of employees who meet voluntarily to identify and solve productivity problems. Following training in group problem-solving techniques, quality circles consisting of three to fifteen members meet once each week for about one hour. At one time, they were the most popular parallel structure approach to EI, and were associated with the Japanese management trend in the 1970s and 1980s.[11]

Parallel structures fall at the lower end of the EI scale. Member participation typically is restricted to making proposals and to offering suggestions for change because subsequent decisions about implementing the proposals are reserved for management. Membership in parallel structures also tends to be limited, primarily to volunteers and to numbers of employees for which there are adequate resources. Management heavily influences the conditions under which parallel structures operate. It controls the amount of authority that members have in making recommendations, the amount of information that is shared with them, the amount of training they receive to increase their knowledge and skills, and the amount of monetary rewards for participation. Because parallel structures offer limited amounts of EI, they are most appropriate for organizations with little or no history of employee participation, top-down management styles, and bureaucratic cultures.

Parallel structures typically are implemented in the following steps:[12]

1. *Define the purpose and scope.* This first step involves defining the purpose for the parallel structure and initial expectations about how it will function. Organizational diagnosis can help clarify which specific problems and issues to address, such as productivity, absenteeism, or service quality. In addition, management training in the use of parallel structures can include discussions about the commitment and resources necessary to implement them; the openness needed to examine organizational practices, operations, and policies; and the willingness to experiment and learn.

2. *Form a steering committee.* Parallel structures typically use a steering committee composed of acknowledged leaders of the various functions and constituencies within the formal organization. This committee performs the following tasks:
   - refining the scope and purpose of the parallel structure
   - developing a vision for the effort
   - guiding the creation and implementation of the structure
   - establishing the linkage mechanisms between the parallel structure and the formal organization
   - creating problem-solving groups and activities
   - ensuring the support of senior management.

   OD practitioners can play an important role in forming the steering committee. First, they can help develop and maintain group norms of learning and innovation. These norms set the tone for problem solving throughout the parallel structure. Second, they can help the committee create a vision statement that refines the structure's purpose and promotes ownership of it. Third, they can help committee members develop and specify objectives and strategies, organizational expectations and required resources, and potential rewards for participation in the parallel structure.

3. *Communicate with organization members.* The effectiveness of a parallel structure depends on a high level of involvement from organization members, and communicating the purpose, procedures, and rewards of participation can promote that involvement. Moreover, employee participation in developing a structure's vision and purpose can increase ownership and visibly demonstrate the "new way" of working. Continued communication concerning parallel structure activities can ensure member awareness.

4. *Form employee problem-solving groups.* These groups are the primary means of accomplishing the purpose of the parallel learning structure. Their formation involves selecting and training group members, identifying problems for the groups to work on, and providing appropriate facilitation. Selecting group members is important because success often is a function of group membership.[13] Members need to represent the appropriate hierarchical levels, expertise, functions, and constituencies that are relevant to the problems at hand. This allows the parallel structure to identify and communicate with the formal structure. It also provides the necessary resources to solve the problems.

Once formed, the groups need appropriate training. This may include discussions about the vision of the parallel structure, the specific problems to be addressed, and the way those problems will be solved. As in the steering committee, group norms promoting openness, creativity, and integration need to be established.

Another key resource for parallel structures is facilitation for the problem-solving groups. Although this can be expensive, it can yield important benefits in problem-solving efficiency and quality. Group members are being asked to solve problems by cutting through traditional hierarchical and functional boundaries. Facilitators can pay special attention to processes that require disparate groups to cooperate. They can help members identify and resolve problem-solving issues within and between groups.

5. *Address the problems and issues.* Generally, groups in parallel structures solve problems by using an action research process. They diagnose specific problems, plan appropriate solutions, and implement and evaluate them. Problem solving can be facilitated when the groups and the steering committee relate effectively to each other. This permits the steering committee to direct problem-solving efforts in an appropriate manner, to acquire the necessary resources and support, and to approve action plans. It also helps ensure that the groups' solutions are linked appropriately to the formal organization. In this manner, early attempts at change will have a better chance of succeeding.

6. *Implement and evaluate the changes.* This step involves implementing appropriate organizational changes and assessing the results. Change proposals need the support of the steering committee and the formal authority structure. As changes are implemented, the organization needs information about their effects. This lets members know how successful the changes have been and if they need to be modified. In addition, feedback on changes helps the organization learn to adapt and innovate.

HIGH-INVOLVEMENT ORGANIZATIONS

Over the past several years, an increasing number of employee involvement projects have been aimed at creating high-involvement organizations (HIOs). These interventions create organizational conditions that support high levels of employee participation. What makes HIOs unique is the comprehensive nature of their design process. Unlike parallel structures that do not alter the formal organization, in HIOs almost all organization features are designed jointly by management and workers to promote high levels of involvement and performance, including structure, work design, information and control systems, physical layout, personnel policies, and reward systems.

Features of High-Involvement Organizations

High-involvement organizations are designed with features congruent with one another. For example, in HIOs employees have considerable influence over decisions. To support such a decentralized philosophy, members receive extensive training in problem-solving techniques, plant operation, and organizational policies. In addition, both operational and issue-oriented information is shared widely and is obtained easily by employees. Finally, rewards are tied closely to unit performance, as well as to knowledge and skill levels. These disparate aspects of the organization are mutually reinforcing and form a coherent pattern that contributes to employee involvement. Table 10.1 presents a list of compatible design elements characterizing HIOs,[14] and most such organizations include several if not all of the following features:

- *Flat, lean organization structures* contribute to involvement by pushing the scheduling, planning, and controlling functions typically performed by management and staff groups toward the shop floor. Similarly, minienterprise, team-based structures that are oriented to a common purpose or outcome help focus employee participation on a shared objective. Participative structures, such as work councils and union–management committees, create conditions in which workers can influence the direction and policies of the organization.

- *Job designs* that provide employees with high levels of discretion, task variety, and meaningful feedback can enhance involvement. They enable workers to influence day-to-day workplace decisions and to receive intrinsic satisfaction by performing work under enriched conditions. Self-managed teams encourage employee responsibility by providing cross-training and job rotation, which give people a chance to learn about the different functions contributing to organizational performance.

Table 10•1	Design Features for a Participative System

□ ORGANIZATIONAL STRUCTURE

1. Flat
2. Lean
3. Minienterprise-oriented
4. Team-based
5. Participative council or structure

□ JOB DESIGN

1. Individually enriched
2. Self-managing teams

□ INFORMATION SYSTEM

1. Open
2. Inclusive
3. Tied to jobs
4. Decentralized; team-based
5. Participatively set goals and standards

□ CAREER SYSTEM

1. Tracks and counseling available
2. Open job posting

□ SELECTION

1. Realistic job preview
2. Team-based
3. Potential and process-skill oriented

□ TRAINING

1. Heavy commitment
2. Peer training
3. Economic education
4. Interpersonal skills

□ REWARD SYSTEM

1. Open
2. Skill-based
3. Gain sharing or ownership
4. Flexible benefits
5. All salaried workforce
6. Egalitarian perquisites

□ PERSONNEL POLICIES

1. Stability of employment
2. Participatively established through representative group

□ PHYSICAL LAYOUT

1. Around organizational structure
2. Egalitarian
3. Safe and pleasant

SOURCE: Reproduced by permission of the publisher from Edward E. Lawler III, "Increasing Worker Involvement to Enhance Organizational Effectiveness: Design Features for a Participation System," in *Change in Organizations*, eds. P. S. Goodman and associates (San Francisco: Jossey-Bass, 1982): 298–99.

- *Open information systems* that are tied to jobs or work teams provide the necessary information for employees to participate meaningfully in decision making. Goals and standards of performance that are set participatively can provide employees with a sense of commitment and motivation for achieving those objectives.

- *Career systems* that provide different tracks for advancement and counseling to help people choose appropriate paths can help employees plan and prepare for long-term development in the organization. Open job posting, for example, makes employees aware of jobs that can further their development.

- *Selection* of employees for high-involvement organizations can be improved through a realistic job preview providing information about what it will be like to work in such situations. Team member involvement in a selection process oriented to potential and process skills of recruits can facilitate a participative climate.

- *Training* employees for the necessary knowledge and skills to participate effectively in decision making is a heavy commitment in HIOs. This effort includes education on the economic side of the enterprise, as well as interpersonal skill development. Peer training is emphasized as a valuable adjunct to formal, expert training.

- *Reward systems* can contribute to employee involvement when information about them is open and the rewards are based on acquiring new skills, as well as sharing gains from improved performance. Similarly, participation is enhanced when people can choose among different fringe benefits and when reward distinctions among people from different hierarchical levels are minimized.

- *Personnel policies* that are participatively set and encourage stability of employment provide employees with a strong sense of commitment to the organization. People feel that the policies are reasonable and that the firm is committed to their long-term development.

- *Physical layouts* of organizations also can enhance employee involvement. Physical designs that support team structures and reduce status differences among employees can reinforce the egalitarian climate needed for employee participation. Safe and pleasant working conditions provide a physical environment conducive to participation.

These HIO design features are mutually reinforcing. "They all send a message to people in the organization that says they are important, respected, valued, capable of growing, and trusted and that their understanding of and involvement in the total organization is desirable and expected."[15] Moreover, these design components tend to motivate and focus organizational behavior in a strategic direction, and thus can lead to superior effectiveness and competitive advantage, particularly in contrast to more traditionally designed organizations.[16]

Application Factors

At present, there is no universally accepted approach to implementing the high-involvement features described here. The actual implementation process often is specific to the situation, and little systematic research has been devoted to understanding the change process itself.[17] Nevertheless, at least two distinct factors seem to characterize how HIOs are implemented. First, implementation generally is guided by an explicit statement of values that members want the new organization to support. Typically, such values as teamwork, equity, quality, and empowerment guide the choice of specific design features. Values that are strongly held and widely shared by organization members can provide the energy, commitment, and direction needed to create high-involvement organizations. A second feature of the implementation process is its participative nature. Managers and employees take active roles in choosing and implementing the design features. They may be helped by OD practitioners, but the locus of control for the change process resides clearly within the organization. This participative change process is congruent with the high-involvement design being created. In essence, high-involvement design processes promote high-involvement organizations.

TOTAL QUALITY MANAGEMENT

Total quality management (TQM) is the most recent and, along with high-involvement organizations, the most comprehensive approach to employee involvement. Also known as "continuous process improvement" and "continuous quality," TQM grew out of a manufacturing emphasis on quality control and represents a long-term effort to orient all of an organization's activities around the concept of quality.[18] Quality is achieved when organizational processes reliably produce products and services that meet or exceed customer expectations. Although it is possible to implement TQM without employee involvement, member participation in the change process increases the likelihood that it will become part of the organization's culture. Quality improvement processes were popular in the 1990s, and many organizations, including Morton Salt, Weyerhaeuser, Xerox, Boeing's Airlift and Tanker Program, Motorola, and Analog Devices, incorporated TQM interventions. Today, continuous quality improvement is essential for global competitiveness.

Like high-involvement designs, TQM pushes decision-making power downward in the organization, provides relevant information to employees, ties rewards to performance, and increases workers' knowledge and skills through extensive training. When implemented successfully, TQM also is aligned closely with a firm's overall business strategy and attempts to change the entire organization toward continuous quality improvement.[19]

TQM typically is implemented in five major steps:

1. *Gain long-term senior management commitment.* This stage involves helping senior executives understand the importance of long-term commitment to TQM. Without a solid understanding of TQM and the key success factors for implementation, managers often believe that workers are solely responsible for quality. Yet only senior executives have the authority and larger perspective to address the organizationwide, cross-functional issues that hold the greatest promise for TQM's success.

    Senior managers' role in TQM implementation includes giving direction and support throughout the change process. For example, establishing organizationwide TQM generally takes three or more years, although technical improvements to the workflow can be as quick as six to eight months. The longer-term and more difficult parts of implementation, however, involve changes in the organization's support systems, such as customer service, finance, sales, and human resources. Often these systems are frozen in place by old policies and norms that can interfere with the new approach. Senior managers have to confront those practices and create new ones that support TQM and the organization's strategic orientation.

Top executives also must be willing to allocate significant resources to TQM implementation, particularly to make large investments in training. For example, as part of its Baldrige Award preparation, Motorola developed Motorola University, a training organization that teaches in twenty-seven languages. Departments at Motorola allocate at least 1.5 percent of their budgets to education, and every employee must take a minimum of forty hours of training per year. This effort supports Motorola's goals of "six sigma" quality (a statistical measure of product quality that implies 99.9997 percent perfection) and of having a workforce that is able to read, write, solve problems, and do math at the seventh-grade level or above. When several business units within Motorola achieved the six-sigma target, the company demonstrated its commitment to continuously improving quality with a new target of tenfold improvement in key goals.

Finally, senior managers need to clarify and communicate throughout the organization a totally new orientation to producing and delivering products and services. At Volvo, for example, CEO Soren Gyll says that the company's three core values—quality, environmental concern and, especially, safety—must never be compromised. Managers are challenged to create a climate "where people can use their analytical skills and their creativity to continuously improve the organization's overall effectiveness and efficiency."

2. *Train members in quality methods.* TQM implementation requires extensive training in the principles and tools of quality improvement. Depending on the organization's size and complexity, such training can be conducted in a few weeks to more than two years. Members typically learn problem-solving skills and simple *statistical process control* (SPC) techniques, usually referred to as the seven tools of quality. At Cedar-Sinai Hospital in Los Angeles, all employees take a three-day course on the applicability of brainstorming, histograms, flowcharts, scatter diagrams, Pareto charts, cause-and-effect diagrams, control charts, and other problem-solving procedures. This training is the beginning of a long-term process in continuous improvement. The knowledge gained is used to understand variations in organizational processes, to identify sources of avoidable costs, to select and prioritize quality improvement projects, and to monitor the effects of changes on product and service quality. By learning to analyze the sources of variation systematically, members can improve the reliability of product manufacturing or service delivery. For example, HCA's West Paces Ferry Hospital used TQM methods to reduce direct costs attributable to antibiotic waste.[20] It used flowcharts, fishbone diagrams, and Pareto charts to determine the major causes of unused intravenous preparations. Changes in the antibiotic delivery process resulted in reduced costs of antibiotics to the hospital of 44.5 percent and to patients of 45 percent.

3. *Start quality improvement projects.* In this phase of TQM implementation, individuals and work groups apply the quality methods to identify the few projects that hold promise for the largest improvements in organizational processes. They identify output variations, intervene to minimize deviations from quality standards, monitor improvements, and repeat this quality improvement cycle indefinitely. Identifying output variations is a key aspect of TQM. Such deviations from quality standards typically are measured by the percentage of defective products or, in the case of customer satisfaction, by on-time delivery percentages or customer survey ratings. For example, VF Corporation, a leading retail apparel firm, found that retailers were out of stock on 30 percent of their items 100 percent of the time. In response, VF revamped its systems to fill orders within twenty-four hours 95 percent of the time.

TQM is concerned not only with variations in the quality of finished products and services but also with variations in the steps of a process that produce a product or service and the levels of internal customer satisfaction. For example, Eastman Chemical Company established a patent process improvement team to enhance the relationship between scientists and lawyers in applying for patent approvals. The team, made up of inventors, lab managers, and attorneys, doubled the number of patent attorneys and relocated their offices near the labs. Attorneys now meet with scientists during the experimental phase of research to discuss ways to increase the chances of yielding a patentable product or process. Patent submissions have increased by 60 percent, and the number of patents issued to the company has doubled.[21]

Based on the measurement of output variations, each individual or work group systematically analyzes the cause of variations using SPC techniques. For example, product yields in a semiconductor manufacturing plant can go down for many reasons, including a high concentration of dust particles, small vibrations in the equipment, poor machine adjustments, and human error. Quality improvement projects often must determine which of the possible causes is most responsible, and, using that information, run experiments and pilot programs to determine which adjustments will cause output variations to drop and quality to improve. Those adjustments that do reduce variations are implemented across the board. Members continue to monitor the quality process to verify improvement and then begin the problem-solving process again for continuous improvement.

4. *Measure progress.* This stage of TQM implementation involves measuring organizational processes against quality standards. Knowing and analyzing the competition's performance are essential for any TQM effort because it sets minimum standards of cost, quality, and service and ensures the organization's position in the industry over the short run. For the longer term, such analytical efforts concentrate on identifying world-class performance, regardless of industry, and creating stretch targets, also known as *benchmarks.* Benchmarks represent the best in organizational achievements and practices for different processes and generally are accepted as "world class." For example, Alaska Airlines is considered the benchmark of customer service in the airline industry, while Disney's customer-service orientation is considered a world-class benchmark.

    The implied goal in most TQM efforts is to meet or exceed a competitor's benchmark. Alcoa's chairman, Paul H. O'Neill, charged all of the company's business units with closing the gap between Alcoa and its competitor's benchmarks by 80 percent within two years.[22] In aluminum sheet for beverage cans, for example, Japan's Kobe Steel, Ltd., was the benchmark, and Wall Street estimated that achieving O'Neill's goal would increase Alcoa's earnings by one dollar per share. The greatest leverage for change often is found in companies from unrelated industries, however. For example, Alcoa might look to Alaska Airlines or Disney to get innovative ideas about customer service. Understanding benchmarks from other industries challenges an organization's thinking about what is possible and promotes what is referred to as "out-of-the-box thinking."

5. *Rewarding accomplishment.* In this final stage of TQM implementation, the organization links rewards to improvements in quality. TQM does not monitor and reward outcomes normally tracked by traditional reward systems, such as the number of units produced. Such measures do not necessarily reflect product quality and can be difficult to replace because they are ingrained in the or-

ganization's traditional way of doing business. Rather, TQM rewards members for "process-oriented" improvements, such as increased on-time delivery, gains in customers' perceived satisfaction with product performance, and reductions in *cycle time*, the time it takes a product or service to be conceived, developed, produced, and sold. Rewards usually are designed initially to promote finding solutions to the organization's key problems. The linkage between rewards and process-oriented improvements reinforces the belief that continuous improvements, even small ones, are an important part of the new organizational culture associated with TQM. According to a survey of five hundred firms in four countries, conducted by Ernst and Young and the American Quality Foundation, more than half of the U.S. companies studied linked executive pay to improving quality and achieving benchmarks.[23]

■ SUMMARY

This chapter described employee involvement interventions. These technostructural change programs are aimed at moving organization decision making downward to improve responsiveness and performance and to increase member flexibility, commitment, and satisfaction. Different approaches to EI can be described by the extent to which power, information, knowledge and skills, and rewards are shared with employees.

The relationship between EI and productivity can be oversimplified. Productivity can be increased through improved employee communication, motivation, and skills and abilities. It also can be affected through increased worker satisfaction, which in turn results in productive employees joining and remaining with the organization.

Major EI interventions are parallel structures, including cooperative union–management projects and quality circles; high-involvement designs; and TQM. Each intervention represents an increase in the amount of power, information, knowledge and skills, and rewards available to employees.

■ NOTES

1. D. Glew, A. O'Leary-Kelly, R. Griffin, and D. Van Fleet, "Participation in Organizations: A Preview of the Issues and Proposed Framework for Future Analysis," *Journal of Management* 21, 3 (1995): 395–421.

2. E. Lawler III, *High-Involvement Management* (San Francisco: Jossey-Bass, 1986).

3. M. Kizilos, "The Relationship Between Employee Involvement and Organization Performance" (unpublished Ph.D. diss., University of Southern California, 1995); M. Huselid, "The Impact of Human Resource Management Practices on Turnover, Productivity, and Corporate Financial Performance," *Academy of Management Journal* 38 (1995): 635–72; M. Kizilos, T. Cummings, and A. Strickstein, "Achieving Superior Customer Service Through Employee Involvement," *Academy of Management Best Paper Proceedings* (1994): 197–201; J. Arthur, "Effects of Human Resources Systems on Manufacturing Performance and Turnover," *Academy of Management Journal* 37 (1994): 670–87; A. Kalleberg and J. Moody, "Human Resource Management and Organizational Performance," *American Behavioral Scientist* 37 (1994): 948–62; D. Denison, *Corporate Culture and Organizational Effectiveness* (New York: John Wiley & Sons, 1990); G. Hansen and B. Wernerfelt, "Determinates of Firm Performance: The Relative Importance of Economic and Organizational Factors," *Strategic Management Journal* 10 (1989): 399–411.

4. E. Lawler III and G. Ledford, "Productivity and the Quality of Work Life," *National Productivity Review* 2 (Winter 1981–82): 23–36.

5. Glew et al., "Participation in Organizations"; J. Wagner, "Participation's Effects on Performance and Satisfaction: A Reconsideration of Research Evidence," *Academy of Management Review* 19 (1994): 312–30.

6. G. Ledford and E. Lawler, "Research on Employee Participation: Beating a Dead Horse?" *Academy of Management Review* 19 (1994): 633–36.

7. E. Lawler III, S. Mohrman, and G. Ledford, *Strategies for High-Performance Organizations* (San Francisco: Jossey-Bass, 1998): 150.

8. G. Bushe and A. Shani, "Parallel Learning Structure Interventions in Bureaucratic Organizations," in *Research in Organizational Change and Development*, vol. 4, eds. W. Pasmore and R. Woodman (Greenwich, Conn.: JAI Press, 1990): 167–94.

9. D. Zand, "Collateral Organization: A New Change Strategy," *Journal of Applied Behavioral Science* 10 (1974): 63–89; S. Goldstein, "Organizational Dualism and Quality Circles," *Academy of Management Review* 10 (1985): 504–17; V. Schein and L. Greiner, "Can Organization Development Be Fine Tuned to Bureaucracies?" *Organizational Dynamics* (Winter 1977): 48–61.

10. L. Davis and C. Sullivan, "A Labor–Management Contract and Quality of Working Life," *Journal of Occupational Behavior* 1 (1979): 29–41; E. Lawler III and J. Drexler Jr., "Dynamics of Establishing Cooperative Quality-of-Work-life Projects," *Monthly Labor Review* 101 (March 1978): 23–28; E. Lawler III and L. Ozler, "Joint Union Management Quality of Work Projects," undated manuscript; D. Nadler, M. Hanlon, and E. Lawler III, "Factors Influencing the Success of Labor–Management Quality of Work Life Projects" (research paper, Columbia University Graduate School of Business, April 1978); J. Drexler Jr., "A Union Management Cooperative Project to Improve the Quality of Work Life," *Journal of Applied Behavioral Science* 13 (1977): 373–86; D. Dinnocenzo, "Labor–Management Cooperation," *Training and Development Journal* 43 (May 1989): 35–40; K. Ropp, "State of the Unions," *Personnel Administrator* 32 (July 1987): 36–40; M. Hilton, "Union and Management: A Strong Case for Cooperation," *Training and Development Journal* 41 (January 1987): 54–55.

11. G. Munchus III, "Employer–Employee Based Quality Circles in Japan: Human Resource Policy Implications for American Firms," *Academy of Management Review* 8 (1983): 255–61; R. Callahan, "Quality Circles: A Program for Productivity Improvement Through Human Resource Development" (unpublished paper, Albers School of Business, Seattle University, 1982).

12. D. Zand, *Information, Organization, and Power: Effective Management in the Knowledge Society* (New York: McGraw-Hill, 1981): 57–88; G. Bushe and A. Shani, *Parallel Learning Structures: Increasing Innovation in Bureaucracies* (Reading, Mass.: Addison-Wesley, 1991).

13. C. Worley and G. Ledford, "The Relative Impact of Group Process and Group Structure on Group Effectiveness" (paper presented at the Western Academy of Management, Spokane, Wash., April 1992).

14. Lawler, *High-Involvement Management.*

15. E. Lawler III, "Increasing Worker Involvement to Enhance Organizational Effectiveness," in *Change in Organizations*, ed. P. Goodman (San Francisco: Jossey-Bass, 1982): 299; R. Walton, "From Control to Commitment in the Workplace," *Harvard Business Review* 63 (1985): 76–84.

16. Lawler, *High-Involvement Management;* E. Lawler, *The Ultimate Advantage* (San Francisco: Jossey-Bass, 1992).

17. Glew et al., "Participation in Organizations."

18. W. Deming, *Quality, Productivity, and Competitive Advantage* (Cambridge: MIT Center for Advanced Engineering Study, 1982); W. Deming, *Out of the Crisis* (Cambridge: MIT Press, 1986); J. Juran, *Quality Control Handbook*, 3d ed. (New York: McGraw-Hill, 1974); J. Juran, *Juran on the Leadership for Quality: An Executive Handbook* (New York: Free Press, 1989); P. Crosby, *Quality Is Free* (New York: McGraw-Hill, 1979); P. Crosby, *Quality Without Tears* (New York: McGraw-Hill, 1984).

19. Y. Shetty, "Product Quality and Competitive Strategy," *Business Horizons* (May-June 1987): 46–52; D. Garvin, "Competing on the Eight Dimensions of Quality," *Harvard Business Review* (November-December 1987): 101–09; D. Garvin, *Managing Quality: The Strategic and Competitive Edge* (New York: Free Press, 1988); "The Quality Imperative," *Business Week*, Special Issue (25 October 1991): 34.

20. C. Caldwell, J. McEachern, and V. Davis, "Measurement Tools Eliminate Guesswork," *Healthcare Forum Journal* (July-August 1990): 23–27.

21. "Quality Imperative," *Business Week*, p. 152.

22. Ibid., p. 14.

23. Ibid.

11

Work Design

This chapter is concerned with work design—creating jobs and work groups that generate high levels of employee fulfillment and productivity. This intervention can be part of a larger employee involvement application, or it can be an independent change program. Work design has been researched and applied extensively in organizations. Recently, organizations have tended to combine work design with formal structure and supporting changes in goal setting, reward systems, work environment, and other performance management practices. These organizational factors can help structure and reinforce the kinds of work behaviors associated with specific work designs. (How performance management interventions can support work design is discussed in Chapter 12.)

This chapter examines three approaches to work design. The engineering approach focuses on efficiency and simplification, and results in traditional job and work group designs. A second approach to work design rests on motivational theories and attempts to enrich the work experience. Job enrichment involves designing jobs with high levels of meaning, discretion, and knowledge of results. The third and most recent approach to work design derives from sociotechnical systems methods, and seeks to optimize both the social and the technical aspects of work systems. This method has led to a popular form of work design called "self-managed teams," which are composed of multiskilled members performing interrelated tasks. Members are given the knowledge, information, and power necessary to control their own task behaviors with relatively little external control. New support systems and supervisory styles are needed to manage them.

The chapter describes each of these perspectives on work design, and then presents a contingency framework for integrating the approaches based on personal and technical factors in the workplace. When work is designed to fit these factors, it is both satisfying and productive.

THE ENGINEERING APPROACH

The oldest and most prevalent approach to designing work is based on engineering concepts and methods. It proposes that the most efficient work designs can be determined by clearly specifying the tasks to be performed, the work methods to be used, and the work flow among individuals. The engineering approach is based on the pioneering work of Frederick Taylor, the father of scientific management. He developed methods for analyzing and designing work and laid the foundation for the professional field of industrial engineering.[1]

The *engineering approach* scientifically analyzes workers' tasks to discover those procedures that produce the maximum output with the minimum input of energies and resources.[2] This generally results in work designs with high levels of specialization and specification. Such designs have several benefits: they enable workers to learn tasks rapidly; they permit short work cycles so performance can take place with little or no mental effort; and they reduce costs because lower-skilled people can be hired and trained easily and paid relatively low wages.

The engineering approach produces two kinds of work design: traditional jobs and traditional work groups. When the work can be completed by one person, such as with bank tellers and telephone operators, traditional jobs are created. These jobs tend to be simplified, with routine and repetitive tasks having clear specifications concerning time and motion. When the work requires coordination among people, such as on automobile assembly lines, traditional work groups are developed. They are composed of members performing relatively routine yet related tasks. The overall group task is typically broken into simpler, discrete parts (often called jobs). The tasks and work methods are specified for each part, and the parts are assigned to group members. Each member performs a routine and repetitive part of the group task. Members' separate task contributions are coordinated for overall task achievement through such external controls as schedules, rigid work flows, and supervisors.[3] In the 1950s and 1960s, this method of work design was popularized by the assembly lines of American automobile manufacturers and was an important reason for the growth of American industry following World War II.

The engineering approach to job design is less an OD intervention than a benchmark in history. Critics of the approach argue that the method ignores workers' social and psychological needs. They suggest that the rising educational level of the workforce and the substitution of automation for menial labor point to the need for more enriched forms of work in which people have greater discretion and are more challenged. Moreover, the current competitive climate requires a more committed and involved workforce able to make online decisions and to develop performance innovations. Work designed with the employee in mind is more humanly fulfilling and productive than that designed in traditional ways. However, it is important to recognize the strengths of the engineering approach. It remains an important work design intervention because its immediate cost savings and efficiency can be measured readily, and because it is well understood and easily implemented and managed.

THE MOTIVATIONAL APPROACH

The *motivational approach* to work design views the effectiveness of organizational activities primarily as a function of member needs and satisfaction, and seeks to improve employee performance and satisfaction by enriching jobs. The motivational method provides people with opportunities for autonomy, responsibility, closure (that is, doing a complete job), and performance feedback. Enriched jobs are popular in the United States at such companies as AT&T Universal Card, TRW, Dayton Hudson, and GTE.

The Core Dimensions of Jobs

Considerable research has been devoted to defining and understanding core job dimensions.[4] Figure 11.1 summarizes the Hackman and Oldham model of job design. Five core dimensions of work affect three critical psychological states, which in turn produce personal and job outcomes. These outcomes include high internal work motivation, high-quality work performance, satisfaction with the work, and low absenteeism and turnover. The five core job dimensions—skill variety, task identity, task significance, autonomy, and feedback from the work itself—are described below and associated with the critical psychological states that they create.

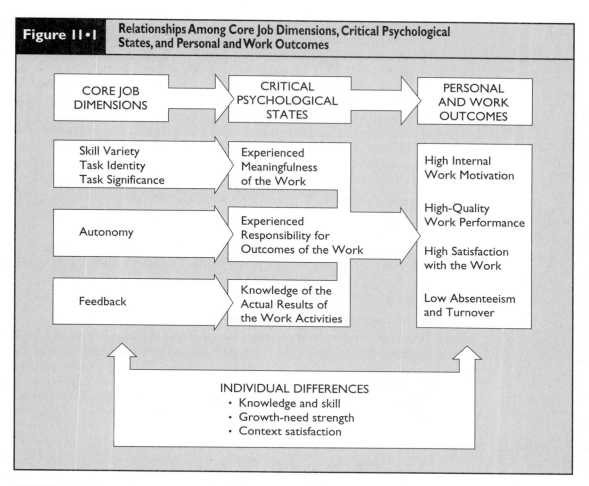

Figure 11•1   Relationships Among Core Job Dimensions, Critical Psychological States, and Personal and Work Outcomes

Skill Variety, Task Identity, and Task Significance

These three core job characteristics influence the extent to which work is perceived as meaningful. *Skill variety* refers to the number and types of skills used to perform a particular task. Employees at Lechmere's, a retail chain in Florida, can work as warehouse stock clerks, cashiers, and salespeople. The more tasks an individual performs, the more meaningful the job becomes. When skill variety is increased by moving a person from one job to another, a form of job enrichment called *job rotation* is accomplished. However, simply rotating a person from one boring job to another is not likely to produce the outcomes associated with a fully enriched job.

Task identity describes the extent to which an individual performs a whole piece of work. For example, an employee who completes an entire wheel assembly for an airplane, including the tire, chassis, brakes, and electrical and hydraulic systems, has more task identity and will perceive the work as more meaningful than someone who only assembles the braking subsystem. *Job enlargement,* another form of job enrichment that combines increases in skill variety with task identity, blends several narrow jobs into one larger, expanded job. For example, separate machine set-up, machining, and inspection jobs might be combined into one. This method can increase meaningfulness, job satisfaction, and motivation when employees comprehend and like the greater task complexity.

Task significance represents the impact that the work has on others. In jobs with high task significance, such as nursing, consulting, or manufacturing something like sensitive parts for the space shuttle, the importance of successful task completion creates meaningfulness for the worker.

Experienced meaningfulness is expressed as an average of these three dimensions. Thus, although it is advantageous to have high amounts of skill variety, task identity, and task significance, a strong emphasis on any one of the three dimensions can, at least partially, make up for deficiencies in the other two.

Autonomy

This refers to the amount of independence, freedom, and discretion that the employee has to schedule and perform tasks. Salespeople, for example, often have considerable autonomy in how they contact, develop, and close new accounts, whereas assembly-line workers often have to adhere to work specifications clearly detailed in a policy-and-procedure manual. Employees are more likely to experience responsibility for their work outcomes when high amounts of autonomy exist.

Feedback from the Work Itself

This core dimension represents the information that workers receive about the effectiveness of their work. It can derive from the work itself, as when determining whether an assembled part functions properly, or it can come from such external sources as reports on defects, budget variances, customer satisfaction, and the like. Because feedback from the work itself is direct and generates intrinsic satisfaction, it is considered preferable to feedback from external sources.

Individual Differences

Not all people react in similar ways to job enrichment interventions. Individual differences—among them, a worker's knowledge and skill levels, growth-need strength, and satisfaction with contextual factors—moderate the relationships among core dimensions, psychological states, and outcomes. "Worker knowledge and skill" refers to the education and experience levels characterizing the workforce. If employees lack the appropriate skills, for example, increasing skill variety may not improve a job's meaningfulness. Similarly, if workers lack the intrinsic motivation to grow and develop personally, attempts to provide them with increased autonomy may be resisted. (We will discuss growth needs more fully in the last section of this chapter.) Finally, contextual factors include reward systems, supervisory style, and co-worker satisfaction. When the employee is unhappy with the work context, attempts to enrich the work itself may be unsuccessful.

Application Stages

The basic steps for job enrichment as described by Hackman and Oldham include making a thorough diagnosis of the situation, forming natural work units, combining tasks, establishing client relationships, vertical loading, and opening feedback channels.[5]

Making a Thorough Diagnosis

The most popular method of diagnosing a job is through the use of the Job Diagnostic Survey (JDS) or one of its variations.[6] An important output of the JDS is the motivating potential score, which is a function of the three psychological states—experienced meaningfulness, autonomy, and feedback. The survey can be used to profile one or more jobs, to determine whether motivation and satisfaction are really problems or whether the job is low in motivating potential, and to isolate specific job aspects that are causing difficulties. The JDS also indicates how ready employees are to accept change. Employees who have high growth needs will respond more readily to job enrichment than will those with low or weak growth needs. A thorough diagnosis of the existing work system should be completed before implementing actual changes. The JDS measures satisfaction with pay, co-workers, and supervision. If there is high dissatisfaction with one or more of these areas, other interventions might be more helpful prior to work redesign.

Forming Natural Work Units

As much as possible, natural work units should be formed. Although there may be a number of technological constraints, interrelated task activities should be grouped together. The basic question in forming natural work units is "How can one increase 'ownership' of the task?" Forming such natural units increases two of the core dimensions—task identity and task significance—that contribute to the meaningfulness of work.

Combining Tasks

Frequently, divided jobs can be put back together to form a new and larger one. In the Medfield, Massachusetts, plant of Corning Glass Works, the task of assembling laboratory hotplates was redesigned by combining a number of previously separate tasks. After the change, each hotplate was completely assembled, inspected, and shipped by one operator, resulting in increased productivity of 84 percent. Controllable rejects dropped from 23 percent to less than 1 percent, and absenteeism dropped from 8 percent to less than 1 percent.[7] A later analysis indicated that the change in productivity was the result of the intervention.[8] Combining tasks increases task identity and allows a worker to use a greater variety of skills. The hotplate assembler can identify with a product finished for shipment, and self-inspection of his or her work adds greater task significance, autonomy, and feedback from the job itself.

Establishing Client Relationships

When jobs are split up, the typical worker has little or no contact with, or knowledge of, the ultimate user of the product or service. Improvements often can be realized simultaneously on three of the core dimensions by encouraging and helping workers to establish direct relationships with the clients of their work. For example, when a typist in a typing pool is assigned to a particular department, feedback increases because of the additional opportunities for praise or criticism of his or her work. Because of the need to develop interpersonal skills in maintaining the client relationship, skill variety may increase. If the worker is given personal responsibility for deciding how to manage relationships with clients, autonomy is increased.

Vertical Loading

The intent of vertical loading is to decrease the gap between *doing* the job and *controlling* the job. A vertically loaded job has responsibilities and controls that formerly were reserved for management. Vertical loading may well be the most crucial of the job-design principles. Autonomy is invariably increased. This approach should lead to greater feelings of personal accountability and responsibility for the work outcomes. For example, at an IBM plant that manufactures circuit boards for personal computers, assembly workers were trained to measure the accuracy and speed of production processes and to test the quality of finished products. Their work is more "whole," they are more autonomous, and the engineers who used to measure and test are free to design better products and more efficient ways to manufacture them.[9]

Opening Feedback Channels

In almost all jobs, approaches exist to open feedback channels and help people learn whether their performance is remaining at a constant level, improving, or deteriorating. The most advantageous and least threatening feedback occurs when a worker learns about performance as the job is performed. In the hotplate department at Corning Glass Works, assembling the entire instrument and inspecting it dramatically increased the quantity and quality of performance information available to the operators. Data given to a manager or supervisor often can be given directly to the employee. Computers and other automated operations can be used to provide people with data not currently accessible to them. Many organizations simply have not realized the motivating impact of direct, immediate feedback.

Barriers to Job Enrichment

As the application of job enrichment has spread, a number of obstacles to significant job restructuring have been identified. Most of these barriers exist in the organizational context within which the job design is executed. Other organizational systems and practices, whether technical, managerial, or personnel, can affect both the implementation of job enrichment and the lifespan of whatever changes are made.

At least four organizational systems can constrain the implementation of job enrichment:[10]

1. *The technical system.* The technology of an organization can limit job enrichment by constraining the number of ways jobs can be changed. For example, long-linked technology like that found on an assembly line can be highly programmed and standardized, thus limiting the amount of employee discretion that is possible. Technology also may set an "enrichment ceiling." Some types of work, such as continuous-process production systems, may be naturally enriched so there is little more that can be gained from a job enrichment intervention.

2. *The personnel system.* Personnel systems can constrain job enrichment by creating formalized job descriptions that are rigidly defined and limit flexibility in changing people's job duties. For example, many union agreements include such narrowly defined job descriptions that major renegotiation between management and the union must occur before jobs can be significantly enriched.

3. *The control system.* Control systems, such as budgets, production reports, and accounting practices, can limit the complexity and challenge of jobs within the system. For example, a company working on a government contract may have such strict quality control procedures that employee discretion is effectively curtailed.

4. *The supervisory system.* Supervisors determine to a large extent the amount of autonomy and feedback that subordinates can experience. To the extent that supervisors use autocratic methods and control work-related feedback, jobs will be difficult, if not impossible, to enrich.

Once these implementation constraints have been overcome, other factors determine whether the effects of job enrichment are strong and lasting.[11] Consistent with the contingency approach to OD, the staying power of job enrichment depends largely on how well it fits and is supported by other organizational practices, such as those associated with training, compensation, and supervision. These practices need to be congruent with and to reinforce jobs having high amounts of discretion, skill variety, and meaningful feedback.

THE SOCIOTECHNICAL SYSTEMS APPROACH

The *sociotechnical systems (STS) approach* currently is the most extensive body of scientific and applied work underlying employee involvement and innovative work designs. Its techniques and design principles derive from extensive action research in both public and private organizations across diverse national cultures.

STS theory is based on two fundamental premises: that an organization or work unit is a combined, social-plus-technical system (sociotechnical), and that this system is open in relation to its environment.[12] The first assumption suggests that whenever human beings are organized to perform tasks, a joint system is operating—a sociotechnical system. This system consists of two independent but related parts: a social part including the people performing the tasks and the relationships among them, and a technical part comprising the tools, techniques, and methods for task performance. These two parts are independent of each other because each follows a different set of behavioral laws. The social part operates according to biological and psychosocial laws, whereas the technical part functions according to mechanical and physical laws. Nevertheless, the two parts are related because they must act together to accomplish tasks. Hence, the term "sociotechnical" signifies the joint relationship that must occur between the social and technical parts, and the word "system" communicates that this connection results in a unified whole.

Because a sociotechnical system is composed of social and technical parts, it follows that it will produce two kinds of outcomes: products, such as goods and services; and social and psychological consequences, such as job satisfaction and commitment. The key issue is how to design the relationship between the two parts so that both outcomes are positive (referred to as *joint optimization*). Sociotechnical practitioners design work and organizations so that the social and technical parts work well together, producing high levels of product and human satisfaction. This effort contrasts with the engineering approach to designing work, which focuses on the technical component, worries about fitting people in later, and often leads to mediocre performance at high social costs. The STS approach also contrasts with the motivational approach that views work design in terms of human fulfillment and can lead to satisfied employees but inefficient work processes.

The second major premise underlying STS theory is that such systems are open to their environments. As discussed in Chapter 4, open systems must interact with their environments to survive and develop. The environment provides the STS with necessary inputs of energy, raw materials, and information, and the STS provides the environment with products and services. The key issue here is how to design the interface between the STS and its environment so that the system has sufficient freedom to function while exchanging effectively with the environment. In what is typically called *boundary management,* STS practitioners structure environmental relationships both to protect the system from external disruptions and to facilitate the exchange of necessary resources and information. This enables the STS to adapt to changing conditions and to influence the environment in favorable directions.

Self-Managed Work Teams

The most prevalent application of the STS approach is self-managed work teams.[13] Alternatively referred to as self-directed, self-regulating, or high-performance work teams, these work designs consist of members performing interrelated tasks.[14] Self-managed teams typically are responsible for a complete product or service, or a major part of a larger production process. They control members' task behaviors and make decisions about task assignments and work methods. In many cases, the team sets its own production goals within broader organizational limits and may be responsible for support services, such as maintenance, purchasing, and quality control. Team members generally are expected to learn many if not all of the jobs within the team's control and frequently are paid on the basis of knowledge and skills rather than seniority. When pay is based on performance, team rather than individual performance is the standard.

Figure 11.2 is a model explaining how self-managed work teams perform. It summarizes current STS research and shows how teams can be designed for high performance. Although the model is based mainly on experience with teams that perform the daily work of the organization (work teams), it also has relevance to other team designs, such as problem-solving teams, management teams, cross-functional integrating teams, and employee involvement teams.[15]

The model shows that team performance and member satisfaction follow directly from how well the team functions: how well members communicate and coordinate with each other, resolve conflicts and problems, and make and implement task-relevant decisions. Team functioning, in turn, is influenced by three major inputs: team task design, team process interventions, and organization support systems. Because these inputs affect how well teams function and subsequently perform, they are key intervention targets for designing and implementing self-managed work teams.

Team Task Design

Self-managed work teams are responsible for performing particular tasks; consequently, how the team is designed for task performance can have a powerful influence on how well it functions. Task design generally follows from the team's

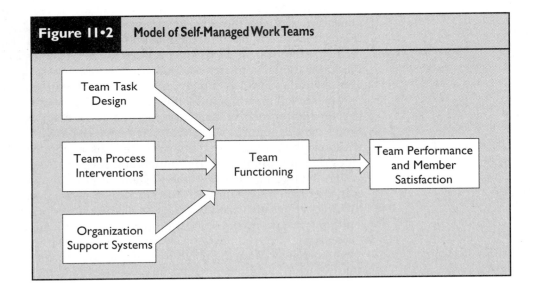

Figure 11•2   Model of Self-Managed Work Teams

mission and goals that define the major purpose of the team and provide direction for task achievement. When a team's mission and goals are closely aligned with corporate strategy and business objectives, members can see how team performance contributes to organization success. This can increase member commitment to team goals.

Team task design links members' behaviors to task requirements and to each other. It structures member interactions and performances. Three task design elements are necessary for creating self-managed work teams: task differentiation, boundary control, and task control.[16] *Task differentiation* involves the extent to which the team's task is autonomous and forms a relatively self-completing whole. High levels of task differentiation provide an identifiable team boundary and a clearly defined area of team responsibility. At Johnsonville Sausage, for example, self-managed teams comprise seven to fourteen members. Each team is large enough to accomplish a set of interrelated tasks but small enough to allow face-to-face meetings for coordination and decision making. In many hospitals, self-managed nursing teams are formed around interrelated tasks that together produce a relatively whole piece of work. Thus, nursing teams may be responsible for particular groups of patients, such as those in intensive care or undergoing cancer treatments, or they may be accountable for specific work processes, such as those in the laboratory, pharmacy, or admissions office.

Boundary control involves the extent to which team members can influence transactions with their task environment—the types and rates of inputs and outputs. Adequate boundary control includes a well-defined work area; group responsibility for boundary-control decisions, such as quality assurance (which reduces dependence on external boundary regulators, such as inspectors); and members sufficiently trained to perform tasks without relying heavily on external resources. Boundary control often requires deliberate cross-training of team members to take on a variety of tasks. This makes members highly flexible and adaptable to changing conditions. It also reduces the need for costly overhead because members can perform many of the tasks typically assigned to staff experts, such as those in quality control, planning, and maintenance.

Task control involves the degree to which team members can regulate their own behavior to provide services or to produce finished products. It includes the freedom to choose work methods, to schedule activities, and to influence production goals to match both environmental and task demands. Task control relies heavily on team members having the power and authority to manage equipment, materials, and other resources needed for task performance. This "work authority" is essential if members are to take responsibility for getting the work accomplished. Task control also requires that team members have accurate and timely information about team performance to allow them to detect performance problems and make necessary adjustments.

Task control enables self-managed work teams to observe and control technical variances as quickly and as close to their source as possible. Technical variances arise from the production process and represent significant deviations from specific goals or standards. In manufacturing, for example, abnormalities in raw material, machine operation, and work flow are sources of variance that can adversely affect the quality and quantity of the finished product. In service work, out-of-the-ordinary requests, special favors or treatment, or unique demands create variances that can place stress on the process. Technical variances traditionally are controlled by support staff and managers, but this can take time and add greatly to costs. Self-managed work teams, on the other hand, have the freedom, skills, and information needed to control technical variances online when they occur. This affords timely responses to production problems and reduces the amount of staff overhead needed.

Team Process Interventions

A second key input to team functioning involves team process interventions. As described in Chapter 8, teams may develop ineffective social processes that impede functioning and performance, such as poor communication among members, dysfunctional roles and norms, and faulty problem solving and decision making. Team process interventions, such as process consultation and team building, can resolve such problems by helping members address process problems and moving the team to a more mature stage of development. Because self-managed work teams need to be self-reliant, members generally acquire their own team process skills. They may attend appropriate training programs and workshops or they may learn on the job by working with OD practitioners to conduct process interventions on their own teams. Although members' process skills generally are sufficient to resolve most of the team's process problems, OD experts occasionally may need to supplement the team's skills and help members address problems that they are unable to resolve.

Organization Support Systems

The final input to team functioning is the extent to which the larger organization is designed to support self-managed work teams. The success of such teams clearly depends on support systems that are quite different from traditional methods of managing.[17] For example, a bureaucratic, mechanistic organization is not highly conducive to self-managed teams. An organic structure, with flexibility among units, relatively few formal rules and procedures, and decentralized authority, is much more likely to support and enhance the development of self-managed work teams. This explains why such teams are so prevalent in high-involvement organizations (described in Chapter 10). Their different features, such as flat, lean structures, open information systems, and team-based selection and reward practices, all reinforce teamwork and responsible self-management.

A particularly important support system for self-managed work teams is the external leadership. Self-managed teams exist along a spectrum from having only mild influence over their work to near-autonomy. In many circumstances, such teams take on a variety of functions traditionally handled by management. These can include assigning members to individual tasks, determining the methods of work, scheduling, setting production goals, and selecting and rewarding members. These activities do not make external supervision obsolete, however. That leadership role usually is changed to two major functions: working with and developing team members, and assisting the team in managing its boundaries.[18]

Working with and developing team members is a difficult process and requires a different style of managing than do traditional systems. The team leader (often called a team facilitator) helps team members organize themselves in a way that allows them to become more independent and responsible. She or he must be familiar with team-building approaches and must assist members in learning the skills to perform their jobs. Recent research suggests that the leader needs to provide expertise in self-management.[19] This may include encouraging team members to be self-reinforcing about high performance, to be self-critical of low performance, to set explicit performance goals, to evaluate goal achievement, and to rehearse different performance strategies before trying them.

If team members are to maintain sufficient autonomy to control variance from goal attainment, the leader may need to help them manage team boundaries. Where teams have limited control over their task environment, the leader may act as a buffer to reduce environmental uncertainty. This can include mediating and negotiating with other organizational units, such as higher management, staff experts, and related work teams. Research suggests that better managers spend more time in lateral interfaces.[20]

These new leadership roles require new and different skills, including knowledge of sociotechnical principles and group dynamics, understanding of both the task environment and the team's technology, and ability to intervene in the team to help members increase their knowledge and skills. Leaders of self-managed teams also should have the ability to counsel members and to facilitate communication among them.

Application Stages

STS work designs have been implemented in a variety of settings, including manufacturing firms, hospitals, schools, and government agencies. Although the specific implementation strategy is tailored to the situation, a common method of change underlies many of these applications. It generally involves high worker participation in work design and implementation. Such participative work design allows employees to translate their special knowledge of the work situation into relevant designs, and employees with ownership over the design process are likely to be highly committed to implementing the outcomes.[21]

STS applications generally proceed in six steps:[22]

1. **Sanctioning the design effort.** At this step, workers receive the necessary protection and support to diagnose their work system and to create an appropriate work design. In many unionized situations, top management and union officials jointly agree to suspend temporarily the existing work rules and job classifications so that employees have the freedom to explore new ways of working. Management also may provide workers with sufficient time and external help to diagnose their work system and devise alternative work structures. In cases of redesigning existing work systems, normal production demands may be reduced during the redesign process. Also, workers may be given some job and wage security so that they feel free to try new designs without fear of losing their jobs or money.

2. **Diagnosing the work system.** This step includes analyzing the work system to discover how it is operating. Knowledge of existing operations (or of intended operations, in the case of a new work system) is the basis for creating an appropriate work design. STS practitioners have devised diagnostic models applicable to work systems that make products or deliver services. The models analyze a system's technical and social parts and assess how well the two fit each other. The task environment facing the system also is analyzed to see how well it is meeting external demands, such as customer quality requirements.

3. **Generating appropriate designs.** Based on the diagnosis, the work system is redesigned to fit the situation. Although this typically results in self-managed work teams, it is important to emphasize that the diagnosis may reveal that tasks are not very interdependent and that an individual-job work design, such as an enriched job, might be more appropriate. Two important STS principles guide the design process.

   The first principle, *compatibility,* suggests that the process of designing work should fit the values and objectives underlying the approach. For example, the major goals of STS design are joint optimization and boundary management. A work-design process compatible with those objectives would be highly participative, involving those having a stake in the work design, such as employees, managers, engineers, and staff experts. They would jointly decide how to create the social and technical components of work, as well as the environmental exchanges. This participative process increases the likelihood that design choices will be based simultaneously on technical, social, and environmental criteria. How well the compatibility guideline is adhered to can determine how well the work design subsequently is implemented.[23]

The second design principle is called *minimal critical specification*. It suggests that STS designers should specify only those critical features needed to implement the work design. All other features of the design should be left free to vary with the circumstances. In most cases, minimal critical specification identifies what is to be done, not how it will be accomplished. This allows employees considerable freedom to choose work methods, task allocations, and job assignments to match changing conditions.

The output of this design step specifies the new work design. In the case of self-managed teams, this includes the team's mission and goals, an ideal work flow, the skills and knowledge required of team members, a plan for training members to meet those requirements, and a list of the decisions the team will make now as well as the ones it should make over time as members develop greater skills and knowledge.

4. *Specifying support systems.* As suggested above, organizational support systems may have to be changed to support new work designs. When self-managed teams are designed, for example, the basis for pay and measurement systems may need to change from individual to team performance to facilitate necessary task interaction among workers.

5. *Implementing and evaluating the work designs.* This stage involves making necessary changes to implement the work design and evaluating the results. For self-managing teams, implementation generally requires a great amount of training so that workers gain the necessary technical and social skills to perform multiple tasks and to control task behaviors. It also may entail developing the team through various team-building and process-consultation activities. OD consultants often help team members carry out these tasks with a major emphasis on helping them gain competence in this area. Evaluation of the work design is necessary both to guide the implementation process and to assess the overall effectiveness of the design. In some cases, the evaluation information suggests the need for further diagnosis and redesign efforts.

6. *Continual change and improvement.* This last step points out that STS designing never is complete but rather continues as new things are learned and new conditions are encountered. Thus, the ability to design and redesign work continually needs to be built into existing work designs. Members must have the skills and knowledge to assess their work unit continually and to make necessary changes and improvements. From this view, STS designing rarely results in a stable work design but instead provides a process for modifying work continually to fit changing conditions and to make performance improvements.

DESIGNING WORK FOR TECHNICAL AND PERSONAL NEEDS

This chapter has described three approaches to work design: engineering, motivational, and sociotechnical. Tradeoffs and conflicts among the approaches must be recognized. The engineering approach produces traditional jobs and work groups and focuses on efficient performance. It downplays employee needs and emphasizes economic outcomes. The motivational approach designs jobs that are stimulating and demanding and highlights the importance of employee need satisfaction. Research suggests, however, that increased satisfaction may not generate improvements in productivity. Finally, the sociotechnical systems approach integrates social and technical aspects, but has not produced consistent research results on its success. In this final section, we attempt to integrate the three perspectives by providing a contingency framework that suggests that any of the three approaches can be effective when applied in the appropriate circumstances. Work design involves creating jobs and work groups for high levels of employee satisfaction and productivity. A large body of research shows that achieving such results depends on designing work to match specific factors operating in the work setting, factors that involve the technology for producing goods and services and the personal needs of employees. When work is designed to fit or match these factors, it is most likely to be both productive and humanly satisfying.

The technical and personal factors affecting work design success provide a contingency framework for choosing among the four different kinds of work designs discussed in the chapter: traditional jobs, traditional work groups, enriched jobs, and self-managed teams.

Technical Factors

Two key dimensions can affect change on the shop floor: technical interdependence, or the extent to which cooperation among workers is required to produce a product or service; and technical uncertainty, or the amount of information processing and decision making employees must do to complete a task.[24] In general, the degree of technical interdependence determines whether work should be designed for individual jobs or for work groups. When interdependence is low and there is little need for worker cooperation—as, for example, in field sales and data entry—work can be designed for individual jobs. Conversely, when interdependence is high and employees must cooperate—as in production processes like coal mining, assembly lines, and writing software—work should be designed for groups composed of people performing interacting tasks.

The second dimension, technical uncertainty, determines whether work should be designed for external forms of control, such as supervision, scheduling, or standardization, or for worker self-control. When technical uncertainty is low and little information has to be processed by employees, work can be designed for external control, such as might be found on assembly lines and in other forms of repetitive work. On the other hand, when technical uncertainty is high and people must process information and make decisions, work should be designed for high levels of employee self-control, such as might be found in professional work and troubleshooting tasks.

Figure 11.3 shows the different types of work designs that are most effective, from a purely technical perspective, for different combinations of interdependence and uncertainty. In quadrant 1, where technical interdependence and uncertainty are both low, such as might be found in data entry, jobs should be designed traditionally with limited amounts of employee interaction and self-control. When task interdependence is high but uncertainty is low (quadrant 2), such as work occurring on assembly lines, work should be designed for traditional work groups in which employee interaction is scheduled and self-control is limited. In quadrant 3, where technical interdependence is low but uncertainty is high, such as in field sales, work should be structured for individual jobs with internal forms of control,

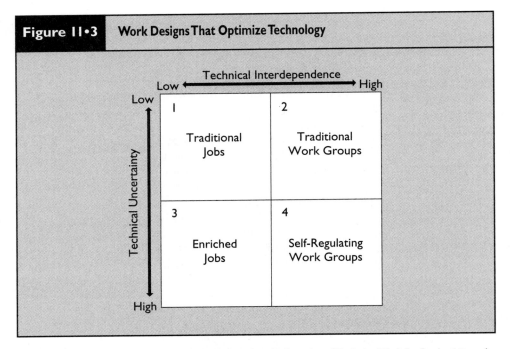

| Figure 11•3 | Work Designs That Optimize Technology |

SOURCE: Reproduced by permission of the publisher from T. Cummings, "Designing Work for Productivity and Quality of Work Life," *Outlook* 6 (1982): 39.

such as in enriched jobs. Finally, when both technical interdependence and uncertainty are high (quadrant 4), such as might be found in a continuous-process chemical plant, work should be designed for self-managed teams in which members have the multiple skills, discretion, and information necessary to control their interactions around the shared tasks.

Personal-Need Factors

Most of the research identifying individual differences in work design has focused on selected personal traits. Two types of personal needs can influence the kinds of work designs that are most effective: social needs, or the desire for significant social relationships; and growth needs, or the desire for personal accomplishment, learning, and development.[25] In general, the degree of *social needs* determines whether work should be designed for individual jobs or work groups. People with low needs for social relationships are more likely to be satisfied working on individualized jobs than in interacting groups. Conversely, people with high social needs are more likely to be attracted to group forms of work than to individualized forms.

The second individual difference, *growth needs*, determines whether work designs should be routine and repetitive or complex and challenging. People with low growth needs generally are not attracted to jobs offering complexity and challenge (that is, enriched jobs) but are more satisfied performing routine forms of work that do not require high levels of decision making. On the other hand, people with high growth needs are satisfied with work offering high levels of discretion, skill variety, and meaningful feedback. Performing enriched jobs allows them to experience personal accomplishment and development.

That some people have low social and growth needs often is difficult for OD practitioners to accept, particularly in light of the social and growth values underlying much OD practice. It is important to recognize, however, that individual differences do exist. Assuming that all people have high growth needs or want high levels of social interaction can lead to inappropriate work designs. For example, a new manager of a clerical support unit was astonished to find the six members using typewriters, even though a significant portion of the work consisted of retyping memos and reports that were produced frequently but changed very little from month to month. In addition, the unit had a terrible record of quality and on-time production. The manager quickly ordered new word processors and redesigned the work flow to increase interaction among members. Worker satisfaction declined, interpersonal conflicts increased, and work quality and on-time performance remained poor. An assessment of the effort revealed that all six of the staff members had low growth needs and low needs for inclusion in group efforts. In the words of one worker, "All I want is to come into work, do my job, and get my paycheck."

It is important to emphasize that people who have low growth or social needs are not inferior to those placing a higher value on those factors; they simply are different. It is necessary also to recognize that people can change their needs through personal growth and experience. OD practitioners must be sensitive to individual differences in work design and careful not to force their own values on others. Many consultants, eager to be seen on the cutting edge of practice, recommend self-managed teams in all situations, without careful attention to technological and personal considerations.

Figure 11.4 shows the different types of work designs that are most effective for the various combinations of social and growth needs. When employees have

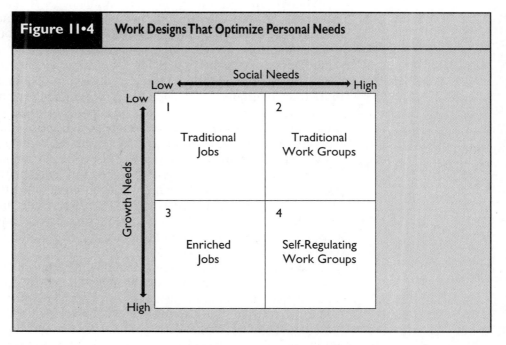

Figure 11•4   Work Designs That Optimize Personal Needs

Social Needs

Low ←———————————→ High

Growth Needs: Low / High

	Low Social Needs	High Social Needs
Low Growth	1 Traditional Jobs	2 Traditional Work Groups
High Growth	3 Enriched Jobs	4 Self-Regulating Work Groups

SOURCE: Reproduced by permission of the publisher from T. Cummings, "Designing Work for Productivity and Quality of Work Life," *Outlook* 6 (1982): 40.

relatively low social and growth needs (quadrant 1), traditional jobs are most effective. In quadrant 2, where employees have high social needs but low growth needs, traditional work groups, such as might be found on an assembly line, are most appropriate. These allow for some social interaction but limited amounts of challenge and discretion. When employees have low social needs but high growth needs (quadrant 3), enriched jobs are most satisfying. Here, work is designed for individual jobs that have high levels of task variety, discretion, and feedback about results. A research scientist's job is likely to be enriched, as is that of a skilled craftsperson. Finally, in quadrant 4, where employees have high social and growth needs, work should be designed for self-managed teams that offer significant social interaction around complex and challenging tasks. A team of astronauts in a space shuttle resembles a self-managed work group, as does a group managing the control room of an oil refinery or a group of nurses in a hospital unit.

Meeting Both Technical and Personal Needs

Jointly satisfying technical and human needs to achieve work-design success is likely to occur only in limited circumstances. When the technical conditions of a company's production processes (as shown in Figure 11.3) are compatible with the personal needs of its employees (as shown in Figure 11.4), the respective work designs combine readily and can satisfy both. On General Motors' assembly lines, for example, the technology is highly interdependent but low in uncertainty (quadrant 2 in Figure 11.3). Much of the production is designed around traditional work groups in which task behaviors are standardized and interactions among workers are scheduled. Such work is likely to be productive and fulfilling to the extent that General Motors' production workers have high social needs and low growth needs (quadrant 2 in Figure 11.4).

When technology and people are incompatible—for example, when an organization has quadrant 1 technology and quadrant 4 worker needs—at least two kinds of changes can be made to design work that satisfies both requirements.[26] One strategy is to change technology or people to bring them more into line with each other. This is a key point underlying sociotechnical systems approaches. For example, technical interdependence can be reduced by breaking long assembly lines into more discrete groups. In Sweden, Volvo redesigned the physical layout and technology for assembling automobiles and trucks to promote self-managed teams. Modifying people's needs is more complex and begins by matching new or existing workers to available work designs. For example, companies can assess workers' needs through standardized paper-and-pencil tests and use the information gleaned from them to counsel employees and help them locate jobs compatible with their needs. Similarly, employees can be allowed to volunteer for specific work designs—a common practice in STS projects. This matching process is likely to require high levels of trust and cooperation between management and workers, as well as a shared commitment to designing work for high performance and employee satisfaction.

A second strategy for accommodating both technical and human requirements is to leave the two components unchanged and create compromise work designs that only partially fulfill the demands of either component. The key issue is to decide to what extent one contingency will be satisfied at the expense of the other. For example, when capital costs are high relative to labor costs, such as in highly automated plants, work design is likely to favor the technology. Conversely, in many service jobs where labor is expensive relative to capital, organizations may design work for employee motivation and satisfaction at the risk of shortchanging their technology. These examples suggest a range of possible compromises based on different weightings of technical and human demands. Careful assessment of both types of contingencies and of the cost–benefit tradeoffs is necessary to design an appropriate compromise work design.

Clearly, the strategy of designing work to bring technology and people more into line with each other is preferable to the compromise work design strategy. Although the latter approach seems necessary when there are heavy constraints on changing the contingencies, in many cases those constraints are more imagined than real. The important thing is to understand the technical and personal factors existing in a particular situation and to design work accordingly. Traditional jobs and traditional work groups will be successful in certain situations (as shown in Figures 11.3 and 11.4); in other settings, enriched jobs and self-managed teams will be more effective.

■ SUMMARY

In this chapter, we discussed three different approaches to work design and described a contingency framework to determine the approach most likely to result in high productivity and worker satisfaction. The contingency framework reconciles the strengths and weaknesses of each approach. The engineering approach produces traditional jobs and traditional work groups. Traditional jobs are highly simplified and involve routine and repetitive forms of work, rather than coordination among people to produce a product or service. Traditional jobs achieve high productivity and worker satisfaction in situations characterized by low technical uncertainty and interdependence and low growth and social needs.

Traditional work groups are composed of members who perform routine yet interrelated tasks. Member interactions are controlled externally, usually by rigid work flows, schedules, and supervisors. Traditional work groups are best suited to conditions of low technical uncertainty but high technical interdependence. They fit people with low growth needs but high social needs.

The motivational approach produces enriched jobs involving high levels of skill variety, task identity, task significance, autonomy, and feedback from the work itself. Enriched jobs achieve good results when the technology is uncertain but does not require high levels of coordination and when employees have high growth needs and low social needs.

Finally, the sociotechnical systems approach is associated with self-managed teams. These groups are composed of members performing interrelated tasks. Members are given the multiple skills, autonomy, and information necessary to control their own task behaviors with relatively little external control. Many OD practitioners argue that self-managed teams represent the work design of the 1990s because high levels of technical uncertainty and interdependence are prevalent in today's workplaces and because today's workers often have high growth and social needs.

■ NOTES

1. F. Taylor, *The Principles of Scientific Management* (New York: Harper & Row, 1911).

2. Ibid.

3. T. Cummings, "Self-Regulating Work Groups: A Socio-Technical Synthesis," *Academy of Management Review* 3

(1978): 625–34; G. Susman, *Autonomy at Work* (New York: Praeger, 1976); J. Slocum and H. Sims, "A Typology of Technology and Job Redesign," *Human Relations* 33 (1983): 193–212.

4. A. Turner and P. Lawrence, *Industrial Jobs and the Worker*

(Cambridge, Mass.: Harvard Graduate School of Business Administration, Division of Research, 1965); J. Hackman and G. Oldham, "Development of the Job Diagnostic Survey," *Journal of Applied Psychology* 60 (April 1975): 159–70; H. Sims, A. Szilagyi, and R. Keller, "The Measurement of Job Characteristics," *Academy of Management Journal* 19 (1976): 195–212.

5. J. Hackman and G. Oldham, *Work Redesign* (Reading, Mass.: Addison-Wesley, 1980); J. Hackman, G. Oldham, R. Janson, and K. Purdy, "A New Strategy for Job Enrichment," *California Management Review* 17 (Summer 1975): 57–71; R. Walters, *Job Enrichment for Results: Strategies for Successful Implementation* (Reading, Mass.: Addison-Wesley, 1975); J. Hackman, "Work Design," in *Improving Life at Work: Behavioral Science Approaches to Organizational Change,* eds. J. Hackman and L. L. Suttle (Santa Monica, Calif.: Goodyear, 1977): 96–163.

6. J. Hackman and G. Oldham, *The Diagnostic Survey: An Instrument for the Diagnosis of Jobs and the Evaluation of Job Redesign Projects,* Technical Report No. 4 (New Haven, Conn.: Yale University, Department of Administrative Sciences, 1974); Sims, Szilagyi, and Keller, "Measurement"; M. Campion, "The Multimethod Job Design Questionnaire," *Psychological Documents* 15 (1985): 1; J. Idaszak and F. Drasgow, "A Revision of the Job Diagnostic Survey: Elimination of a Measurement Artifact," *Journal of Applied Psychology* 72 (1987): 69–74.

7. E. Huse and M. Beer, "Eclectic Approach to Organizational Development," *Harvard Business Review* 49 (September-October 1971): 103–12.

8. A. Armenakis and H. Field, "Evaluation of Organizational Change Using Nonindependent Criterion Measures," *Personnel Psychology* 28 (Spring 1975): 39–44.

9. R. Henkoff, "Make Your Office More Productive," *Fortune* (25 February 1991): 84.

10. G. Oldham and J. Hackman, "Work Design in the Organizational Context," in *Research in Organizational Behavior,* vol. 2, eds. B. Staw and L. Cummings (Greenwich, Conn.: JAI Press, 1980): 247–78; J. Cordery and T. Wall, "Work Design and Supervisory Practice: A Model," *Human Relations* 38 (1985): 425–41.

11. Hackman and Oldham, *Work Redesign.*

12. E. Trist, B. Higgin, H. Murray, and A. Pollock, *Organizational Choice* (London: Tavistock, 1963); T. Cummings and S. Srivastva, *Management of Work: A Socio-Technical Systems Approach* (San Diego: University Associates, 1977); A. Cherns, "Principles of Sociotechnical Design Revisited," *Human Relations* 40 (1987): 153–62.

13. Cummings, "Self-Regulating Work Groups"; J. Hackman, *The Design of Self-Managing Work Groups,* Technical Report No. 11 (New Haven, Conn.: Yale University, School of Organization and Management, 1976); Cummings and Srivastva, *Management of Work;* Susman, *Autonomy at Work;* H. Sims and C. Manz, "Conversations Within Self-Managed Work Groups," *National Productivity Review* 1 (Summer 1982): 261–69; T. Cummings, "Designing Effective Work Groups," in *Handbook of Organizational Design: Remodeling Organizations and Their Environments,* vol. 2, eds. P. C. Nystrom and W. H. Starbuck (New York: Oxford University Press, 1981): 250–71.

14. C. Manz, "Beyond Self-Managing Teams: Toward Self-Leading Teams in the Workplace," in *Research in Organizational Change and Development,* vol. 4, eds. W. Pasmore and R. Woodman (Greenwich, Conn.: JAI Press, 1990): 273–99; C. Manz and H. Sims Jr., "Leading Workers to Lead Themselves: The External Leadership of Self-Managed Work Teams," *Administrative Science Quarterly* 32 (1987): 106–28.

15. B. Dumaine, "The Trouble with Teams," *Fortune* (5 September 1994): 86–92.

16. Cummings, "Self-Regulating Work Groups."

17. Cummings, "Self-Regulating Work Groups"; J. Pearce II and E. Ravlin, "The Design and Activation of Self-Regulating Work Groups," *Human Relations* 40 (1987): 751–82; J. R. Hackman, "The Design of Work Teams," in *Handbook of Organizational Behavior,* ed. J. Lorsch (Englewood Cliffs, N.J.: Prentice Hall, 1987): 315–42.

18. Ibid.

19. C. Manz and H. Sims, "The Leadership of Self-Managed Work Groups: A Social Learning Theory Perspective" (paper delivered at meeting of National Academy of Management, New York, August 1982); C. Manz and H. Sims Jr., "Searching for the 'Unleader': Organizational Member Views on Leading Self-Managed Groups," *Human Relations* 37 (1984): 409–24.

20. H. Mintzberg, *The Nature of Managerial Work* (New York: Harper & Row, 1973); L. Sayles, *Managerial Behavior: Administration in Complex Organizations* (New York: McGraw-Hill, 1964).

21. M. Weisbord, "Participative Work Design: A Personal Odyssey," *Organizational Dynamics* (1984): 5–20.

22. T. Cummings, "Socio-Technical Systems: An Intervention Strategy," in *New Techniques in Organization Development,* ed. W. Burke (New York: Basic Books, 1975): 228–49; Cummings and Srivastva, *Management of Work;* T.

Cummings and E. Molloy, *Improving Productivity and the Quality of Work Life* (New York: Praeger, 1977).

23. Cherns, "Sociotechnical Design Revisited."

24. T. Cummings, "Self-Regulating Work Groups"; Susman, *Autonomy at Work;* Slocum and Sims, "Typology of Technology"; M. Kiggundu, "Task Interdependence and Job Design: Test of a Theory," *Organizational Behavior and Human Performance* 31 (1983): 145–72.

25. Hackman and Oldham, *Work Redesign;* K. Brousseau,

"Toward a Dynamic Model of Job–Person Relationships: Findings, Research Questions, and Implications for Work System Design," *Academy of Management Review* 8 (1983): 33–45; G. Graen, T. Scandura, and M. Graen, "A Field Experimental Test of the Moderating Effects of Growth Needs Strength on Productivity," *Journal of Applied Psychology* 71 (1986): 484–91.

26. T. Cummings, "Designing Work for Productivity and Quality of Work Life," *Outlook* 6 (1982): 35–39.

12. Human Resources Management Interventions

In this chapter, we discuss three human resources management interventions: performance management, career planning and development, and workforce diversity. These change processes typically are carried out by personnel or human resources specialists in organizations. Recently, however, human resources management has been more integrated with OD processes. In many companies, such as Johnson & Johnson, GTE, and Shell Oil, the OD function is located in the human resources department. Moreover, as OD practitioners increasingly have become involved in organization design, they have sought help from human resources professionals to bring personnel practices more in line with the new designs.

Performance management involves goal setting, performance appraisal, and reward systems interventions that align member work behavior with business strategy, employee involvement, and workplace technology. Career planning and development processes help employees set and attain career objectives at each stage of their careers. Workforce diversity interventions modify organizational practices to fit the needs of an increasingly diverse workforce.

PERFORMANCE MANAGEMENT

Performance management is an integrated process of defining, assessing, and reinforcing employee work behaviors and outcomes.[1] Organizations with a well-developed performance management process often outperform those without this element of organization design.[2] As shown in Figure 12.1, performance management includes practices and methods for goal setting, performance appraisal, and reward systems. These practices jointly influence the performance of individuals and work groups. Goal setting specifies the kinds of performances that are desired; performance appraisal assesses those outcomes; reward systems provide the reinforcers to ensure that desired outcomes are repeated. Because performance management occurs in a larger organizational context, at least three contextual factors determine how these practices affect work performance: business strategy, workplace technology, and employee involvement.[3] High levels of work performance tend to occur when goal setting, performance appraisal, and reward systems are aligned jointly with these contextual factors.

Business strategy defines the goals and objectives that are needed for an organization to compete successfully, and performance management focuses, assesses, and reinforces member work behaviors toward those objectives. This ensures that work behaviors are strategically driven.

Workplace technology affects whether performance management practices should be based on the individual or the group. When technology is low in interdependence and work is designed for individual jobs, goal setting, performance appraisal, and reward systems should be aimed at individual work behaviors. Conversely, when technology is highly interdependent and work is designed for groups, performance management should be aimed at group behaviors.[4]

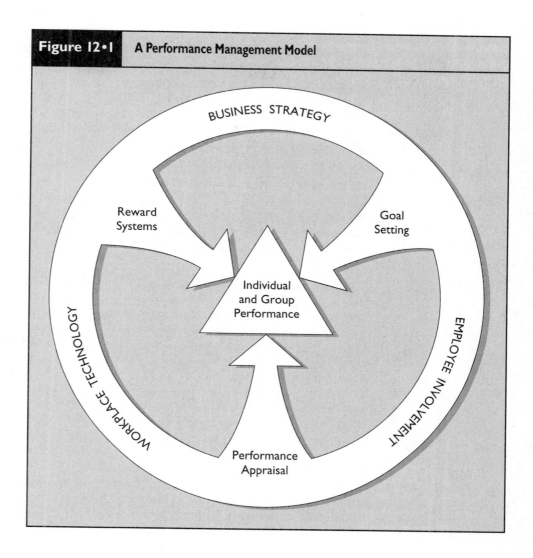

Figure 12•1   A Performance Management Model

BUSINESS STRATEGY

Reward Systems

Goal Setting

Individual and Group Performance

WORKPLACE TECHNOLOGY

EMPLOYEE INVOLVEMENT

Performance Appraisal

Finally, the level of employee involvement in an organization should determine the nature of performance management practices. When organizations are highly bureaucratic with low levels of participation, goal setting, performance appraisal, and reward systems should be formalized and administered by management and staff personnel. In high-involvement situations, on the other hand, performance management should be heavily participative, with both management and employees setting goals and appraising and rewarding performance. In high-involvement organizations, for example, employees participate in all stages of performance management, and are heavily involved in both designing and administering its practices.

Goal Setting

Goal setting involves managers and subordinates in jointly establishing and clarifying employee goals. In some cases, such as management by objectives, it also can facilitate employee counseling and support. The process of establishing challenging goals involves managing the level of participation and goal difficulty. Once goals have been established, the way they are measured is an important determinant of member performance.[5]

Goal setting can affect performance in several ways. It influences what people think and do by focusing their behavior in the direction of the goals, rather than elsewhere. Goals energize behavior, motivating people to put forth the effort to reach difficult goals that are accepted, and when goals are difficult but achievable, goal setting prompts persistence over time. Goal-setting interventions have been implemented in such organizations as GE, 3M, AT&T Universal Card, and Occidental Petroleum's subsidiary Oxy-USA.

Characteristics of Goal Setting

An impressive amount of research underlies goal-setting interventions and practices,[6] and has revealed that goal setting works equally well in both individual and group settings.[7] This research has identified two major processes that affect positive outcomes: establishment of challenging goals and clarification of goal measurement.

Establishing Challenging Goals. The first element of goal setting concerns establishing goals that are perceived as challenging but realistic and to which there is a high level of commitment. This can be accomplished by varying the goal difficulty and the level of employee participation in the goal-setting process. Increasing the difficulty of employee goals, also known as "stretch goals," can increase their perceived challenge and enhance the amount of effort expended to achieve them.[8] Thus, more difficult goals tend to lead to increased effort and performance, as long as they are seen as feasible. If goals are set too high, however, they may lose their motivating potential and employees will give up when they fail to achieve them. An important method for increasing the acceptance of a challenging goal is to collect benchmarks or best-practice referents. When employees see that other people, groups, or organizations have achieved a specified level of performance, they are more motivated to achieve that level themselves.

Another aspect of establishing challenging goals is to vary the amount of participation in the goal-setting process. Having employees participate can increase motivation and performance, but only to the extent that members set higher goals than those typically assigned to them. Participation also can convince employees that the goals are achievable and can increase their commitment to achieving them.

All three contextual factors play an important role in establishing challenging goals. First, there must be a clear "line of sight" between the business strategy goals and the goals established for individuals or groups. When the group is trying to achieve goals that are not aligned with the business strategy, performance can suffer and organization members can become frustrated. Second, employee participation in goal setting is more likely to be effective if employee involvement policies in the organization support it. Under such conditions, participation in goal setting is likely to be seen as legitimate, resulting in the desired commitment to challenging goals. Third, when tasks are highly interdependent and work is designed for groups, group-oriented participative goal setting tends to increase commitment.[9]

Clarifying Goal Measurement. The second element in the goal-setting process involves specifying and clarifying the goals. When given specific goals, workers perform higher than when they are simply told to "do their best" or when they receive no guidance at all. Specific goals reduce ambiguity about expectations and focus the search for appropriate behaviors.

To clarify goal measurement, objectives should be operationally defined. For example, a group of employees may agree to increase productivity by 5 percent, a challenging and specific goal. But there are a variety of ways to measure productivity, and it is important to define the goal operationally to be sure that the measure can be influenced by employee or group behaviors. For example, a productivity goal defined by sales per employee may be inappropriate for a manufacturing group.

Clarifying goal measurement also requires that employees and supervisors negotiate the resources necessary to achieve the goals—for example, time, equipment, raw materials, and access to information. If employees cannot have appropriate resources, the targeted goal may have to be revised.

Contextual factors also play an important role in the clarifying process. Goal specification and clarity can be difficult in high-technology settings where the work often is uncertain and highly interdependent. Increasing employee participation in clarifying goal measurement can give employees ownership of a nonspecific but challenging goal. Employee involvement policies also can impact the way goals are clarified. The entire goal-setting process can be managed by employees and work teams when employee involvement policies and work designs favor it. Finally, the process of specifying and clarifying goals is extremely difficult if the business strategy is unclear. Under such conditions, attempting to gain consensus on the measurement and importance of goals can lead to frustration and resistance to change.

Application Stages

Based on these features of the goal-setting process, OD practitioners have developed specific approaches to goal setting. The following steps characterize those applications:

1. *Diagnosis.* The first step is a thorough diagnosis of the job or work group; employee needs; and the three context factors, business strategy, workplace technology, and level of employee involvement. This provides information about the nature and difficulty of specific goals, the appropriate types and levels of participation, and the necessary support systems.

2. *Preparation for goal setting.* This step prepares managers and employees to engage in goal setting, typically by increasing interaction and communication between managers and employees, and offering formal training in goal-setting methods. Specific action plans for implementing the program also are made at this time.

3. *Setting of goals.* In this step challenging goals are established and methods for goal measurement are clarified. Employees participate in the process to the extent that contextual factors support such involvement and to the extent that they are likely to set higher goals than those assigned by management.

4. *Review.* At this final step the goal-setting process is assessed so that modifications can be made, if necessary. The goal attributes are evaluated to see whether the goals are energizing and challenging and whether they support the business strategy and can be influenced by the employees.

Performance Appraisal

Performance appraisal is a feedback system that involves the direct evaluation of individual or work group performance by a supervisor, manager, or peers. Most organizations have some kind of evaluation system that is used for performance feedback, pay administration, and, in some cases, counseling and developing employees.[10] Thus, performance appraisal represents an important link between goal-setting processes and reward systems. Abundant evidence, however, indicates that organizations do a poor job appraising employees.[11] Consequently, a growing number of firms have sought ways to improve performance appraisal. Some innovations have been made in enhancing employee involvement, balancing organizational and employee needs, and increasing the number of raters.[12] These newer forms of appraisal are being used in such organizations as AT&T, Raychem, Levi Strauss, Intel, and Monsanto.

The Performance Appraisal Process

Table 12.1 summarizes several common elements of performance appraisal systems.[13] For each element, two contrasting features are presented, representing traditional bureaucratic approaches and newer, high-involvement approaches. Performance appraisals are conducted for a variety of purposes, including affirmative action, pay and promotion decisions, and human resources planning and development.[14] Because each purpose defines what performances are relevant and how they should be measured, separate appraisal systems are often used. For example, appraisal methods for pay purposes are often different from systems that assess employee development or promotability. Employees also have a variety of reasons for wanting appraisal, such as receiving feedback for career decisions, getting a raise, and being promoted. Rather than trying to meet these multiple purposes with a few standard appraisal systems, the new appraisal approaches are more tailored to balance the multiple organizational and employee needs. This is accomplished by actively involving the appraisee, co-workers, and managers in assessing the purposes of the appraisal at the time it takes place and adjusting the process to fit that purpose. Thus, at one time the appraisal process might focus on pay decisions, another time on employee development, and still another time on employee promotability. Actively involving all relevant participants can increase the chances that the purpose of the appraisal will be correctly identified and understood and that the appropriate appraisal methods will be applied.

The new methods tend to expand the appraiser role beyond managers to include multiple raters, such as the appraisee, co-workers, and others having direct exposure to the employee's performance. Also known as *360-degree feedback,* this broader approach is used more for member development than for compensation purposes.[15] This wider involvement provides a number of different views of the appraisee's performance. It can lead to a more comprehensive assessment of the employee's performance and can increase the likelihood that both organizational and

Table 12•1	Performance Appraisal Elements	
ELEMENTS	**TRADITIONAL APPROACHES**	**HIGH-INVOLVEMENT APPROACHES**
Purpose	Organizational, legal Fragmented	Developmental Integrative
Appraiser	Supervisor, managers	Appraisee, co-workers, and others
Role of appraisee	Passive, recipient	Active participant
Measurement	Subjective Concerned with validity	Objective and subjective
Timing	Periodic, fixed, administratively driven	Dynamic, timely, employee- or work-driven

personal needs will be taken into account. The key task is to form an overarching view of the employee's performance that incorporates all of the different appraisals. Thus, the process of working out differences and arriving at an overall assessment is an important aspect of the appraisal process. This improves the appraisal's acceptance, the accuracy of the information, and its focus on activities that are critical to the business strategy.

The newer methods also expand the role of the appraisee. Traditionally, the employee is simply a receiver of feedback. The supervisor unilaterally completes a form concerning performance on predetermined dimensions, usually personality traits, such as initiative or concern for quality, and presents its contents to the appraisee. The newer approaches actively involve appraisees in all phases of the appraisal process. The appraisee joins with superiors and staff personnel in gathering data on performance and identifying training needs. This active involvement increases the likelihood that the content of the performance appraisal will include the employee's views, needs, and criteria, along with those of the organization. This newer role for employees increases their acceptance and understanding of the feedback process.

Performance measurement is typically the source of many problems in appraisal because it is seen as subjective. Traditionally, performance evaluation focused on the consistent use of prespecified traits or behaviors. To improve consistency and validity of measurement, considerable training is used to help raters (supervisors) make valid assessments. This concern for validity stems largely from legal tests of performance appraisal systems and leads organizations to develop measurement approaches, such as the behaviorally anchored rating scale (BARS) and its variants. In newer approaches validity is not only a legal or methodological issue but a social issue as well; all appropriate participants are involved in negotiating acceptable ways of measuring and assessing performance. Increased participation in goal setting is a part of this new approach. All participants are trained in methods of measuring and assessing performance. Because it focuses on both objective and subjective measures of performance, the appraisal process is more understood, accepted, and accurate.

The timing of performance appraisals traditionally is fixed by managers or staff personnel and is based on administrative criteria, such as yearly pay decisions. Newer approaches increase the frequency of feedback. Although it may not be practical to increase the number of formal appraisals, the frequency of informal feedback can increase, especially when strategic objectives change or when the technology is highly uncertain. In those situations, frequent performance feedback is necessary for appropriate adaptations in work behavior. The newer approaches to appraisal increase the timeliness of feedback and give employees more control over their work.

Application Stages

The process of implementing a performance appraisal system has received increasing attention. OD practitioners have recommended the following six steps:[16]

1. *Select the right people.* For political and legal reasons, the design process needs to include human resources staff, legal representatives, senior management, and system users. Failure to recognize performance appraisal as part of a complex performance management system is the single most important reason for design problems. Members representing a variety of functions need to be involved in the design process so that the essential strategic and organizational issues are addressed.

2. *Diagnose the current situation.* A clear picture of the current appraisal process is essential to designing a new one. Diagnosis involves assessing the contextual factors (business strategy, workplace technology, and employee involvement), current appraisal practices and satisfaction with them, work design, and the current goal-setting and reward system practices. This information is used to define the current system's strengths and weaknesses.

3. *Establish the system's purposes and objectives.* The ultimate purpose of an appraisal system is to help the organization achieve better performance. Managers, staff, and employees can have more specific views about how the appraisal process can be used. Potential purposes can include serving as a basis for rewards, career planning, human resources planning, and performance improvement or simply giving performance feedback.

4. *Design the performance appraisal system.* Given the agreed-upon purposes of the system and the contextual factors, the appropriate elements of an appraisal system can be established. These should include choices about who performs the appraisal, who is involved in determining performance, how performance is measured, and how often feedback is given. Criteria for designing an effective performance appraisal system include timeliness, accuracy, acceptance, understanding, focus on critical control points, and economic feasibility.

   First, the timeliness criterion recognizes the time value of information. Individuals and work groups need to get performance information before evaluation or review. When the information precedes performance evaluation, it can be used to engage in problem-solving behavior that improves performance and satisfaction. Second, the information contained in performance feedback needs to be accurate. Inaccurate data prevent employees from determining whether their performance is above or below the goal targets and discourage problem-solving behavior. Third, the performance feedback must be accepted and owned by the people who use it. Participation in the goal-setting process can help to ensure this commitment to the performance appraisal system. Fourth, information contained in the appraisal system needs to be understood if it is to have problem-solving value. Many organizations use training to help employees understand the operating, financial, and human resources data that will be fed back to them. Fifth, appraisal information should focus on critical control points. The information received by employees must be aligned with important elements of the business strategy, employee performance, and reward system. For example, if the business strategy requires cost reduction but workers are measured and rewarded on the basis of quality, the performance management system may produce the wrong kinds of behavior. Finally, the economic feasibility criterion suggests that an appraisal system should meet a simple cost–benefit test. If the costs associated with collecting and feeding back performance information exceed the benefits derived from using the information, then a simpler system should be installed.

5. *Experiment with implementation.* The complexity and potential problems associated with performance appraisal processes strongly suggest using a pilot test of the new process to spot, gauge, and correct any flaws in the design before it is implemented systemwide.

6. *Evaluate and monitor the system.* Although the experimentation step may have uncovered many initial design flaws, ongoing evaluation of the system once it is implemented is important. User satisfaction, from human resources staff, manager, and employee viewpoints, is an essential input. In addition, the

legal defensibility of the system should be tracked by noting the distribution of appraisal scores against age, sex, and ethnic categories.

Reward Systems

Organizational rewards are powerful incentives for improving employee and work group performance. As pointed out in Chapter 11, rewards also can produce high levels of employee satisfaction. OD traditionally has relied on intrinsic rewards, such as enriched jobs and opportunities for decision making, to motivate employee performance. Early quality-of-work-life interventions were based mainly on the intrinsic satisfaction derived from performing challenging, meaningful types of work. More recently, OD practitioners have expanded their focus to include extrinsic rewards: pay; various incentives, such as stock options, bonuses, and gain sharing; promotions; and benefits. They have discovered that both intrinsic and extrinsic rewards can enhance performance and satisfaction.[17]

OD practitioners increasingly are attending to the design and implementation of reward systems. This recent attention to rewards has derived partly from research in organization design and employee involvement. These perspectives treat rewards as an integral part of organizations.[18] They hold that rewards should be congruent with other organizational systems and practices, such as the organization's structure, top management's human relations philosophy, and work designs. Many features of reward systems contribute to both employee fulfillment and organizational effectiveness. In this section, we describe how rewards affect individual and group performance and then discuss three specific rewards: pay, promotions, and benefits.

How Rewards Affect Performance

Considerable research has been done on how rewards affect individual and group performance. The most popular model describing this relationship is value expectancy theory. In addition to explaining how performance and rewards are related, it suggests requirements for designing and evaluating reward systems.

The *value expectancy model* posits that employees will expend effort to achieve performance goals that they believe will lead to outcomes that they value.[19] This effort will result in the desired performance goals if the goals are realistic, if employees fully understand what is expected of them, and if they have the necessary skills and resources. Ongoing motivation depends on the extent to which attaining the desired performance goals actually results in valued outcomes. Consequently, key objectives of reward systems interventions are to identify the intrinsic and extrinsic outcomes (rewards) that are highly valued and to link them to the achievement of desired performance goals.

Based on value expectancy theory, the ability of rewards to motivate desired behavior depends on these six factors:[20]

1. *Availability.* For rewards to reinforce desired performance, they must be not only desired but also available. Too little of a desired reward is no reward at all. For example, pay increases are often highly desired but unavailable. Moreover, pay increases that are below minimally accepted standards may actually produce negative consequences.[21]

2. *Timeliness.* Like effective performance feedback, rewards should be given in a timely manner. A reward's motivating potential is reduced to the extent that it is separated in time from the performance it is intended to reinforce.

3. *Performance contingency.* Rewards should be closely linked with particular performances. If the goal is met, the reward is given; if the target is missed, the reward is reduced or not given. The clearer the linkage between performance and rewards, the better able rewards are to motivate desired behavior. Unfortunately, this criterion often is neglected in practice. Forty percent of employees nationwide believe that there is no linkage between pay and performance.[22] From another perspective, merit increases in 1988 were concentrated between 4 and 5 percent nationwide. That is, almost everyone, regardless of performance level, got about the same raise.

4. *Durability.* Some rewards last longer than others. Intrinsic rewards, such as increased autonomy and pride in workmanship, tend to last longer than extrinsic rewards. Most people who have received a salary increase realize that it gets spent rather quickly.

5. *Equity.* Satisfaction and motivation can be improved when employees believe that the pay policies of the organization are equitable or fair. Internal equity concerns comparison of personal rewards to those holding similar jobs or performing similarly in the organization. Internal inequities typically occur when employees are paid a similar salary or hourly wage regardless of their level of performance. External equity concerns comparison of rewards with those of other organizations in the same labor market. When an organization's reward level does not compare favorably with the level of other organizations, employees are likely to feel inequitably rewarded.

6. *Visibility.* To leverage a reward system, it must be visible. Organization members must be able to see who is getting the rewards. Visible rewards, such as placement on a high-status project, promotion to a new job, and increased authority, send signals to employees that rewards are available, timely, and performance contingent.

Reward systems interventions are used to elicit and maintain desired levels of performance. To the extent that rewards are available, durable, equitable, timely, visible, and performance contingent, they can support and reinforce organizational goals, work designs, and employee involvement. The next sections describe three types of rewards—pay, fringe benefits, and promotions—that are particularly effective in improving employee performance and satisfaction.

Pay

In recent years, interest has grown in using various forms of pay to improve employee satisfaction and increase both individual and organizational performance. This has resulted in a number of innovative pay schemes, including skill-based pay, all-salaried workforce, lump-sum salary increases, performance-based pay, and gain sharing.[23] Each of these systems is described and discussed below.

Skill-Based Pay Plans. Traditionally, organizations design pay systems by evaluating jobs. The characteristics of a particular job are determined, and pay is made comparable to what other organizations pay for jobs with similar characteristics. This job evaluation method tends to result in pay systems with high external and internal equity. However, it fails to reward employees for all of the skills that they have, discourages people from learning new skills, and results in a view of pay as an entitlement.[24]

Some organizations, such as General Mills, Northern Telecom, United Technologies, and General Foods, have worked to resolve these problems by designing pay systems according to people's skills and abilities. By focusing on the person rather than the job, skill-based pay systems reward learning and growth.

Skill-based pay systems contribute to organizational effectiveness by providing a more flexible workforce and by giving employees a broad perspective on how the entire plant operates. This flexibility can result in leaner staffing and fewer problems with absenteeism, turnover, and work disruptions. Skill-based pay can lead to durable employee satisfaction by reinforcing individual development and by producing an equitable wage rate.

Major drawbacks of skill-based pay schemes are the tendency to "top out," extra costs, and the lack of performance contingency. Top-out occurs when employees learn all the skills there are to learn and then run up against the top end of the pay scale, with no higher levels to attain. Some organizations have resolved this topping-out effect by installing a gain-sharing plan (see below) after most employees have learned all relevant jobs. Gain sharing ties pay to organizational effectiveness, allowing employees to push beyond previous pay ceilings. Other organizations have resolved this effect by making base skills obsolete and adding new ones, thus raising the standards of employee competence. Skill-based pay systems also require a heavy investment in training, as well as a measurement system capable of telling when employees have learned the new jobs. They typically increase direct labor costs, as employees are paid highly for learning multiple tasks. In addition, because pay is based on skill and not performance, the workforce could be highly paid and flexible but not productive.

Lump-Sum Salary Increases. Traditionally, organizations have distributed annual pay increases by adjusting the regular paychecks of employees. For example, weekly paychecks are increased to reflect the annual raise. This tradition has two major drawbacks. It makes employees wait a full year before they receive the full amount of their annual increase. Second, it makes the raise hardly visible to employees because once added to regular pay checks, it may mean little change in take-home pay.

Aetna, BFGoodrich, Timex, and Westinghouse, among others, have tried to make annual salary increases more flexible and visible[25] by instituting a lump-sum increase program that gives employees the freedom to decide when they receive their annual raise. For example, an employee can choose to receive it all at once at the start of the year. The money advanced to the employee is treated as a loan, usually at a modest interest rate. If the person quits before the end of the year, the proportion of the raise that has not been earned has to be paid back.

Lump-sum increase programs can contribute to employee satisfaction by tailoring the annual raise to individual needs. Such programs can improve organizational effectiveness by making the organization more attractive and reducing turnover. They can increase employee motivation in situations where pay is linked to performance. By making the amount of the salary increase highly visible, employees can see a clear relationship between their performance and their annual raise. The major disadvantages of lump-sum programs are the extra costs of administering the plan and the likelihood that some employees will quit and not pay back the company.

Performance-Based Pay Systems. Organizations have devised many ways of linking pay to performance,[26] making it the fastest-growing segment of pay-based reward systems development. They are used in such organizations as Monsanto, Behlen Mfg., DuPont, American Express, and Herman Miller.[27] Such plans tend to vary along three dimensions: (1) the organizational unit by which performance is measured for reward purposes—an individual, group, or organization basis; (2) the way performance is measured—the subjective measures used in supervisors' ratings or objective measures of productivity, costs, or profits; and (3) what rewards are given for good performance—salary increases, stock, or cash bonuses. Table 12.2 lists different types of performance-based pay systems varying along these dimensions and rates them in terms of other relevant criteria.

In terms of linking pay to performance, individual pay plans are rated highest, followed by group plans and then organization plans. The last two plans score lower on this factor because pay is not a direct function of individual behavior. At the group and organization levels, an individual's pay is influenced by the behavior of others and by external market conditions. Objective measures are more credible, and people are more likely to see the link between pay and objective measures. Second, most of the pay plans do not produce negative side effects, such as workers falsifying data and restricting performance. The major exceptions are individual bonus plans. These plans, such as piece-rate systems, tend to result in negative effects, particularly when trust in the plan is low. Third, as might be expected, group- and organization-based pay plans encourage cooperation among workers more than do individual plans. Under the former, it is generally to everyone's

Table 12•2	Ratings of Various Pay-for-Performance Plans*				
		TIE PAY TO PERFORMANCE	PRODUCE NEGATIVE SIDE EFFECTS	ENCOURAGE COOPERATION	EMPLOYEE ACCEPTANCE
SALARY REWARD					
Individual plan	Productivity	4	1	1	4
	Cost-effectiveness	3	1	1	4
	Superiors' rating	3	1	1	3
Group	Productivity	3	1	2	4
	Cost-effectiveness	3	1	2	4
	Superiors' rating	2	1	2	3
Organizationwide	Productivity	2	1	3	4
	Cost-effectiveness	2	1	2	4
STOCK/BONUS REWARD					
Individual plan	Productivity	5	3	1	2
	Cost-effectiveness	4	2	1	2
	Superiors' rating	4	2	1	2
Group	Productivity	4	1	3	3
	Cost-effectiveness	3	1	3	3
	Superiors' rating	3	1	3	3
Organizationwide	Productivity	3	1	3	4
	Cost-effectiveness	3	1	3	4
	Profit	2	1	3	3

*Ratings: 1 = lowest rating, 5 = highest rating.

SOURCE: Reproduced by permission of the publisher from E. Lawler III, "Reward Systems," in *Improving Life at Work*, eds. J. Hackman and J. Suttle (Santa Monica, Calif.: Goodyear, 1977): 195.

advantage to work well together because all share in the financial rewards of higher performance. The organization plans also promote cooperation among functional departments. Because members from different departments feel that they can benefit from each others' performance, they encourage and help each other make positive contributions. Finally, from an employee's perspective, Table 12.2 suggests that the least acceptable pay plans are individual bonus programs. Employees tend to dislike such plans because they encourage competition among individuals and because they are difficult to administer fairly. Table 12.2 also suggests that employees favor salary increases over bonuses. This follows from the simple fact that a salary increase becomes a permanent part of a person's pay, but a bonus does not.

The overall ratings in Table 12.2 suggest that no one pay-for-performance plan scores highest on all criteria. Rather, each plan has certain strengths and weaknesses that depend on a variety of contingencies. As business strategies, organization performance, and other contingencies change, the pay-for-performance system also must change. When all criteria are taken into account, however, the best performance-based pay systems seem to be group and organization bonus plans that are based on objective measures of performance and individual salary-increase plans. These plans are relatively good at linking pay to performance. They have few negative side effects and at least modest employee acceptance. The group and organization plans promote cooperation and should be used where there is high task interdependence among workers, such as might be found on assembly lines. The individual plan promotes competition and should be used where there is little required cooperation among employees, such as in field sales jobs.

Gain Sharing. As the name implies, gain sharing involves paying employees a bonus based on improvements in the operating results of an organization. Gain-sharing plans tie the workers' goals to the organization's goals. It is to the financial advantage of employees to work harder, to cooperate with each other, to make suggestions, and to implement improvements. Although not traditionally associated with employee involvement, gain-sharing plans such as the Scanlon Plan, the Rucker Plan, or Improshare increasingly have been included in comprehensive employee involvement projects. Many organizations, such as Georgia-Pacific, Huffy Bicycle Company, Inland Container Corp., TRW, and General Electric, are discovering that when designed correctly, gain-sharing plans can contribute to employee motivation, involvement, and performance.

Developing a gain-sharing plan requires making choices about the following design elements:[28]

- *Process of design.* This factor concerns whether the plan will be designed participatively or in a top-down manner. Because the success of gain sharing depends on employee acceptance and cooperation, it is recommended that a task force composed of a cross section of employees design the plan and be trained in gain-sharing concepts and practice. The task force should include people who are credible and represent both management and nonmanagement interests.

- *Organizational unit covered.* The size of the unit included in the plan can vary widely, from departments or plants with fewer than fifty employees to companies with several thousand people. A plan covering the entire plant would be ideal in situations where there is a freestanding plant with good performance measures and an employee size of fewer than five hundred. When the number of employees exceeds five hundred, multiple plans may be installed, each covering a relatively discrete part of the company.

- *Bonus formula.* Gain-sharing plans are based on a formula that generates a bonus pool, which is divided among those covered by the plan. Although most plans are custom-designed, there are two general considerations about the nature of the bonus formula. First, a standard of performance must be developed that can be used as a baseline for calculating improvements or losses. Some plans use past performance to form a historical standard, whereas others use engineered or estimated standards. When available, historical data provide a relatively fair standard of performance; engineer-determined data can work, however, if there is a high level of trust in the standard and how it is set. Second, the costs included in arriving at the bonus must be chosen. The key is to focus on those costs that are most controllable by employees. Some plans use labor costs as a proportion of total sales; others include a wider range of controllable costs, such as those for materials and utilities.

- *Sharing process.* Once the bonus formula is determined, it is necessary to decide how to share gains when they are obtained. This decision includes choices about what percentage of the bonus pool should go to the company and what percentage to employees. In general, the company should take a low-enough percentage to ensure that the plan generates a realistic bonus for employees. Other decisions about dividing the bonus pool include who will share in the bonus and how the money will be divided among employees. Typically, all employees included in the organizational unit covered by the plan share in the bonus. Most plans divide the money on the basis of a straight percentage of total salary payments.

- *Frequency of bonus.* Most plans calculate a bonus monthly. This typically fits with organizational recording needs and is frequent enough to spur employee motivation. Longer payout periods generally are used in seasonal businesses or where there is a long production or billing cycle for a product or service.

- *Change management.* Organizational changes, such as new technology and product mixes, can disrupt the bonus formula. Many plans include a steering committee to review the plan and to make necessary adjustments, especially in light of significant organizational changes.

- *The participative system.* Many gain-sharing plans include a participative system that helps to gather, assess, and implement employee suggestions and improvements. These systems generally include a procedure for formalizing suggestions and different levels of committees for assessing and implementing them.

Promotions

Like decisions about pay increases, many decisions about promotions and job movements in organizations are made in a top-down, closed manner: higher-level managers decide whether lower-level employees will be promoted. This process can be secretive, with people often not knowing that a position is open, that they are being considered for promotion, or the reasons why some people are promoted but others are not. Without such information, capable people who might be interested in a new job may be overlooked. Furthermore, because employees may fail to see the connection between good performance and promotions, the motivational potential of promotions is reduced.

Fortunately, this is changing. Most organizations today have tried to reduce the secrecy surrounding promotions and job changes by openly posting the availability of new jobs and inviting people to nominate themselves.[29] Although open job posting entails extra administrative costs, it can lead to better promotion decisions.

Open posting increases the pool of available personnel by ensuring that interested people will be considered for new jobs and that capable people will be identified. Open posting also can increase employee motivation by showing that a valued reward is available and contingent on performance.

Some organizations have increased the accuracy and equity of job-change decisions by including peers and subordinates in the decision-making process. Peer and subordinate judgments about a person's performance and promotability help bring all relevant data to bear on promotion decisions. Such participation can increase the accuracy of these decisions and can make people feel that the basis for promotions is equitable. In many self-regulating work teams, for example, the group interviews and helps select new members and supervisors. This helps ensure that new people will fit in and that the group is committed to making that happen. Evidence from high-involvement plants suggests that participation in selecting new members can lead to greater group cohesiveness and task effectiveness.[30]

Benefits

In addition to pay and promotions, organizations provide a variety of other extrinsic rewards in the form of benefits. Some of these are mandated by law, such as unemployment insurance and workers' compensation; others are a matter of long tradition, such as paid vacations and health insurance; and still others have emerged to keep pace with the needs of the changing labor force, such as maternity leave, educational benefits, retirement plans, and child care. Organizations, such as Genentech, Johnson & Johnson, Xerox, Allstate, and Bank of America, increasingly are using benefits to attract and retain good employees, to help them better integrate work with home life, and to improve the quality of work life. These benefits can translate into economic gains through reduced absenteeism and turnover, and greater organizational commitment and performance.

Examples of some of the more recent trends in benefits include various forms of early and flexible retirement and preretirement counseling to meet the demands of the greying labor force. Maternity and paternity leaves and child care are designed to satisfy the needs of dual-career couples and single parents. For example, Genentech underwrites half the operating expenses of its child care facility, and Johnson & Johnson, along with ten other corporations, formed an alliance among 145 providers to offer child and dependent care services. There also has been increased attention to providing educational programs, financial services, and pension and investing plans to help employees develop themselves and prepare for secure futures.

Organizations generally provide equal benefit packages to all employees at similar organizational levels. Employees are treated essentially the same, with major differences occurring between hierarchical levels, which therefore tests the equity criterion. This approach also does not account for the kinds of benefits that different people value and therefore may not pass the availability test. For example, younger workers may want more vacation time, whereas older employees may desire more retirement benefits. By treating employees the same, a company spends money for benefits that some people do not value. This also can lead to employee dissatisfaction and reduced motivation. Finally, benefits cannot be manipulated during the year and fail to be timely or performance contingent.

Most large companies are tailoring benefit plans to employee needs through the use of cafeteria-style programs.[31] These plans give employees some choice over how they receive their total fringe-benefit payment. The company tells workers how much it will spend on the total benefit package, and employees use that amount to buy only the fringe benefits they want. In some plans, the employee can spend less than the allocated amount and receive the balance as an increase in pay.

For example, one employee might decide to sign up for a less expensive health maintenance organization benefit plan and allocate the remaining amount toward a cash payment; another might allocate the benefit amount equally between paid vacations, life insurance, and health insurance. These plans also allow the employee to purchase additional benefits, such as life, dental, optical, and family health insurance, often at preferred rates.

Reward-System Process Issues

Thus far, we have discussed different reward systems and assessed their strengths and weaknesses. Considerable research has been conducted on the process aspect of reward systems. *Process* refers to how pay and other rewards typically are administered in the organization. At least two process issues affect employees' perceptions of the reward system: who should be involved in designing and administering the reward system, and what kind of communication should exist with respect to rewards.[32]

Traditionally, reward systems are designed by top managers and compensation specialists and simply are imposed on employees. Although this top-down process may result in a good system, it cannot ensure that employees will understand and trust it. In the absence of trust, workers are likely to have negative perceptions of the reward system. There is growing evidence that employee participation in the design and administration of a reward system can increase employee understanding and can contribute to feelings of control over and commitment to the plan.[33]

Communication about reward systems also can have a powerful impact on employee perceptions of pay equity and on motivation. Most organizations maintain secrecy about pay rates, especially in the managerial ranks. Managers typically argue that secrecy is preferred by employees. It also gives managers freedom in administering pay because they do not have to defend their judgments. There is evidence to suggest, however, that pay secrecy can lead to dissatisfaction with pay and to reduced motivation. Dissatisfaction derives mainly from people's misperceptions about their pay relative to the pay of others. Research shows that managers tend to overestimate the pay of peers and of people below them in the organization and that they tend to underestimate the pay of superiors. These misperceptions contribute to dissatisfaction with pay because regardless of a manager's pay level, it will seem small in comparison to the perceived pay level of subordinates and peers. Perhaps worse, potential promotions will appear less valuable than they actually are.

Secrecy can reduce motivation by obscuring the relationship between pay and performance. For organizations having a performance-based pay plan, secrecy prevents employees from testing whether the organization is actually paying for performance; employees come to mistrust the pay system, fearing that the company has something to hide. Secrecy can also reduce the beneficial impact of accurate performance feedback. Pay provides people with feedback about how they are performing in relation to some standard. Because managers overestimate the pay of peers and subordinates, they will consider their own pay low and thus perceive performance feedback more negatively than it really is. Such misperceptions about performance discourage those managers who are actually performing effectively.

For organizations having a history of secrecy, initial steps toward an open reward system should be modest. For example, an organization could release information on pay ranges and median salaries for different jobs. Organizations with unions generally publish such data for lower-level jobs, and extending that information to all jobs would not be difficult. Once organizations have established higher levels of trust about pay, they might publicize information about the size of raises and who receives them. Finally, as organizations become more democratic, with high levels of trust among managers and workers, they can push toward complete openness about all forms of rewards.

It is important to emphasize that both the amount of participation in designing reward systems and the amount of frankness in communicating about rewards should fit the rest of the organization design and managerial philosophy. Clearly, high levels of participation and openness are congruent with democratic organizations. It is questionable whether authoritarian organizations would tolerate either one.

CAREER PLANNING AND DEVELOPMENT INTERVENTIONS

Career planning and development have been receiving increased attention in organizations. Growing numbers of managers and professional staff are seeking more control over their work lives. As organizations downsize and restructure, there is less trust in the organization to provide job security. Employees are not willing to have their careers "just happen" and are taking an active role in planning and managing them. This is particularly true for women, midcareer employees, and college recruits, who are increasingly asking for career planning assistance.[34] For example, a recent study by the Hay Group found that technology professionals were willing to leave their jobs for better career development opportunities.[35] On the other hand, organizations are becoming more and more reliant on their "intellectual capital." Providing career planning and development opportunities for organization members helps to recruit and retain skilled and knowledgeable workers. Many talented job candidates, especially minorities and women, are showing a preference for employers who offer career advancement opportunities.

Many organizations—General Electric, Xerox, Intel, Ciba-Geigy, Cisco Systems, Quaker Oats, and Novotel UK, among others—have adopted career planning and development programs. These programs have attempted to improve the quality of work life for managers and professionals, to improve their performance, to increase employee retention, and to respond to equal employment and affirmative action legislation. Companies have discovered that organizational growth and effectiveness require career development programs to ensure that needed talent will be available. Competent managers are often the scarcest resource. Many companies also have experienced the high costs of turnover among recent college graduates, including MBAs, which can reach 50 percent after five years. Career planning and development help attract and hold such highly talented employees and can increase the chances that their skills and knowledge will be used.

Recent legislation and court actions have motivated many firms to set up career planning and development programs for minority and female employees, who are in short supply at the middle- and upper-management levels. Organizations are discovering that the career development needs of women and minorities often require special programs and the use of nontraditional methods, such as integrated systems for recruitment, placement, and development. Similarly, age-discrimination laws have led many organizations to set up career programs aimed at older managers and professionals. Thus, career planning and development are increasingly being applied to people at different ages and stages of development—from new recruits to those nearing retirement age.

Career Stages

A career consists of a sequence of work-related positions occupied by a person during the course of a lifetime.[36] Traditionally, careers were judged in terms of advancement and promotion upward in the organizational hierarchy. Today, they are defined in more holistic ways to include a person's attitudes and experiences. For example, a person can remain in the same job, acquiring and developing new skills, and have a successful career without ever getting promoted. Similarly, people may move horizontally through a series of jobs in different functional areas of the firm. Although they may not be promoted upward in the hierarchy, their broadened job experiences constitute a successful career.

Considerable research has been devoted to understanding how aging and experience affect people's careers. This research has drawn on the extensive work done on adult growth and development[37] and has adapted that developmental perspective to work experience.[38] Results suggest that employees progress through at least four distinct career stages as they mature and gain experience. Each stage has unique concerns, needs, and challenges.

1. *The establishment stage (ages 21–26).* This phase is the outset of a career when people are generally uncertain about their competence and potential. They are dependent on others, especially bosses and more experienced employees, for guidance, support, and feedback. At this stage, people are making initial choices about committing themselves to a specific career, organization, and job. They are exploring possibilities while learning about their own capabilities.

2. *The advancement stage (ages 26–40).* During this phase, employees become independent contributors who are concerned with achieving and advancing in their chosen careers. They have typically learned to perform autonomously and need less guidance from bosses and closer ties with colleagues. This settling-down period also is characterized by attempts to clarify the range of long-term career options.

3. *The maintenance stage (ages 40–60).* This phase involves leveling off and holding on to career successes. Many people at this stage have achieved their greatest advancements and are now concerned with helping less-experienced subordinates. For those who are dissatisfied with their career progress, this period can be conflictual and depressing, as characterized by the term "midlife crisis." People often reappraise their circumstances, search for alternatives, and redirect their career efforts. Success in these endeavors can lead to continuing growth, whereas failure can lead to early decline.

4. *The withdrawal stage (ages 60 and above).* This final stage is concerned with leaving a career. It involves letting go of organizational attachments and getting ready for greater leisure time and retirement. The employee's major contributions are imparting knowledge and experience to others. For those people who are generally satisfied with their careers, this period can result in feelings of fulfillment and a willingness to leave the career behind.

The different career stages represent a broad developmental perspective on people's jobs. They provide insight about the personal and career issues that people are likely to face at different career phases. These issues can be potential sources of stress. Employees are likely to go through the phases at different rates, and to experience personal and career issues differently at each stage. For example, one person may experience the maintenance stage as a positive opportunity to develop less-experienced employees; another person may experience the maintenance stage as a stressful leveling off of career success.

Career Planning

Career planning involves setting individual career objectives. It is highly personalized and generally includes assessing one's interests, capabilities, values, and goals; examining alternative careers; making decisions that may affect the current job; and planning how to progress in the desired direction. This process results in people choosing occupations, organizations, and jobs. It determines, for example, whether individuals will accept or decline promotions and transfers and whether they will stay or leave the company for another job or for retirement.

The four career stages can be used to make career planning more effective. Table 12.3 shows the different career stages and the career planning issues relevant at each phase. Applying the table to a particular employee involves first diagnosing the person's existing career stage—establishment, advancement, maintenance, or withdrawal. Next, available career planning resources, such as workshops, career counseling, assessment programs, and self-directed materials, are used to help the employee address pertinent issues.

According to Table 12.3, employees who are just becoming established in careers can be stressed by concerns for identifying alternatives, assessing their interests and capabilities, learning how to perform effectively, and finding out how they are doing. At this stage, the company should provide considerable communication and counseling about available career paths and the skills and abilities needed to progress in them. Workshops, self-development materials, and assessment techniques should be aimed at helping employees assess their interests, aptitudes, and capabilities and at linking that information to possible careers and jobs. Considerable attention should be directed to giving employees continual feedback about job performance and to

Table 12·3	Career Stages and Career Planning Issues
CAREER STAGE	**CAREER-PLANNING ISSUES**
Establishment	What are alternative occupations, organizations, and jobs? What are my interests and capabilities? How do I get the work accomplished? Am I performing as expected? Am I developing the necessary skills for advancement?
Advancement	Am I advancing as expected? How can I advance more effectively? What long-term options are available? How do I get more exposure and visibility? How do I develop more effective peer relationships? How do I better integrate career choices with my personal life?
Maintenance	How do I help others become established and advance? Should I reassess myself and my career? Should I redirect my actions?
Withdrawal	What are my interests outside of work? What postretirement work options are available to me? How can I be financially secure? How can I continue to help others?

counseling them about how to improve it. The supervisor–subordinate relationship is especially important for these feedback and development activities.

People at the advancement stage are concerned mainly with getting ahead, discovering long-term career options, and integrating career choices, such as transfers or promotions, with their personal lives. Here, the company should provide employees with communication and counseling about challenging assignments and possibilities for more exposure and demonstration of skills. It should help clarify the range of possible long-term career options and provide members with some idea about where they stand in achieving them. Workshops, developmental materials, and assessment methods should be aimed at helping employees develop wider collegial relationships, join with effective mentors and sponsors, and develop more creativity and innovation. These activities also should help people assess both career and personal life spheres and integrate them more successfully.

At the maintenance stage, individuals are concerned with helping newer employees become established and grow in their careers. This phase also may involve a reassessment of self and career and a possible redirection to something more rewarding. The firm should provide individuals with communications about the broader organization and how their roles fit into it. Workshops, developmental materials, counseling, and assessment techniques should be aimed at helping employees assess and develop skills in order to train and coach others. For those experiencing a midlife crisis, career planning activities should be directed at helping them reassess their circumstances and develop in new directions. Midlife crises generally are caused by perceived threats to people's career or family identities.[39] Career planning should help people deal effectively with identity issues, especially in the context of an ongoing career. This may include workshops and close interpersonal counseling to help people confront identity issues and reorient their thinking about themselves in relation to work and family. These activities also might help employees deal with the emotions evoked by a midlife crisis and develop the skills and confidence to try something new.

Employees who are at the withdrawal stage can experience stress about disengaging from work and establishing a secure leisure life. Here, the company should provide communications and counseling about options for postretirement work and financial security, and it should convey the message that the employee's experience in the organization is still valued. Retirement planning workshops and materials can help employees gain the skills and information necessary to make a successful transition from work to nonwork life. They can prepare people to shift their attention away from the organization to other interests and activities.

Career Development

Career development helps people achieve their career objectives. It follows closely from career planning and includes organizational practices that help employees implement those plans. These may include skill training, performance feedback and coaching, planned job rotation, mentoring, and continuing education.

Career development can be integrated with people's career needs by linking it to different career stages. Table 12.4 identifies career development interventions, lists the career stages to which they are most relevant, and defines their key purposes and intended outcomes. It shows that career development practices may apply to one or more career stages. Performance feedback and coaching, for example, are relevant to both the establishment and advancement stages. Career development interventions also can serve a variety of purposes, such as helping members identify a career path or providing feedback on career progress and work effectiveness. They can contribute to different organizational outcomes such as lowering turnover and costs and enhancing member satisfaction.

Career development interventions traditionally have been applied to younger employees who have a longer time period to contribute to the firm than do older members. Managers often stereotype older employees as being less creative, alert, and productive than younger workers and consequently provide them with less career development support.[40] Similarly, Table 12.4 suggests that the OD field has been relatively lax in developing methods for helping older members cope with the withdrawal stage because only two of the eleven interventions presented there

Table 12•4	Career Development Interventions		
INTERVENTION	**CAREER STAGE**	**PURPOSE**	**INTENDED OUTCOMES**
Realistic job preview	Establishment Advancement	To provide members with an accurate expectation of work requirements	Reduce turnover Reduce training costs Increase commitment Increase job satisfaction
Job pathing	Establishment Advancement	To provide members with a sequence of work assignments leading to a career objective	Reduce turnover Build organizational knowledge
Performance feedback and coaching	Establishment Advancement	To provide members with knowledge about their career progress and work effectiveness	Increase productivity Increase job satisfaction Monitor human resources development
Assessment centers	Establishment Advancement	To select and develop members for managerial and technical jobs	Increase person–job fit Identify high-potential candidates
Mentoring	Establishment Advancement Maintenance	To link a less-experienced member with a more-experienced member for member development	Increase job satisfaction Increase member motivation
Developmental training	Establishment Advancement Maintenance	To provide education and training opportunities that help members achieve career goals	Increase organizational capability
Work–life balance planning	Establishment Advancement Maintenance	To help members balance work and personal goals	Improve quality of life Increase productivity
Job rotation and challenging assignments	Advancement Maintenance	To provide members with interesting work	Increase job satisfaction Maintain member motivation
Dual-career accommodations	Advancement Maintenance	To assist members with significant others to find satisfying work assignments	Attract and retain high-quality members Increase job satisfaction
Consultative roles	Maintenance Withdrawal	To help members fill productive roles later in their careers	Increase problem-solving capacity Increase job satisfaction
Phased retirement	Withdrawal	To assist members in moving into retirement	Increase job satisfaction Lower stress during transition

apply to the withdrawal stage—consultative roles and phased retirement. This relative neglect can be expected to change in the near future, however, as the U.S. workforce continues to grey. To sustain a highly committed and motivated workforce, organizations increasingly will have to address the career needs of older employees. They will have to recognize and reward the contributions that older workers make to the company. Workforce diversity interventions, discussed later in this chapter, are a positive step in that direction.

Realistic Job Preview

This intervention provides people with realistic expectations about the job during the recruitment process. It provides recruits with information about whether the job is likely to be consistent with their needs and career plans. Such knowledge is especially useful during the establishment stage, when people are most in need of realistic information about organizations and jobs. It also can help employees during the advancement stage, when job changes are likely to occur because of promotion.[41]

Job Pathing

This intervention provides members in the establishment and advancement career stages with a carefully developed sequence of work assignments leading to a career objective, although the notion of a job path in the new economy is being challenged.[42] Job pathing helps employees develop new competencies by performing jobs that require new skills and abilities. Research suggests that employees who receive challenging job assignments early in their careers do better in later jobs.[43] Career pathing allows for a gradual stretching of people's talents by moving them through selected jobs of increasing challenge and responsibility. As a person gains experience and demonstrates competence in the job, she or he moves to another job with more advanced skills and knowledge. Performing well on one job increases the chance of being assigned to a more demanding job.

Performance Feedback and Coaching

One of the most effective interventions during the establishment and advancement phases includes feedback about job performance and coaching to improve performance. As suggested in the discussions of goal setting and performance appraisal interventions, employees need continual feedback about goal achievement as well as support and coaching to improve their performances. Feedback and coaching are particularly relevant when employees are establishing careers. They have concerns about how to perform the work, whether they are performing up to expectations, and whether they are gaining the necessary skills for advancement. A manager can facilitate career establishment by providing feedback on performance, coaching, and on-the-job training. These activities can help employees get the job done while meeting their career development needs.[44]

Assessment Centers

This intervention traditionally was designed to help organizations select and develop employees with high potential for managerial jobs. More recently, assessment centers have been extended to career development and to selection of people to fit new work designs, such as self-managing teams.[45] For example, when used to evaluate managerial capability, assessment centers typically process twelve to fifteen people at a time and require them to spend two to three days on site. Participants are given a comprehensive interview, take several tests of mental ability and knowledge, and participate in individual and group exercises intended to simulate managerial work. An assessment team consisting of experienced managers and human resources specialists observes the behaviors and performance of each candidate. This team arrives at an overall assessment of each participant's managerial potential, including a rating on several items believed to be relevant to managerial success in the organization, and pass the results to management for use in making promotion decisions.

Mentoring

One of the most useful ways to help employees advance in their careers is sponsorship.[46] This involves establishing a close link between a manager or someone more experienced and another organization member who is less experienced. Mentoring is a powerful intervention that assists members in the establishment, advancement, and maintenance stages of their careers. For those in the establishment stage, a sponsor or mentor takes a personal interest in the employee's career and guides and sponsors it. This ensures that a person's hard work and skill translate into actual opportunities for promotion and advancement.[47] For older employees in the maintenance stage, mentoring provides opportunities to share knowledge and experience with others who are less experienced. Older managers may mentor younger employees who are in the establishment and advancement career stages. Mentors do not have to be the direct supervisors of the younger employees but can be hierarchically or functionally distant from them. Other mentoring opportunities include temporarily assigning veteran managers to newer managers to help them gain managerial skills and knowledge.

Developmental Training

A large number of organizations offer developmental training programs, including Procter & Gamble, Cisco Systems, IBM, and Hewlett-Packard. This intervention helps employees gain the skills and knowledge for training and coaching others. It may include workshops and training materials oriented to human relations, communications, active listening, and mentoring. It also can involve substantial investments in education, such as tuition reimbursement programs that assist members in achieving advanced degrees. Developmental training interventions generally are aimed at increasing the organization's reservoir of skills and knowledge. This enhances its capability to implement personal and organizational strategies.

Work–Life Balance Planning

Work–life balance planning involves a variety of programs to help members better manage the interface between work and family. These include such organizational practices as flexible hours, job sharing, and daycare, as well as interventions to help employees identify and achieve both career and family goals. A popular program is called *middlaning*, a metaphor for a legitimate, alternative career track that acknowledges choices about living life in the "fast lane."[48] Middlaning helps people redesign their work and income-generating activities so that more time and energy are available for family and personal needs. It involves education in work addiction, guilt, anxiety, and perfectionism; skill development in work contract negotiation; examination of alternatives such as changing careers, freelancing, and entrepreneuring; and exploration of options for controlling financial pressures by improving income/expense ratios, limiting "black hole" worries such as college tuition for children and retirement expenses, and replacing financial worrying with financial planning. Because concerns about work–life balance are unlikely to abate and may even increase in the near future, we can expect requisite OD interventions, such as middlaning, to proliferate throughout the public and private sectors.

Job Rotation and Challenging Assignments

The purpose of these interventions is to provide employees with the experience and visibility needed for career advancement or with the challenge needed to revitalize a stagnant career at the maintenance stage. Unlike job pathing, which specifies a sequence of jobs to reach a career objective, job rotation and challenging assignments are less planned and may not be as oriented to promotion opportunities. Companies such as Corning Glass Works, Hewlett-Packard, American Crystal Sugar Company, and Fidelity Investments identify "comers" (managers under forty years old with potential for assuming top management positions) and "hipos" (high-potential candidates) and provide them with cross-divisional job experiences during the advancement stage. In the maintenance stage, challenging assignments can help revitalize veteran employees by providing them with new challenges and opportunities for learning and contribution.

Dual-Career Accommodations

These are practices for helping employees cope with the problems inherent in "dual careers"—that is, both the employee and a spouse or significant other pursuing full-time careers. Dual careers are becoming more prevalent as women increasingly enter the workforce. The U.S. Department of Labor reports that more than 80 percent of all marriages involve dual careers.[49] A survey of companies reported the following dual-career accommodations: recognition of problems in dual careers, help with relocation, flexible working hours, counseling for dual-career employees, family daycare centers, improved career planning, and policies making it easier for two members of the same family to work in the same organization or department.[50] Some companies also have established cooperative arrangements with other firms to provide sources of employment for the other partner.[51]

Consultative Roles

These provide late-career employees with opportunities to apply their wisdom and knowledge to helping others develop in their careers and solve organizational problems. Such roles, which can be structured around specific projects or problems, involve offering advice and expertise to those responsible for resolving the issues. In contrast to mentoring roles, consultative roles are not focused directly on guiding or sponsoring younger employees' careers. They are directed at helping others deal with complex problems or projects. Similarly, in contrast to managerial positions, consultative roles do not include the performance evaluation and control inherent in being a manager. They are based more on wisdom and experience than on authority. Consequently, consultative roles provide an effective transition for moving preretirement managers into more support-staff positions. They free up managerial positions for younger employees while allowing older managers to apply their experience and skills in a more supportive and less threatening way than might be possible from a strictly managerial role.

Phased Retirement

This provides older employees with an effective way of withdrawing from the organization and establishing a productive leisure life. It includes various forms of part-time work. Employees gradually devote less of their time to the organization and more time to leisure pursuits (which to some might include developing a new career). Phased retirement allows older employees to make a gradual transition from organizational to leisure life. It enables them to continue contributing to the firm while it gives them time to establish themselves outside of work. For example, people may use the extra time off work to take courses, to gain new skills and knowledge, and to create opportunities for productive leisure. IBM, for example, offers tuition rebates for courses on any topic taken within three years of retirement.[52] Many IBM preretirees have used this program to prepare for second careers.

WORKFORCE DIVERSITY INTERVENTIONS

Several profound trends are shaping the labor markets of modern organizations. Researchers suggest that contemporary workforce characteristics are radically different from what they were just twenty years ago. Employees represent every ethnic background and color; range from highly educated to illiterate; vary in age from eighteen to eighty; may appear perfectly healthy or may have a terminal illness; may be single parents or part of dual-income, divorced, same-sex, or traditional families; and may be physically or mentally challenged.

Workforce diversity is more than a euphemism for cultural or ethnic differences. Such a definition is too narrow and focuses attention away from the broad range of issues that a diverse workforce poses. Diversity results from people who bring different resources and perspectives to the workplace and who have distinctive needs, preferences, expectations, and lifestyles.[53] Organizations must design human resources systems that account for these differences if they are to attract and retain a productive workforce and if they want to turn diversity into a competitive advantage.[54]

Unfortunately, organizations have tended to address workforce diversity pressures in a piecemeal fashion; only 5 percent of more than fourteen hundred companies surveyed thought they were doing a "very good job" of managing diversity.[55] As each trend makes itself felt, the organization influences appropriate practices and activities. For example, as the percentage of women in the workforce increased, many organizations simply added maternity leaves to their benefits packages; as the number of physically challenged workers increased and when Congress passed the Americans with Disabilities Act in 1990, organizations changed their physical settings to accommodate wheelchairs. Demographers warn, however, that these trends are not only powerful by themselves but will likely interact with each other to force organizational change. Thus, a growing number of organizations, such as MBNA Corporation, Lockheed Martin, the St. Paul Companies, Levi Strauss, Procter & Gamble, Monsanto, and Wisconsin Electric, are taking bolder steps. They are not only adopting learning perspectives with respect to diversity, but systemically weaving diversity-friendly values and practices into the cultural fabric of the organization.

Many of the OD interventions described in this book can be applied to the strategic responses and implementation of workforce diversity, as shown in Table 12.5. It summarizes several of the internal and external pressures facing organizations, including age, gender, disability, culture and values, and sexual orientation.[56] The table also reports the major trends characterizing those dimensions, organizational implications and workforce needs, and specific OD interventions that can address those implications.

Age

The average age of the U.S. workforce is rising and changing the distribution of age groups. Between 1998 and 2008, the category of workers aged twenty-five to fifty-four will grow 5.5 percent, and the fifty-five and over age category is expected to increase almost 48 percent. This skewed distribution is mostly the result of the baby boom between 1946 and 1964. As a result, organizations will face a predominantly

Table 12•5	Workforce Diversity Dimensions and Interventions		
WORKFORCE DIFFERENCES	**TRENDS**	**IMPLICATIONS AND NEEDS**	**INTERVENTIONS**
Age	Median age up Distribution of ages changing	Health care Mobility Security	Wellness program Job design Career planning and development Reward systems
Gender	Percentage of women increasing Dual-income families	Child care Maternity/paternity leave Single parents	Job design Fringe benefit rewards
Disability	The number of people with disabilities entering the workforce is increasing	Job challenge Job skills Physical space Respect and dignity	Performance management Job design Career planning and development
Culture and values	Rising proportion of immigrant and minority-group workers Shift in rewards	Flexible organizational policies Autonomy Affirmation Respect	Career planning and development Employee involvement Reward systems
Sexual orientation	Number of single-sex households up More liberal attitudes toward sexual orientation	Discrimination	Equal employment opportunities Fringe benefits Education and training

middle-aged and older workforce. Even now, many organizations are reporting that the average age of their workforce is over forty. Such a distribution will place special demands on the organization.

For example, the personal needs and work motivation of the different cohorts will require differentiated human resources practices. Older workers place heavy demands on health-care services, are less mobile, and will have fewer career advancement opportunities. This situation will require specialized work designs that account for physical capabilities of older workers, career development activities that address and use their experience, and benefit plans that accommodate their medical and psychological needs. Demand for younger workers, on the other hand, will be intense. To attract and retain this more mobile group, jobs will have to be more challenging, advancement opportunities more prevalent, and an enriched quality of work life more common.

Organization development interventions, such as work design, wellness programs (discussed below), career planning and development, and reward systems must be adapted to these different age groups. For the older employee, work designs can reduce the physical components or increase the knowledge and experience components of a job. At Builder's Emporium, a chain of home improvement centers, the store clerk job was redesigned to eliminate heavy lifting by assigning night crews to replenish shelves and emphasizing sales ability instead of strength. Younger workers will likely require more challenge and autonomy. Wellness programs can be used to address the physical and mental health of both generations. Career planning and development programs will have to recognize the different career stages of each cohort and offer resources tailored to that stage. Finally, reward system interventions may offer increased health benefits, time off, and other perks for the older worker while using promotion, ownership, and pay to attract and motivate the scarcer, younger workforce.

Gender

Another important trend is the increasing percentage of female workers in the labor force. By the year 2008, almost 48 percent of the U.S. workforce will be women, and they will represent more than half of the new entrants between 1998 and 2008. The organizational implications of these trends are sobering. Three-quarters of all working women are in their childbearing years, and more than half of all mothers work. Health-care costs will likely increase at even faster rates, and costs associated with absenteeism and turnover will rise. In addition, demands for child care, maternity and paternity leaves, and flexible working arrangements will place pressure on work systems to maintain productivity and teamwork. From a management perspective, there will be more men and women working together as peers, more women entering the executive ranks, greater diversity of management styles, and changing definitions of managerial success.

Work design, reward systems, and career development are among the more important interventions for addressing issues arising out of the gender trend. For example, jobs can be modified to accommodate the special demands of working mothers. A number of organizations, such as Digital Equipment, Steelcase, and Hewlett-Packard, have instituted job sharing, by which two people perform the tasks associated with one job. The firms have done this to allow their female employees to pursue both family and work careers. Reward system interventions, especially fringe benefits, can be tailored to offer special leaves to both mothers and fathers, child-care options, flexible working hours, and health and wellness benefits. Career development interventions help maintain, develop, and retain a competent and diverse workforce. Organizations such as Polaroid, Hoechst Celanese, and Ameritech have instituted job pathing, challenging assignments, and mentoring programs to retain key female members.

Disability

A third trend is the increasing number of men and women with disabilities entering the workforce. The workforce of the twenty-first century will comprise people with a variety of physical and mental disabilities. In 1990, the federal Americans with Disabilities Act banned all forms of discrimination on the basis of physical or mental disability in the hiring and promotion process. It also required many organizations to modify physical plants and office buildings to accommodate people with disabilities.

The organizational implications of the disability trend represent both opportunity and adjustment. The productivity of physically and mentally disabled workers often surprises managers, and training is required to increase managers' awareness of this opportunity. Employing disabled workers, however, also means a need for more comprehensive health care, new physical workplace layouts, new attitudes toward working with the disabled, and challenging jobs that use a variety of skills.

OD interventions, including work design, career planning and development, and performance management, can be used to integrate the disabled into the workforce. For example, traditional approaches to job design can simplify work to permit physically handicapped workers to complete an assembly task. Career planning and development programs need to focus on making disabled workers aware of career opportunities. Too often, these employees do not know that advancement is possible, and they are left feeling frustrated. Career tracks need to be developed for these workers.

Performance management interventions, including goal setting, monitoring, and coaching performance, aligned with the workforce's characteristics are important. At Blue Cross and Blue Shield of Florida, for example, a supervisor learned sign language to communicate with a deaf employee whose productivity was low but whose quality of work was high. Two other deaf employees were transferred to that supervisor's department, and over a two-year period, the performance of the deaf workers improved 1,000 percent with no loss in quality.

Culture and Values

Immigration into the United States from the Pacific Rim, South America, Europe, the Middle East, and the former Soviet states will alter drastically the cultural diversity of the workplace. Between 1998 and 2008, the U.S. civilian labor force will increase by 12 percent, while the Asian and Hispanic population in the United States will increase by 40 and 37 percent, respectively. Approximately six hundred thousand people will immigrate (legally and illegally) into the United States, mostly from Latin America and Asia, and about two-thirds of those immigrants will enter the workforce. In California, 50 percent of the population will be people of color by the year 2005, and they will speak more than eighty languages.

Cultural diversity has broad organizational implications. Different cultures represent a variety of values, work ethics, and norms of correct behavior. Not all cultures want the same things from work, and simple, piecemeal changes in specific organizational practices will be inadequate if the workforce is culturally diverse. Management practices will have to be aligned with cultural values and support both career and family orientations. English is a second language for many people, and jobs of all types (processing, customer contact, production, and so on) will have to be adjusted accordingly. Finally, the organization will be expected to satisfy both extrinsic and monetary needs, as well as intrinsic and personal growth needs.

Several planned change interventions, including employee involvement, reward systems, and career planning and development, can be used to adapt to cultural diversity. Employee involvement practices can be adapted to the needs for participation in decision making. People from certain cultures, such as Scandinavia, are more likely to expect and respond to high-involvement policies; other cultures, such as Latin America, view participation with reservation. (See the discussion of cultural values in Chapter 15.) Participation in an organization can take many forms, from suggestion systems and attitude surveys to high-involvement work designs and performance management systems. Organizations can maximize worker productivity by basing the amount of power and information workers have on cultural and value orientations.

Reward systems can focus on increasing flexibility. For example, flexible working hours and locations permit employees to meet personal obligations without sacrificing organizational objectives. Many organizations have implemented this innovation, and most report that the positive benefits outweigh the costs. For example, Pacific Telesis, Eddie Bauer, and Marriott allow workers to spend part of their time telecommuting from home. Other flexible benefits, such as floating holidays, allow people from different cultures to match important religious and family occasions with work schedules.

Finally, career planning and development programs can help workers identify advancement opportunities that are in line with their cultural values. Some cultures value technical skills over hierarchical advancement; others see promotion as a prime indicator of self-worth and accomplishment. By matching programs with people, job satisfaction, productivity, and employee retention can be improved.

Sexual Orientation

Finally, diversity in sexual and affectional orientation, including gay, lesbian, and bisexual individuals and couples, increasingly is affecting the way that organizations think about human resources. Accurate data on the number of gay men and lesbians in the workforce are difficult to obtain because laws and social norms do not support self-disclosure of a person's sexual orientation. However, a 1998 U.S. Census report showed the number of same-sex-partner households as 1.67 million, and a number of studies have estimated the number of gay men and lesbians at between 6 and 10 percent of the population.

The primary organizational implication of sexual orientation diversity is discrimination. People can have strong emotional reactions to sexual orientation. When these feelings interact with the gender, culture, and values trends described above, the likelihood of both overt and unconscious discrimination is high. An important aspect to this discrimination is the misperceived relationship between sexual orientation and AIDS/HIV. Overall, although 47,000 new cases of HIV and AIDS were reported in the twelve months ending July 1999, the data suggest that the growth of AIDS/HIV is lowest within the gay and lesbian community and highest among drug users and teenagers. The common perception, however, does not fit the facts and gay men and lesbians often are reticent to discuss how organizational policies can be less discriminatory because they fear their openness will lead to unfair treatment.

Interventions aimed at this dimension of workforce diversity are relatively new in OD and are being developed as organizations encounter sexual orientation issues in the workplace. The most frequent response is education and training. This intervention increases members' awareness of the facts and decreases the likelihood of overt discrimination. Human resources practices having to do with equal employment opportunity (EEO) and fringe benefits also can help address sexual orientation parity issues. Some organizations have modified their EEO statements to address sexual orientation. Firms such as Advanced Micro Devices, Fujitsu, Ben & Jerry's, and Dow Chemical have communicated strongly to members and outsiders that decisions with respect to hiring, promotion, transfer, and so on cannot (and will not) be made with respect to a person's sexual orientation. Similarly, organizations increasingly are offering domestic-partner benefit plans. Companies such as Microsoft, Apple, Lotus Development Corporation, and Inprise/Borland have extended health-care and other benefits to the same-sex partners of their members. A 1992 *Newsweek* poll found that 78 percent of the respondents favored extending employee benefits to the domestic partners of lesbians and gay men.

Workforce diversity interventions are growing rapidly in OD. A national survey revealed that 75 percent of firms either have, or plan to begin, diversity efforts.[57] Research suggests that diversity interventions are especially prevalent in large organizations with diversity-friendly senior management and human resources policies.[58] Although existing evidence shows that diversity interventions are growing in popularity, there is still ambiguity about the depth of organizational commitment to such practices and their personal and organizational consequences. A great deal more research is needed to understand these newer interventions and their outcomes.

■ SUMMARY

This chapter presented three types of human resources management interventions—performance management, career planning and development, and workforce diversity. Although all three change programs are relatively new to organization development, they offer powerful methods for managing employee and work group performance. They also help enhance worker satisfaction and support work design, business strategy, and employee involvement practices.

Performance management includes goal setting, performance appraisal, and reward systems. Goal setting is accomplished by setting difficult but feasible goals, managing participation in the goal-setting process, and being sure that the goals can be measured and influenced by the employee or work group. Performance appraisals represent an important link between goal setting and reward systems. As part of an organization's feedback and control system, they provide employees and work groups with information they can use to improve work outcomes. Appraisals are becoming more participative and developmental. Finally, reward systems interventions elicit and maintain desired performance. They can be oriented to both individual jobs or work groups and affect both performance and employee well-being. Three major kinds of reward systems interventions are the design of pay, promotions, and benefits.

Career planning involves helping people choose occupations, organizations, and jobs at different stages of their careers. Employees typically pass through four different career stages—establishment, advancement, maintenance, and withdrawal—with different career planning issues relevant to each stage. Career development helps employees achieve career objectives. Effective efforts in that direction include linking corporate business objectives, human resources needs, and the personal needs of employees. Different career development needs and practices exist and are relevant to each of the four stages of people's careers.

Workforce diversity interventions are designed to adapt human resources practices to an increasingly diverse workforce. Demographic, gender, disability, and culture and values trends point to a more complex set of human resources demands. Within such a context, OD interventions (for example, job design, performance management, and employee involvement practices) have to be adapted to a diverse set of personal preferences, needs, and lifestyles.

■ NOTES

1. A. Mohrman, S. Mohrman, and C. Worley, "High-Technology Performance Management," in *Managing Complexity in High-Technology Organizations,* eds. M. Von Glinow and S. Mohrman (New York: Oxford University Press, 1990): 216–36.

2. D. McDonald and A. Smith, "A Proven Connection: Performance Management and Business Results," *Compensation and Benefits Review* 27 (1995): 59–64.

3. J. Riedel, D. Nebeker, and B. Cooper, "The Influence of Monetary Incentives on Goal Choice, Goal Commitment, and Task Performance," *Organizational Behavior and Human Decision Processes* 42 (1988): 155–80; P. Earley, T. Connolly, and G. Ekegren, "Goals, Strategy Development,

and Task Performance: Some Limits on the Efficacy of Goal Setting," *Journal of Applied Psychology* 74 (1989): 24–33; N. Perry, "Here Come Richer, Riskier Pay Plans," *Fortune* (19 December 1988): 50–58; A. Mohrman, S. Resnick-West, and E. Lawler III, *Designing Performance Appraisal Systems* (San Francisco: Jossey-Bass, 1990).

4. Mohrman, Mohrman, and Worley, "High-Technology Performance Management."

5. E. Locke and G. Latham, *A Theory of Goal Setting and Task Performance* (Englewood Cliffs, N.J.: Prentice Hall, 1990).

6. Locke and Latham, *Theory of Goal Setting;* E. Locke, R. Shaw, L. Saari, and G. Latham, "Goal Setting and Task Performance: 1969–1980," *Psychological Bulletin* 97 (1981):

125–52; M. Tubbs, "Goal Setting: A Meta-Analytic Examination of the Empirical Evidence," *Journal of Applied Psychology* 71 (1986): 474–83.

7. A. O'Leary-Kelly, J. Martocchio, and D. Frink, "A Review of the Influence of Group Goals on Group Performance," *Academy of Management Journal* 37 (1994): 1285–1301.

8. S. Sherman, "Stretch Goals: The Dark Side of Asking for Miracles," *Fortune* (13 November 1995): 231–32; S. Tully, "Why to Go for Stretch Targets," *Fortune* (14 November 1994): 145–58.

9. D. Crown and J. Rosse, "Yours, Mine, and Ours: Facilitating Group Productivity Through the Integration of Individual and Group Goals," *Organizational Behavior and Human Decision Processes* 64, 2 (1995): 138–50.

10. G. Latham and R. Wexley, *Increasing Productivity Through Performance Appraisal* (Reading, Mass.: Addison-Wesley, 1981).

11. C. Peck, "Pay and Performance: The Interaction of Compensation and Performance Appraisal," *Research Bulletin* 155 (New York: Conference Board, 1984).

12. S. Mohrman, G. Ledford Jr., E. Lawler III, and A. Mohrman, "Quality of Work Life and Employee Involvement," in *International Review of Industrial and Organizational Psychology 1986*, eds. C. Cooper and I. Robertson (New York: John Wiley, 1986); G. Yukl and R. Lepsinger, "How to Get the Most out of 360-Degree Feedback," *Training* 32, 21 (1995): 45–50.

13. Mohrman et al., "Quality of Work Life."

14. E. Huse, "Performance Appraisal—A New Look," *Personnel Administration* 30 (March-April 1967): 3–18.

15. S. Gebelein, "Employee Development: Multi-Rater Feedback Goes Strategic," *HR Focus* 73, 1 (1996): 1, 4; B. O'Reilly, "360 Feedback Can Change Your Life," *Fortune* (17 October 1994): 93–100.

16. Mohrman, Resnick-West, and Lawler, *Designing Performance Appraisal Systems;* E. Lawler, "Performance Management: The Next Generation," *Compensation and Benefits Review* 26, 3 (1994): 16–19.

17. W. Scott, J. Farh, and P. Podsakoff, "The Effects of 'Intrinsic' and 'Extrinsic' Reinforcement Contingencies on Task Behavior," *Organizational Behavior and Human Decision Processes* 41 (1988): 405–25; E. Lawler III, *Strategic Pay* (San Francisco: Jossey-Bass, 1990).

18. E. Lawler, *Rewarding Excellence: Pay Strategies for the New Economy* (San Francisco: Jossey-Bass, 2000).

19. J. Campbell, M. Dunnette, E. Lawler III, and K. Weick, *Managerial Behavior, Performance, and Effectiveness* (New York: McGraw-Hill, 1970).

20. S. Kerr, "Risky Business: The New Pay Game," *Fortune* (22 July 1996): 94–96.

21. C. Worley, D. Bowen, and E. Lawler III, "On the Relationship Between Objective Increases in Pay and Employees' Subjective Reactions," *Journal of Organization Behavior* 13 (1992): 559–71.

22. Perry, "Richer, Riskier Pay Plans."

23. S. Tully, "Your Paycheck Gets Exciting," *Fortune* (1 November 1993): 83–98.

24. V. Gibson, "The New Employee Reward System," *Management Review* (February 1995): 13–18.

25. Lawler, *Pay and Organization Development*, pp. 69–72.

26. Ibid., p. 113.

27. H. Gleckman, S. Atchison, T. Smart, and J. Bryne, "Bonus Pay: Buzzword or Bonanza?" *Business Week* (14 November 1994): 62–67.

28. M. Schuster, J. Schuster, and M. Montague, "Excellence in Gainsharing: From the Start to Renewal," *Journal for Quality and Participation* 17, 3 (1994): 18–25; D. Band, G. Scanlon, and C. Tustin, "Beyond the Bottom Line: Gainsharing and Organization Development," *Personnel Review* 23, 8 (1994): 17–32; J. Belcher, "Gainsharing and Variable Pay: The State of the Art," *Compensation and Benefits Review* 26, 3 (1994): 50–60.

29. E. Lawler III, "Reward Systems," in *Improving Life at Work*, eds. J. Hackman and J. Suttle (Santa Monica, Calif.: Goodyear, 1977): 176.

30. R. Walton, "How to Counter Alienation in the Plant," *Harvard Business Review* 50 (November-December 1972): 70–81.

31. Lawler, "Reward Systems," pp. 180–82; J. Haslinger, "Flexible Compensation: Getting a Return on Benefit Dollars," *Personnel Administrator* 30 (1985): 39–46.

32. Lawler, *Pay and Organization Development*, pp. 101–11.

33. E. Lawler III and G. Jenkins, *Employee Participation in Pay Plan Development* (unpublished technical report to U.S. Department of Labor, Ann Arbor, Mich.; Institute for Social Research, University of Michigan, 1976).

34. J. Fierman, "Beating the Midlife Career Crisis," *Fortune* (6 September 1993): 52–62; L. Richman, "How to Get Ahead in America," *Fortune* (16 May 1994): 46–54.

35. "IT Workers Expect Career Development and Job Satisfaction," *HR Focus* (1 August 1999): 4.

36. D. Feldman, *Managing Careers in Organizations* (Glenview, Ill.: Scott, Foresman, 1988).

37. E. Erikson, *Childhood and Society* (New York: Norton, 1963); G. Sheehy, *Passages: Predictable Crises of Adult Life* (New York: E. P. Dutton, 1974); D. Levinson, *Seasons of a Man's Life* (New York: Alfred A. Knopf, 1978); R. Gould, *Transformations: Growth and Change in Adult Life* (New York: Simon & Schuster, 1978).

38. D. Super, *The Psychology of Careers* (New York: Harper & Row, 1957); D. T. Hall, *Careers in Organizations* (Santa Monica, Calif.: Goodyear, 1976); E. Schein, *Career Dynamics: Matching Individual and Organizational Needs* (Reading, Mass.: Addison-Wesley, 1978); L. Baird and K. Kram, "Career Dynamics: The Superior/Subordinate Relationship," *Organizational Dynamics* 11 (Spring 1983): 46–64; J. Slocum and W. Cron, "Job Attitudes and Performance During Three Career Stages" (working paper, Edwin L. Cox School of Business, Southern Methodist University, Dallas, Tex., 1984).

39. M. McGill, "Facing the Mid-Life Crisis," *Business Horizons* 16 (November 1977): 5–13.

40. B. Rosen and T. Jerdee, "Too Old or Not Too Old," *Harvard Business Review* 55 (November-December 1977): 97–106; N. Munk, "Finished at Forty," *Fortune* (1 February 1999): 50–66.

41. S. Premack and J. Wanous, "A Meta-Analysis of Realistic Job Preview Experiments," *Journal of Applied Psychology* 70 (1985): 706–19; B. M. Meglino, A. DeNisi, S. Youngblood, and K. Williams, "Effects of Realistic Job Previews: A Comparison Using an Enhancement and a Reduction Preview," *Journal of Applied Psychology* 73 (1988): 259–66; J. Vandenberg and V. Scarpello, "The Matching Method: An Examination of the Processes Underlying Realistic Job Previews," *Journal of Applied Psychology* 75 (1990): 60–67.

42. L. Thurow, "Building Wealth," *Atlantic Monthly* (June 1999): 57–69.

43. D. Bray, R. J. Campbell, and D. Grant, *Formative Years in Business: A Long Term AT&T Study of Managerial Lives* (New York: John Wiley & Sons, 1974).

44. F. Balcazar, B. Hopkins, and Y. Suarez, "A Critical Objective Review of Performance Feedback," *Journal of Organizational Behavior Management* 7 (1986): 65–89; J. Chobbar and J. Wallin, "A Field Study on the Effect of Feedback Frequency on Performance," *Journal of Applied Psychology* 69 (1984): 524–30; R. Waldersee and F. Luthans, "A Theoretically Based Contingency Model of Feedback: Implications for Managing Service Employees," *Journal of Organizational Change Management* 3 (1990): 46–56.

45. G. Thornton, *Assessment Centers* (Reading, Mass.: Addison-Wesley, 1992); A. Engelbrecht and H. Fischer, "The Managerial Performance Implications of a Developmental Assessment Center Process," *Human Relations* 48 (1995): 387–404.

46. J. Clawson, "Mentoring in Managerial Careers," in *Family and Career*, ed. C. B. Derr (New York: Praeger, 1980); K. Kram, *Mentoring at Work* (Glenview, Ill.: Scott, Foresman, 1984); A. Geiger-DuMond and S. Boyle, "Mentoring: A Practitioner's Guide," *Training and Development* (March 1995): 51–54; G. Shea, *Mentoring: How to Develop Successful Mentor Behaviors* (Menlo Park, Calif.: Crisp Publications, 1998).

47. E. Collins and P. Scott, "Everyone Who Makes It Has a Mentor," *Harvard Business Review* 56 (July-August 1978): 100; M. Murray, *Beyond the Myths and Magic of Mentoring* (San Francisco: Jossey-Bass, 1991).

48. D. Hitchin and J. Hitchin, "Middlaning: Living a Reasonable and Appropriately Balanced Life," *Graziadio Business Report* (Summer 1998): http://bschool.pepperdine.edu/gbr/982/middlani.html.

49. R. Karanbayya and A. Reilly, "Dual Earner Couples: Attitudes and Actions in Restructuring Work for Family," *Journal of Organizational Behavior* 13 (1992): 585–603; J. Schneer and F. Reitman, "Effects of Alternate Family Structures on Managerial Careers," *Academy of Management Journal* 36 (1993): 830–43.

50. D. T. Hall and M. Morgan, "Career Development and Planning," in *Contemporary Problems in Personnel*, 3d ed., eds. K. Pearlman, F. Schmidt, and W. C. Hamnek (New York: John Wiley & Sons, 1983): 232–33.

51. M. Bekas, "Dual-Career Couples—A Corporate Challenge," *Personnel Administrator* (April 1984): 37–44.

52. J. Ivancevich and W. Glueck, *Foundations of Personnel/Human Resource Management*, 3d ed. (Plano, Tex.: Business Publications, 1986): 541.

53. D. Jamieson and J. O'Mara, *Managing Workforce 2000: Gaining the Diversity Advantage* (San Francisco: Jossey-Bass, 1991).

54. F. Rice, "How to Make Diversity Pay," *Fortune* (8 August 1994): 78–86; R. Thomas Jr., "From Affirmative Action to Affirming Diversity," *Harvard Business Review* (March-April 1990): 107–17; K. Labich, "Making Diversity Pay," *Fortune* (9 September 1996): 177–80.

55. Rice, "How to Make Diversity Pay," p. 79.

56. This section benefited greatly from the advice and assistance of Pat Pope, president of Pope and Associates, Cincinnati, Ohio. Much of the data and many examples cited in support of each trend can be found in the following references and Websites: Munk, "Finished at Forty"; M. Galen, "Equal Opportunity Diversity: Beyond the Numbers Game," *Business Week* (14 August 1995): 60–61; K. Hammon and A. Palmer, "The Daddy Trap," *Business Week* (21 September 1998): 56–64; H. Kahan and D. Mulryan, "Out of the Closet," *American Demographics* (May

1995): 40–47; http://stats.bls.gov; http://nces.ed.gov; http://census.gov; http://cdc.gov.

57. Towers Perrin, *Workforce 2000 Today: A Bottom-Line Concern—Revisiting Corporate Views on Workforce Change* (New York: Author, 1992).

58. S. Rynes and B. Rosen, "A Field Survey of Factors Affecting the Adoption and Perceived Success of Diversity Training," *Personnel Psychology* 48 (1995): 247–70; Labich, "Making Diversity Pay."

13

Organization and Environment Relationships

This chapter concerns interventions that address the relationship between an organization and its environment. These change programs are relatively recent additions to the OD field. They focus on helping organizations position themselves strategically in their competitive environments and achieve a better fit with the external forces affecting their goal achievement and performance. Practitioners are discovering that additional knowledge and skills in such areas as competitive strategy, finance, marketing, and political science are necessary to implement these strategic interventions.

The chapter begins with a description of an organization and environment framework. Organizations are open systems and must relate to their environments. They must acquire the resources and information needed to function and they must deliver products or services that are valued by customers. An organization's strategy—how it acquires resources and delivers outputs—is shaped by particular aspects and features of the environment. Organizations can devise a number of responses for managing environmental interfaces, from internal administrative responses, such as creating special units to scan the environment, to external collective responses, such as forming strategic alliances with other organizations.

Three organization and environment interventions are described next. Integrated strategic change, transorganizational development, and merger and acquisition integration help organizations gain a comprehensive understanding of their environments and devise appropriate responses to external demands.

ORGANIZATION AND ENVIRONMENT FRAMEWORK

This section provides a framework for understanding how environments affect organizations and, in turn, how organizations can affect environments. First we describe different *types* of environments that can affect organizations. Then we identify environmental *dimensions* that influence organizational responses to external forces. Finally, we review the different ways that organizations can respond to their environments. This material provides an introductory context for describing interventions that concern organization and environment relationships: integrated strategic change, transorganizational development, and mergers and acquisitions.

Environmental Types

Organizational environments are everything beyond the boundaries of organizations that can directly or indirectly affect performance and outcomes. That includes external agents that directly affect the organization, such as suppliers, customers, regulators, and competitors, as well as indirect influences in the wider cultural, political, and economic context. These two classes of environments are called the task environment and the general environment, respectively.[1] We will also describe the enacted environment, which reflects members' perceptions of the general and task environments.

As described in Chapter 4, the *general environment* consists of all external forces that can influence an organization. It can be categorized into technological, legal and regulatory, political, economic, social, and ecological components. Each of these forces can affect the organization in both direct and indirect ways. For example, economic recessions can directly impact demand for a company's product. The general environment also can affect organizations indirectly by virtue of the linkages between external agents. For example, an organization may have trouble obtaining raw materials from a supplier because the supplier is embroiled in a labor dispute with a national union, a lawsuit with a government regulator, or a boycott by a consumer group. Thus, components of the general environment can affect the organization without having any direct connection to it.

The *task environment* consists of the specific individuals and organizations that interact directly with the organization and can affect goal achievement: customers, suppliers, competitors, producers of substitute products or services, labor unions, financial institutions, and so on. These direct relationships are the medium through which organizations and environments mutually influence one another. Customers, for example, can demand changes in the organization's products, and the organization can try to influence customers' tastes and desires through advertising.

The *enacted environment* consists of the organization's perception and representation of its general and task environments. Weick suggested that environments must be perceived before they can influence decisions about how to respond to them.[2] Organization members must actively observe, register, and make sense of the environment before it can affect their decisions about what actions to take. Thus, only the enacted environment can affect which organizational responses are chosen. The general and task environments, however, can influence whether those responses are successful or ineffective. For example, members may perceive customers as relatively satisfied with their products and may decide to make only token efforts at developing new products. If those perceptions are wrong and customers are dissatisfied with the products, the meager product development efforts can have disastrous organizational consequences. As a result, an organization's enacted environment should accurately reflect its general and task environments if members' decisions and actions are to be effective.

Environmental Dimensions

Environments also can be characterized along dimensions that describe the organization's context and influence its responses. One perspective views environments as information flows and suggests that organizations need to process information to discover how to relate to their environments.[3] The key dimension of the environment affecting information processing is *information uncertainty*, or the degree to which environmental information is ambiguous. Organizations seek to remove uncertainty from the environment so that they know best how to transact with it. For example, organizations may try to discern customer needs through focus groups and surveys and attempt to understand competitor strategies through press releases, salesforce behaviors, and knowledge of key personnel. The greater the uncertainty, the more information processing is required to learn about the environment. This is particularly evident when environments are complex and rapidly changing. These kinds of environments pose difficult information processing problems for organizations. For example, global competition, technological change, and financial markets have created highly uncertain and complex environments for many multinational firms and have severely strained their information processing capacity.

Another perspective views environments as consisting of resources for which organizations compete.[4] The key environmental dimension is *resource dependence,* or the degree to which an organization relies on other organizations for resources. Organizations seek to manage critical sources of resource dependence while remaining as autonomous as possible. For example, firms may contract with several suppliers of the same raw material so that they are not overly dependent on one vendor. Resource dependence is extremely high for an organization when other organizations control critical resources that cannot be obtained easily elsewhere. Resource criticality and availability determine the extent to which an organization is dependent on the environment and must respond to its demands. An example is the tight labor market for information systems experts experienced by many firms in the late 1990s.

These two environmental dimensions—information uncertainty and resource dependence—can be combined to show the degree to which organizations are constrained by their environments and consequently must be responsive to their demands.[5] As shown in Figure 13.1, organizations have the most freedom from external forces when information uncertainty and resource dependence are both low. In such situations, organizations do not need to respond to their environments and can behave relatively independently of them. U.S. automotive manufacturers faced these conditions in the 1950s and operated with relatively little external constraint or threat. Organizations are more constrained and must be more responsive to external demands as information uncertainty and resource dependence increase. They

Figure 13•1	**Environmental Dimensions and Organizational Transactions**

RESOURCE DEPENDENCE

	Low	High
INFORMATION UNCERTAINTY — Low	Minimal environmental constraint and need to be responsive to environment	Moderate constraint and responsiveness to environment
INFORMATION UNCERTAINTY — High	Moderate constraint and responsiveness to environment	Maximal environmental constraint and need to be responsive to environment

SOURCE: Adapted from H. Aldrich, *Organizations and Environments* (New York: Prentice Hall, 1979): 133.

must perceive the environment accurately and respond to it appropriately. As described in Chapter 1, organizations such as financial institutions, high-technology firms, and health-care facilities are facing unprecedented amounts of environmental uncertainty and resource dependence. Their existence depends on recognizing external challenges and responding quickly and appropriately to them.

Organizational Responses

Organizations must have the capacity to monitor and make sense of their environments if they are to respond appropriately. They must identify and attend to those environmental factors and features that are highly related to goal achievement and performance. Moreover, they must have the internal capacity to develop effective responses. Organizations employ a number of methods to influence and respond to their environments, to buffer their technology from external disruptions, and to link themselves to sources of information and resources. These responses are generally designed by senior executives responsible for setting corporate strategy and managing external relationships. Three classes of responses are described below: administrative, competitive, and collective.

Administrative Responses

The most common organizational responses to the environment are administrative, including the formation or clarification of the organization's mission; the development of objectives, policies, and budgets; or the creation of scanning units. These responses can be either proactive or reactive and are aimed at defining the organization's purpose and key tasks in relationship to particular environments. As discussed in Chapter 7, an organization's *mission* describes its long-term purpose, including the products or services to be offered and the markets to be served. An effective mission clearly differentiates the organization from others in its competitive environment.[6] For example, 3M's core purpose is to solve unsolved problems innovatively. 3M is distinguished from its competitors by its attention to unsolved problems and its core competence of innovation. Similarly, an organization's *objectives, policies, and budgets* signal which parts of the environment are important. They allocate and direct resources to particular environmental relationships.[7] Intel's new product development objectives and allocation of more than 20 percent of revenues to research and development signal the importance of its linkage to the technological environment. Finally, organizations may create *scanning units*, such as market research and regulatory relations departments, to respond administratively to the environment. These units scan particular parts or aspects of the environment, interpret relevant information, and communicate it to decision makers who develop appropriate responses.[8] Scanning units generally include specialists with expertise in a particular segment of the environment. For example, market researchers provide information to marketing executives about customer tastes and preferences. Such information guides choices about product development, pricing, and advertising.

Competitive Responses

Competitive responses to the environment typically are associated with for-profit firms but can also apply to nonprofit and governmental organizations. Such actions seek to enhance the organization's performance by establishing a competitive advantage over its rivals. To sustain competitive advantage, organizations must achieve an external position vis-à-vis their competitors or perform internally in ways that are unique, valuable, and difficult to imitate.[9]

Uniqueness. An organization first must identify the bundle of resources and processes that make it distinct from other firms. These can include financial resources, such as access to low-cost capital; reputational resources, such as brand image or a history of product quality; technological resources, such as patents or a strong research and development department; and human resources, such as excellent labor–management relationships or scarce and valuable skill sets. Based on this list, the organization then determines how the resources apply to key organizational processes—regular patterns of organizational activity that involve a sequence of tasks performed by individuals.[10] For example, a software development process combines computer resources, software programs, typing skills, knowledge of computer languages, and customer requirements. Other organizational processes include new product development, strategic planning, appraising member performance, making sales calls, fulfilling customer orders, and the like. Processes and capabilities that are unique to the organization are called *distinctive competencies* and represent the cornerstone of competitive advantage.[11]

Value. Organizations achieve competitive advantage when their resources and processes deliver outputs that either warrant a higher-than-average price or are exceptionally low in cost. Both advantages are valuable according to a performance/price criterion. Products and services with highly desirable features or capabilities, although expensive, are valuable because of their ability to satisfy customer demands for high quality or some other performance dimension. Mercedes automobiles are valuable because the perceived benefits of ownership, including engineering performance, reliability, and prestige, exceed the price paid. On the other hand, outputs that cost little to produce are valuable because of their ability to satisfy customer demands at a low price. Chevrolet automobiles are valuable because they provide basic transportation at a low price. Mercedes and Chevrolet are both profitable, but achieve that outcome through different value propositions.

Imitability. Finally, sustainable competitive advantage is achieved when unique and valuable resources and processes are difficult to mimic or duplicate by other organizations.[12] For example, organizations can protect their competitive advantage by making it difficult for other firms to identify their distinctive competence. Disclosing unimportant information at trade shows or forgoing superior profits can make it difficult for competitors to identify an organization's strengths. Organizations can aggressively pursue a range of opportunities, thus raising the cost for competitors who try to replicate their success. Organizations can seek to retain key human resources through attractive compensation and reward practices like those described in Chapter 12, thereby making it more difficult and costly for competitors to attract such talent.

Collective Responses

Organizations can cope with problems of environmental dependence and uncertainty through increased coordination with other organizations. Collective responses help control interdependencies among organizations and include such methods as bargaining; contracting; coopting; and creating joint ventures, federations, strategic alliances, and consortia.[13] Contemporary organizations increasingly are turning to joint ventures and partnerships with other organizations to manage environmental uncertainty and perform tasks that are too costly and complicated for single organizations to perform. These multiorganization arrangements are being used as a means of sharing resources for large-scale research and development, for spreading the risks of innovation, for applying diverse expertise to complex problems and tasks, and for overcoming barriers to entry into foreign markets. For example, pharmaceutical firms are forming strategic alliances to distribute noncompeting medications and avoid the high costs of establishing sales organizations; firms from different countries are forming joint ventures to overcome restrictive trade barriers; and high-technology firms are forming research consortia to undertake significant and costly research and development for their industries.

INTEGRATED STRATEGIC CHANGE

Integrated strategic change (ISC) is a recent intervention that brings an OD perspective to traditional strategic planning. It was developed in response to managers' complaints that good business strategies often are not implemented. The research suggested that too little attention was being given to the change process and human resources issues necessary to execute the strategy.[14] For example, the predominant paradigm in strategic planning and implementation artificially separates strategic thinking from operational and tactical actions; it ignores the contributions that planned change processes can make to implementation.[15] In the traditional process, senior managers and strategic planning staff prepare economic forecasts, competitor analyses, and market studies. They discuss these studies and rationally align the firm's strengths and weaknesses with the environmental opportunities and threats to form the organization's strategy.[16] Implementation occurs as middle managers, supervisors, and employees hear about the new strategy through memos, restructuring announcements, changes in job responsibilities, or new departmental objectives. Consequently, because participation has been limited to top management, there is little understanding of the need for change and little ownership of the new behaviors, initiatives, and tactics required to achieve the announced objectives.

Key Features

ISC, in contrast, was designed to be a highly participative process. It has three key features:[17]

1. The relevant unit of analysis is the organization's *strategic orientation* comprising its strategy and organization design. Strategy and the design that supports it must be considered as an integrated whole.

2. Creating the strategic plan, gaining commitment and support for it, planning its implementation, and executing it are treated as one integrated process. The ability to repeat such a process quickly and effectively when conditions warrant represents a sustainable competitive advantage.[18]

3. Individuals and groups throughout the organization are integrated into the analysis, planning, and implementation process to create a more achievable plan, to maintain the firm's strategic focus, to direct attention and resources on the organization's key competencies, to improve coordination and integration within the organization, and to create higher levels of shared ownership and commitment.

Application Stages

The ISC process is applied in four phases: performing a strategic analysis, exercising strategic choice, designing a strategic change plan, and implementing the plan. The four steps are discussed sequentially here but actually unfold in overlapping and integrated ways. Figure 13.2 displays the steps in the ISC process and its change

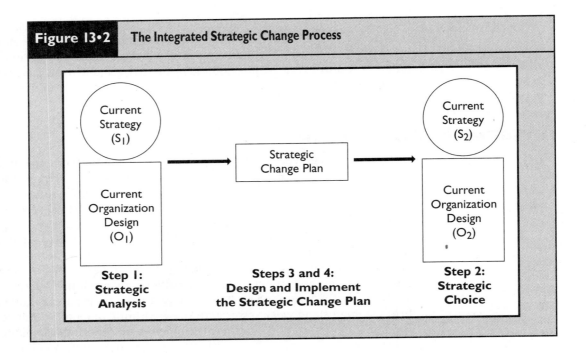

Figure 13•2   The Integrated Strategic Change Process

components. An organization's existing strategic orientation, identified as its current strategy (S_1) and organization design (O_1), is linked to its future strategic orientation (S_2/O_2) by the strategic change plan.

1. *Performing the strategic analysis.* The ISC process begins with a diagnosis of the organization's readiness for change and its current strategy and organization (S_1/O_1). The most important indicator of readiness is senior management's willingness and ability to carry out strategic change. Greiner and Schein suggest that the two key dimensions in this analysis are the leader's willingness and commitment to change and the senior team's willingness and ability to follow the leader's initiative.[19] Organizations whose leaders are not willing to lead and whose senior managers are not willing and able to support the new strategic direction when necessary should consider team-building processes to ensure their commitment.

    The second stage in strategic analysis is understanding the current strategy and organization design. The process begins with an examination of the organization's industry as well as its current financial performance and effectiveness. This information provides the necessary context to assess the current strategic orientation's viability. Porter's model of industry attractiveness[20] as well as the environmental framework introduced at the beginning of this chapter are the two most relevant models for analyzing the environment. Next, the current strategic orientation is described to explain current levels of performance and human outcomes. Several models for guiding this diagnosis exist.[21] For example, the current strategic orientation can be assessed according to the model and methods introduced in Chapter 4. The strategy is represented by the organization's mission, goals and objectives, intent, and business policies. The organization design is described by the structure, work, information, and human resource systems. Other models for understanding the organization's strategic orientation include the competitive positioning model[22] and other typologies.[23] These frameworks assist in assessing customer satisfaction; product and service offerings; financial health; technological capabilities; and organizational culture, structure, and systems.

Strategic analysis actively involves organization members in the process. Search conferences; employee focus groups; interviews with salespeople, customers, purchasing agents; and other methods allow a variety of employees and managers to participate in the diagnosis and increase the amount and relevance of the data collected. This builds commitment to and ownership of the analysis; should a strategic change effort result, members are more likely to understand why and be supportive of it.

2. *Exercising strategic choice.* Once the existing strategic orientation is understood, a new one must be designed. For example, the strategic analysis may reveal misfits among the organization's environment, strategic orientation, and performance. These misfits can be used as inputs to workshops where the future strategy and organization design are crafted. Based on this analysis, senior management formulates visions for the future and broadly defines two or three alternative sets of objectives and strategies for achieving those visions. Market forecasts, employees' readiness and willingness to change, competitor analyses, and other projections can be used to develop the alternative future scenarios.[24] The different sets of objectives and strategies also include projections about the organizational design changes that will be necessary to support each alternative. Although participation from other organizational stakeholders is important in the alternative generation phase, choosing the appropriate strategic orientation ultimately rests with top management and cannot easily be delegated. Senior executives are in the unique position of viewing strategy from a general management position. When major strategic decisions are given to lower-level managers, the risk of focusing too narrowly on a product, market, or technology increases.

   This step determines the content or "what" of strategic change. The desired strategy (S_2) defines the products or services to offer, the markets to be served, and the way these outputs will be produced and positioned. The desired organization design (O_2) specifies the organizational structures and processes necessary to support the new strategy. Aligning an organization's design with a particular strategy can be a major source of superior performance and competitive advantage.[25]

3. *Designing the strategic change plan.* The strategic change plan is a comprehensive agenda for moving the organization from its current strategy and organization design to the desired future strategic orientation. It represents the process or "how" of strategic change. The change plan describes the types, magnitude, and schedule of change activities, as well as the costs associated with them. It also specifies how the changes will be implemented, given power and political issues, the nature of the organizational culture, and the current ability of the organization to implement change.[26]

4. *Implementing the strategic change plan.* The final step in the ISC process is the actual implementation of the strategic change plan. This draws heavily on knowledge of motivation, group dynamics, and change processes. It deals continuously with such issues as alignment, adaptability, teamwork, and organizational and personal learning. Implementation requires senior managers to champion the different elements of the change plan. They can, for example,

initiate action and allocate resources to particular activities, set high but achievable goals, and provide feedback on accomplishments. In addition, leaders must hold people accountable to the change objectives, institutionalize each change that occurs, and be prepared to solve problems as they arise. This final point recognizes that no strategic change plan can account for all of the contingencies that emerge. There must be a willingness to adjust the plan as implementation unfolds to address unforeseen and unpredictable events and to take advantage of new opportunities.

TRANSORGANIZATIONAL DEVELOPMENT

Transorganizational development (TD) is a form of planned change aimed at helping organizations develop collective and collaborative strategies with other organizations. Many of the tasks, problems, and issues facing organizations today are too complex and multifaceted to be addressed by a single organization. Multiorganization strategies and arrangements are increasing rapidly in today's highly competitive, global environment. In the private sector, research and development consortia allow companies to share resources and risks associated with large-scale research efforts. For example, Sematech involved many large organizations, such as Intel, AT&T, IBM, Xerox, and Motorola, that joined together to improve the competitiveness of the U.S. semiconductor industry. Joint ventures between domestic and foreign firms, such as Fuji-Xerox, can help overcome trade barriers and facilitate technology transfer across nations. The New United Motor Manufacturing, Inc., in Fremont, California, for example, is a joint venture between General Motors and Toyota to produce automobiles using Japanese teamwork methods. In the public sector, partnerships between government and business provide the resources and initiative to undertake complex urban renewal projects, such as Baltimore's Inner Harbor Project and Pittsburgh's Neighborhood Housing Services. Alliances among public service agencies in a region, such as the Human Services Council of Grand River, Michigan, and OuR TOWN, a cooperative project between local governments to promote rural tourism, can help coordinate services, promote economies, and avoid costly overlap and redundancy.

Transorganizational Systems and Their Problems

Cummings has referred to these multiorganization structures as *transorganizational systems* (TSs)—groups of organizations that have joined together for a common purpose.[27] TSs include a range of collective responses, including licensing agreements, strategic alliances, joint ventures, and public–private partnerships. They are functional social systems existing intermediately between single organizations and societal systems. TSs make decisions and perform tasks on behalf of their member organizations, although members maintain their separate organizational identities and goals. This separation distinguishes them from mergers and acquisitions. In contrast to most organizations, TSs tend to be underorganized: relationships among member organizations are loosely coupled; leadership and power are dispersed among autonomous organizations, rather than hierarchically centralized; and commitment and membership are tenuous as member organizations act to maintain their autonomy while jointly performing.

These characteristics make creating and managing TSs difficult.[28] Potential member organizations may not perceive the need to join with other organizations. They may be concerned with maintaining their autonomy or have trouble identifying potential partners. U.S. firms, for example, are traditionally "rugged individualists" preferring to work alone rather than to join with other organizations. Even if organizations decide to join together, they may have problems managing their relationships and controlling joint performances. Because members typically are accustomed to hierarchical forms of control, they may have difficulty managing lateral relations among independent organizations. They also may have difficulty managing different levels of commitment and motivation among members and sustaining membership over time.

Application Stages

Given these problems, transorganizational development has evolved as a unique form of planned change aimed at creating TSs and improving their effectiveness. In laying out the conceptual boundaries of TD, Cummings described the practice of TD as following the phases of planned change appropriate for underorganized systems (see Chapter 2).[29] These stages parallel other process models that have been proposed for creating and managing joint ventures, strategic alliances, and interorganizational collaboration.[30] The four stages are shown in Figure 13.3, along with key issues that need to be addressed at each stage. The stages and issues are described below.

1. *Identification stage.* This initial stage of TD involves identifying potential member organizations of the TS. For example, in the case of a strategic alliance or joint venture, this stage involves identifying the potential partners best suited to achieving the organization's objectives. Identifying potential members can be difficult because organizations may not perceive the need to join together or may not know enough about each other to make membership choices. These problems are typical when trying to create a new TS. Relationships among potential members may be loosely coupled or nonexistent; thus, even if organizations see the need to form a TS, they may be unsure about who should be included.

   The identification stage generally is carried out by one or a few organizations interested in exploring the possibility of creating a TS. Change agents work with these initiating organizations to clarify their own goals, such as product or technology exchange, learning, or market access; to explore collaboration alternatives,

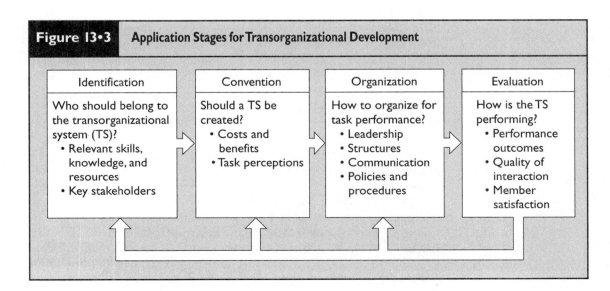

Figure 13•3   Application Stages for Transorganizational Development

Identification	Convention	Organization	Evaluation
Who should belong to the transorganizational system (TS)? • Relevant skills, knowledge, and resources • Key stakeholders	Should a TS be created? • Costs and benefits • Task perceptions	How to organize for task performance? • Leadership • Structures • Communication • Policies and procedures	How is the TS performing? • Performance outcomes • Quality of interaction • Member satisfaction

including internal development, purchasing skills or resources, or making an acquisition; and understanding the tradeoff between the loss of autonomy and the value of collaboration. OD practitioners also help specify criteria for membership in the TS and identify organizations meeting those standards. Because TSs are intended to perform specific tasks, a practical criterion for membership is how much organizations can contribute to task performance. Potential members can be identified and judged in terms of the skills, knowledge, and resources that they bring to bear on the TS task. TD practitioners warn, however, that identifying potential members also should take into account the political realities of the situation.[31] Consequently, key stakeholders who can affect the creation and subsequent performance of the TS are identified as possible members.

During the early stages of creating a TS, there may be insufficient leadership and cohesion among participants to choose potential members. In these situations, participants may contract with an outside change agent who can help them achieve sufficient agreement on TS membership. In several cases of TD, change agents helped members create a special leadership group that could make decisions on behalf of the participants.[32] This leadership group comprised a small cadre of committed members and was able to develop enough cohesion among members to carry out the identification stage.

2. *Convention stage.* Once potential members of the TS are identified, the convention stage is concerned with bringing them together to assess whether creating a TS is desirable and feasible. This face-to-face meeting enables potential members to explore mutually their motivations for joining and their perceptions of the joint task. They work to establish sufficient levels of motivation and of task consensus to form the TS.

Like the identification stage, this phase of TD generally requires considerable direction and facilitation by change agents. Existing stakeholders may not have the legitimacy or skills to perform the convening function, and change agents can serve as conveners if they are perceived as legitimate and credible by the attending organizations. In many TD cases, conveners came from research centers or universities with reputations for neutrality and expertise in TD.[33] Because participating organizations tend to have diverse motives and views and limited means for resolving differences, change agents may need to structure and manage interactions to facilitate airing of differences and arriving at consensus about forming the TS. They may need to help organizations work through differences and reconcile self-interests with those of the larger TS.

3. *Organization stage.* When the convention stage results in a decision to create a TS, members then begin to organize themselves for task performance. This involves establishing structures and mechanisms that promote communication and interaction among members and that direct joint efforts to the task at hand.[34] For example, members may create a coordinating council to manage the TS, and they might assign a powerful leader to head that group. They might choose to formalize exchanges among members by developing rules, policies, and formal operating procedures. When members are required to invest large amounts of resources in the TS, such as might occur in an industry-based research consortium, the organizing stage typically includes voluminous contracting and negotiating about members' contributions and returns. Here, corporate lawyers and financial analysts play key roles in structuring the TS. They determine how costs and benefits will be allocated among member organizations as well as the legal obligations, decision-making responsibilities, and contractual rights of members.

In the case of strategic alliances and joint ventures, explicit strategies must be created for how the TS will perform its work. Change agents can help members define competitive advantage for the TS as well as the structural requirements necessary to support achievement of its goals.

4. *Evaluation stage.* This final stage of TD involves assessing how the TS is performing. Members need feedback so that they can identify problems and begin to resolve them. Feedback data generally include performance outcomes and member satisfactions, as well as indicators of how well members are interacting jointly. Change agents, for example, can periodically interview or survey member organizations about various outcomes and features of the TS and feed that data back to TS leaders. Such information will enable leaders to make necessary operational modifications and adjustments. It may signal the need to return to previous stages of TD to make necessary corrections, as shown by the feedback arrows in Figure 13.2.

MERGERS AND ACQUISITIONS

Mergers and acquisitions (M&As) involve the combination of two organizations. *Merger* refers to the integration of two previously independent organizations into a completely new organization; *acquisition* involves the purchase of one organization by another for integration into the acquiring organization. M&As are distinct from TSs, such as alliances and joint ventures, because at least one of the organizations ceases to exist. The stressful dynamics associated with M&As led one researcher to call them the "ultimate change management challenge."[35]

M&A Rationale

Organizations have a number of reasons for wanting to acquire or merge with other firms, including diversification or vertical integration; gaining access to global markets, technology, or other resources; and achieving operational efficiencies, improved innovation, or resource sharing.[36] As a result, M&As have become a preferred method for rapid growth and strategic change. For example, the value of U.S. domestic M&A transactions was more than $488 billion in 1997 and more than $800 billion in 1998.[37] The total value of M&A activity on a worldwide basis was expected to exceed $2 trillion in 1999. Recent large transactions include Chrysler and Daimler-Benz, CBS and Viacom, Ford and Volvo, Boeing and McDonnell Douglas, and WorldCom and MCI. Despite M&A popularity, they have a questionable record of success.[38] Among the reasons commonly cited for merger failure are inadequate due diligence processes, lack of a compelling strategic rationale, unrealistic expectations of synergy, paying too much for the transaction, conflicting corporate cultures, and failure to move quickly.[39]

M&A interventions typically are preceded by an examination of corporate and business strategy. Corporate strategy describes the range of businesses within which the firm will participate, and business strategy specifies how the organization will compete in any particular business. Organizations must decide whether their corporate and strategic goals should be achieved through administrative or competitive responses, such as ISC, or through collective responses, such as TD or M&As. Mergers and acquisitions are preferred when internal development is too slow, or when alliances or joint ventures do not offer sufficient control over key resources to meet the firm's objectives.

M&As are complex strategic changes that involve various legal and financial requirements beyond the scope of this text. OD practitioners are encouraged to seek out and work with specialists in these other relevant disciplines. The focus here is on how OD can contribute to M&A success.

Application Stages

Mergers and acquisitions involve three major phases as shown in Table 13.1: precombination, legal combination, and operational combination.[40] OD practitioners can make substantive contributions to the precombination and operational combination phases as described below.

Precombination Phase

This first phase consists of planning activities designed to ensure the success of the combined organizations. The organization that initiates the strategic change must identify a candidate organization, work with it to gather information about each other, and plan the implementation and integration activities. The evidence is growing that precombination phase activities are critical to M&A success.[41]

1. *Search for and select candidate.* This involves developing screening criteria to assess and narrow the field of candidate organizations, agreeing on a first-choice candidate, assessing regulatory compliance, establishing initial contacts, and formulating a letter of intent. Criteria for choosing an M&A partner can include leadership and management characteristics, market access resources, technical or financial capabilities, physical facilities, and so on. OD practitioners can add value at this stage of the process by encouraging screening criteria that include managerial, organizational, and cultural components as well as technical and

Table 13·1	Major Phases and Activities in Merger and Acquisitions	
MAJOR M&A PHASES	**KEY STEPS**	**OD AND CHANGE MANAGEMENT ISSUES**
Precombination	• Search for and select candidate • Create M&A team • Establish business case • Perform due diligence assessment • Develop merger integration plans	• Ensure that candidates are screened for cultural as well as financial, technical, and physical asset criteria • Define a clear leadership structure • Establish a clear strategic vision, competitive strategy, and systems integration potential • Specify the desirable organization design features • Specify an integration action plan
Legal combination	• Complete financial negotiations • Close the deal • Announce the combination	
Operational combination	• Day 1 activities • Organizational and technical integration activities • Cultural integration activities	• Implement changes quickly • Communicate • Solve problems together and focus on the customer • Conduct an evaluation to learn and identify further areas of integration planning

financial aspects. In practice, financial issues tend to receive greater attention at this stage, with the goal of maximizing shareholder value. Failure to attend to cultural and organizational issues, however, can result in diminished shareholder value during the operational combination phase.[42]

Identifying potential candidates, narrowing the field, agreeing on a first choice, and checking regulatory compliance are relatively straightforward activities. They generally involve investment brokers and other outside parties who have access to databases of organizational, financial, and technical information. The final two activities, making initial contacts and creating a letter of intent, are aimed at determining the candidate's interest in the proposed merger or acquisition.

2. *Create an M&A team.* Once there is initial agreement between the two organizations to pursue a merger or acquisition, senior leaders from the respective organizations appoint an M&A team to establish the business case, to oversee the due diligence process, and to develop a merger integration plan.[43] This team typically comprises senior executives and experts in such areas as business valuation, technology, organization, and marketing. OD practitioners can facilitate formation of this team through human process interventions, such as team building and process consultation, and help the team establish clear goals and action strategies. They also can help members define a clear leadership structure, apply relevant skills and knowledge, and ensure that both organizations are represented appropriately. The group's leadership structure, or who will be accountable for the team's accomplishments, is especially critical. In an acquisition, an executive from the acquiring firm is typically the team's leader. In a merger of equals, the choice of a single individual to lead the team is more difficult, but must be made. The outcome of this decision and the process used to make it form the first outward symbol of how this strategic change will be conducted.

3. *Establish the business case.* The purpose of this activity is to develop a prima facie case that combining the two organizations will result in a competitive advantage that exceeds their separate advantages.[44] It includes specifying the strategic vision, competitive strategy, and systems integration potential for the M&A. OD practitioners can facilitate this discussion to ensure that each issue is fully explored. If the business case cannot be justified on strategic, financial, and operational grounds, the M&A should be revisited or terminated, or another candidate should be sought.

Strategic vision represents the organizations' combined capabilities. It synthesizes the strengths of the two organizations into a viable new organization. For example, AT&T had a clear picture of its intentions in acquiring NCR: to "link people, organizations, and their information in a seamless global computer network."

Competitive strategy describes the business model for how the combined organization will add value in a particular product market or segment of the value chain, how that value proposition is best performed by the combined organization (compared with competitors), and how that proposition will be difficult to imitate. The purpose of this activity is to force the two organizations to go beyond the rhetoric of "these two organizations should merge because it's a good fit." The AT&T and NCR acquisition struggled, in part, because NCR management was told simply to "look for synergies."[45]

Systems integration specifies how the two organizations will be combined. It addresses how and if they can work together. It includes such key questions as

Will one firm be acquired and operated as a wholly owned subsidiary? Does the transaction imply a merger of equals? Are layoffs implied, and if so, where? On what basis can promised synergies or cost savings be achieved?

4. ***Perform a due diligence assessment.*** This involves evaluating whether the two organizations actually have the managerial, technical, and financial resources that each assumes the other possesses. It includes a comprehensive review of each organization's articles of incorporation, stock option plans, organization charts, and so on. Financial, human resources, operational, technical, and logistical inventories are evaluated along with other legally binding issues. The discovery of previously unknown or unfavorable information can stop the M&A process from going forward.

    Although due diligence assessment traditionally emphasizes the financial aspects of M&As, this focus is increasingly being challenged by evidence that culture clashes between two organizations can ruin expected financial gains.[46] Thus, attention to the cultural features of M&As is becoming more prevalent in due diligence assessment. For example, Abitibi-Price applied a cultural screen as part of its due diligence activities along with financial and operational criteria. The process sought to identify the fit between Abitibi's values and those of possible merger candidates. Stone Consolidated emerged as both a good strategic and cultural fit with Abitibi. This cultural assessment contributed heavily to the success of the subsequent merger.

    The scope and detail of due diligence assessment depend on knowledge of the candidate's business, the complexity of its industry, the relative size and risk of the transaction, and the available resources. Due diligence activities must reflect symbolically the vision and values of the combined organizations. An overly zealous assessment, for example, can contradict promises of openness and trust made earlier in the transaction. Missteps at this stage can lower or destroy opportunities for synergy, cost savings, and improved shareholder value.[47]

5. ***Develop merger integration plans.*** This stage specifies how the two organizations will be combined.[48] It defines integration objectives; the scope and timing of integration activities; organization design criteria; Day 1 requirements; and who does what, where, and when. The scope of these plans depends on how integrated the organizations will be. If the candidate organization will operate as an independent subsidiary with an "arm's-length" relationship to the parent, merger integration planning need only specify those systems that will be common to both organizations. A full integration of the two organizations requires a more extensive plan.

    Merger integration planning starts with the business case conducted earlier and involves more detailed analyses of the strategic vision, competitive strategy, and systems integration for the M&A. For example, assessment of the organizations' markets and suppliers can reveal opportunities to serve customers better and to capture purchasing economies of scale. Examination of business processes can identify best operating practices; which physical facilities should be combined, left alone, or shutdown; and which systems and procedures are redundant. Capital budget analysis can show which investments should be continued or dropped. Typically, the M&A team appoints subgroups composed of members from both organizations to perform these analyses. OD practitioners can conduct team building and process consultation interventions to improve how those groups function.

    Next, plans for designing the combined organization are developed. They include the organization's structure, reporting relationships, human resources policies, information and control systems, operating logistics, work designs, and customer-focused activities.

The final task of integration planning involves developing an action plan for implementing the M&A. This specifies tasks to be performed, decision-making authority and responsibility, and timelines for achievement. It also includes a process for addressing conflicts and problems that will invariably arise during the implementation process.

Legal Combination Phase

This phase of the M&A process involves the legal and financial aspects of the transaction. The two organizations settle on the terms of the deal, register the transaction with and gain approval from appropriate regulatory agencies, communicate with and gain approval from shareholders, and file appropriate legal documents. In some cases, an OD practitioner can provide advice on negotiating a fair agreement, but this phase generally requires knowledge and expertise beyond that typically found in OD practice.

Operational Combination Phase

This final phase involves implementing the merger integration plan. In practice, it begins during due diligence assessment and may continue for months or years following the legal combination phase.[49] M&A implementation includes the three kinds of activities described below.

1. *Day 1 activities.* These include communications and actions that officially start the implementation process. For example, announcements may be made about key executives of the combined organization, the location of corporate headquarters, the structure of tasks, and areas and functions where layoffs will occur. M&A practitioners pay special attention to sending important symbolic messages to organization members, investors, and regulators about the soundness of the merger plans and those changes that are critical to accomplishing strategic and operational objectives.[50]

2. *Operational and technical integration activities.* These involve the physical moves, structural changes, work designs, and procedures that will be implemented to accomplish the strategic objectives and expected cost savings of the M&A. The merger integration plan lists these activities, which can be large in number and range in scope from seemingly trivial to quite critical. For example, American Airlines' acquisition of Reno Air involved changing Reno's employee uniforms, the signage at all airports, marketing and public relations campaigns, repainting airplanes, and integrating the route structures, among others. When these integration activities are not executed properly, the M&A process can be set back. American's poor job of clarifying the wage and benefit programs caused an unauthorized pilot "sickout" that cancelled many flights and left thousands of travelers stranded. Finally, integrating the reservation, scheduling, and pricing systems was a critical activity. Failure to execute this task quickly could have caused tremendous logistical problems, increased safety risks, and further alienated customers.

3. *Cultural integration activities.* These tasks are aimed at building new values and norms in the organization. Successful implementation melds both the technical and cultural aspects of the combined organization. For example, members from both organizations can be encouraged to solve business problems together, thus addressing operational and cultural integration issues simultaneously.[51]

The M&A literature contains several practical suggestions for managing the operational combination phase. First, the merger integration plan should be implemented sooner rather than later, and quickly rather than slowly. Integration of two organizations generally involves aggressive financial targets, short timelines, and intense public scrutiny.[52] Moreover, the change process is often plagued by culture clashes and political fighting. Consequently, organizations need to make as many changes as possible in the first one hundred days following the legal combination phase.[53] Quick movement in key areas has several advantages: it preempts unanticipated organization changes that might thwart momentum in the desired direction, it reduces organization members' uncertainty about when things will happen, and it reduces the anxiety of the activity's impact on the individual's situation. All three of these conditions can prevent desired collaboration and other benefits from occurring.

Second, integration activities must be communicated clearly and in a timely fashion to a variety of stakeholders, including shareholders, regulators, customers, and organization members. M&As can increase uncertainty and anxiety about the future, especially for members of the involved organizations who often inquire, "Will I have a job? Will my job change? Will I have a new boss?" These kind of questions can dominate conversations, reduce productive work, and spoil opportunities for collaboration. To reduce ambiguity, organizations can provide concrete answers through a variety of channels including company newsletters, email and intranet postings, press releases, video and in-person presentations, one-on-one interaction with managers, and so on.

Third, members from both organizations need to work together to solve implementation problems and to address customer needs. Such coordinated tasks can clarify work roles and relationships; they can contribute to member commitment and motivation. Moreover, when coordinated activity is directed at customer service, it can assure customers that their interests will be considered and satisfied during the merger.

Fourth, organizations need to assess the implementation process continually to identify integration problems and needs. The following questions can guide the assessment process:[54]

- Have savings estimated during precombination planning been confirmed or exceeded?
- Has the new entity identified and implemented shared strategies or opportunities?
- Has the new organization been implemented without loss of key personnel?
- Was the merger and integration process seen as fair and objective?
- Is the combined company operating efficiently?
- Have major problems with stakeholders been avoided?
- Did the process proceed according to schedule?
- Were substantive integration issues resolved?
- Are people highly motivated (more so than before)?

■ SUMMARY

In this chapter, we presented interventions aimed at improving organization and environment relationships. Organizations are open systems that exist in environmental contexts and they must establish and maintain effective linkages with the environment to survive and prosper. Three types of environments affect organizational functioning: the general environment, the task environment, and the enacted environment. Only the last environment can affect organizational choices about behavior, but the first two impact the consequences of those actions. Two environmental dimensions, information uncertainty and resource dependence, affect the degree to which organizations are constrained by their environments and need to be responsive to them. For example, when information uncertainty and resource dependence are high, organizations are maximally constrained and need to be responsive to their environments.

Integrated strategic change is a comprehensive intervention for addressing organization and environment issues. It gives equal weight to the strategic and organizational factors affecting organization performance and effectiveness. In addition, these factors are highly integrated during the process of assessing the current strategy and organization design, selecting the desired strategic orientation, developing a strategic change plan, and implementing it.

Transorganizational development is a form of planned change aimed at helping organizations create partnerships with other organizations to perform tasks or to solve problems that are too complex and multifaceted for single organizations to carry out. Because these multiorganization systems tend to be underorganized, TD follows the stages of planned change relevant to underorganized systems: identification, convention, organization, and evaluation.

Mergers and acquisitions involve combining two or more organizations to achieve strategic and financial objectives. It generally involves three phases: precombination, legal combination, and operational combination. The M&A process has been dominated by financial and technical concerns, but experience and research strongly support the contribution that OD practitioners can make to M&A success.

■ NOTES

1. R. Miles, *Macro Organization Behavior* (Santa Monica, Calif.: Goodyear, 1980); R. Daft, *Organization Theory and Design* (Cincinnati, Ohio: South-Western College Publishing, 1998).

2. K. Weick, *The Social Psychology of Organizing*, 2d ed. (Reading, Mass.: Addison-Wesley, 1979).

3. J. Galbraith, *Competing with Flexible Lateral Organizations*, 2d ed. (Reading, Mass.: Addison-Wesley, 1994); P. Evans and T. Wurster, "Strategy and the New Economics of Information," *Harvard Business Review* 75 (1997): 70–83.

4. J. Pfeffer and G. Salancik, *The External Control of Organizations: A Resource Dependence Perspective* (New York: Harper & Row, 1978).

5. H. Aldrich, *Organizations and Environments* (New York: Prentice Hall, 1979); L. Hrebiniak and W. Joyce, "Organizational Adaptation: Strategic Choice and Environmental Determinism," *Administrative Science Quarterly* 30 (1985): 336–49.

6. J. Collins and J. Porras, "Building Your Company's Vision," *Harvard Business Review* (September-October 1996): 65–77; D. Calfee, "Get Your Mission Statement Working," *Management Review* (January 1993): 54–57; J. Pearce II and F. David, "Corporate Mission Statements: The Bottom Line," *Academy of Management Executive* 1 (1987): 109–16; F. David, "How Companies Define Their Mission," *Long-Range Planning* 22 (1989): 90–97; Peter F. Drucker Foundation, *The Drucker Foundation Self-Assessment Tool: Process Guide* (San Francisco: Peter F. Drucker Foundation and Jossey-Bass, 1999), http://www.pfdf.org/leaderbooks/sat/ mission.html.

7. C. Hofer and D. Schendel, *Strategy Formulation: Analytic Concepts* (St. Paul, Minn.: West Publishing, 1978).

8. Pfeffer and Salancik, *External Control of Organizations*.

9. J. Barney, *Gaining and Sustaining Competitive Advantage* (Reading, Mass.: Addison-Wesley, 1996).

10. R. Nelson and S. Winter, *An Evolutionary Theory of Economic Change* (Cambridge, Mass.: Belknap Press, 1982).

11. P. Selznick, *Leadership in Administration* (New York: Harper & Row, 1957); M. Peteraf, "The Cornerstones of Competitive Advantage: A Resource-Based View," *Strategic Management Journal* 14 (1993): 179–92.

12. R. Grant, *Contemporary Strategy Analysis,* 3d ed. (Malden, Mass.: Blackwell, 1998); Barney, *Competitive Advantage.*

13. Aldrich, *Organizations and Environments.*

14. M. Jelinek and J. Litterer, "Why OD Must Become Strategic," in *Organizational Change and Development,* vol. 2, eds. W. Pasmore and R. Woodman (Greenwich, Conn.: JAI Press, 1988): 135–62; A. Bhambri and L. Pate, "Introduction—The Strategic Change Agenda: Stimuli, Processes, and Outcomes," *Journal of Organization Change Management* 4 (1991): 4–6; D. Nadler, M. Gerstein, R. Shaw, and associates, eds., *Organizational Architecture* (San Francisco: Jossey-Bass, 1992); C. Worley, D. Hitchin, and W. Ross, *Integrated Strategic Change: How Organization Development Builds Competitive Advantage* (Reading, Mass.: Addison-Wesley, 1996).

15. C. Worley, D. Hitchin, R. Patchett, R. Barnett, and J. Moss, "Unburn the Bridge, Get to Bedrock, and Put Legs on the Dream: Looking at Strategy Implementation with Fresh Eyes" (paper presented to the Western Academy of Management, Redondo Beach, Calif., March 1999).

16. H. Mintzberg, *The Rise and Fall of Strategic Planning* (New York: Free Press, 1994).

17. Worley, Hitchin, and Ross, *Integrated Strategic Change.*

18. P. Senge, *The Fifth Discipline* (New York: Doubleday, 1990); E. Lawler, *The Ultimate Advantage* (San Francisco: Jossey-Bass, 1992); Worley, Hitchin, and Ross, *Integrated Strategic Change.*

19. L. Greiner and V. Schein, *Power and Organization Development* (Reading, Mass.: Addison-Wesley, 1988).

20. M. Porter, *Competitive Strategy* (New York: Free Press, 1980).

21. Grant, *Contemporary Strategy Analysis.*

22. M. Porter, *Competitive Advantage* (New York: Free Press, 1985).

23. R. Miles and C. Snow, *Organization Strategy, Structure, and Process* (New York: McGraw-Hill, 1978); M. Tushman and E. Romanelli, "Organizational Evolution: A Metamorphosis Model of Convergence and Reorientation," in *Research in Organizational Behavior,* vol. 7, eds. L. Cummings and B. Staw (Greenwich, Conn.: JAI Press, 1985).

24. J. Naisbitt and P. Aburdene, *Reinventing the Corporation* (New York: Warner Books, 1985); A. Toffler, *The Third Wave* (New York: McGraw-Hill, 1980); A. Toffler, *The Adaptive Corporation* (New York: McGraw-Hill, 1984); M. Weisbord, *Productive Workplaces* (San Francisco: Jossey-Bass, 1987).

25. E. Lawler III, *The Ultimate Advantage* (San Francisco: Jossey-Bass, 1992); M. Tushman, W. Newman, and E. Romanelli, "Convergence and Upheaval: Managing the Unsteady Pace of Organizational Evolution," *California Management Review* 29 (1987): 1–16; Nadler et al., *Organizational Architecture;* R. Buzzell and B. Gale, *The PIMS Principles* (New York: Free Press, 1987).

26. L. Hrebiniak and W. Joyce, *Implementing Strategy* (New York: Macmillan, 1984); J. Galbraith and R. Kazanjian, *Strategy Implementation: Structure, Systems, and Process,* 2d ed. (St. Paul, Minn.: West Publishing, 1986).

27. T. Cummings, "Transorganizational Development," in *Research in Organizational Behavior,* vol. 6, eds. B. Staw and L. Cummings (Greenwich, Conn.: JAI Press, 1984): 367–422.

28. B. Gray, "Conditions Facilitating Interorganizational Collaboration," *Human Relations* 38 (1985): 911–36; K. Harrigan and W. Newman, "Bases of Interorganization Co-Operation: Propensity, Power, Persistence," *Journal of Management Studies* 27 (1990): 417–34; Cummings, "Transorganizational Development."

29. Cummings, "Transorganizational Development."

30. C. Raben, "Building Strategic Partnerships: Creating and Managing Effective Joint Ventures," in *Organizational Architecture,* eds. Nadler et al. (San Francisco: Jossey-Bass, 1992): 81–109; B. Gray, *Collaborating: Finding Common Ground for Multiparty Problems* (San Francisco: Jossey-Bass, 1989); Harrigan and Newman, "Bases of Interorganization Co-operation"; P. Lorange and J. Roos, "Analytical Steps in the Formation of Strategic Alliances," *Journal of Organizational Change Management* 4 (1991): 60–72; B. Gomes-Casseres, "Managing International Alliances: Conceptual Framework," *Harvard Business School Note* 9-793-133 (Boston: Harvard Business School Publishing, 1993).

31. D. Boje, "Towards a Theory and Praxis of Transorganizational Development: Stakeholder Networks and Their Habitats" (working paper 79-6, Behavioral and Organizational Science Study Center, Graduate School of Management, University of California, Los Angeles, February 1982); B. Gricar, "The Legitimacy of Consultants and Stakeholders in Interorganizational Problems" (paper presented at annual meeting of the Academy of Management, San Diego, Calif., August 1981); T. Williams, "The Search Conference in Active Adaptive Planning," *Journal*

of *Applied Behavioral Science* 16 (1980): 470–83; B. Gray and T. Hay, "Political Limits to Interorganizational Consensus and Change," *Journal of Applied Behavioral Science* 22 (1986): 95–112.

32. E. Trist, "Referent Organizations and the Development of Interorganizational Domains" (paper presented at annual meeting of the Academy of Management, Atlanta, August 1979).

33. Cummings, "Transorganizational Development."

34. Raben, "Building Strategic Partnerships."

35. T. Galpin and D. Robinson, "Merger Integration: The Ultimate Change Management Challenge," *Mergers and Acquisitions* 31(1997): 24–29.

36. M. Marks and P. Mirvis, *Joining Forces: Making One Plus One Equal Three in Mergers, Acquisitions, and Alliances* (San Francisco: Jossey-Bass, 1998).

37. R. Smith and I. Walter, "1998 Global Capital Market Activity and Market Shares of Leading Competitors." http:\\www.stern.edu/~rsmith/Gorilla_Tables.htm, accessed December 2, 1999.

38. A variety of studies have questioned whether merger and acquisition activity actually generates benefits to the organization or its shareholders, including M. Porter, "From Competitive Advantage to Corporate Strategy," *Harvard Business Review* (May-June 1978): 43–59; "Merger Integration Problems," *Leadership and Organization Development Journal* 19 (1998): 59–60; "Why Good Deals Miss the Bull's-Eye: Slow Integration, Poor Communication Torpedo Prospects for Creating Value," *Mergers and Acquisitions* 33 (1999): 5; T. Brush, "Predicted Change in Operational Synergy and Post-Acquisition Performance of Acquired Businesses," *Strategic Management Journal* 17 (1996): 1–24; and P. Zweig with J. Perlman, S. Anderson, and K. Gudridge, "The Case Against Mergers," *Business Week* (30 October 1995): 122–30. The research includes an A. T. Kearney study of 115 multibillion-dollar, global mergers between 1993 and 1996 where 58 percent failed to create "substantial returns for shareholders," measured by tangible returns in the form of dividends and stock price appreciation; a Mercer Management Consulting study of all mergers from 1990 to 1996 where nearly half "destroyed" shareholder value; a PriceWaterhouseCoopers study of 97 acquirers that completed deals worth $500 million or more from 1994 to 1997 and where two-thirds of the buyer's stocks dropped on announcement of the transaction and "a year later" a third of the losers still were lagging the levels of peer-company shares or the stock market in general; and a European study of 300 companies

that found that planning for restructuring was poorly thought out and underfunded. Similarly, despite the large amount of writing on the subject, a large proportion of firms involved in mergers have not gotten the message that postmerger integration is the key to success. For example, in the A. T. Kearny study, only 39 percent of the cases had set up a management team in the first one hundred days and only 28 percent had a clear vision of corporate goals when the acquisition began.

39. Zweig et al., "Case Against Mergers."

40. Marks and Mirvis, *Joining Forces;* R. Ashkenas, L. DeMonaco, and S. Francis, "Making the Deal Real: How GE Capital Integrates Acquisitions," *Harvard Business Review* (January-February 1998); B. Brunsman, S. Sanderson, and M. Van de Voorde, "How to Achieve Value Behind the Deal During Merger Integration," *Oil and Gas Journal* 96 (1998): 21–30; A. Fisher, "How to Make a Merger Work," *Fortune* (24 January 1994): 66–70; K. Kostuch, R. Malchione, and I. Marten, "Post-Merger Integration: Creating or Destroying Value?" *Corporate Board* 19 (1998): 7–11; A. Kruse, "Merging Cultures: How OD Adds Value in Mergers and Acquisitions" (presentation to the ODNetwork meeting, San Diego, Calif., October 1999); M. Sirower, "Constructing a Synergistic Base for Premier Deals," *Mergers and Acquisitions* 32 (1998): 42–50; D. Jemison and S. Sitkin, "Corporate Acquisitions: A Process Perspective," *Academy of Management Review* 11 (1986): 145–63.

41. Ashkenas, DeMonaco, and Francis, "Making the Deal Real"; G. Ledford, C. Siehl, M. McGrath, and J. Miller, "Managing Mergers and Acquisitions" (working paper, Center for Effective Organizations, University of Southern California, Los Angeles, 1985).

42. Ledford et al., "Managing Mergers and Acquisitions"; B. Blumenthal, "The Right Talent Mix to Make Mergers Work," *Mergers and Acquisitions* (September-October 1995): 26–31; A. Buono, J. Bowditch, and J. Lewis, "When Cultures Collide: The Anatomy of a Merger," *Human Relations* 38 (1985): 477–500; D. Tipton, "Understanding Employee Views Regarding Impending Mergers to Minimize Integration Turmoil" (unpublished Master's thesis, Pepperdine University, 1998).

43. Marks and Mirvis, *Joining Forces;* Ashkenas, DeMonaco, and Francis, "Making the Deal Real."

44. Sirower, "Constructing a Synergistic Base"; Brunsman, Sanderson, and Van de Voorde, "How to Achieve Value."

45. Sirower, "Constructing a Synergistic Base."

46. Ledford et al., "Managing Mergers and Acquisitions."

47. S. Elias, "Due Diligence," http://www.eliasondeals.com/duedilig.html, 1998.

48. Brunsman, Sanderson, and Van de Voorde. "How to Achieve Value."

49. Ashkenas, DeMonaco, and Francis, "Making the Deal Real."

50. Ashkenas, DeMonaco, and Francis, "Making the Deal Real"; Brunsman, Sanderson, and Van de Voorde, "How to Achieve Value."

51. Galpin and Robinson, "Merger Integration."

52. Ibid.

53. Ashkenas, DeMonaco, and Francis, "Making the Deal Real."

54. Kostuch, Malchione, and Marten, "Post-Merger Integration."

14. Organization Transformation

This chapter presents interventions aimed at transforming organizations. It describes activities directed at changing the basic character or culture of the organization. These interventions bring about important alignments among the organization's strategies, design elements, and culture, and between the organization and its competitive environment.[1] They are directed mostly at the culture or dominant paradigm within the organization. These frame-breaking and sometimes revolutionary interventions typically go beyond improving the organization incrementally and focus on changing the way it views itself and its environment.

Organization transformation is a recent advance in organization development, and there is some confusion about its meaning and definition. This chapter starts with a description of several major features of transformational change. Against this background, three kinds of interventions are discussed: culture change, self-design, and organization learning and knowledge management.

CHARACTERISTICS OF TRANSFORMATIONAL CHANGE

Organization transformation implies radical changes in how members perceive, think, and behave at work. These changes go far beyond making the existing organization better or fine-tuning the status quo. They are concerned with fundamentally altering the organizational assumptions about its functioning and how it relates to the environment. Changing these assumptions entails significant shifts in corporate philosophy and values and in the numerous structures and organizational arrangements that shape members' behaviors. Not only is the magnitude of change greater, but the change fundamentally alters the qualitative nature of the organization. Examination of the rapidly growing literature on the topic suggests the following distinguishing features of these revolutionary change efforts.

Change Is Triggered by Environmental and Internal Disruptions

Organizations are unlikely to undertake transformational change unless significant reasons to do so emerge. Power, sentience, and expertise are vested in the existing organizational arrangements, and when faced with problems, members are more likely to fine-tune those structures than to alter them drastically.

Transformational change typically occurs in response to at least three kinds of disruption:[2]

1. *Industry discontinuities*—sharp changes in legal, political, economic, and technological conditions that shift the basis for competition within industries
2. *Product life-cycle shifts*—changes in product life cycle that require different business strategies
3. *Internal company dynamics*—changes in size, corporate portfolio strategy, executive turnover, and the like.

These disruptions severely jolt organizations and push them to alter business strategy and, in turn, their mission, values, structure, systems, and procedures.

Change Is Systemic and Revolutionary

Transformational change can be characterized as systemic and revolutionary because the entire nature of the organization is altered fundamentally. It is systemic because the different features of the organization, such as structure, information systems, human resources practices, and work design tend to reinforce one another, thus making it difficult to change them in a piecemeal manner.[3] Long-term studies of organizational evolution underscore the revolutionary nature of transformational change and point to the benefits of changing as rapidly as possible.[4] The faster the organization can respond to disruptions, the quicker it can attain the benefits of operating in a new way. Rapid change enables the organization to reach a period of smooth growth and functioning sooner, thus providing it with a competitive advantage over those firms that change more slowly.

Change Demands a New Organizing Paradigm

Transformational change, by definition, involves discontinuous shifts in how organizations structure and manage themselves.[5] Creative metaphors, such as "organization learning" or "continuous improvement," often are used to help members visualize the new paradigm.[6] During the 1980s, increases in technological change, concern for quality, and worker participation led to at least one shift in organizing paradigm. Characterized as the transition from a "control-based" to a "commitment-based" organization, the features of the new paradigm included leaner, more flexible structures; information and decision making pushed down to the lowest levels; decentralized teams and business units accountable for specific products, services, or customers; and participative management and teamwork. This new organizing paradigm is well suited to changing conditions.

Change Is Driven by Senior Executives and Line Management

A key feature of organization transformation is the active role of senior executives and line managers in all phases of the change process.[7] They are responsible for the strategic direction and operation of the organization and actively lead the transformation. They decide when to initiate transformational change, what the change should be, how it should be implemented, and who should be responsible for directing it. The work of Nadler, Tushman, and others points to three key roles for executive leadership of such change:[8]

1. *Envisioning.* Executives must articulate a clear and credible vision of the new strategic orientation. They also must set new and difficult standards for performance, and generate pride in past accomplishments and enthusiasm for the new strategy.

2. *Energizing.* Executives must demonstrate personal excitement for the changes and model the behaviors that are expected of others. They must communicate examples of early success to mobilize energy for change.

3. *Enabling.* Executives must provide the resources necessary for undertaking significant change and use rewards to reinforce new behaviors. Leaders also must build an effective top-management team to manage the new organization and develop management practices to support the change process.

Continuous Learning and Change

Transformational change requires considerable innovation and learning.[9] Organizational members must learn how to enact the new behaviors required to implement new strategic directions. This typically is a continuous learning process of trying new behaviors, assessing their consequences, and modifying them if necessary. Because members usually must learn qualitatively different ways of perceiving, thinking, and behaving, the learning process is likely to be substantial and to involve much unlearning. It is directed by a vision of the future organization and by the values and norms needed to support it. Learning occurs at all levels of the organization, from senior executives to lower-level employees.

Because the environment itself is likely to be changing during the change process, transformational change rarely has a delimited timeframe but is likely to persist as long as the firm needs to adapt to change. Learning how to manage change in a continuous manner can help the organization keep pace with a dynamic environment. It can provide the built-in capacity to fit the organization continually to its environment.

CULTURE CHANGE

The topic of organization culture has become extremely important to American companies in the past ten years, and culture change is the most common form of organization transformation. The number of culture change interventions has grown accordingly as organizations have come to appreciate the power of corporate culture in shaping employee beliefs and actions. A well-conceived and well-managed organization culture, closely linked to an effective business strategy, can mean the difference between success and failure in today's demanding environments.

Despite the increased attention to culture change, there is still some confusion about what the term "culture" really means when applied to organizations.[10] Examination of the different definitions suggests that organization culture is the pattern of basic assumptions, values, norms, and beliefs shared by organization members. These shared meanings help members make sense out of everyday life in the organization. The meanings signal how work is to be done and evaluated, and how employees are to relate to each other and to significant others, such as customers, suppliers, and government agencies.

Corporate culture is the product of long-term social learning and reflects what has worked in the past.[11] It represents those basic assumptions, values, norms, and beliefs that have worked well enough to be passed on to succeeding generations of employees. For example, the cultures of many companies (for example, IBM, J.C.Penney, Sony, and Hewlett-Packard) are rooted deeply in the firm's history. They were laid down by a strong founder and have been reinforced by top executives and corporate success into customary ways of perceiving and acting. These customs provide organization members with clear and widely shared answers to such practical issues as "what really matters around here," "how do we do things around here," and "what we do when a problem arises."[12]

Diagnosing Organization Culture

Culture change interventions generally start by diagnosing the organization's existing culture to assess its fit with current or proposed business strategies. This requires uncovering and understanding the shared assumptions, values, norms, and beliefs that characterize an organization's culture. OD practitioners have developed a number of useful approaches for diagnosing organization culture. These fall into three different yet complementary perspectives: the behavioral approach, the competing values approach, and the deep assumption approach. Each diagnostic perspective focuses on particular aspects of organization culture, and together the approaches can provide a comprehensive assessment of these complex phenomena.

The Behavioral Approach

This method of diagnosis emphasizes the pattern of behaviors that produce business results.[13] It is among the more practical approaches to culture diagnosis because it assesses key work behaviors that can be observed.[14] The behavioral approach provides specific descriptions about how tasks are performed and how relationships are managed in an organization. For example, organization members may be asked to describe "the way the game is played," as if they were coaching a new organization member. They may be asked to give their impressions of some key relationships, such as boss–subordinate, peer, and interdepartment, and of such tasks as innovating, decision making, communicating, and appraising/rewarding. These perceptions can reveal implicit norms for how tasks are performed and relationships are managed in the organization.

Cultural diagnosis derived from a behavioral approach also can be used to assess the cultural risk of trying to implement organizational changes needed to support a new strategy. Significant cultural risks result when changes that are highly important to implementing a new strategy are incompatible with the existing patterns of behavior. Knowledge of such risks can help managers determine whether implementation plans should be changed to manage around the existing culture, whether the culture should be changed, or whether the strategy itself should be modified or abandoned.

The Competing Values Approach

This perspective assesses an organization's culture in terms of how it resolves a set of value dilemmas.[15] The approach suggests that an organization's culture can be understood in terms of two important "value pairs"; each pair consists of contradictory values placed at opposite ends of a continuum. The two value pairs are (1) internal focus and integration versus external focus and differentiation and (2) flexibility and discretion versus stability and control. Organizations continually struggle to satisfy the conflicting demands placed on them by these competing values. For example, when faced with the competing values of internal versus external focus, organizations must choose between attending to the integration problems of internal operations or the competitive issues in the external environment. Too much emphasis on the environment can result in neglect of internal efficiencies. Conversely, too much attention to the internal aspects of organizations can result in missing important changes in the competitive environment. The competing values approach commonly collects diagnostic data about the competing values with a survey designed specifically for that purpose.[16] It provides measures of where an organization's existing values fall along each of the dimensions.

The Deep Assumptions Approach

This final diagnostic approach emphasizes the deepest levels of organization culture—the generally unexamined, but tacit and shared assumptions that guide member behavior and that often have a powerful impact on organization effectiveness. Diagnosing organization culture at the deep assumptions level poses at least three difficult problems for collecting pertinent information.[17] First, culture reflects shared assumptions about what is important, how things are done, and how people should behave in organizations. People generally take cultural assumptions for granted and rarely speak of them directly. Rather, the company's culture is implied in concrete behavioral examples, such as daily routines, stories, rituals, and language. This means that considerable time and effort must be spent observing, sifting through, and asking people about these cultural outcroppings to understand their deeper significance for organization members. Second, some values and beliefs that people espouse have little to do with the ones they really hold and follow. People are reluctant to admit this discrepancy, yet somehow the real assumptions underlying idealized portrayals of culture must be discovered. Third, large, diverse organizations are likely to have several subcultures, including countercultures going against the grain of the wider organization culture. Assumptions may not be shared widely and may differ across groups in the organization. This means that focusing on limited parts of the organization or on a few select individuals may provide a distorted view of the organization's culture and subcultures. All relevant groups in the organization must be discovered and their cultural assumptions sampled. Only then can practitioners judge the extent to which assumptions are shared widely.

Changing Corporate Culture

Although knowledge about changing corporate culture is in a formative stage, the following practical advice can serve as guidelines for cultural change:[18]

1. *Formulate a clear strategic vision.* Effective cultural change should start from a clear vision of the firm's new strategy and of the shared values and behaviors needed to make it work.[19] This vision provides the purpose and direction for cultural change. It serves as a yardstick for defining the firm's existing culture and for deciding whether proposed changes are consistent with core values of the organization. A useful approach to providing clear strategic vision is development of a statement of corporate purpose, listing in straightforward terms the firm's core values. For example, Johnson & Johnson calls its guiding principles "Our Credo." It describes several basic values that guide the firm, including, "We believe our first responsibility is to the doctors, nurses and patients, to mothers and all others who use our products and services"; "Our suppliers and distributors must have an opportunity to make a fair profit"; "We must respect [employees'] dignity and recognize their merit"; and "We must maintain in good order the property we are privileged to use, protecting the environment and natural resources."[20]

2. *Display top-management commitment.* Cultural change must be managed from the top of the organization. Senior managers and administrators have to be strongly committed to the new values and need to create constant pressures for change. They must have the staying power to see the changes through.[21] For example, Jack Welch, CEO at General Electric, has enthusiastically pushed a policy of cost cutting, improved productivity, customer focus, and bureaucracy busting for more than ten years to every plant, division, group, and sector in his organization. His efforts were rewarded with a *Fortune* cover story lauding his organization for creating more than $52 billion in shareholder value during his tenure.[22]

3. *Model culture change at the highest levels.* Senior executives must communicate the new culture through their own actions. Their behaviors need to symbolize

the kinds of values and behaviors being sought. In the few publicized cases of successful culture change, corporate leaders have shown an almost missionary zeal for the new values; their actions have symbolized the values forcefully.[23] For example, Jim Treybig, CEO of Tandem, the computer manufacturer, decided not to fire an employee whose performance had slipped until he could investigate the reason for the employee's poor performance. It turned out that the employee was having family problems, and therefore Treybig gave him another chance. To the people at Tandem, the story symbolized the importance of consideration in leading people.[24] Donald Kendall, the chief executive of PepsiCo, demonstrated the kind of ingenuity and dedication he expects from his staff by using a snowmobile to get to work in a blizzard.

4. *Modify the organization to support organizational change.* Cultural change generally requires supporting modifications in organizational structure, human resources systems, information and control systems, and management styles. These organizational features can help to orient people's behaviors to the new culture.[25] They can make people aware of the behaviors required to get things done in the new culture and can encourage performance of those behaviors. For example, Phil Condit and Harry Stonecipher of Boeing realized that more than culture change in the commercial aircraft division was necessary to turn around the organization's poor performance in 1997 and 1998. To alter the "warm and fuzzy" culture of the division radically, they initiated workforce reductions, fired key executives, made changes in the production standards, and initiated continuous improvement processes in production. These changes reinforced and symbolized the importance of financial performance, accountability, and global leadership in the industry.[26]

5. *Select and socialize newcomers and terminate deviants.* One of the most effective methods for changing corporate culture is to change organizational membership. People can be selected and terminated in terms of their fit with the new culture. This is especially important in key leadership positions, where people's actions can significantly promote or hinder new values and behaviors. For example, Gould, in trying to change from an auto parts and battery company to a leader in electronics, replaced about two-thirds of its senior executives with people more in tune with the new strategy and culture. Jan Carlzon of Scandinavian Airlines (SAS) replaced thirteen out of fifteen top executives in his turnaround of the airline. Another approach is to socialize newly hired people into the new culture. People are most open to organizational influences during the entry stage, when they can be effectively indoctrinated into the culture. For example, companies with strong cultures like Samsung, Procter & Gamble, and 3M attach great importance to socializing new members into the company's values.

6. *Develop ethical and legal sensitivity.* Cultural change can raise significant tensions between organization and individual interests, resulting in ethical and legal problems for practitioners. This is particularly pertinent when organizations are trying to implement cultural values promoting employee integrity, control, equitable treatment, and job security—values often included in cultural change efforts. Statements about such values provide employees with certain expectations about their rights and about how they will be treated in the organization. If the organization does not follow through with behaviors and procedures supporting and protecting these implied rights, it may breach ethical principles and, in some cases, legal employment contracts. Recommendations for reducing the chances

of such ethical and legal problems include setting realistic values for culture change and not promising what the organization cannot deliver; encouraging input from throughout the organization in setting cultural values; providing mechanisms for member dissent and diversity, such as internal review procedures; and educating managers about the legal and ethical pitfalls inherent in cultural change and helping them develop guidelines for resolving such issues.

SELF-DESIGNING ORGANIZATIONS

A growing number of researchers and practitioners have called for self-designing organizations that have the built-in capacity to transform themselves to achieve high performance in today's competitive and changing environment.[27] Mohrman and Cummings have developed a self-design change strategy that involves an on-going series of designing and implementing activities carried out by managers and employees at all levels of the firm.[28] The approach helps members translate corporate values and general prescriptions for change into specific structures, processes, and behaviors suited to their situations. It enables them to tailor changes to fit the organization and helps them continually to adjust the organization to changing conditions.

The Demands of Transformational Change

Mohrman and Cummings developed the self-design strategy in response to a number of demands facing organizations engaged in transformational change. These demands strongly suggest the need for self-design, in contrast to more traditional approaches to organization change that emphasize ready-made programs and quick fixes. Although organizations prefer the control and certainty inherent in programmed change, the five requirements for organizational transformation reviewed below argue against this strategy:

1. Transformational change generally involves altering most features of the organization and achieving a fit among them and with the firm's strategy. This suggests the need for a *systemic* change process that accounts for these multiple features and relationships.

2. Transformational change generally occurs in situations experiencing heavy change and uncertainty. This means that changing is never totally finished, as new structures and processes will continually have to be modified to fit changing conditions. Thus, the change process needs to be *dynamic and iterative*, with organizations continually changing themselves.[29]

3. Current knowledge about transforming organizations provides only general prescriptions for change. Organizations need to learn how to translate that information into specific structures, processes, and behaviors appropriate to their situations. This generally requires considerable on-site innovation and learning as members learn by doing—trying out new structures and behaviors, assessing their effectiveness, and modifying them if necessary. Transformational change needs to facilitate this *organizational learning*.[30]

4. Transformational change invariably affects many organization stakeholders, including owners, managers, employees, and customers. These different stakeholders are likely to have different goals and interests related to the change process. Unless the differences are revealed and reconciled, enthusiastic support

for change may be difficult to achieve. Consequently, the change process must attend to the interests of *multiple stakeholders.*[31]

5.   Transformational change needs to occur at *multiple levels of the organization* if new strategies are to result in changed behaviors throughout the firm. Top executives must formulate a corporate strategy and clarify a vision of what the organization needs to look like to support it. Middle and lower levels of the organization need to put those broad parameters into operation by creating structures, procedures, and behaviors to implement the strategy.[32]

Application Stages

The self-design strategy accounts for these demands of organization transformation. It focuses on all features of the organization (for example, structure, human resources practices, and technology) and designs them to support the business strategy mutually. It is a dynamic and an iterative process aimed at providing organizations with the built-in capacity to change and redesign themselves continually as the circumstances demand. The approach promotes organizational learning among multiple stakeholders at all levels of the firm, providing them with the knowledge and skills needed to transform the organization and continually to improve it.

Figure 14.1 outlines the self-design approach. Although the process is described in three stages, in practice the stages merge and interact iteratively over time. Each stage is described below:

1.   *Laying the foundation.* This initial stage provides organization members with the basic knowledge and information needed to get started with organization transformation. It involves three kinds of activities. The first is acquiring knowledge about how organizations function, about organizing principles for achieving high performance, and about the self-design process. This information is generally gained through reading relevant material, attending in-house workshops, and visiting other organizations that successfully have transformed themselves. This learning typically starts with senior executives or with those managing the transformation process and cascades to lower organizational levels if a decision is made to proceed with self-design. The second activity in laying the

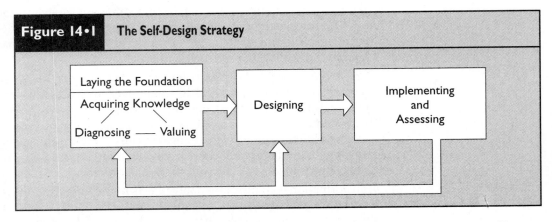

| Figure 14•1 | The Self-Design Strategy |

Laying the Foundation
Acquiring Knowledge
Diagnosing — Valuing
→ Designing →
Implementing and Assessing

SOURCE: S. Mohrman and T. Cummings, *Self-Designing Organizations: Learning How to Create High Performance,* page 37. © 1989 by Addison-Wesley Publishing Co., Inc. Reprinted by permission of Addison Wesley Longman.

foundation involves valuing—determining the corporate values that will guide the transformation process. These values represent those performance outcomes and organizational conditions that will be needed to implement the corporate strategy. They are typically written in a values statement that is discussed and negotiated among multiple stakeholders at all levels of the organization. The third activity is diagnosing the current organization to determine what needs to be changed to enact the corporate strategy and values. Organization members generally assess the different features of the organization, including its performance. They look for incongruities between its functioning and its valued performances and conditions. In the case of an entirely new organization, members diagnose constraints and contingencies in the situation that need to be taken into account in designing the organization.

2. *Designing.* In this second stage of self-design, organization designs and innovations are generated to support corporate strategy and values. Only the broad parameters of a new organization are specified; the details are left to be tailored to the levels and groupings within the organization. Referred to as minimum specification design, this process recognizes that designs need to be refined and modified as they are implemented throughout the firm.

3. *Implementing and assessing.* This last stage involves implementing the designed organization changes. It includes an ongoing cycle of action research: changing structures and behaviors, assessing progress, and making necessary modifications. Information about how well implementation is progressing and how well the new organizational design is working is collected and used to clarify design and implementation issues and to make necessary adjustments. This learning process continues not only during implementation but indefinitely as members periodically assess and improve the design and alter it to fit changing conditions. The feedback loops shown in Figure 14.1 suggest that the implementing and assessing activities may lead back to affect subsequent designing, diagnosing, valuing, and acquiring knowledge activities. This iterative sequence of activities provides organizations with the capacity to transform and improve themselves continually.

The self-design strategy is applicable to existing organizations needing to transform themselves, as well as to new organizations just starting out. It is also applicable to changing the total organization or subunits. The way self-design is managed and unfolds can also differ. In some cases, it follows the existing organization structure, starting with the senior executive team and cascading downward across organizational levels. In other cases, the process is managed by special design teams that are sanctioned to set broad parameters for valuing and designing for the rest of the organization. The outputs of these teams then are implemented across departments and work units, with considerable local refinement and modification.

ORGANIZATION LEARNING AND KNOWLEDGE MANAGEMENT

The third organizational transformation intervention is aimed at helping organizations develop and use knowledge to change and improve themselves continually. It includes two interrelated change processes. Organization learning (OL) interventions emphasize the organizational structures and social processes that enable employees and teams to learn and to share knowledge. They draw heavily on the social sciences for conceptual grounding and on OD interventions, such as team building, structural design, and employee involvement, for practical guidance. In organizations, OL change processes typically are associated with the human resources function and may be assigned to a special leadership role, such as chief learning officer. Knowledge management (KM) interventions, on the other hand, focus on the tools and techniques that enable organizations to collect, organize, and translate information into useful knowledge. They are rooted conceptually in the information and computer sciences and, in practice, emphasize electronic forms of knowledge storage and transmission such as intranets, data warehousing, and knowledge repositories. Organizationally, KM applications often are located in the information systems function and may be under the direction of a chief technology officer.

Both OL and KM are crucial in today's complex, rapidly changing environments, and their importance is likely to increase in the future. They can be a source of strategic renewal, and they can enable organizations to acquire and apply knowledge more quickly and effectively than competitors thus establishing a sustained competitive advantage.[33] Moreover, when knowledge is translated into new products and services, it can become a key source of wealth creation for organizations.[34] OL and KM are among the most widespread and fastest-growing interventions in OD. They are the focus of an expanding body of research and practice, and have been applied in such diverse firms as Andersen Consulting, Boeing, General Motors, Microsoft, Mobil Oil, and the U.S. Army.

Conceptual Framework

Based on existing research and practice, Figure 14.2 provides an integrative framework for understanding OL and KM interventions,[35] summarizing the elements of these change processes and showing how they combine to affect organization performance. This framework suggests that specific characteristics, such as structure and human resources systems, influence how well organization learning processes

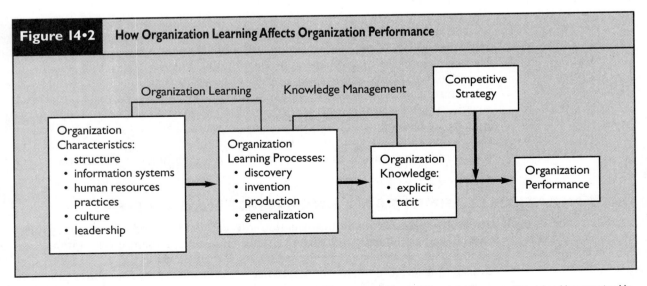

Figure 14·2   How Organization Learning Affects Organization Performance

SOURCE: Reproduced by permission from W. Snyder and T. Cummings, "Organization Learning Disorders: Conceptual Model and Intervention Hypotheses," *Human Relations* 51 (1998): 873–895.

are carried out. These learning processes affect the amount and kind of knowledge that an organization possesses; that knowledge, in turn, directly influences performance outcomes, such as product quality and customer service. As depicted in Figure 14.2, the linkage between organization knowledge and performance depends on the organization's competitive strategy. Organization knowledge will lead to high performance to the extent that it is both relevant and applied effectively to the strategy. For example, customer-driven organizations require timely and relevant information about customer needs. Their success relies heavily on members having that knowledge and applying it effectively in their work with customers.

Figure 14.2 also shows how OL and KM are interrelated. OL interventions address how organizations can be designed to promote effective learning processes, and how those learning processes themselves can be improved. KM interventions focus on the outcomes of learning processes, on how strategically relevant knowledge can be effectively organized and used throughout the organization. Each of the key elements of OL and KM—organization characteristics, organization learning processes, and organization knowledge—are described below along with the interventions typically associated with them.

Characteristics of a Learning Organization

As shown in Figure 14.2, there are several organization features that can promote effective learning processes, including structure, information systems, human resources practices, culture, and leadership. Consequently, many of the interventions described in this book can help organizations develop more effective learning capabilities. For example, human resources management interventions—performance appraisal, reward systems, and career planning and development—can reinforce members' motivation to gain new skills and knowledge.

OL practitioners have combined many of these interventions into the design and implementation of what is commonly referred to as the *learning organization*, a term used to describe organizations that are capable of effective learning.[36] Much of the literature on the learning organization is prescriptive and proposes how organizations should be designed and managed to promote effective learning. Although there is relatively little systematic research to support these premises, there is growing consensus among researchers and practitioners about specific organizational features that characterize the learning organization.[37] These qualities are mutually reinforcing and fall into five interrelated categories.

Structure

Learning organizations are structured to facilitate OL. Their structures emphasize teamwork, strong lateral relations, and networking across organizational boundaries both internal and external to the firm. These features promote the information sharing, systems thinking, and openness to information that are necessary for OL. They help members scan wider parts of the organization and its environment and reduce barriers to shared learning. Learning organizations also have relatively flat managerial hierarchies that enhance opportunities for employee involvement in the organization. Members are empowered to make relevant decisions and to influence the organization significantly, thus nurturing the personal mastery and efficacy that are essential to OL.

Information Systems

Organization learning involves gathering and processing information, and consequently, the information systems of learning organizations provide an infrastructure for OL. Organizations traditionally rely on information systems for control purposes: they use information to detect and correct errors in organizational functioning. In today's environments where learning is directed increasingly at transformational change, organizations require more sophisticated information systems to support these higher levels of OL. They need systems that facilitate rapid acquisition, processing, and sharing of rich, complex information and that enable people to manage knowledge for competitive advantage. For example, Monsanto has developed a "knowledge management architecture" that uses Lotus Notes to link salespeople, account managers, and competitor analysts to shared customer and competitor databases that are updated continually.[38] Change processes aimed at information systems will be discussed more thoroughly below when KM interventions are described.

Human Resources Practices

Because organization members are the ultimate creators and users of OL, the human resources practices of learning organizations are designed to promote member learning. These include appraisal and reward systems that account for long-term performance and knowledge development; they reinforce the acquisition and sharing of new skills and knowledge. For example, General Mills uses skill-based pay to motivate employees to learn multiple skills and jobs. Similarly, the training and development programs of learning organizations emphasize continuous learning and improvement. They are directed at enhancing human capital and opportunities for OL. Taco, a New England pump and valve manufacturer, has developed a "learning center" that includes classrooms, a computer lab, and a library.[39] Employees take advantage of more than six dozen courses offered at the center to improve their work skills and, in some cases, to earn college credit or a high school equivalency diploma.

Organization Culture

The shared assumptions, values, and norms that form an organization's culture can influence strongly how members gather, process, and share information. Learning organizations have strong cultures that promote openness, creativity, and experimentation among members. These values and norms provide the underlying social support needed for successful learning. They encourage members to acquire, process, and share information; they nurture innovation and provide the freedom to try new things, to risk failure, and to learn from mistakes. Hewlett-Packard, for example, has strong values and norms fostering innovation and experimentation.[40] Members are encouraged to think and behave differently. Mistakes and errors are treated as a normal part of the innovation process, and members actively learn from their failures how to change and improve both themselves and the organization.

Leadership

Like most interventions aimed at organization transformation, OL and KM depend heavily on effective leadership throughout the organization. The leaders of learning organizations are actively involved in OL.[41] They model the openness, risk taking, and reflection necessary for learning. They also communicate a compelling vision of the learning organization and provide the empathy, support, and personal advocacy needed to lead others in that direction. During Motorola's early efforts at total quality management, for example, CEO Bob Galvin championed the quality vision, attended the first classes on quality, and placed it first on the agenda at his monthly executive meetings.[42]

Organization Learning Processes

The organization characteristics described above affect how well members carry out organization learning processes. As shown in Figure 14.2, these processes consist of four interrelated activities: discovery, invention, production, and generalization.[43] Learning starts with discovery when errors or gaps between desired and actual conditions are detected. For example, sales managers may discover that sales are falling below projected levels and set out to solve the problem. Invention is aimed at devising solutions to close the gap between desired and current conditions, and includes diagnosing the causes of the gap and creating appropriate solutions to reduce it. The sales managers may learn that poor advertising is contributing to the sales problem and may devise a new sales campaign to improve sales. Production processes involve implementing solutions, and generalization includes drawing conclusions about the effects of the solutions and extending that knowledge to other relevant situations. For instance, the new advertising program would be implemented, and if successful, the managers might use variations of it with other product lines. Thus, these four learning processes enable members to generate the knowledge necessary to change and improve the organization.

Organizations can apply the learning processes described above to three levels of learning.[44] The lowest level is called *single-loop learning* or *adaptive learning* and is focused on learning how to improve the status quo. This is the most prevalent form of learning in organizations and enables members to reduce errors or gaps between desired and existing conditions. It can produce incremental change in how organizations function. The sales managers described above engaged in single-loop learning when they looked for ways to reduce the difference between current and desired levels of sales.

Double-loop learning or *generative learning* is aimed at changing the status quo. It operates at a more abstract level than does single-loop learning because members learn how to change the existing assumptions and conditions within which single-loop learning operates. This level of learning can lead to transformational change, where the status quo itself is radically altered. For example, the sales managers may learn that sales projections are based on faulty assumptions and models about future market conditions. This knowledge may result in an entirely new conception of future markets with corresponding changes in sales projections and product development plans. It may lead the managers to drop some products that had previously appeared promising, develop new ones that were not considered before, and alter advertising and promotional campaigns to fit the new conditions.

The highest level of OL is called *deuterolearning,* which involves learning how to learn. Here learning is directed at the learning process itself and seeks to improve how organizations perform single- and double-loop learning. For example, the sales managers might periodically examine how well they perform the processes of discovery, invention, production, and generalization. This could lead to improvements and efficiencies in how learning is conducted throughout the organization.

Practitioners have developed change strategies designed specifically for organization learning processes. Although these interventions are relatively new in OD and do not follow a common change process, they tend to focus on cognitive aspects of learning and how members can become more effective learners. In describing these change strategies, we draw heavily on the work of Argyris and Schon and of Senge and his colleagues because it is the most developed and articulated work in OL practice.[45]

From this perspective, organization learning is not concerned with the organization as a static entity but as an active process of sense making and organizing.

Members socially construct the organization as they continually act and interact with each other and learn from those actions how to organize themselves for productive achievement. This active learning process enables members to develop, test, and modify mental models or maps of organizational reality. Called *theories in use*, these cognitive maps inform member behavior and organizing.[46] They guide how members make decisions, perform work, and organize themselves. Unfortunately, members' theories in use can be faulty, resulting in ineffective behaviors and organizing efforts. They can be too narrow and fail to account for important aspects of the environment; they can include erroneous assumptions that lead to unexpected negative consequences. Effective OL can resolve these problems by enabling members to learn from their actions how to detect and correct errors in their mental maps, and thus it can promote more effective organizing efforts.

The predominant mode of learning in most organizations is ineffective, however, and may even intensify errors. Referred to as *Model I* learning, it includes values and norms that emphasize unilateral control of environments and tasks, and protection of oneself and others from information that may be hurtful.[47] These norms result in a variety of defensive routines that inhibit learning, such as withholding information and feelings, competition and rivalry, and little public testing of theories in use and the assumptions underlying them. Model I is limited to single-loop learning, where existing theories in use are reinforced.

A more effective approach to learning, called *Model II*, is based on values promoting valid information, free and informed choice, internal commitment to the choice, and continuous assessment of its implementation.[48] This results in minimal defensiveness with greater openness to information and feedback, personal mastery and collaboration with others, and public testing of theories in use. Model II applies to double-loop learning, where theories in use are changed, and to deutero-learning, where the learning process itself is examined and improved.

OL interventions are aimed at helping organization members learn how to change from Model I to Model II learning. Like all learning, this change strategy includes the learning processes of discovery, invention, production, and generalization. Although the phases are described linearly below, in practice they form a recurrent cycle of overlapping learning activities.

1. *Discover theories in use and their consequences.* This first step involves uncovering members' mental models or theories in use and the consequences that follow from behaving and organizing according to them. Depending on the size of the client system, this may directly involve all members, such as a senior executive team, or it may include representatives of the system, such as a cross section of members from different levels and areas. Because these theories generally are taken for granted and rarely examined, members need to generate and analyze data to infer the theories' underlying assumptions. For example, members may engage in genuine exchange about how they currently address problems, make decisions, and interact with each other and relevant others, such as suppliers, customers, and competitors. They may be open and frank with each other, treat each other as colleagues, and suspend individual assumptions as much as possible. This exchange, known as *dialogue*, can result in clearer understanding of existing theories in use and their behavioral consequences and enable members to uncover faulty assumptions that lead to ineffective behaviors and organizing efforts.

2. *Invent and produce more effective theories in use.* Based on what is discovered in the first phase of this change process, members invent and produce theories

in use that lead to more effective actions and that are more closely aligned with Model II learning. This involves double-loop learning as members try to create and enact new theories. In essence, members learn by doing; they learn from their invention and production actions how to invent and produce more effective theories in use. As might be expected, learning how to change theories in use can be extremely difficult. There is a strong tendency for members to revert to habitual behaviors and modes of learning. They may have trouble breaking out of existing mindsets and seeing new realities and possibilities. OL practitioners have developed both behavioral and conceptual interventions to help members overcome these problems.

Behaviorally, OD practitioners help members apply the values underlying Model II learning. They can encourage members to confront and talk openly about how habitual actions and learning methods prevent them from creating and enacting more effective theories. Once these barriers to change are discussed openly, members typically discover that they are changeable. This shared insight often leads to the invention of more effective theories for behaving, organizing, and learning. Subsequent experimentation with trying to enact those theories in the workplace is likely to produce more effective change because the errors that invariably occur when trying new things now can be discussed and hence corrected.

Conceptually, OL practitioners teach members *system thinking* to help them invent more effective theories in use.[49] It provides concepts and tools for detecting subtle but powerful structures that underlie complex situations. Learning to see such structures can help members understand previously unknown forces operating in the organization. This information is essential for developing effective theories for organizing, particularly in today's complex, changing world.

3. ***Continuously monitor and improve the learning process.*** This final stage involves deuterolearning—learning how to learn. Here, learning is directed at the learning process itself and at how well Model II learning characteristics are reflected in it. This includes assessing OL strategies and the organizational structures and processes that contribute to them. Members assess periodically how well these elements facilitate single- and double-loop learning. They generalize positive findings to new or changing situations and make appropriate modifications to improve OL. Because these activities reflect the highest and most difficult level of OL, they depend heavily on members' capability to do Model II learning. Members must be willing to question openly their theories in use about OL; they must be willing to test publicly the effectiveness both of their learning strategies and of the wider organization.

Organization Knowledge

The key outcome of organization learning processes is organization knowledge. It includes what members know about organizational processes, products, customers, and competitive environments. Such knowledge may be *explicit* and exist in codified forms such as documents, manuals, and databases; or it may be *tacit* and reside mainly in members' skills, memories, and intuitions.[50] Fueled by innovations in information technology, KM interventions have focused heavily on codifying organization knowledge so it can be readily accessed and applied to organizational tasks. Because tacit knowledge is difficult if not impossible to codify, attention also has been directed at how such knowledge can be shared informally across members and organizational units.

Organization knowledge contributes to organization performance to the extent that it is relevant and applied effectively to the organization's competitive strategy, as shown in Figure 14.2. Moreover, organization knowledge is particularly valuable when it is unique and cannot easily be obtained by competitors.[51] Thus, organizations seek to develop or acquire knowledge that distinctly adds value for customers and that can be leveraged across products, functions, business units, or geographical regions. For example, Wal-Mart excels at managing its unique distribution system across a wide variety of regional stores. Honda is particularly successful at leveraging its competence in producing motors across a number of product lines, including automobiles, motorcycles, and lawn mowers.[52] These knowledge capabilities have been described as "core competencies,"[53] "invisible assets,"[54] and "intellectual capital,"[55] thus suggesting their contribution to organization performance.

KM interventions are growing rapidly in OD and include a range of change strategies and methods. Although there is no universal approach to KM, these change processes address the essential steps for generating, organizing, and distributing knowledge within organizations.

1. *Generating knowledge.* This stage involves identifying the kinds of knowledge that will create the most value for the organization and then creating mechanisms for increasing that stock of knowledge. It starts with examination of the organization's competitive strategy—how it seeks to create customer value to achieve profitable results. Strategy provides the focus for KM; it identifies those areas where knowledge is likely to have the biggest payoff. For example, competitive strategies that emphasize customer service, such as those found at McKinsey and Nordstrom, place a premium on knowledge about customer needs, preferences, and behavior. Strategies favoring product development, like those at Microsoft and Hoffman-LaRoche, benefit from knowledge about research and development. Strategies focusing on operational excellence, such as those at Motorola and Chevron, value knowledge about manufacturing and quality improvement processes.

   Once the knowledge required for competitive strategy is identified, organizations need to devise mechanisms for acquiring or creating that knowledge. Externally, organizations can acquire other companies that possess the needed knowledge, or they can rent it from knowledge sources such as consultants and university researchers.[56] Internally, organizations can facilitate *communities of practice:* informal networks among employees performing similar work who share expertise and solve problems together.[57] They can also create more formal groups for knowledge generation, such as R&D departments, corporate universities, and centers of excellence. Organizations can bring together people with different skills, ideas, and values to generate new products or services. Called *creative abrasion,* this process breaks traditional frames of thinking by having diverse perspectives rub creatively against each other to develop innovative solutions.[58]

2. *Organizing knowledge.* This phase includes putting valued knowledge into a form that organizational members can use readily. It also may involve refining knowledge to increase its value to users. KM practitioners have developed tools and methods for organizing knowledge that form two broad strategies: codification and personalization.[59] *Codification* approaches rely heavily on information technology. They categorize and store knowledge in databases where it can be accessed and used by appropriate members. This strategy works best for explicit forms of knowledge that can be extracted from people, reports, and other data

sources, and then organized into meaningful categories called "knowledge objects" that can be reused for various purposes. The economic rationale underlying this strategy is to invest once in a knowledge asset and then to reuse it many times.

Personalization strategies for organizing knowledge focus on the people who develop knowledge and on how they can share it person-to-person. This approach emphasizes tacit knowledge, which cannot be codified and stored effectively in computerized information systems. Such knowledge is typically accessed through personal conversations, direct contact, and ongoing dialogue with the people who possess it.

3. ***Distributing knowledge.*** This final stage of KM creates mechanisms for members to gain access to needed knowledge. It overlaps with the previous phase of KM and involves making knowledge easy for people to find and encouraging its use and reuse. KM practitioners have developed a variety of methods for distributing knowledge, generally grouped as three approaches: self-directed distribution, knowledge services and networks, and facilitated transfer.[60]

Self-directed methods rely heavily on member control and initiative for knowledge distribution. They typically include databases for storing knowledge and locator systems for helping members find what they want. Databases can include diverse information such as articles, analytical reports, customer data, and best practices. Locator systems can range from simple phone directories to elaborate search engines.

Knowledge services and networks promote knowledge transfer by providing specific assistance and organized channels for leveraging knowledge throughout the organization. KM services include a variety of support for knowledge distribution, such as help desks, information systems, and knowledge packages. They also may involve special units and roles that scan the flow of knowledge and organize it into more useful forms, such as "knowledge departments," "knowledge managers," or "knowledge integrators."[61] Knowledge networks create linkages among organizational members for sharing knowledge and learning from one another. These connections can be electronic, such as those occurring in chat rooms, intranets, and discussion databases, or they may be personal like those taking place in talk rooms, knowledge fairs, and communities of practice.

Facilitated transfer of organization knowledge involves specific people who assist and encourage knowledge distribution. These people are trained to help members find and transmit knowledge as well as gain access to databases and other knowledge services. They also may act as change agents helping members implement knowledge to improve organization processes and structures. For example, Amoco's "Shared Learning Program" includes dedicated practitioners, called "quality/progress professionals," who coach employees in best practices and how to use them.[62]

■ SUMMARY

In this chapter, we presented interventions for helping organizations transform themselves. These changes can occur at any level in the organization, but their ultimate intent is to change the total system. They typically happen in response to or in anticipation of significant environmental, technological, or internal changes. These changes may require alterations in the firm's strategy, as described in Chapter 13, but are aimed mostly at altering corporate culture, vision, and mental models within the organization.

Corporate culture includes the pattern of basic assumptions, values, norms, and beliefs shared by organization members. It influences how members perceive, think, and behave at work. Culture change interventions start with diagnosing the organization's existing culture. This can include assessing the cultural risks of making organizational changes needed to implement strategy. Changing corporate culture can be extremely difficult and requires clear strategic vision, top-management commitment, symbolic leadership, supporting organizational changes, selection and socialization of newcomers and termination of deviants, and sensitivity to legal and ethical issues.

A self-design change strategy helps a firm gain the built-in capacity to design and implement its own organizational transformation. Self-design involves multiple levels of the firm and multiple stakeholders, and includes an iterative series of activities: acquiring knowledge, valuing, diagnosing, designing, implementing, and assessing.

Organization learning and knowledge management interventions help organizations develop and use knowledge to change and improve themselves continually. Organization learning interventions address how organizations can be designed to promote effective learning processes and how those learning processes themselves can be improved. An organization designed to promote learning over a sustained period of time is called a learning organization. Knowledge management focuses on how that knowledge can be organized and used to improve organization performance.

■ NOTES

1. C. Lundberg, "On Organizational Learning: Implications and Opportunities for Expanding Organizational Development," in *Research in Organizational Change and Development*, vol. 3, eds. W. Pasmore and R. Woodman (Greenwich, Conn.: JAI Press, 1989): 61–82.

2. M. Tushman, W. Newman, and E. Romanelli, "Managing the Unsteady Pace of Organizational Evolution," *California Management Review* (Fall 1986): 29–44.

3. A. Meyer, A. Tsui, and C. Hinings, "Guest Co-Editors Introduction: Configurational Approaches to Organizational Analysis," *Academy of Management Journal* 36 (1993): 1175–95.

4. Tushman, Newman, and Romanelli, "Managing the Unsteady Pace"; L. Greiner, "Evolution and Revolution as Organizations Grow," *Harvard Business Review* (July-August 1972): 37–46.

5. R. Golembiewski, K. Billingsley, and S. Yeager, "Measuring Change and Persistence in Human Affairs: Types of Changes Generated by OD Designs," *Journal of Applied Behavioral Science* 12 (1975): 133–57.

6. J. Sackmann, "The Role of Metaphors in Organization Transformation," *Human Relations* 42 (1989): 463–85.

7. R. Waldersee, "Becoming a Learning Organization: The Transformation of the Workplace," *Journal of Management Development* 16 (1997): 262–74; A. Pettigrew, *The Awakening Giant: Continuity and Change in Imperial Chemical Industries* (Oxford: Blackwell, 1985); A. Pettigrew, "Context and Action in the Transformation of the Firm," *Journal of Management Studies* 24 (1987): 649–70; M. Tushman and E. Romanelli, "Organizational Evolution: A Metamorphosis Model of Convergence and Reorientation," in *Research in Organizational Behavior*, vol. 7, eds. L. Cummings and B. Staw (Greenwich, Conn.: JAI Press, 1985): 171–222.

8. P. Nutt and R. Backoff, "Facilitating Transformational Change," *Journal of Applied Behavioral Science* 33 (1997): 490–508; M. Tushman, W. Newman, and D. Nadler, "Executive Leadership and Organizational Evolution: Managing Incremental and Discontinuous Change," in *Corporate Transformation: Revitalizing Organizations for a Competitive World*, eds. R. Kilmann and T. Covin (San Francisco: Jossey-Bass, 1988): 102–30; W. Bennis and B. Nanus, *Leaders: The Strategies for Taking Charge* (New York: Harper & Row, 1985); Pettigrew, "Context and Action."

9. T. Cummings and S. Mohrman, "Self-Designing Organizations: Towards Implementing Quality-of-Work-Life

Innovations," in *Research in Organizational Change and Development,* vol. 1, eds. R. Woodman and W. Pasmore (Greenwich, Conn.: JAI Press, 1987): 275–310.

10. D. Meyerson and J. Martin, "Cultural Change: An Integration of Three Different Views," *Journal of Management Studies* 24 (1987): 623–47; D. Denison and G. Spreitzer, "Organizational Culture and Organizational Development: A Competing Values Approach," in *Research in Organizational Change and Development,* vol. 5, eds. R. Woodman and W. Pasmore (Greenwich, Conn.: JAI Press, 1991): 1–22; E. Schein, *Organizational Culture and Leadership,* 2d ed. (San Francisco: Jossey-Bass, 1992).

11. Schein, *Organizational Culture.*

12. M. Louis, "Toward a System of Inquiry on Organizational Culture" (paper delivered at the Western Academy of Management meetings, Colorado Springs, Colo., April 1982).

13. D. Hanna, *Designing Organizations for High Performance* (Reading, Mass.: Addison-Wesley, 1988).

14. H. Schwartz and S. Davis, "Matching Corporate Culture and Business Strategy," *Organizational Dynamics* (Summer 1981): 30–48; S. Davis, *Managing Corporate Culture* (Cambridge, Mass.: Ballinger, 1984).

15. K. Cameron and R. Quinn, *Diagnosing and Changing Organizational Culture* (Reading, Mass.: Addison-Wesley, 1999); Denison and Spreitzer, "Organizational Culture"; R. E. Quinn, *Beyond Rational Management: Mastering the Paradoxes and Competing Demands of High Performance* (San Francisco: Jossey-Bass, 1988).

16. R. Quinn and G. Spreitzer, "The Psychometrics of the Competing Values Culture Instrument and an Analysis of the Impact of Organizational Culture on Quality of Life," in *Research in Organizational Change and Development,* vol. 5, eds. R. Woodman and W. Pasmore (Greenwich, Conn.: JAI Press, 1991): 115–42.

17. Schein, *Organizational Culture.*

18. E. Schein, *The Corporate Culture Survival Guide* (San Francisco: Jossey-Bass, 1999); Schwartz and Davis, "Matching Corporate Culture"; B. Uttal, "The Corporate Culture Vultures," *Fortune* (17 October 1983): 66–72; Davis, *Managing Corporate Culture;* R. Kilmann, M. Saxton, and R. Serpa, eds., *Gaining Control of the Corporate Culture* (San Francisco: Jossey-Bass, 1985); P. Frost, L. Moore, M. Louis, C. Lundberg, and J. Martin, eds., *Organizational Culture* (Beverly Hills, Calif.: Sage, 1985): 95–196; V. Sathe, "Implications of Corporate Culture: A Manager's Guide to Action," *Organizational Dynamics* (Autumn 1983): 5–23; B.

Drake and E. Drake, "Ethical and Legal Aspects of Managing Corporate Cultures," *California Management Review* (Winter 1988): 107–23.

19. C. Worley, D. Hitchin, and W. Ross, *Integrated Strategic Change* (Reading, Mass.: Addison-Wesley, 1996); R. Beckhard and W. Pritchard, *Changing the Essence* (San Francisco: Jossey-Bass, 1992).

20. F. Aguilar and A. Bhambri, *Johnson and Johnson (A)* (Boston: HBS Case Services, 1983).

21. Dumaine, "Creating a New Company Culture"; C. O'Reilly, "Corporations, Culture, and Commitment: Motivation and Social Control in Organizations," *California Management Review* 31 (Summer 1989): 9–25; Pettigrew, "Context and Action."

22. Tichy and Sherman, *Control Your Destiny;* B. Morris, "The Wealth Builders," *Fortune* (11 December 1995): 80–96.

23. Dumaine, "Creating a New Company Culture."

24. Ibid.

25. Tichy and Sherman, *Control Your Destiny.*

26. K. Labich, "Boeing Finally Hatches a Plan," *Fortune* (1 March 1999): 101–06.

27. B. Hedberg, P. Nystrom, and W. Starbuck, "Camping on Seesaws: Prescriptions for a Self-Designing Organization," *Administrative Science Quarterly* 21 (1976): 41–65; K. Weick, "Organization Design: Organizations as Self-Designing Systems," *Organizational Dynamics* 6 (1977): 30–46.

28. S. Mohrman and T. Cummings, *Self-Designing Organizations: Learning How to Create High Performance* (Reading, Mass.: Addison-Wesley, 1989); Cummings and Mohrman, "Self-Designing Organizations."

29. P. Lawrence and D. Dyer, *Renewing American Industry* (New York: Free Press, 1983).

30. C. Argyris, R. Putnam, and D. Smith, *Action Science* (San Francisco: Jossey-Bass, 1985); C. Lundberg, "On Organizational Learning: Implications and Opportunities for Expanding Organizational Development," in *Research on Organizational Change and Development,* vol. 3, eds. R. Woodman and W. Pasmore (Greenwich, Conn.: JAI Press, 1989): 61–82; P. Senge, *The Fifth Discipline* (New York: Doubleday, 1990).

31. M. Weisbord, *Productive Workplaces* (San Francisco: Jossey-Bass, 1987); R. Freeman, *Strategic Management* (Boston: Ballinger, 1984).

32. D. Miller and P. Friesen, *Organizations: A Quantum View* (Englewood Cliffs, N.J.: Prentice Hall, 1984).

33. M. Crossan, H. Lane, and R. White, "An Organizational Learning Framework: From Intuition to Institution," *Academy of Management Review* 24 (1999): 522–37; S. Prokesch, "Unleashing the Power of Learning: An Interview with British Petroleum's John Browne," *Harvard Business Review* (September-October 1997): 147–68; J.-C. Spender, "Making Knowledge the Basis of a Dynamic Theory of the Firm," *Strategic Management Journal* 17 (1996): 45–62; R. Strata, "Organizational Learning: The Key to Management Innovation," *Sloan Management Review* 30 (1989): 63–74.

34. D. Teece, "Capturing Value from Knowledge Assets: The New Economy, Market for Know-How, and Intangible Assets," *California Management Review* 40 (Spring 1998): 55–79.

35. This framework draws heavily on the work of W. Snyder and T. Cummings, "Organization Learning Disorders: Conceptual Model and Intervention Hypotheses," *Human Relations* 51 (1998): 873–95.

36. Senge, *Fifth Discipline*; S. Chawla and J. Renesch, eds., *Learning Organizations: Developing Cultures for Tomorrow's Workplace* (Portland, OR: Productivity Press, 1995).

37. M. McGill, J. Slocum, and D. Lei, "Management Practices in Learning Organizations," *Organizational Dynamics* (Autumn 1993): 5–17; E. Nevis, A. DiBella, and J. Gould, "Understanding Organizations as Learning Systems," *Sloan Management Review* (Winter 1995): 73–85.

38. T. Stewart, "Getting Real About Brain Power," *Fortune* (27 November 1995): 201–03.

39. T. Stewart, "How a Little Company Won Big by Betting on Brainpower," *Fortune* (4 September 1995): 121–22.

40. Nevis, DiBella, and Gould, "Understanding Organizations."

41. M. Beer, "Leading Learning and Learning to Lead: An Action Learning Approach to Developing Organizational Fitness," in *The Leader's Change Handbook: An Essential Guide to Setting Direction and Action Taking*, eds. J. Conger, G. Spreitzer, and E. Lawler III (San Francisco: Jossey-Bass, 1999): 127–61.

42. Ibid.

43. J. Dewey, *How We Think* (Boston: D.C. Heath, 1933).

44. C. Argyris and D. Schon, *Organizational Learning: A Theory of Action Perspective* (Reading, Mass.: Addison-Wesley, 1978); C. Argyris and D. Schon, *Organizational Learning II: Theory, Method, and Practice* (Reading, Mass.: Addison-Wesley, 1996); Senge, *Fifth Discipline*.

45. Argyris and Schon, *Organizational Learning II*; Senge, *Fifth Discipline*; P. Senge, C. Roberts, R. Ross, B. Smith, and A. Kleiner, *The Fifth Discipline Fieldbook: Strategies for Building a Learning Organization* (New York: Doubleday, 1995).

46. Argyris and Schon, *Organizational Learning II*.

47. Ibid.

48. Argyris and Schon, *Organizational Learning II*; C. Argyris, *Intervention Theory and Method* (Reading, Mass.: Addison-Wesley, 1970).

49. Senge, *Fifth Discipline*.

50. M. Polanyi, *The Tacit Dimension* (New York: Doubleday, 1966); I. Nonaka and H. Takeuchi, *The Knowledge-Creating Company: How Japanese Companies Foster Creativity and Innovation for Competitive Advantage* (New York: Oxford University Press, 1995).

51. J. Barney, "Looking Inside for Competitive Advantage," *Academy of Management Executive* 9 (4, 1995): 49–61; M. Peteraf, "The Cornerstones of Competitive Advantage," *Strategic Management Journal* 14, 3 (1993): 179–92; Worley, Hitchin, and Ross, *Integrated Strategic Change*.

52. W. Snyder, "Organization Learning and Performance: An Exploration of the Linkages Between Organizational Learning, Knowledge, and Performance" (unpublished Ph.D. diss., University of Southern California, Los Angeles, 1996).

53. C. Prahalad and G. Hamel, "The Core Competencies of the Corporation," *Harvard Business Review* 68 (1990): 79–91.

54. H. Itami, *Mobilizing for Invisible Assets* (Cambridge: Harvard University Press, 1987).

55. L. Edvinsson and M. Malone, *Intellectual Capital: Realizing Your Company's True Value by Finding Its Hidden Brainpower* (New York: Harper Business, 1997); T. Stewart, *Intellectual Capital: The New Wealth of Organizations* (New York: Doubleday, 1997); J. Nahapiet and S. Ghoshal, "Social Capital, Intellectual Capital, and the Organizational Advantage," *Academy of Management Review* 23 (1998): 242–66.

56. V. Anand, C. Manz, and W. Glick, "An Organizational Memory Approach to Information Management," *Academy of Management Review* 23 (1998): 796–809.

57. J. Lave and E. Wenger, *Situated Learning: Legitimate Peripheral Participation* (New York: Cambridge University Press, 1993); J. Brown and P. Duguid, "Organizational Learning and Communities of Practice: Towards a Unified View of Working, Learning, and Innovation," *Organization Science* 2 (1991): 40–57.

58. D. Leonard-Barton, *Wellsprings of Knowledge: Building and Sustaining the Sources of Innovation* (Boston: Harvard Business School Press, 1995); D. Leonard-Barton and S. Sensiper, "The Role of Tacit Knowledge in Group Innovation," *California Management Review* 40 (Spring 1998): 112–32.

59. M. Hansen, N. Nohria, and T. Tierney, "What's Your Strategy for Managing Knowledge?" *Harvard Business Review* (March-April 1999): 106–16.

60. C. O'Dell and C. Grayson, *If Only We Knew What We Know* (New York: Free Press, 1998).

61. Ibid.

62. Ibid.

The Future of Organization Development

4

15. Organization Development in Global Settings

This chapter describes the practice of organization development in international settings. It presents the contingencies and practice issues associated with OD in organizations outside the United States, in worldwide organizations, and in global social change organizations. The increasing applicability and effectiveness of OD in countries and cultures outside of the United States is debatable, however. Because OD was developed predominantly by American and Western European practitioners, its practices and methods are heavily influenced by the values and assumptions of industrialized cultures. Thus, the traditional approaches to planned change may promote management practices that conflict with the values and assumptions of other societies. Some practitioners believe, on the other hand, that OD can result in organizational improvements in any culture. Despite different points of view on this topic, the practice of OD in international settings can be expected to expand dramatically. The rapid development of foreign economies and firms, along with the evolution of the global marketplace, is creating organizational needs and opportunities for change.

ORGANIZATION DEVELOPMENT OUTSIDE THE UNITED STATES

Organization development is being practiced increasingly in organizations outside of the United States.[1] Survey feedback interventions have been used at Air New Zealand and at the Air Emirates (United Arab Republic); work design interventions have been implemented in Gamesa (Mexico); merger and acquisition integration interventions have been used in Korea, The Netherlands, and Europe; and reward system changes have been implemented at the Weili Washing Machine Factory in Zhongshan, China.[2]

The success of OD in settings outside the United States depends on two key contingencies. First, OD interventions need to be responsive to the cultural values and organizational customs of the host country if the changes are to produce the kinds of positive results shown in the United States.[3] Second, a country's economic development can affect the success of OD interventions.[4]

Cultural Context

Researchers have proposed that applying OD in different countries requires a "context-based" approach to planned change.[5] This involves fitting the change process to the organization's cultural context, including the values held by members in the particular country or region. These beliefs inform people about which behaviors are important and acceptable in their culture. Cultural values play a major role in shaping the customs and practices that occur within organizations as well, influencing how members react to phenomena having to do with power, conflict, ambiguity, time, and change.

There is a growing body of knowledge about cultural diversity and its effect on organizational and management practices.[6] Researchers have identified five key values that describe national cultures and influence organizational customs: context orientation, power distance, uncertainty avoidance, achievement orientation, and individualism (Table 15.1).[7]

Context Orientation

This value describes how information is conveyed and time is valued in a culture. In low-context cultures, such as Scandinavia and the United States, information is communicated in words and phrases. By using more specific words, more meaning is expressed. In addition, time is viewed as discrete and linear—as something that can be spent, used, saved, or wasted. In high-context cultures, on the other hand, the communication medium reflects the message more than the words, and time is a fluid and flexible concept. For example, social cues in Japan and Venezuela provide as much, if not more, information about a particular situation than do words alone. Organizations in high-context cultures emphasize ceremony and ritual. How one behaves is an important signal of support and compliance with the way things are done. Structures are less formal in high-context cultures; there are few written policies and procedures to guide behavior. Because high-context cultures

Table 15•1	Cultural Values and Organization Customs		
VALUE	**DEFINITION**	**ORGANIZATION CUSTOMS WHEN THE VALUE IS AT ONE EXTREME**	**REPRESENTATIVE COUNTRIES**
Context	The extent to which words carry the meaning of a message; how time is viewed	Ceremony and routines are common. Structure is less formal; fewer written policies exist. People are often late for appointments.	*High:* Asian and Latin American countries *Low:* Scandinavian countries, United States
Power distance	The extent to which members of a society accept that power is distributed unequally in an organization	Decision making is autocratic. Superiors consider subordinates as part of a different class. Subordinates are closely supervised. Employees are not likely to disagree. Powerful people are entitled to privileges.	*High:* Latin American and Eastern European countries *Low:* Scandinavian countries
Uncertainty avoidance	The extent to which members of an organization tolerate the unfamiliar and unpredictable	Experts have status/authority. Clear roles are preferred. Conflict is undesirable. Change is resisted. Conservative practices are preferred.	*High:* Asian countries *Low:* European countries
Achievement orientation	The extent to which organization members value assertiveness and the acquisition of material goods	Achievement is reflected in wealth and recognition. Decisiveness is valued. Larger and faster are better. Gender roles are clearly differentiated.	*High:* Asian and Latin American countries, South Africa *Low:* Scandinavian countries
Individualism	The extent to which people believe they should be responsible for themselves and their immediate families	Personal initiative is encouraged. Time is valuable to individuals. Competitiveness is accepted. Autonomy is highly valued.	*High:* United States *Low:* Latin American and Eastern European countries

view time as fluid, punctuality for appointments is less a priority than is maintaining relationships.

Power Distance

This value concerns the way people view authority, status differences, and influence patterns. People in high power distance regions, such as Latin America and Eastern Europe, tend to favor unequal distributions of power and influence, and consequently autocratic and paternalistic decision-making practices are accepted. Organizations in high power distance cultures tend to be highly centralized with several hierarchical levels and a large proportion of supervisory personnel. Subordinates in these organizations represent a lower social class. They expect to be supervised closely and believe that power holders are entitled to special privileges. Such practices would be inappropriate in low power distance regions, such as Scandinavia, where participative decision making and egalitarian methods prevail.

Uncertainty Avoidance

This value reflects a preference for conservative practices and familiar and predictable situations. People in high uncertainty avoidance regions, such as Asia, prefer stable routines, resist change, and act to maintain the status quo. They do not like conflict and believe that company rules should not be broken. In regions where uncertainty avoidance is low, such as in many European countries, ambiguity is less threatening. Organizations in these cultures tend to favor fewer rules, higher levels of participation in decision making, more organic structures, and more risk taking.

Achievement Orientation

This value concerns the extent to which the culture favors the acquisition of power and resources. Employees from achievement-oriented cultures, such as Asia and Latin America, place a high value on career advancement, freedom, and salary growth. Organizations in these cultures pursue aggressive goals and have high levels of stress and conflict. Organizational success is measured in terms of size, growth, and speed. On the other hand, workers in cultures where achievement is less of a driving value, such as those in Scandinavia, prize the social aspects of work including working conditions and supervision, and typically favor opportunities to learn and grow at work.

Individualism

This value is concerned with looking out for oneself as opposed to one's group or organization. In high individualism cultures, such as the United States and Canada, personal initiative and competitiveness are valued strongly. Organizations in individualistic cultures often have high turnover rates and individual rather than group decision-making processes. Employee empowerment is supported when members believe that it improves the probability of personal gain. These cultures encourage personal initiative, competitiveness, and individual autonomy. Conversely, in low individualism countries, such as Taiwan, Japan, and Peru, allegiance to one's group is paramount. Organizations operating in these cultures tend to favor cooperation among employees and loyalty to the company.

Economic Development

In addition to cultural context, an important contingency affecting OD success internationally is a country's level of industrial and economic development. It can be judged from social, economic, and political perspectives.[8] For example, economic development can be reflected in a country's management capability as measured by information systems and skills; decision-making and action-taking capabilities; project planning and organizing abilities; evaluation and control technologies; leadership, motivational, and reward systems; and human selection, placement, and development levels. Similarly, the United Nations' Human Development Programme has created a Human Development Index that assesses a country's economic development in terms of life expectancy, educational attainment, and income.

Subsistence Economies

Countries such as Bangladesh, Nepal, Afghanistan, India, and Nigeria have relatively low degrees of development and their economies are agriculturally based. Their populations consume most of what they produce, and any surplus is used to barter for other needed goods and services. A large proportion of the population is unfamiliar with the concept of "employment." Working for someone else in exchange for wages is not common or understood, and consequently few large organizations exist outside of the government. In subsistence economies, OD interventions emphasize global social change and focus on creating conditions for sustainable social and economic progress. These change methods are described in the last section of this chapter.

Industrializing Economies

These countries, which include South Africa, the Philippines, Brazil, Iran, and the People's Republic of China, are moderately developed and tend to be rich in natural resources. An expanding manufacturing base that accounts for increasing amounts of the country's gross domestic product fuels economic growth. The rise of manufacturing also contributes to the formation of a class system including upper-, middle-, and low-income groups. Organizations operating in these nations generally focus on efficiency of operations and revenue growth. Consequently, OD interventions address strategic, structural, and work design issues.[9] They help organizations identify domestic and international markets, develop clear and appropriate goals, and structure themselves to achieve efficient performance and market growth.

Industrial Economies

Highly developed countries, such as Scandinavia, Japan, France, and the United States, emphasize nonagricultural industry. In these economies, manufactured goods are exported and traded with other industrialized countries; investment funds are available both internally and externally; the workforce is educated and skilled; and technology often is substituted for labor. Because the OD interventions described in this book were developed primarily in industrial economies, they can be expected to have their strongest effects in those contexts. Their continued success cannot be ensured, however, because these countries are advancing rapidly to postindustrial conditions. Here, OD interventions will need to fit into economies driven by information and knowledge, where service outpaces manufacturing, and where national and organizational boundaries are more open and flexible.

How Cultural Context and Economic Development Affect OD Practice

The contingencies of cultural context and economic development can have powerful effects on the way OD is carried out in different countries.[10] They can determine whether change processes proceed slowly or quickly; involve few or many members; are directed by hierarchical authority or by consensus; and focus on business, organizational, or human process issues.

When the two contingencies are considered together, they reveal four different international settings for OD practice, as shown in Figure 15.1. These different

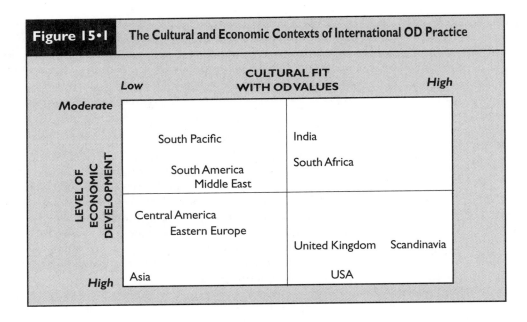

Figure 15•1   The Cultural and Economic Contexts of International OD Practice

situations reflect the extent to which a country's culture fits with traditional OD values of direct and honest communication, sharing power, and improving their effectiveness and the degree to which the country is economically developed.[11] In Figure 15.1, the degree of economic development is restricted to moderately and highly industrialized regions. Subsistence economies are not included because they afford little opportunity to practice traditional OD; in those contexts, a more appropriate strategy is global social change, discussed later in this chapter. In general, however, the more developed the economy, the more OD is applied to the organizational and human process issues described in this book. In less developed situations, OD focuses on business issues, such as procuring raw materials, producing efficiently, and marketing successfully.[12] On the other hand, when the country's culture supports traditional OD values, the planned change process can be applied with only small adjustments.[13] The more the cultural context differs from OD's traditional values profile, the more the planned change process will need to be modified to fit the situation.

Low Cultural Fit, Moderate Industrialization

This context is least suited to traditional OD practice. It includes industrializing economies with cultural values that align poorly with OD values, including many Middle East nations, such as Iraq, Iran, and the United Arab Republic; the South Pacific region, including Malaysia and the Philippines; and certain South American countries, such as Brazil, Ecuador, Guatemala, and Nicaragua. These regions are highly dependent on their natural resources and have a relatively small manufacturing base. They tend to be high-context cultures with values of high power distance and achievement orientation and of moderate uncertainty avoidance. They are not a bad fit with OD values because these cultures tend toward moderate or high levels of collectivism, especially in relation to family.

These settings require change processes that fit local customs and that address business issues. As might be expected, little is written on applying OD in these countries, and there are even fewer reports of OD practice. Cultural values of high power distance and achievement are inconsistent with OD activities emphasizing openness, collaboration, and empowerment. Moreover, executives in industrializing economies frequently equate OD with human process interventions, such as team building, conflict management, and process consultation. They perceive OD as too soft to meet their business needs. For example, Egyptian and Filipino managers tend to be autocratic, engage in protracted decision making, and focus on economic and business problems. Consequently, organizational change is slow paced, centrally controlled, and aimed at achieving technical rationality and efficiency.[14]

High Cultural Fit, Moderate Industrialization

This international context includes subsistence and industrializing economies with cultures that align with traditional OD values. Such settings support the kinds of OD processes described in this book, especially technostructural and strategic interventions that focus on business development. According to data on economic development and cultural values, relatively few countries fit this context. India's industrial base is growing rapidly and may fit this contingency. Similarly, South Africa's recent political and cultural changes make it one of the most interesting settings in which to practice OD.[15]

South Africa is an industrializing economy. Its major cities are the manufacturing hubs of the economy, although agriculture and mining still dominate in rural areas. The country's values are in transition and may become more consistent with OD values. South Africans customarily have favored a low-context orientation; relatively high levels of power distance; and moderate levels of individualism, uncertainty avoidance, and achievement orientation. Organizations typically have been bureaucratic with authoritarian management, established career paths, and job security primarily for Caucasian employees. These values and organizational conditions are changing, however, as the nation's political and governance structures are transformed. Formerly, apartheid policies reduced uncertainty and defined power differences among citizens. Today, free elections and the abolishment of apartheid have increased uncertainty drastically and established legal equality among the races. These changes are likely to move South Africa's values closer to those underlying OD.[16] If so, OD interventions should become increasingly relevant to that nation's organizations.

Low Cultural Fit, High Industrialization

This international setting includes industrialized countries with cultures that fit poorly with traditional OD values. Many countries in Central America, Eastern Asia, and Eastern Europe fit this description. Reviews of OD practice in those regions suggest that planned change includes all four types of interventions described in this book, although the change process itself is adapted to local conditions.[17] For example, Mexico, Venezuela, China, Japan, and Korea are high-context cultures where knowledge of local mannerisms, customs, and rituals is required to understand the meaning of communicated information.[18] To function in such settings, OD practitioners not only must know the language but the social customs as well. Similarly, cultural values emphasizing high levels of power distance, uncertainty avoidance, and achievement orientation foster organizations where roles, status differences, and working conditions are clear; where autocratic and paternalistic decisions are expected; and where the acquisition of wealth and influence by the powerful is accepted. OD interventions that focus on social processes and employee empowerment are not favored naturally in this cultural context and consequently need to be modified to fit the situations.

Asian organizations, such as Matsushita, Nissan, Toyota, Fujitsu, NEC, and Hyundai, provide good examples of how OD interventions can be tailored to this global setting. These firms are famous for continuous improvement and TQM practices; they adapt these interventions to fit the Asian culture. Roles and behaviors required to apply TQM are highly specified, thereby holding uncertainty to a relatively low level. Teamwork and consensus decision-making practices associated with quality improvement projects also help manage uncertainty. When large numbers of employees are involved, information is spread quickly and members are kept informed about the changes taking place. Management controls the change process by regulating the implementation of suggestions made by the problem-solving groups. Because these interventions focus on work processes, teamwork and employee involvement do not threaten the power structure. Moreover, TQM and continuous improvement do not alter the organization radically but produce small, incremental changes that can add up to impressive gains in long-term productivity and cost reduction.

In these cultures, OD practitioners also tailor the change process itself to fit local conditions. Mexican companies, for example, expect OD practitioners to act as experts and to offer concrete advice on how to improve the organization. To be successful, OD practitioners need sufficient status and legitimacy to work with senior management and to act in expert roles.[19] Status typically is associated with academic credentials, senior management experience, high-level titles, or recommendations by highly placed executives and administrators. As might be expected, the change process in Latin America is autocratic and driven downward from the top of the organization. Subordinates or lower-status people generally are not included in diagnostic or implementation activities because inclusion might equalize power differences and threaten the status quo. Moreover, cultural norms discourage employees from speaking out or openly criticizing management. There is relatively little resistance to change because employees readily accept changes dictated by management.

In Asia, OD is an orderly process, driven by consensus and challenging performance goals.[20] Organizational changes are implemented slowly and methodically, so trust builds and change-related uncertainty is reduced. Changing too quickly is seen as arrogant, divisive, and threatening. At the China Association for the International Exchange of Personnel, the move from a government bureau to a "market-facing" organization has been gradual but consistent. Managers have been encouraged to contact more and more foreign organizations, to develop relationships and contracts, and to learn marketing and organization development skills. Because Asian values promote a cautious and somewhat closed culture that prizes consensus, dignity, and respect, OD tends to be impersonal and to focus mainly on work-flow improvements. Human process issues are rarely addressed because people are expected to act in ways that do not cause others to "lose face" or bring shame to the group.

High Cultural Fit, High Industrialization

This last setting includes industrialized countries with cultural contexts that fit well with traditional OD values. Much of the OD practice described in this book was developed in these situations, particularly in the United States.[21] To extend our learning, we will focus on how OD is practiced in other nations in this global setting, including the Scandinavian countries—Sweden, Norway, Finland, and Denmark—and countries with a strong British heritage, such as Great Britain, Northern Ireland, Australia, and New Zealand.

Scandinavians enjoy a high standard of living and strong economic development.[22] Because their cultural values most closely match those traditionally espoused in OD, organizational practices are highly participative and egalitarian. OD practice tends to mirror these values. Multiple stakeholders, such as managers, unionists, and staff personnel, actively are involved in all stages of the change process, from entry and diagnosis to intervention and evaluation. This level of involvement is much higher than typically occurs in the United States. It results in a change process that is heavily oriented to the needs of shop-floor participants. Norwegian labor laws, for example, give unionists the right to participate in technological innovations that can affect their work lives. Such laws also mandate that all employees in the country have the right to enriched forms of work.

Given this cultural context, Scandinavian companies pioneered sociotechnical interventions to improve productivity and quality of work life.[23] Sweden's Saab-Scania and Volvo restructured automobile manufacturing around self-managed work groups. Denmark's Patent Office and Norway's Shell Oil demonstrated how union–management cooperative projects can enhance employee involvement throughout the organization. In many cases, national governments were involved heavily in these change projects by sponsoring industrywide improvement efforts. The Norwegian government, for example, was instrumental in introducing industrial democracy to that nation's companies. It helped union and management in selected industries implement pilot projects to enhance productivity and quality of work life. The results of these sociotechnical experiments were then diffused throughout the Norwegian economy. In many ways, the Scandinavian countries have gone further than other global regions in linking OD to national values and policies.

Countries associated with the United Kingdom tend to have values consistent with a low-context orientation, moderate to high individualism and achievement orientation, and moderate to low power distance and uncertainty avoidance. This cultural pattern results in personal relationships that often seem indirect to Americans. For example, a British subordinate who is told to think about a proposal is really being told that the suggestion has been rejected. These values also promote organizational policies that are steeped in formality, tradition, and politics. The United Kingdom's long history tends to reinforce the status quo, and consequently resistance to change is high.

OD practice in the United Kingdom parallels the cultural pattern described above. In Great Britain, for example, sociotechnical systems theory was developed by practitioners at the Tavistock Institute of Human Relations.[24] Applications, such as self-managed work groups, however, have not readily diffused within British organizations. The individualistic values and inherently political nature of this culture tend to conflict with interventions emphasizing employee empowerment and teamwork. In contrast, the Scandinavian cultures are far more supportive of sociotechnical practice and have been instrumental in diffusing it worldwide.

The emergence of the European Union has served as a catalyst for change in many British organizations. Companies such as Akzo Nobel, British Aerospace, International Computers Ltd. (ICL), and Reuters are actively engaged in strategic change interventions. At British Petroleum, chairman Robert B. Horton is implementing a flexible organization to compete better in the emerging economy. He is reducing the number of levels in the structure, discontinuing long-standing committees, eliminating staff, and empowering employees in teams.[25] More limited interventions, such as team building, conflict resolution, and work redesign, are being carried out in such organizations as Unilever and SmithKline Beecham.

WORLDWIDE ORGANIZATION DEVELOPMENT

An important trend facing many business firms is the emergence of a global marketplace. Driven by competitive pressures, lowered trade barriers, and advances in information technologies, the number of companies offering products and services in multiple countries is increasing rapidly. The organizational growth and complexity associated with worldwide operations pose challenging managerial problems. Executives must choose appropriate strategic orientations for operating across cultures and geographical locations, and under diverse governmental and environmental requirements. They must be able to adapt corporate policies and procedures to a range of local conditions. Moreover, the tasks of controlling and coordinating operations in different nations place heavy demands on information and control systems and on managerial skills and knowledge.

Worldwide organization development applies to organizations that are operating across multiple geographic and cultural boundaries. This contrasts with OD in organizations that operate outside the United States but within a single cultural and economic context. This section describes the emerging practice of OD in worldwide organizations, a relatively new but important area of planned change.

What Is a Worldwide Organization?

Worldwide organizations can be defined in terms of three key facets.[26] First, they offer products or services in more than one country and actively manage substantial direct investments in those countries. Consequently, they must relate to a variety of demands, such as unique product requirements, tariffs, value-added taxes, transportation laws, and trade agreements. Second, worldwide firms must balance product and functional concerns with geographic issues of distance, time, and culture. American tobacco companies, for example, face technological, moral, and organizational issues in determining whether to market cigarettes in less-developed countries, and if they do, they must decide how to integrate manufacturing and distribution operations on a global scale. Third, worldwide companies must carry out coordinated activities across cultural boundaries using a wide variety of personnel. Workers with different cultural backgrounds must be managed in ways that support the overall goals and image of the organization.[27] The company must therefore adapt its human resources policies and procedures to fit the culture and accomplish operational objectives. From a managerial perspective, selecting executives to head foreign operations is an important decision in worldwide organizations.

Worldwide Strategic Orientations

A key contingency in designing OD interventions in worldwide organizations is how products, organizational units, and personnel are arranged to form strategic orientations that enable firms to compete in the global marketplace.[28] Worldwide organizations can offer certain products or services in some countries and not in others; they can centralize or decentralize operations; and they can determine how to work with people from different cultures. Despite the many possible combinations of characteristics, researchers have found that worldwide organizations generally implement one of three types of strategic orientations: global, multinational, or transnational. Table 15.2 presents these orientations in terms of the diagnostic framework described in Chapter 4. Each strategic orientation is geared to specific market, technological, and organizational requirements. OD interventions that can help organizations meet these demands also are included in Table 15.2.

Table 15•2	Characteristics and Interventions for Worldwide Strategic Orientations				
WORLDWIDE STRATEGIC ORIENTATION	**STRATEGY**	**STRUCTURE**	**INFORMATION SYSTEM**	**HUMAN RESOURCES**	**OD INTERVENTIONS**
Global	Standardized products Goals of efficiency through volume	Centralized, balanced, and coordinated activities Global product division	Formal	Ethnocentric selection	Career planning Role clarification Employee involvement Senior management team building Conflict management
Multinational	Tailored products Goals of local responsiveness through specialization	Decentralized operations; centralized planning Global geographic divisions	Profit centers	Regiocentric or polycentric selection	Intergroup relations Local management team building Management development Reward systems Strategic alliances
Transnational	Tailored products Goals of learning and responsiveness through integration	Decentralized, worldwide coordination Global matrix or network	Subtle, clan-oriented controls	Geocentric selection	Extensive selection and rotation Cultural development Intergroup relations Building corporate vision

Global Orientation

This orientation is characterized by a strategy of marketing standardized products in different countries. It is an appropriate orientation when there is little economic reason to offer products or services with special features or locally available options. Manufacturers of office equipment, consumer goods, computers, tires, and containers, for example, can offer the same basic product in almost any country.

The goal of efficiency dominates this orientation. Production efficiency is gained through volume sales and a small number of large manufacturing plants, and managerial efficiency is achieved by centralizing product design, manufacturing, distribution, and marketing decisions. Tight coordination is achieved by the close physical proximity of major functional groups and formal control systems that balance inputs, production, and distribution with worldwide demand. Many Japanese firms, such as Honda, Sony, NEC, and Matsushita, used this strategy in the 1970s and early 1980s to grow in the international economy. In Europe, Nestlé exploits economies of scale in marketing by advertising well-known brand names around the world. The increased number of microwaves and two-income families allowed Nestlé to push its Nescafé coffee and Lean Cuisine low-calorie frozen dinners to dominant market-share positions in Europe, North America, Latin America, and Asia. Similarly, Korean noodle maker, Nong Shim Company, avoided the 1999 financial crisis by staying focused on efficiency. Yoo Jong Suk, Nong Shim's head of strategy, went against recommendations to diversify and stated, "All we want is to be globally recognized as a ramyon maker."[29]

In the global orientation, the organization tends to be centralized with a global product structure. Presidents of each major product group report to the CEO and form the line organization. Each of these product groups is responsible for worldwide operations. Information systems in global orientations tend to be quite formal with local units reporting sales, costs, and other data directly to the product president. The predominant human resources policy integrates people into the organization through ethnocentric selection and staffing practices. These methods seek to fill key foreign positions with personnel, or expatriates, from the home country where the corporation headquarters is located.[30] Managerial jobs at Volvo and Michelin, for example, are occupied by Swedish and French citizens, respectively.[31] Ethnocentric policies support the global orientation because expatriate managers are more likely than host-country nationals to recognize and comply with the need to centralize decision making and to standardize processes, decisions, and relationships with the parent company. Although many Japanese automobile manufacturers have decentralized production, Nissan's global strategy has been to retain tight, centralized control of design and manufacturing, ensure that almost all of its senior foreign managers are Japanese, and have even low-level decisions emerge from face-to-face meetings in Tokyo.[32]

Several OD interventions can be used to support the global strategic orientation, including career planning, role clarification, employee involvement, conflict management, and senior management team building. Each of these interventions can help the organization achieve improved operational efficiency. For example, role clarification interventions, such as job enrichment, goal setting, and conflict management, can formalize and standardize organizational activities. This ensures that each individual knows specific details about how, when, and why a job needs to be done. As a result, necessary activities are described and efficient transactions and relationships are created. Senior management team building can improve the quality of strategic decisions. Centralized policies make the organization highly dependent on this group and can exaggerate decision-making errors. In addition, interpersonal conflict can increase the cost of coordination or cause significant coordination mistakes. Process interventions at this level can help improve the speed and quality of decision making and improve interpersonal relationships.

Multinational Orientation

This strategic orientation, characterized by a product line that is tailored to local conditions, is best suited to markets that vary significantly from region to region or country to country. At American Express, for example, charge card marketing is fitted to local values and tastes. The "Don't leave home without it" and "Membership has its privileges" themes seen in the United States were translated to "Peace of mind only for members" in Japan.[33]

The multinational orientation emphasizes a decentralized, global division structure. Each region or country is served by a divisional organization that operates autonomously and reports to headquarters. This results in a highly differentiated and loosely coordinated corporate structure. Operational decisions, such as product design, manufacturing, and distribution, are decentralized and tightly integrated at the local level. For example, laundry soap manufacturers offer product formulas, packaging, and marketing strategies that conform to the different environmental regulations, types of washing machines, water hardness, and distribution channels in each country. On the other hand, planning activities often are centralized at corporate headquarters to achieve important efficiencies necessary for worldwide coordination of emerging technologies and of resource allocation. A profit-center control system allows local autonomy as long as profitability is maintained. Examples of multinational corporations include Hoechst and BASF of Germany, IBM and Merck of the United States, and Honda of Japan. Each of these organizations encourages local subsidiaries to maximize effectiveness within their geographic region.

People are integrated into multinational firms through polycentric or regiocentric personnel policies because these firms believe that host-country nationals can understand native cultures most clearly.[34] By filling positions with local citizens who appoint and develop their own staffs, the organization aligns the needs of the market with the ability of its subsidiaries to produce customized products and services. The distinction between a polycentric and a regiocentric selection process is one of focus. In a polycentric selection policy, a subsidiary represents only one country; in the regiocentric selection policy, a slightly broader perspective is taken and key positions are filled by regional citizens (that is, people who might be called Europeans, as opposed to Belgians or Italians).

The decentralized and locally coordinated multinational orientation suggests the need for a complex set of OD interventions. When applied to a subsidiary operating in a particular country or region, the OD process described above for organizations outside the United States is relevant. The key is to tailor OD to fit the specific cultural and economic context where the subsidiary is located.

When OD is applied across different regions and countries, interventions must account for differences in cultural and economic conditions that can affect its success. Appropriate interventions for multinational corporations include intergroup relations, local management team building, sophisticated management selection and development practices, and changes to reward systems. Intergroup interventions to improve relations between local subsidiaries and the parent company also are important for multinational companies. Decentralized decision making and regiocentric selection can strain corporate–subsidiary relations. Local management teams, operating in ways appropriate to their cultural context, may not be understood by corporate managers from another culture. OD practitioners can help both groups understand these differences by offering training in cultural diversity and appreciation. They also can smooth parent–subsidiary relationships by focusing on the profit-center control system or other criteria as the means for monitoring and measuring subsidiary effectiveness.

Management selection, development, and reward systems also require special attention in multinational firms. Managerial selection for local or regional subsidiaries requires finding technically and managerially competent people who also possess the interpersonal competence needed to interface with corporate headquarters. Because these people may be difficult to find, management development programs can teach these cross-cultural skills and abilities. Such programs typically involve language, cultural awareness, and technical training; they also can include managers and staff from subsidiary and corporate offices to improve communications between the two areas. Finally, reward systems need to be aligned with the decentralized structure. Significant proportions of managers' total compensation could be tied to local profit performance, thereby aligning reward and control systems.

Transnational Orientation

The transnational strategy combines customized products with both efficient and responsive operations; the key goal is learning. This is the most complex worldwide strategic orientation because transnationals can manufacture products, conduct research, raise capital, buy supplies, and perform many other functions wherever in the world the job can be done optimally. They can move skills, resources, and knowledge to regions where they are needed.

The transnational orientation combines the best of global and multinational orientations and adds a third attribute—the ability to transfer resources both within the firm and across national and cultural boundaries. Otis Elevator, a division of United Technologies, developed a new programmable elevator using six research centers in five countries: a United States group handled the systems integration; Japan designed the special motor drives that make the elevators ride smoothly; France perfected the door systems; Germany created the electronics; and Spain produced the small-geared components.[35] Other examples of transnational firms include General Electric, Asea Brown Boveri, Motorola, Electrolux, and Hewlett-Packard.

Transnational firms organize themselves into global matrix and network structures especially suited for moving information and resources to their best use. In the matrix structure, local divisions similar to the multinational structure are crossed with product groups at the headquarters office. The network structure treats each local office, including headquarters, product groups, and production facilities, as self-sufficient nodes that coordinate with each other to move knowledge and resources to their most valued place. Because of the heavy information demands needed to operate these structures, transnationals have sophisticated information systems. State-of-the-art information technology is used to move strategic and operational information throughout the system rapidly and efficiently. Organizational learning and knowledge management practices (Chapter 14) gather, organize, and disseminate the knowledge and skills of members who are located around the world.

People are integrated into transnational firms through a geocentric selection policy that staffs key positions with the best people, regardless of nationality.[36] This staffing practice recognizes that the distinctive competence of a transnational firm is its capacity to optimize resource allocation on a worldwide basis. Unlike global and multinational firms that spend more time training and developing managers to fit the strategy, the transnational firm attempts to hire the right person from the beginning. Recruits at any of Hewlett-Packard's foreign locations, for example, are screened not only for technical qualifications but for personality traits that match HP's cultural values.[37]

Transnational companies require OD interventions that can improve their ability to achieve efficient worldwide integration under highly decentralized decision-making conditions. These interventions include extensive management selection and development practices in support of the geocentric policies described above, intergroup relations, and development and communication of a strong corporate vision and culture. Knowledge management interventions help develop a worldwide repository of information that enables members' learning.

Effective transnational firms have well-developed vision and mission statements that communicate the values and beliefs underlying the firm's culture and guide its operational decisions. ABB's mission statement, for example, went through a multicultural rewriting when they recognized that talking about profit was an uncomfortable activity in some cultures.[38] OD processes that increase member participation in the construction or modification of these statements can help members gain ownership of them. Research into the development of corporate credos at the British computer manufacturer ICL, SAS, and Apple Computer showed that success was more a function of the heavy involvement of many managers than the quality of the statements themselves.[39]

Once vision and mission statements are crafted, management training can focus on clarifying their meaning, the values they express, and the behaviors required to support those values. This process of gaining shared meaning and developing a strong culture provides a basis for social control. Because transnationals need flexibility and coordination, they cannot rely solely on formal reports of sales, costs, or demand to guide behavior. This information often takes too much time to compile and distribute. Rather, the corporate vision and culture provide transnational managers with the reasoning and guidelines for why and how they should make decisions.

This form of social control supports OD efforts to improve management selection and development, intergroup relationships, and strategic change. The geocentric selection process can be supplemented by a personnel policy that rotates managers through different geographical regions and functional areas to blend people, perspectives, and practices. At such organizations as GE, ABB, Coca-Cola, and Colgate, a cadre of managers with extensive foreign experience is being developed. Rotation throughout the organization also improves the chances that when two organizational units must cooperate, key personnel will know each other and make coordination more likely. The corporate vision and culture can also become important tools in building cross-functional or interdepartmental processes for transferring knowledge, resources, or products. Moreover, they can provide guidelines for formulating and implementing strategic change, and serve as a social context for designing appropriate structures and systems at local subsidiaries.

Changing Worldwide Strategic Orientations

In addition to implementing planned changes that support the development of the three basic worldwide strategic orientations, OD can help firms change from one orientation to another. Researchers have found that many organizations that sell products or services to other countries start with either global or multinational orientations. They also have suggested that global and multinational organizations tend to evolve into a transnational orientation.[40]

Changing from Domestic to Global or Multinational

At first, OD can help organizations make the transition from a domestic to a worldwide strategic orientation. Team building, large-group interventions, and integrated strategic change, for example, can aid the process through which senior executives gather appropriate information about international markets, distinctive competencies, and culture, and choose a strategic orientation. Based on that decision, OD interventions can help the organization implement the change. For instance, members can use technostructural interventions to design an appropriate structure, to define new tasks and work roles, and to clarify reporting relationships between corporate headquarters and foreign-based units. Managers and staff can apply human resources management interventions to train and prepare managers and their families for international assignments and to develop selection methods and reward systems relevant to operating internationally.[41]

Changing from Global to Transnational

In the transition from a global to a transnational orientation, the firm must acquire the know-how to operate a decentralized organization and learn to transfer knowledge, skills, and resources among disparate organizational units operating in different countries. In this situation, the administrative challenge is to encourage creative over centralized thinking and to let each functional area operate in a way that best suits its context. OD interventions that can help this transition include training efforts that increase the tolerance for differences in management practices, control systems, performance appraisals, and policies and procedures; reward systems that encourage entrepreneurship and performance at each foreign subsidiary; and efficient organization designs at the local level. Training interventions that help managers develop an appreciation for the different ways that effectiveness can be achieved will aid the global organization's move toward transnationalism. More flexible reward systems promote coordination among subsidiaries, product lines, and staff groups. In addition, OD practitioners can work with individual business units rather than with senior management at headquarters. Working with each subsidiary on issues relating to its own structure and function sends an important message about the significance of decentralized operations.

Changing from Multinational to Transnational

In moving from a multinational to a transnational orientation, products, technologies, and regulatory constraints can become more homogeneous and require more efficient operations. The competencies required to compete on a transnational basis, however, may be located in many different geographic areas. The need to balance local responsiveness against the need for coordination among organizational units is new to multinational firms. They must create interdependencies among organizational units through the flow of parts, components, and finished goods; the flow of funds, skills, and other scarce resources; or the flow of intelligence, ideas, and knowledge.

In such situations, OD is an important activity because complex interdependencies require sophisticated and nontraditional coordinating mechanisms.[42] OD interventions, such as intergroup team building or cultural awareness and interpersonal skills training, can help develop the communication linkages necessary for successful coordination. In addition, the inherently "matrixed" structures of worldwide firms and the cross-cultural context of doing business in different countries tend to create conflict. OD interventions, such as role clarification, third-party consultation, and mediation techniques, can help to solve such problems. OD practitioners also can help increase coordination by modifying reward systems to encourage cooperation and spelling out clearly the behaviors required for success.

GLOBAL SOCIAL CHANGE

The newest and perhaps most exciting applications of organization development in international settings are occurring in global social change organizations (GSCOs).[43] These organizations generally are not for profit and nongovernmental. They typically are created at the grassroots level to help communities and societies address such important problems as unemployment, race relations, sustainable development, homelessness, hunger, disease, and political instability. In international settings, GSCOs are heavily involved in the developing nations. Examples include the World Conservation Union, the Hunger Project, the Nature Conservancy, the Mountain Forum, International Physicians for the Prevention of Nuclear War, International Union for the Conservation of Nature and Natural Resources, and the Asian Coalition for Agrarian Reform and Rural Development. Many practitioners who help create and develop these GSCOs come from an OD background and have adapted their expertise to fit highly complex, global situations. This section describes global social change organizations and how OD is practiced in them.

Global Social Change Organizations: What Are They?

Global social change organizations are part of a social innovation movement to foster the emergence of a global civilization.[44] They exist under a variety of names, including development organizations (DOs), international nongovernmental organizations (INGOs), social movement organizations (SMOs), international private voluntary organizations, and bridging organizations.[45] They exist to address complex social problems, including overpopulation, ecological degradation, the increasing concentration of wealth and power, the lack of management infrastructures to facilitate growth, and the lack of fundamental human rights.

GSCOs differ from traditional for-profit firms on several dimensions.[46] First, they typically advocate a mission of social change—the formation and development of better societies and communities. "Better" typically means more just (Amnesty International, Hunger Project), peaceful (International Physicians for the Prevention of Nuclear War), or ecologically conscious (Nature Conservancy, the Global Village of Beijing, the Mountain Forum, International Union for the Conservation of Nature and Natural Resources). Second, the mission is supported by a network structure. Most GSCO activity occurs at the boundary or periphery between two or more organizations.[47] Unlike most industrial firms that focus on internal effectiveness, GSCOs are directed at changing their environmental context. For example, World Vision coordinated the efforts of more than one hundred organizations to address the human consequences of Ceausescu's Romanian government.[48] Third, GSCOs generally have strong values and ideologies that justify and motivate organization behavior. These "causes" provide intrinsic rewards to GSCO members and a blueprint for action.[49] Fourth, GSCOs interact with a broad range of external and often conflicting constituencies. To help the poor, GSCOs often must work with the rich; to save the ecology, they must work with developers; to empower the masses, they must work with the powerful few. This places a great deal of pressure on GSCOs to reconcile pursuit of a noble cause with the political reality of power and wealth. Fifth, managing these diverse external constituencies often creates significant organizational conflict. On the one hand, GSCOs need to create specific departments to serve and represent particular stakeholders. On the other hand, they are strongly averse to bureaucracy and desire collegial and consensus-seeking cultures. The conflicting perspectives of the stakeholders, the differentiated departments, and the ideological basis of the organization's mission can produce a contentious internal environment. Sixth, GSCO membership often is transitory. Many people are volunteers, and the extent and depth of their involvement varies over time and by issue. Turnover is quite high.

Application Stages

Global social change organizations are concerned with creating sustainable change in communities and societies. This requires a form of planned change in which the practitioner is heavily involved, many stakeholders are encouraged and expected to participate, and "technologies of empowerment" are used.[50] Often referred to as "participatory action research,"[51] planned change in GSCOs involves three types of activities: building local organization effectiveness, creating bridges and linkages with other relevant organizations, and developing vertical linkages with policymakers.

Building the Local Organization

Although GSCOs are concerned primarily with changing their environments, a critical issue in development projects is recognizing the potential problems inherent in the GSCO itself. Because the focus of change is their environment, members of GSCOs are often oblivious to the need for internal development. Moreover, the complex organizational arrangements of a network make planned change in GSCOs particularly challenging.

OD practitioners focus on three activities in helping GSCOs build themselves into viable organizations: using values to create the vision, recognizing that internal conflict is often a function of external conditions, and understanding the problems of success. For leadership to function effectively, the broad purposes of the GSCO must be clear and closely aligned with the ideologies of its members. Singleness of purpose can be gained from tapping into the compelling aspects of the values and principles that the GSCO represents. For example, the Latin American Division of the Nature Conservancy holds an annual two-day retreat. Each participant prepares a white paper concerning his or her area of responsibility: the issues, challenges, major dilemmas or problems, and ideas for directions the division could take. Over the course of the retreat, participants actively discuss each paper. They have broad freedom to challenge the status quo and to question previous decisions. By the end of the retreat, discussions have produced a clear statement about the course that the division will take for the following year. People leave with increased clarity about and commitment to the purpose and vision of the division.[52] Developing a shared vision results in the alignment of individual and organizational values.

Because of the diverse perspectives of the different stakeholders, GSCOs often face multiple conflicts. In working through them, the organizational vision can be used as an important rallying point for discovering how each person's role contributes to the GSCO's purpose. The affective component of the vision is what allows GSCO members to give purpose to their lives and work.[53]

Finally, a GSCO's success can create a number of problems. The very accomplishment of its mission can take away its reason for existence, thus causing an identity crisis. For example, a GSCO that succeeds in creating jobs for underprivileged youth can be dissolved because its funding is redirected toward organizations that have not yet met their goals, because its goals change, or simply because it has accomplished its purpose. During these times, the vital social role that these organizations play needs to be emphasized. GSCOs often represent bridges between the powerful and powerless, between the rich and poor, and between the elite and oppressed, and as such may need to be maintained as legitimate parts of the community.

Another problem can occur when GSCO success produces additional demands for greater formalization. New people must be hired and acculturated; greater control over income and expenditures has to be developed; new skills and behaviors have to be learned. The need for more formal systems often runs counter to ideological principles of autonomy and freedom and can produce a profound resistance to change. Employees' participation during diagnosis and implementation can help them commit to the new systems. In addition, new employment opportunities, increased job responsibilities, and improved capabilities to carry out the GSCO's mission can be used to encourage commitment and reduce resistance to the changes.

Creating Horizontal Linkages

Successful social change projects often require a network of local organizations with similar views and objectives. Consequently, an important planned change activity in GSCOs is creating strong linkages to organizations in the community or society where the development project is taking place. For example, GSCOs aimed at job development not only must recruit, train, and market potential job applicants but also must develop relationships with local job providers and government authorities. The GSCO must help these organizations commit to the GSCO's vision, mobilize resources, and create policies to support development efforts.

Unfortunately, members of GSCOs often view local government officials, community leaders, or for-profit organizations as part of the problem. Rather than interacting with these stakeholders, GSCOs often "protect" themselves and their ideologies from contamination by these outsiders. Planned change efforts to overcome this myopia are similar to the transorganizational development interventions discussed in Chapter 13. GSCO members are helped to identify, convene, and organize these key external organizations. For example, following the earthquakes in Mexico City in 1985, the Committee of Earthquake Victims was established to prevent the government and landlords from evicting low-income tenants from their destroyed housing. The committee formed relationships with other GSCOs concerned with organizing the poor or with responding to the disaster. The committee also linked up with local churches, universities, charitable organizations, and poor urban neighborhood organizations. It bargained with the government and appealed to the media to scuttle attempts at widespread eviction proceedings. This pressure culminated in agreement around a set of principles for reconstruction in Mexico City.[54]

Developing Vertical Linkages

GSCOs also must create channels of communication and influence upward to governmental and policy-level decision-making processes. These higher-level decisions often affect the creation and eventual success of GSCO activities. For example, the Global Village of Beijing (GVB) is a nongovernmental organization that raises the environmental consciousness of people in China. GVB leveraged its relationships with journalists and the government to produce a weekly television series on government channels to discuss and promote environmentally friendly practices, such as recycling, and to expose the Chinese people to environmental projects in different countries. When the Chinese government proposed new environmental regulations and policies as part of the World Trade Organization admission process, GVB helped assess the proposals.[55]

Vertical linkages also can be developed by building on a strong record of success. The Institute of Cultural Affairs (ICA) is concerned with the "application of methods of human development to communities and organizations all around the world." With more than one hundred offices in thirty-nine nations, ICA trains and consults with small groups, communities, organizations, and voluntary associations, in addition to providing leadership training for village leaders, conducting community education programs, and running ecological preservation projects. Its reputation has led to recognition and credibility: it was given consultative status by the United Nations in 1985, and it has category II status with the Food and Agriculture Organization, working relation status with the World Health Organization, and consultative status with UNICEF.[56]

■ SUMMARY

This chapter has examined the practice of international organization development in three areas. In organizations outside the United States, the traditional approaches to OD need to be adapted to fit the cultural and economic development context in which they are applied. This adaptation approach recognizes that OD practices may be culture-bound: what works in one culture may be inappropriate in another. The cultural contexts of different geographical regions were examined in terms of five values: context orientation, power distance, uncertainty avoidance, achievement orientation, and individualism. This approach also recognizes that not all OD interventions may be appropriate. The prevailing economic situation may strongly favor business-oriented over process-oriented interventions. The process of OD under different cultural and economic conditions was also described, although the descriptions are tentative. As OD matures, its methods will become more differentiated and adaptable.

OD activities to improve global, multinational, and transnational strategic orientations increasingly are in demand. Each of these strategies responds to specific environmental, technological, and economic conditions. Interventions in worldwide organizations require a strategic and organizational perspective on change to align people, structures, and systems.

Finally, OD process in global social change organizations was discussed. This relatively new application of OD promotes the establishment of a global civilization. Strong ideological positions regarding the fair and just distribution of wealth, resources, and power fuel this movement. By strengthening local organizations, building horizontal linkages with other like-minded GSCOs, and developing vertical linkages with policy-making organizations, a change agent can help the GSCO become more effective and alter its external context. To support roles of stewardship and bridging, change agents need communication, negotiation, and networking skills.

■ NOTES

1. P. Sorensen Jr., T. Head, K. Johnson, N. Mathys, J. Preston, and D. Cooperrider, eds., *Global and International Organization Development* (Champaign, Ill.: Stipes, 1995); D. Berlew and W. LeClere, "Social Intervention in Curaçao: A Case Study," *Journal of Applied Behavioral Science* 10 (1974): 29–52; B. Myers and J. Quill, "The Art of O.D. in Asia: Never Take Yes for an Answer," *Proceedings of the O.D. Network Conference, Seattle* (Fall 1981): 52–58; R. Boss and M. Mariono, "Organization Development in Italy," *Group and Organization Studies* 12 (1987): 245–56.

2. B. Moore, "The Service Profit Chain—A Tale of Two Airlines" (unpublished Master's thesis, Pepperdine University, 1999); P. Engardino and L. Curry, "The Fifth Tiger Is on China's Coast," *Business Week* (6 April 1992): 43.

3. L. P. Evans, "Organization Development in the Transnational Enterprise," in *Research in Organizational Change and Development*, vol. 3, eds. R. Woodman and W. Pasmore (Greenwich, Conn.: JAI Press, 1989): 1–38; L. Brown, "Is Organization Development Culture Bound?" *Academy of Management Newsletter* (Winter 1982); L. Bourgeois and M. Boltvinik, "OD in Cross-Cultural Settings: Latin America," *California Management Review* 23 (Spring 1981): 75–81; W. Ouchi, *Theory Z* (Reading, Mass.: Addison-Wesley, 1981).

4. T. Head, "The Role of a Country's Economic Development in Organization Development Implementation," in *Global and International Organization Development*, Sorensen et al., pp. 18–25; W. Woodworth, "Privatization in Be-

larussia: Organizational Change in the Former USSR," *Organization Development Journal* 3 (1993): 53–59.

5. E. Schein, *Organization Culture and Leadership*, 2d ed. (San Francisco: Jossey-Bass, 1992); Evans, "Organization Development," p. 11.

6. G. Hofstede, *Culture's Consequences* (Beverly Hills, Calif.: Sage, 1980); A. Jaeger, "Organization Development and National Culture: Where's the Fit?" *Academy of Management Journal* 11 (1986): 178–90; N. Margulies and A. Raia, "The Significance of Core Values on the Theory and Practice of Organizational Development," *Journal of Organizational Change and Management* 1 (1988): 6–17; A. Francesco and B. Gold, *International Organizational Behavior* (Upper Saddle River, N.J.: Prentice Hall, 1998).

7. Hofstede, *Culture's Consequences*; E. Hall and M. Hall, "Key Concepts: Understanding Structures of Culture" in *International Management Behavior*, eds. H. Lane, J. DiStefano, and M. Maznevski, 3d ed. (Cambridge, Mass.: Blackwell); F. Kluckhohn and F. Strodtbeck, *Variations in Value Orientations* (Evanston, Ill.: Peterson, 1961); F. Trompenaars, *Riding the Waves of Culture* (London: Economist Press, 1993).

8. K. Murrell, "Management Infrastructure in the Third World," in *Global Business Management in the 1990s*, ed. R. Moran (New York: Beacham, 1990); The United Nations Development Programme, *Human Development Report* (New York: Oxford University Press, 1994); P. Kotler, *Marketing Management*, 9th ed. (Englewood Cliffs, N.J.: Prentice Hall, 1997).

9. B. Webster, "Organization Development: An International Perspective" (unpublished Master's thesis, Pepperdine University, 1995).

10. Jaeger, "Organization Development and National Culture."

11. The dearth of published empirical descriptions of OD in particular countries and organizations necessitates a regional focus. The risk is that these descriptions may generalize too much. Practitioners should take great care in applying these observations to specific situations.

12. Woodworth, "Privatization in Belarussia."

13. K. Johnson, "Estimating National Culture and O. D. Values," in *Global and International Organization Development*, Sorensen et al., pp. 266–81; Jaeger, "Organization Development and National Culture."

14. A. Shevat, "The Practice of Organizational Development in Israel," in *Global and International Organization Development*, Sorensen et al., pp. 180–83; W. Fisher, "Organization Development in Egypt," in *Global and International Organization Development*, Sorensen et al., pp. 184–90.

15. J. Preston, L. DuToit, and I. Barber, "A Potential Model of Transformational Change Applied to South Africa," in *Research in Organizational Change and Development*, vol. 9, eds. R. Woodman and W. Pasmore (Greenwich, Conn.: JAI Press, 1998); G. Sigmund, "Current Issues in South African Corporations: An Internal OD Perspective" (unpublished Master's thesis, Pepperdine University, 1996).

16. Johnson, "Estimating National Culture."

17. Webster, "Organization Development"; I. Perlaki, "Organization Development in Eastern Europe," *Journal of Applied Behavioral Science* 30 (1994): 297–312; J. Putti, "Organization Development Scene in Asia: The Case of Singapore," in *Global and International Organization Development*, Sorensen et al., pp. 215–23; M. Rikuta, "Organizational Development within Japanese Industry: Facts and Prospects," in *Global and International Organization Development*, Sorensen et al., pp. 231–47; J. Reeder, "When West Meets East: Cultural Aspects of Doing Business in Asia," *Business Horizons* (January-February 1987): 69–74; Myers and Quill, "Art of O.D."; I. Nonaka, "Creating Organizational Order out of Chaos: Self-Renewal in Japanese Firms," *California Management Review* (Spring 1988): 57–73; S. Redding, "Results-Orientation and the Orient: Individualism as a Cultural Determinant of Western Managerial Techniques," *International HRD Annual*, vol. 1 (Alexandria, Va.: American Society for Training & Development, 1985); K. Johnson, "Organizational Development in Venezuela," in *Global and International Organization Development*, Sorensen et al., pp. 259–64; C. Fuchs, "Organizational Development Under Political, Economic and Natural Crisis," in *Global and International Organization Development*, Sorensen et al., pp. 248–58; R. Babcock and T. Head, "Organization Development in the Republic of China (Taiwan)," in *Global and International Organization Development*, Sorensen et al., pp. 224–30; R. Marshak, "Training and Consulting in Korea," *OD Practitioner* 25 (Summer 1993): 16–21.

18. Babcock and Head, "Organization Development"; Johnson, "Organizational Development."

19. Johnson, "Organizational Development"; A. Mueller, "Successful and Unsuccessful OD Interventions in a Venezuelan Banking Organization: The Role of Culture" (unpublished Master's thesis, Pepperdine University, 1995).

20. Rikuta, "Organizational Development."

21. Webster, "Organization Development"; B. Gustavsen, "The LOM Program: A Network-Based Strategy for Organization Development in Sweden," in *Research in Organizational Change and Development*, vol. 5, eds. R. Woodman and W. Pasmore (Greenwich, Conn.: JAI Press, 1991): 285–316; P. Sorensen Jr., H. Larsen, T. Head, and H. Scoggins, "Organization Development in Denmark," in *Global and International Organization Development*, Sorensen et al., pp. 48–64; A. Derefeldt, "Organization Development in Sweden," in *Global and International Organization Development*, Sorensen et al., pp. 65–73; J. Norsted and S. Aguren, *The Saab-Scania Report* (Stockholm: Swedish Employer's Confederation, 1975); B. Jonsson, "Corporate Strategy for People at Work—The Volvo Experience," (paper presented at the International Conference on the Quality of Working Life, Toronto, Canada, August 30–September 3, 1981).

22. Johnson, "Estimating National Culture."

23. Norsted and Aguren, *Saab-Scania Report*; Jonsson, "Corporate Strategy."

24. E. Trist, "On Socio-Technical Systems," in *The Planning of Change*, 2d ed., eds. W. Bennis, K. Benne, and R. Chin (New York: Holt, Rinehart & Winston, 1969): 269–72; A. Cherns, "The Principles of Sociotechnical Design," *Human Relations* 19 (1976): 783–92; E. Jacques, *The Changing Culture of a Factory* (New York: Dryden, 1952).

25. P. Nulty, "Batman Shakes BP to Bedrock," *Fortune* (19 November 1990): 155–62.

26. C. Bartlett and S. Ghoshal, *Transnational Management*, 3d ed. (Boston: Irwin McGraw-Hill, 2000).

27. H. Lancaster, "Global Managers Need Boundless

Sensitivity, Rugged Constitutions," *Wall Street Journal* (13 October 1998): B1.

28. Bartlett and Ghoshal, *Transnational Management*; D. Heenan and H. Perlmutter, *Multinational Organization Development* (Reading, Mass.: Addison-Wesley, 1979); Evans, "Organization Development," pp. 15–16; Y. Doz, *Strategic Management in Multinational Companies* (Oxford: Pergamon Press, 1986); C. Bartlett, Y. Doz, and G. Hedlund, *Managing the Global Firm* (London: Routledge, 1990).

29. M. Ihlwan, "Doing a Bang-up Business," *Business Week* (18 May 1999): 50.

30. Heenan and Perlmutter, *Multinational Organization Development*, p. 13.

31. A. Borrus, "The Stateless Corporation," *Business Week* (14 May 1990): 103.

32. Ibid., p. 105.

33. J. Main, "How to Go Global—And Why," *Fortune* (28 August 1989): 76.

34. Heenan and Perlmutter, *Multinational Organization Development*, p. 20.

35. Borrus, "Stateless Corporation," p. 101.

36. Heenan and Perlmutter, *Multinational Organization Development*, p. 20.

37. Evans, "Organization Development."

38. T. Stewart, "A Way to Measure Worldwide Success," *Fortune* (15 March 1999): 196–98.

39. Evans, "Organization Development."

40. C. Bartlett and S. Ghoshal, "Organizing for Worldwide Effectiveness: The Transnational Solution," *California Management Review* (Fall 1988): 54–74.

41. R. Tung, "Expatriate Assignments: Enhancing Success and Minimizing Failure," *Academy of Management Executive* (Summer 1987): 117–26; J. Roure, J. Alvarez, C. Garcia-Pont, and J. Nueno, "Managing Internationally: The International Dimensions of the Managerial Task," *European Management Journal* 11 (1993): 485–92; A. Mamman, "Expatriate Adjustment: Dealing with Hosts' Attitudes in a Foreign Assignment," *Journal of Transitional Management Development* 1 (1995).

42. Evans, "Organization Development in the Transnational Enterprise."

43. L. Brown and J. Covey, "Development Organizations and Organization Development: Toward an Expanded Paradigm for Organization Development," in *Research in Organizational Change and Development*, vol. 1, eds. R. Woodman and W. Pasmore (Greenwich, Conn.: JAI Press, 1987): 59–88; P. Tuecke, "Rural International Development," in *Discovering Common Ground*, ed. M. Weisbord (San Francisco: Berrett-Koehler, 1993).

44. P. Freire, *Pedagogy of the Oppressed* (Harmondsworth, England: Penguin, 1972); H. Perlmutter and E. Trist, "Paradigms for Societal Transition," *Human Relations* 39 (1986): 1–27; F. Westley, "Bob Geldof and Live Aid: The Affective Side of Global Social Innovation," *Human Relations* 44 (1991): 1011–36; D. Cooperrider and W. Pasmore, "Global Social Change: A New Agenda for Social Science," *Human Relations* 44 (1991): 1037–55; H. Perlmutter, "On the Rocky Road to the First Global Civilization," *Human Relations* 44 (1991): 897–920; E. Boulding, "The Old and New Transnationalism: An Evolutionary Perspective," *Human Relations* 44 (1991): 789–805; P. Johnson and D. Cooperrider, "Finding a Path with a Heart: Global Social Change Organizations and Their Challenge for the Field of Organizational Development," in *Research in Organizational Change and Development*, vol. 5, eds. R. Woodman and W. Pasmore (Greenwich, Conn.: JAI Press, 1991): 223–84.

45. D. Cooperrider and T. Thachankary, "Building the Global Civic Culture: Making Our Lives Count," in *Global and International Organization Development*, Sorensen et al., pp. 282–306; Brown and Covey, "Development Organizations."

46. L. Brown, "Bridging Organizations and Sustainable Development," *Human Relations* 44 (1991): 807–31; Johnson and Cooperrider, "Finding a Path"; Cooperrider and Thachankary, "Building the Global Civil Culture."

47. L. D. Brown and D. Ashman, "Social Capital, Mutual Influence, and Social Learning in Intersectoral Problem Solving in Africa and Asia," in *Organizational Dimensions of Global Change*, eds. Cooperrider and Dutton (Newbury Park, Calif.: Sage, 1999): 139–167.

48. W. Pasmore, "OD and the Management of Global Social Change: Implications and Opportunities," *ODC Newsletter* (Winter 1994): 8–11.

49. F. Westley, "Not on Our Watch," in *Organizational Dimensions of Global Change*, Cooperrider and Dutton, pp. 88–113.

50. Johnson and Cooperrider, "Finding a Path"; Cooperrider and Thachankary, "Building the Global Civic Culture."

51. W. Whyte, *Participatory Action Research* (Newbury Park, Calif.: Sage, 1991).

52. Johnson and Cooperrider, "Finding a Path," pp. 240–41.

53. P. Vaill, "The Purposing of High Performing Organizations," *Organization Dynamics* 11 (Autumn 1982): 23–39.

54. S. Annis, "What Is Not the Same about the Urban Poor: The Case of Mexico City," in *Strengthening the Poor:* *What Have We Learned?* ed. J. Lewis (Washington, D.C.: Overseas Development Council, 1988): 138–43.

55. Personal communication with members of the Global Village of Beijing, March 28, 2000.

56. Johnson and Cooperrider, "Finding a Path."

16

Future Directions in Organization Development

The field of organization development continues to grow and mature. New theories and concepts are being developed, more complex and rigorous research is being conducted, new methods and interventions are being applied, and organizations from more diverse countries and cultures are becoming involved. Because so much change has occurred in a relatively brief period, predicting the future of OD is risky if not foolhardy. However, several trends can be identified at the turn of the twenty-first century that provide clues about the larger context within which OD will operate. These may be used to speculate about where the field is heading. In this concluding chapter, we first describe these trends and then draw implications for future directions in OD.[1]

TRENDS IN THE CONTEXT OF ORGANIZATION DEVELOPMENT

As summarized in Figure 16.1, several interrelated trends are affecting the context within which OD will be applied in the near future. They concern various aspects of the economy, the workforce, technology, and organizations. In some cases, the trends will affect OD practice directly. Technology trends, such as groupware and Internet conferencing, surely will influence how OD practitioners facilitate teams and manage change. Other trends, such as the increasing concentration of wealth, represent important contextual forces that will affect OD indirectly through their interaction with other trends.

The Economy

Researchers have described a variety of alternative economic futures and there is substantial agreement that the world's economy is undergoing an important transition from the industrial age which characterized much of the twentieth century.[2] Those scenarios differ in their particulars, but many of the same trends are identified as drivers of economic change—globalization, the increasing concentration of wealth, and concerns for the ecosystem, among others. Trends such as technology and workforce changes also are mentioned and they will be discussed separately.

As noted in Chapter 1, the economy rapidly is becoming global. The shift in manufacturing from high- to low-labor-cost countries, the growth of international mergers and acquisitions, and the spread of worldwide service businesses suggest that the emergence of a global economy is well under way. Today, almost any product or service can be made, bought, and delivered anywhere in the world.

Globalization can help companies reduce costs, gain resources, expand markets, and develop new products and practices more quickly. In addition, because globalization and growth often work together, organization members are provided with opportunities for development and advancement. But globalization also can present difficulties. Managing a worldwide organization is a daunting task, as described in Chapter 15, and it can present difficult problems for national governments. Because a global economy transcends national borders, it has evolved with relatively little

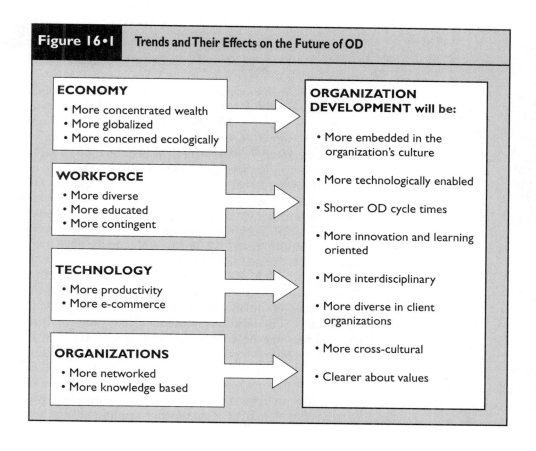

Figure 16•1   Trends and Their Effects on the Future of OD

ECONOMY
- More concentrated wealth
- More globalized
- More concerned ecologically

WORKFORCE
- More diverse
- More educated
- More contingent

TECHNOLOGY
- More productivity
- More e-commerce

ORGANIZATIONS
- More networked
- More knowledge based

ORGANIZATION DEVELOPMENT will be:
- More embedded in the organization's culture
- More technologically enabled
- Shorter OD cycle times
- More innovation and learning oriented
- More interdisciplinary
- More diverse in client organizations
- More cross-cultural
- Clearer about values

order and organization.[3] This makes it difficult for governments to control how globalization develops and affects them. For example, China is trying diligently to preserve its cultural and communist underpinnings while facing a rapid influx of capitalist goods and services,[4] and many other developing nations face pressures to move to a western capitalism model despite questions about whether it is appropriate for their cultures.

A second trend in the economy is the increasingly concentrated wealth in relatively few individuals, corporations, and nations. Over the past two decades, for example, the ratio of CEO compensation to that of the average employee grew from 35:1 to 150:1 in large U.S. firms;[5] the number of billionaires in the world increased over fourteen-fold;[6] the world's five hundred largest corporations, which employ 0.05 of 1 percent of the world's population, produced about 25 percent of the world's economic output;[7] and fifty corporations achieved sufficient wealth to place them among the *world's* one-hundred largest economies. At the same time, 4.8 billion of the world's 6 billion people lived in developing countries, and 3 billion of them existed on less than $2 a day.[8]

The concentration of wealth may be a natural outcome of capitalism, but it also can contribute to misallocation of resources, environmental degradation, and short-term thinking.[9] For example, Wall Street's current focus on quarterly earnings can skew decision-making criteria to delay preventive maintenance or safety initiatives, to postpone implementation of necessary environmental protection equipment, or to forego important long-term capital investments. The concentration of wealth also can contribute to social conflict driven by fears that the wealthy will act in their own self-interest at the expense of those who are financially less fortunate. The bloody demonstrations that occurred at the December 1999 meeting of the World Trade Organization in Seattle derived in part from such fear and people's willingness to act on it.

Finally, our view of the natural environment as a consumable in economic success is being challenged. There are ever more clear warnings that the ecosystem no longer can be treated as a factor of production, and that success cannot be defined as the accumulation of wealth and material goods at the expense of the environment. These concerns arise in part from the proliferation of capitalism, but also from the growing realization that free and open markets can have negative unintended consequences for the global ecosystem. Recent studies suggest that industrialization is a controversial but probable cause of global warming,[10] and several traditional organizations, such as BP Amoco and Royal Dutch/Shell, are reversing long-held opinions about their contribution to environmental decay by setting aggressive goals to reduce greenhouse gases.[11] Unfortunately, many developing economies, including China, the Philippines, and Mexico, continue to operate with loose environmental controls. As a result, there are more calls for change in the values underlying capitalism—from consumption to investment,[12] from open to mindful markets,[13] and from wealth accumulation as an end in itself to an examination of the return on living capital.[14] Some observers note that such value shifts are already under way in many nations and organizations. For example, traditional business models which assume that labor is scarce and natural resources are abundant are being tempered by models that emphasize the abundance of knowledge and the scarcity of natural resources. IKEA, the Dutch furniture manufacturer, has altered its environmental policies and practices radically to reduce emissions, waste, and environmental degradation and increase sustainability, profits, and customer satisfaction.[15]

The Workforce

The workforce is becoming more diverse, educated, and contingent. Chapter 12 documented the diversity trend and suggested that organizations, whether they operate primarily in their home country or abroad, will need to develop policies and operating styles that embrace the changing cultural, ethnic, gender, and age diversity of the workforce. Similarly, a more educated workforce is likely to demand higher wages, more involvement in decision making, and continued investment in knowledge and skills. For example, the current half-life of information systems personnel is about two years and requires continual updating of their knowledge and skills to remain competent in these jobs. In response, organizations are increasing their training and management development budgets significantly.[16] They are investing far more in corporate universities and corporate–university partnerships, and many organizations, such as Motorola, 3M, and Xerox, have policies outlining the minimum hours of technical and managerial training that each employee will receive yearly. Finally, the continued high rate of downsizings, reengineering efforts, and mergers and acquisitions described in Chapters 9 and 13 is forcing the workforce to become more contingent and less loyal. The implicit psychological contract that governs relationships between employers and employees is being rewritten with new assumptions about long-term employment and rewards in exchange for commitment and loyalty.

Technology

Information technology is changing internal operations and increasing productivity. For years, economists were puzzled by a "productivity paradox." Despite a thirty-year, $2 trillion investment in computers and technology, productivity rose very slowly during the 1970s and 1980s. But in 1999, productivity rose 2.9 percent in the United States (and 5 percent in the last six months of 1999), nearly twice the 1.5 percent average annual gains seen since the early 1970s. The biggest gains were in manufacturing, but service businesses such as transportation, trade, and finance also have started to see the payoff from new technology investments. The productivity lag apparently resulted from the relatively long time it took for organizations to adopt the new technology and learn how to apply it.[17] For example, Countrywide Home Loans, one of the largest mortgage lenders in the United States, has been experimenting with technology solutions since the late 1980s. But only recently have the benefits of technology paid off. The 1997 implementation of an automated information system in its customer service center has helped reduce the average cost per call from $4 to less than $0.60 on more than twenty thousand calls per day. The increased productivity has not cost jobs; Countrywide nearly doubled its workforce between 1996 and 1999.

Information technology is also fueling the growth of e-commerce, an economy that knows no boundaries.[18] E-commerce concerns the buying and selling of products and services over the Internet, and ranges from withdrawing cash from an automatic teller machine to more complex interactions such as purchasing products from a Website. Of the three types of e-commerce transactions—business-to-business, business-to-consumer, and consumer-to-consumer—the first two forms provide the radically new context for OD.

The business-to-consumer, or e-tailer, market is expected to grow to over $184 billion in revenues by 2004. Although Amazon.com and E*TRADE get the publicity, the business transformations fueled by information technology are likely to be the focus of OD attention in the future. Dell Computer, for instance, sells custom-made computers to consumers and businesses, but it started out as a mail-order company advertising in the back of magazines. Today, 25 percent of its computer sales comes through the Internet. The shift in organization structures, labor skill sets, work designs, and work processes in the transformation from a mail-order business to a leader in e-commerce represents the kind of change that many organizations will face and the challenges OD practitioners must meet.

The issues in the business-to-business market are even more complex. Estimates suggest that this form of e-commerce will grow to over $2.7 trillion by 2004. A good example of the implications and potential of this market is the online store being created by General Motors, Ford, and DaimlerChrysler. It represents the first major migration of an entire industry's supply chain onto the Internet, and will reengineer radically the way businesses interact with each other. This virtual marketplace will handle $250 billion in parts and supplies purchased from sixty thousand suppliers each year, automate routine transactions, and streamline the bidding process for everything from car windows to paper clips and paint. Web-based transactions will replace the inefficient phone, mail, and face-to-face sales call processes that dominated this industry for decades. Such business-to-business marketplaces are expected to be adopted by other auto makers as well as other industries, such as aerospace, construction, and office supplies.[19]

The Organization

The interventions described in this book represent the best practices in OD. They help organizations become more streamlined and flexible, and more capable of improving themselves continuously in response to trends in the economy, workforce, and technology. But many organizations are not aware of these practices and still others resist applying them.[20] For example, despite the attention to them in the business press, only a small percentage of organizations use self-managed work teams, are organized into networks, or successfully manage strategic alliances. But these are the organizations of the future, and they will invent entirely new, entrepreneurial structures capable of exploiting new ideas and technologies quickly. The "dot-coms" so prominent in the technology industry represent one vision of the future.

Organizations clearly will be more networked. As explained in Chapter 9, network or "fishnet" structures rely on strategic alliances, joint ventures, and other transorganization relationships.[21] These configurations enable single organizations to partner with other organizations to develop, manufacture, and distribute goods and services. Networks are highly adaptable and can disband and reform along different task or market lines as the circumstances demand. To succeed, organizations are learning how to assess quickly whether they are compatible with network partners and whether the joint product/service is successful. They are gaining competence to enter into and to breakup networks swiftly, thus enabling them to exploit product/market opportunities rapidly and to "fail quickly" when the network is unproductive.[22]

Network structures also are enabling organizations to gain many of the efficiencies traditionally reserved for large firms while remaining small and nimble. Organizations have tended to grow large to gain economies of scale in manufacturing, distribution, and marketing. Large size, however, can lead to rigid and slow responses that can be disastrous in rapidly changing environments. Network structures can help small organizations combine to produce goods and services efficiently. Small, focused firms that perform particular tasks with excellence can align with organizations that have complimentary resources and expertise. Thus, the network can gain economies of scale while each of the partner organizations remains small and flexible.

As discussed in Chapter 14, knowledge is becoming a key source of organizational competence and competitive advantage. Organizations increasingly will structure themselves around knowledge processes rather than functions, products, or geography. Such structures typically transcend both internal and external organizational boundaries. They remove barriers to learning and facilitate how employees acquire, organize, and disseminate knowledge assets. For example, at HP Consulting, a five thousand–person global consulting organization within Hewlett-Packard, learning communities, project snapshots, and knowledge maps are used to give members access to all of the organization's knowledge and experience when they are consulting. Learning communities are informal groups composed of organization members who operate in different parts of the organization but whose success is dependent on each other's knowledge. Current and former clients also can be part of the learning community. They are encouraged to discuss best practices, issues, or skills that they want to learn about through whatever means possible, including face-to-face meetings, electronic chats, emails, or conference calls. More formally, project snapshots are organized meetings of team members who have collaborated on a project to discuss learnings that can be applied to future projects. Through this knowledge management process, the HP consulting organization is building a knowledge base that can be shared by all members and applied to their client's problems.[23]

IMPLICATIONS FOR OD'S FUTURE

The economic, workforce, technology, and organization trends outlined above have significant implications for how OD will be conceived and practiced in the coming years. Figure 16.1 summarizes them. A global economy populated with flexible, networked organizations and driven by information technology and a diverse workforce will require OD to be more embedded in the organization's operations, more technologically enabled, shorter in cycle time, more innovation and learning oriented, more interdisciplinary, applied to more diverse clients, more cross-cultural, and clearer about values.

OD Will Be More Embedded in the Organization's Operations

As the economic and technical demands facing organizations require faster, more flexible organizations, the ability to manage change continuously will become a key source of competitive advantage. This suggests that OD practices will become more embedded in the organization's normal operating routines. For example, Chapter 1 defined three types of OD practitioners, including line managers who applied OD principles to their work. OD activities such as diagnosis, intervention planning, and change management can and should become part of the daily work of managers and employees. When managers integrate OD knowledge into their role, change capabilities will be diffused throughout the organization rather than located in a special function or role. That would permit faster and more flexible reactions to challenges faced by the organization. In addition to embedding OD skills into managerial roles, OD interventions themselves will be integrated into core business processes, such as product development, strategic planning, and order fulfillment. This should provide a closer linkage between OD and business results.

This does not mean that the role of the professional OD practitioner will go away. Professionals will be needed to help organization members gain change management competencies. Small, entrepreneurial firms will need specialized assistance in bringing on new members rapidly and organizing their efforts. Organizations involved in strategic alliances and mergers and acquisitions will need professional help managing interorganizational interfaces and integrating diverse corporate cultures and business practices. OD professionals also will be needed to assist in the implementation of new technologies, particularly knowledge management practices. The demand for OD practitioners is likely to increase rather than decrease. For example, there is some anecdotal evidence to suggest that as line and senior managers learn more about the knowledge and skills associated with OD practice, their requests for assistance in formulating change processes increase. Managers will look more frequently for a partner and coach to help them lead and facilitate organization change.

OD Processes Will Be More Technologically Enabled

Information technology is pervasive; it will effect not only organizations, work, and the economy but will have a significant affect on OD practice. First, it will enable OD processes to be both synchronous and asynchronous (anytime, anywhere) as well as more virtual and less face-to-face. In global organizations, members work in a variety of locations, cultures, and time zones. OD interventions, such as team building, employee involvement, and integrated strategic change, will have to be planned and implemented in ways that encourage contributions from a variety of stakeholders at times that are convenient or at times when creative ideas emerge. Information technology, such as email, newsgroups, and bulletin boards, allow organization members to make these contributions at any time they are ready. In addition, groupware technologies allow members to discuss issues in chat rooms, in Web and video conferences, and on the more traditional telephone conference.

As a result, the process of OD is likely to change. For example, using these technologies to exchange ideas, discuss policies, or decide on change processes will produce different types of group dynamics from those found in face-to-face meetings. OD practitioners not only will need to be comfortable with this technology but also will need to develop virtual facilitation skills that recognize these dynamics. In many cases, a more structured and assertive approach will be necessary to ensure that all members have an opportunity to share their ideas. The effect of these technologically mediated exchanges on work satisfaction, productivity, and quality is not yet known. In addition, processes of visioning, diagnosis, data feedback, and action planning will have to be reengineered to leverage new technologies.

Second, information technology will provide much more information about the organization to a greater number of participants in a shorter period of time. OD processes will be adapted to recognize that members have more information at their fingertips. For example, organization intranets provide members with an information channel that is richer, more efficient, more interactive, and more dynamic than are such traditional channels as newsletters and memos. Thus, intranets can provide a timely method for collecting data on emerging issues, to provide performance feedback on key operational measures, and to involve members in key decisions.

OD Cycle Times Will Be Shorter

Trends in the economy and technology are shortening product, organization, and industry life cycles. Pressures to reduce the cycle time of OD activities are also likely to increase. To be seen as relevant, OD practitioners must be mindful of opportunities to quicken the pace of key processes, and contemporaneously remain aware of the practices and processes that cannot be hurried.

New information technologies and interventions will expedite certain steps in the change process. For example, a large-scale organization diagnosis involving member interviews and surveys used to take as long as six months. By the time the data were ready, many of the pressing issues had faded because of new developments in the marketplace, turnover in personnel, or proactive management. Today, with electronic surveys and large-group designs, organization diagnosis can be completed in as little as a few hours. In coming years, new technologies, such as groupware and video conferencing, increasingly will be used to bring more people together faster than ever before. In short, there is real potential to reduce dramatically the time required to perform many OD practices.

There are physical and psychological limits to reductions in the OD change cycle, however, and it is not realistic to expect change to be instantaneous.[24] For example, managers often are disturbed by estimates that major structural or cultural changes take two to five years. A new organization chart or a new vision and values statement hung on members' office walls often gives the illusion that change has occurred, but the working relationships, process improvements, and other aspects of fully implementing these large-scale changes often take longer than expected. Similarly, most organization members are not capable of dropping a well-known and understood set of behaviors one day and picking up a new set of behaviors the next with the same level of efficiency. There are clear minimums with respect to the speed of change in individual behavior, and members may face a steep learning curve when they are asked to change their routines.

OD Will Be More Innovation and Learning Oriented

Given the emerging context facing OD, change processes are more likely to be aimed at creating entirely new structures, processes, and behaviors than at fine-tuning the status quo. Christos Cotsakos, CEO of E*TRADE, has suggested that organizations that are "managing change" are behind; successful organizations in the future will be the ones *creating* change. This will require unprecedented amounts of innovation and learning. Multiple stakeholders representing a diversity of interests will come together to envision a shared future and to learn how to enact it. Because this process typically leads into uncharted waters, both organizational members and change agents will be joint learners, exploring new territory together. Implementing new organizational innovations will require significant amounts of experimentation as participants try out new ways of operating, assess progress, and make necessary adjustments. In essence, they will learn from their actions how to create a new strategy, organization, or service. A collaborative learning effort is capable of implementing radically new possibilities and ways of functioning that could not be envisioned beforehand. Thus, it is a process of innovation, not of detection and correction of errors. In turn, the new structures and systems increase feedback and information flow to the organization, thereby improving its capacity to learn and adapt in a rapidly changing technological and economic environment. OD interventions such as action science,[25] appreciative inquiry,[26] self-designing organizations,[27] and learning organizations[28] are forerunners of the innovation and learning that will evolve in the coming years.

OD Will Be More Interdisciplinary

Globalization, technology, diversity, and other trends rapidly are broadening the focus of OD and making other social sciences more relevant to planned change. This suggests that OD will continue to become more interdisciplinary and rely on a variety of perspectives and approaches to developing and changing organizations. Historically, the focus of OD expanded from small groups and social process to organization structures and work design, and more recently, to strategic and global social change.[29] Along the way, different disciplines have been applied to OD practice, including organization theory, industrial engineering, labor relations, comparative management, and corporate strategy. In the future, OD will be called on to help organizations address issues related to global networks, e-commerce, ecological sustainability, temporary employment, entrepreneurial growth, and economic and workforce diversity. This enlarged sphere of practice will require new approaches to planned change informed by such fields as information systems, international relations, social ecology, entrepreneurship, and labor economics. Fortunately, many of these other disciplines are expanding their boundaries and becoming more aware of the contributions that OD can make. For example, strategic management, sociology, and economics, fields that traditionally focused on technology, product development, class structure, and economic performance, are integrating human resources, change, and other organizational processes into their models of profitability, corporate valuation, and social development.[30]

As OD becomes more interdisciplinary, the prospects for an integrated approach to planned change seem near. Recent developments in complexity science and chaos theory, for example, provide fascinating new conceptual frameworks and metaphors for OD practitioners and represent how other disciplines, such as mathematics and physics, might contribute to a unified theory of change.[31] Ideally, an integrated perspective will balance human fulfillment and economic performance, provide a fuller recognition of the systemic and dynamic nature of organizations, and develop improved techniques for managing large-scale, transformational change within and across national cultures. For OD practice, the benefit will be organizations where all employees think strategically, guided jointly by self-interest and organizational and ecological welfare.

OD Will Work with More Diverse Client Organizations

The changes occurring in OD's context suggest that in the future, planned change will be applied to a more diverse client base. Traditionally, OD was focused on large business organizations, but three other types of organizations increasingly will become targets of planned change: small entrepreneurial startups, government organizations, and global social change organizations. Small, entrepreneurial startups are an important and underserved market for OD. Many of these organizations are at the forefront of the technology trends cited earlier. Because they are operating on scarce and finite venture capital, time is their most valuable asset and the one most critical to their success. As a result, there is a clear action orientation, little perceived need to reflect and learn, and few structures and systems to guide behaviors and decisions.[32] This is a context that can be well served by fast, flexible change processes orienting new people quickly to the business strategy, integrating them rapidly into new work roles, increasing the efficiency of work processes, and helping founders and key managers think about how the market, competitors, and technology are changing. Entrepreneurs are not inclined to think about nor are they trained to examine these issues. OD can help them address such matters and gain needed competence.

The economic, workforce, technology, and organization trends also are pushing government organizations to become more efficient, flexible, and networked. As a result, government increasingly is applying OD interventions such as strategic planning, employee involvement, and performance management, and we expect that the demand for change management assistance in the public sector will grow. Moreover, in combination with the globalization trend, governments will become more proactive in managing the effects of economic development. Public–private partnerships, a form of transorganization development, also are likely to flourish and will require the assistance of OD practitioners sensitive to the differences between these two types of organizations and to the demands the partnerships will be under, such as environmental protection, employment, corporate citizenship, and taxation.

Chapter 15 described the application of OD in global social change organizations. The increasing concentration of wealth and globalization of the economy will create a plethora of opportunities for OD to assist developing countries, disadvantaged citizens, and the ecology. In China, for example, as the government reduces bureaucracy and creates state-owned enterprises, the need for nongovernment organizations to take over the delivery of social services is great. In response, the Global Village of Beijing has begun practical campaigns to involve the Chinese people in pro-environment practices and to develop leaders for other nongovernment organizations. OD practices and processes can help these organizations achieve their objectives, manage their resources, and improve their functioning through team building, transorganization development, and strategic planning.

Similarly, limits to the world's ecosystem, including its capacity to absorb population growth, function with a depleted ozone layer, and operate with polluted waters, are causing a rethinking of the traditional business model. The revised model, in turn, will require a new organization that values different outcomes and processes. For example, the Natural Step model stresses the importance of organization strategies and designs that work within a sustainability framework, and the natural capitalism model argues that business strategies built around the productive use of natural resources can solve environmental problems at a profit.[33] Organizations, such as IKEA, Interface, and Motorola, are rethinking their business models to address these issues. For example, Interface, a manufacturer of carpet products, has pioneered the idea of "leasing" its carpets. Under its "Evergreen Lease," they accept responsibility for keeping the carpet clean and fresh in exchange for a monthly fee. By installing carpet tiles instead of large rolls, and because only a small fraction of carpeting actually gets used, they can replace the tiles and save approximately 80 percent of the cost of carpeting materials. OD practitioners will need to make themselves aware of these alternative models and can help organizations develop and implement practices that are more environmentally sustainable.

OD Will Become More Cross-Cultural

As organizations and the economy become more global, the recent growth of OD applications in international and cross-cultural situations is a harbinger of the future. Despite increased research and practice in this area, we know little about planned change processes in cross-cultural settings. Traditionally, OD has been practiced in organizations *within* specific cultures: British-trained OD practitioners helped British organizations in Great Britain; Mexican OD practitioners helped Latin American organizations; and so on. But the current trends clearly point to the need for OD applications that work *across* cultures. Team-building interventions need to be modified to help a team composed of Americans, Indians, Chinese, Koreans, and French Canadians who have never met face-to-face but are charged with developing a new product in a short period of time. The merger and acquisition process needs to be adapted to help a Japanese and U.S. firm implement a new organization structure that honors both cultures. Because the number of organizations operating in multiple countries is growing rapidly, opportunities for OD in these situations seem endless: interorganizational and transorganizational relationships between subsidiaries, operating units, and headquarters organizations; team building across cultural boundaries; working out global logistic and supply chain processes; implementing diversity-centric values in ethnocentric cultures; designing strategic planning exercises at multiple levels. Moreover, OD is likely to find increased opportunities in GSCO organizations that are often part of an international network. Transorganization development processes and network structure development interventions adapted for cross-cultural contexts have yet to be developed and will have important applications in the future.

OD Will Become More Clear About Values

The economic and technological trends suggest that OD practitioners are likely to face more value dilemmas in the coming years. For example, the increasing concentration of wealth conflicts with OD's traditional values of equality and egalitarianism, and OD practitioners will need to be clear about how they are helping to centralize or decentralize power. Similarly, technology can isolate people or bring them together. The choices OD practitioners make in incorporating technology into change management processes will have an important effect on feelings of inclusion, influence, and participation. Finally, despite OD's best efforts to embrace diversity, it is common to find practitioners frustrated by differences in cultural assumptions.

As discussed in Chapter 1, OD professionals initially promoted a coherent set of humanistic and democratic values for organizations. Over time, those values were supplemented with values favoring organizational effectiveness, thus creating potential conflicts in trying to jointly satisfy both humanistic and effectiveness outcomes. The field currently reflects that division. Many practitioners believe that OD has become too corporate and is in danger of colluding with powerful managers to concentrate wealth further. They argue that OD should return to its original values and focus on liberating the human potential inside organizations. Other practitioners argue that focusing on human potential exclusively will doom OD to irrelevance and limit its contribution to a better world. This is an important and ongoing debate within OD, and it is likely to become even more intense as additional values, such as ecological sustainability and economic equality, enter the field of planned change. OD practitioners will be called on more often to help organization members balance personal development and work demands, increase the organization's short-term profitability, and maximize its long-term environmental sustainability. Balancing these diverse values will be extremely difficult. OD will be able to influence the future of organizations if practitioners clearly recognize these value dilemmas and help clients develop strategies for resolving them.

■ SUMMARY

In this concluding chapter, we described four interrelated trends—the economy, the workforce, technology, and organizations—likely to affect the context within which organization development will be practiced. Each trend has been proposed as an important driver of the future. The chapter went on to propose several themes or directions that OD will be likely to take. If our speculations prove accurate, the practice of OD will be more embedded in the organization's key functions, more technologically enabled, expected to operate within shorter cycle times, more collaborative and oriented toward action learning, more interdisciplinary, more likely to serve a diverse client base, more cross-culturally oriented, and more confronted with values conflicts.

To be relevant, OD practitioners and the field as a whole must act together to influence the future they prefer or adjust to the future that is coming. Our hope is that this text was able to inform and equip the reader with the skills, knowledge, and value awareness necessary to shape the future.

■ NOTES

1. The authors wish to thank many people who responded to requests for their thoughts on the future of OD, including Stan Herman, Jay Hays, Vana Prewitt, Diane Hildebrand, Martin Nelson, Nancy Taylor, Herb Kessner, Lori Preston, Don Cole, Nancy Polend, Ann Kruse, Connie Fuller, and Ivy Gordon. The content of the chapter was greatly influenced by their thoughts and our hope is that it reflects their inputs as well as our own beliefs.

2. D. Bell, *The Coming of Post-Industrial Society: A Venture in Social Forecasting* (New York: Basic Books, 1973); A. Toffler, *The Third Wave* (New York: Morrow, 1980); D. Korten, *When Corporations Rule the World* (West Hartford, Conn.: Kumarian Press; San Francisco: Berrett-Koehler, 1995); L. Thurow, *The Future of Capitalism* (New York: William Morrow, 1996).

3. R. Wright, "The New Mantra of Globalization: Inclusion Conference," *Los Angeles Times* (8 February 2000): A-10; Thurow, *Future of Capitalism*.

4. T. Carrel, "Beijing: New Face for the Ancient Capital," *National Geographic* 197 (2000): 116–37.

5. L. Thurow, "Building Wealth," *Atlantic Monthly* (June 1999): 57–69; R. Senser, "Loaded at the Top: The Growing Inequalities in Wealth and Income in the United States," www.senser.com/loaded.htm, accessed on December 11, 1999. The article, in a slightly different form, first appeared in *Commonweal* (1 December 1995).

6. Thurow, "Building Wealth."

7. Korten, *When Corporations Rule.*

8. Wright, "New Mantra."

9. Thurow, *Future of Capitalism;* Korten, *When Corporations Rule;* N. Mankiw, *Principles of Economics* (Fort Worth, Tex.: Dryden Press, 1997).

10. U. McFarling, "Climate Is Warming at Steep Rate Study Says," *Los Angeles Times* (23 February 2000): A1.

11. J. Guyon, "A Big Oil Man Gets Religion," *Fortune* (6 March 2000): F87–F89.

12. Thurow, *Future of Capitalism*.

13. Korten, *When Corporations Rule*.

14. A. Lovins, L. Lovins, and P. Hawken, "A Road Map for Natural Capitalism," *Harvard Business Review* (May-June, 1999): 145–58.

15. Information on IKEA's transformation can be found at http://www.naturalstep.org/event/cases.

16. L. Bassi and M. Van Buren, "The 1999 ASTD State of the Industry Report," *Training & Development*, supplement (January 1999).

17. E. Sanders, "Tech-Driven Efficiency Spurs Economic Boom," *Los Angeles Times* (22 February 2000): A-1.

18. P. Drucker, "Beyond the Information Revolution," *Atlantic Monthly* (October 1999): 47–57.

19. A. Dunn and J. O'Dell, "Auto Makers Plan Behemoth E-Business," *Los Angeles Times* (26 February 2000): A-1.

20. G. Colvin, "Managing in the Info Era," *Fortune* (6 March 2000): F6–F9.

21. Institute for the Future, "21st Century Organizations: Reconciling Control and Empowerment," http://www.iftf.org, accessed December 4, 1999.

22. From remarks of Kirby Dyess, vice president for business development, Intel, in a speech at Pepperdine University's MSOD alumni conference, Watsonville, Calif., July 1999.

23. M. Martiny, "Knowledge Management at HP Consulting," *Organizational Dynamics* 27 (1998): 71–77.

24. C. Worley and R. Patchett, "Myth and Hope Meet Reality: The Fallacy of and Opportunities for Reducing Cycle Time in Strategic Change," in M. Anderson, *Fast-Cycle Organization Development* (Cincinnati, Ohio: South-Western College Publishing, 2000); C. Worley, T. Cummings, and P. Monge, "A Critique, Test, and Refinement of the Punctuated Equilibrium Model of Strategic Change" (working paper, Pepperdine University, 1999).

25. C. Argyris, R. Putnam, and D. Smith, *Action Science* (San Francisco: Jossey-Bass, 1985).

26. D. Cooperrider, P. Sorensen, D. Whitney, and T. Yaeger, *Appreciative Inquiry: Rethinking Human Organization Toward a Positive Theory of Change* (Champaign, IL: Stipes, 2000).

27. L. D. Brown and J. Covey, "Development Organizations and Organization Development: Toward an Expanding Paradigm for Organization Development," in *Research in Organizational Change and Development*, vol. 1, eds. R. Woodman and W. Pasmore (Greenwich, Conn.: JAI Press, 1987): 59–87.

28. P. Senge, *The Fifth Discipline: The Art and Practice of the Learning Organization* (New York: Doubleday, 1990).

29. R. Jacobs, *Real Time Strategic Change* (San Francisco: Berrett-Koehler, 1994): C. Worley, D. Hitchin, and W. Ross, *Integrated Strategic Change* (Reading, Mass.: Addison-Wesley, 1996); J. Preston, L. DuToit, and I. Barber, "A Potential Model of Transformational Change Applied to South Africa" in *Research in Organizational Change and Development*, vol. 9, eds. R.Woodman and W. Pasmore (Greenwich, Conn.: JAI Press, 1998).

30. D. Hambrick, "Strategic Awareness Within Top Management Teams," *Strategic Management Journal* 2 (1981): 263–79; S. Finkelstein and D. Hambrick, "Top Management Team Tenure and Organizational Outcomes: The Moderating Role of Managerial Discretion" (working paper, Center for Effective Organizations, University of Southern California, Los Angeles, 1989); L. Greiner and A. Bhambri, "New CEO Intervention and Dynamics of Deliberate Strategic Change," *Strategic Management Review* 10 (Summer 1989): 67–86; Thurow, *Future of Capitalism*; R. Winter and S. Nelson, *An Evolutionary Theory of Economic Change* (Cambridge, Mass.: Belknap Press, 1982).

31. M. Wheatley, *Leadership and the New Science: Learning about Organization from an Orderly Universe* (San Francisco: Berrett-Koehler, 1992).

32. K. Chee, "Strategic and Organization Development Challenges Faced by High-Technology Startup Chief Executive Officers" (unpublished Master's thesis, Pepperdine University, 1999).

33. Lovins, Lovins, and Hawken, "Road Map"; information on the Natural Step can be found at http://www.naturalstep.org.

Name Index

Numbers following *n* or *nn* indicate note numbers.

Subject Index

Page numbers followed by an *f* or *t* indicate a figure or table, respectively.